THE
MESSIANIC
LEGACY

by the same author
HOLY BLOOD, HOLY GRAIL

THE MESSIANIC LEGACY

*Michael Baigent, Richard Leigh,
and Henry Lincoln*

HENRY HOLT AND COMPANY
NEW YORK

Dedication

Aborde la Nef ensablée
Et jeûne à ton clou subtil
Et à ton marteau lourd.
Console-toi. Du tombeau vide
Poussera un rejecton générreux.

Bientost d'une âme heureuse
Le chant se lèvera.
Joue, Nymphaea,
Joue ta musique céleste.
Ta boudego bourdonne
Comme la voix du Verbe.
Sa chaleureuse mélodie nous attire.
Comme la Rose rose, Apiphile
Et la Rose rouge, l'Abeille.

Jehan l'Ascuiz

Copyright © 1986 by Michael Baigent, Richard Leigh, Henry Lincoln
All rights reserved, including the right to reproduce this book
or portions thereof in any form.
First published in the United States in 1987
by Henry Holt and Company, Inc.,
521 Fifth Avenue, New York, New York 10175.

Library of Congress Cataloging-in-Publication Data
Baigent, Michael.
The messianic legacy.
Reprint. Originally published: London : Cape, 1986.
Bibliography: p.
Includes index.
1. Messianism—History. 2. Prieuré de Sion.
I. Leigh, Richard. II. Lincoln, Henry. III. Title.
BL475.B3 1987 909 87-14832
ISBN 0-8050-0568-4

Permission from Faber & Faber Ltd to quote from
Nikos Kazantzakis's *The Last Temptation* (translated by P. A. Bien,
1961) on p. 78 and from William Collins Sons & Co. Ltd to quote
from Michel Tournier's *The Erl King* (translated by Barbara Bray,
1972) on pp. 140–1 is gratefully acknowledged.

First American Edition
Printed in the United States of America
10 9 8 7 6 5 4 3 2 1

ISBN 0-8050-0568-4

Contents

PART THREE THE CABAL

Illustrations

The authors and publisher would like to thank the following for providing photographs: Archives du Loiret, Orléans (31, 32), Michael Baigent, London (1, 3, 4, 5, 9, 27, 30, 33, 34, 35), Bibliothèque Nationale, Paris (28, 29), Bodleian Library, Oxford (17), Werner Braun, Jerusalem (18), Trustees of the British Museum, London (14), Commissioners of Public Works in Ireland, Dublin (10, 13, 16), Coptic Museum, Cairo (11), José Dominguez García, Madrid (6, 7, 8, 12), Gisbert Gramberg, Greven (21–3), Israel Department of Antiquities and Museums, Jerusalem (2), Henry Lincoln, London (36, 37), Novosti Press Agency, London (25, 26), Scala, Florence (24), Ronald Sheridan, London (38), Board of Trinity College, Dublin (15), Wiener Library, London (19, 20).

Plates

between pages 48 and 49

1   The Garden of Gethsemane, Jerusalem.
2   The archaeological evidence that Pontius Pilate existed: an inscription found at Caesarea in 1961.
3   Qumran: Cave 4, where the Dead Sea Scrolls were found.
4   The remains of the Qumran community buildings.
5   Qumran, with the ruins of the tower.
6   The Cathedral at Santiago de Compostela, north-west Spain.
7   Fourth- and fifth-century Christian burials at Santiago de Compostela.
8   Santa Maria de Bretoña, north-west Spain.
9   Kidron Valley, Jerusalem.
10   Kilfenora Cross, Co. Clare.

Maps and charts

Acknowledgments

Once again, we should like to thank Ann Evans, whose rare dexterity in trivariance accounts in large part for this book's existence.

We should also like to thank: Juan Atienza, Andrew Baker, Michael Bentine, Ernest Bigland, Colin Bloy, Brie Burkeman, Derek Burton, Liz Calder, Philippe de Chérisey, Jonathan Clowes, Lindy and Ramon del Corral, Ian Craig, Neville Barker Cryer, Robert Eisenman, Geoff Elkin, Patrick J. Freeman, Jim Garrets, Janice Glaholm, Denis Graham, Joy Hancox, Nigel Horne, Douglas Lockhart, Lydia Ludlow, Linda MacFadyen, Jania McGillivray, Rosalind Maiden, Alison Mansbridge, Tom Maschler, Robert Matthews, Roberta Matthews, Robin Mosley, Michael Myfsud, William Phillips, Pierre Plantard de Saint-Clair, John Prudhoe, Bob Quinn, David Rolfe, Gino Sandri, John Saul, Hugh Schonfield, Rosalie Siegel, Gordon Thomas, Jonathan Tootell, Louis Vazart, Gérard Watelet, Lilianne Ziegel, the staff of the Wiener Library and the British Library Reading Room, and, of course, our ladies.

Introduction

In 1982, some twelve years of research into a small local mystery in the south of France culminated in the publication of *The Holy Blood and the Holy Grail*. Bérenger Saunière, an obscure Languedoc priest of the late nineteenth century, had metaphorically taken us by the hand and directed us to the stones we had to turn in order to discern the pattern underlying his story. He led us to a secret, or semi-secret, society, the Prieuré de Sion, which could be traced back nearly a thousand years, which included in its membership a number of illustrious figures and which remained active in France and possibly elsewhere to the present day. The avowed objective of the Prieuré de Sion was to restore to the throne of modern France the Merovingian bloodline – a bloodline which had vanished from the stage of history more than thirteen hundred years ago. This appeared to make no sense. What could possibly be so special about the Merovingian bloodline? Why should its restoration be of interest to men such as Leonardo da Vinci and Victor Hugo – and, more recently, to men such as André Malraux, Marshal Alphonse Juin and perhaps Charles de Gaulle?

A partial, but crucial, answer to this question emerged when we discovered that the Merovingians themselves claimed direct lineal descent from the Old Testament House of David – and that that claim was acknowledged to be valid by the dynasty which supplanted them, by other monarchs and by the Roman Church of the time. Gradually, the evidence assembled itself, as if with a momentum of its own. It led us into the sensitive territory of biblical scholarship. It prompted us to suggest a provocative hypothesis – that Jesus had been a legitimate king of Israel, that he had been married and had sired children, that these children had perpetuated his bloodline until, some three and a half centuries later, it merged with the Merovingian dynasty of France.

Our conclusions, as they crystallised, were initially as startling to us as they subsequently proved to our readers. But for us, the import of what we were uncovering had become apparent only by degrees, seeping into our consciousness piecemeal over a period of years. For our readers, the same process of discovery was compressed into the confines of a single book, and its effect was therefore more sudden, more unexpected and more disturbing – or more exhilarating. It involved no slow, painstaking, week-by-week and month-by-month assembly of facts, correlation of data and shuffling of confused jig-saw pieces into a coherent picture. On the contrary, it occurred with the disorienting abruptness of a detonation. Given the sphere in which this detonation occurred, the results were perhaps inevitable. For many of our readers, the primary – if not, indeed the only – point of discussion in our book was 'the Jesus material'.

Jesus projected our work on to front pages around the world and invested it with an element of 'sensationalism'. So far as the media in particular were concerned, everything else we had written took second place, if it was assigned a place at all. The excitement we had felt when, for instance, we discovered a new dimension to the Crusades, a new fragment of information concerning the creation of the Knights Templar or new evidence about the source of the notorious Protocols of Sion, was not generally shared. All such discoveries were eclipsed by the shadow of Jesus and our hypothesis about him.

For us, however, our hypothesis about Jesus was by no means the only aspect of our research. Nor, ultimately, was it the most important one. Even while the media, and many readers, were concentrating on our biblical conclusions, we could perceive the direction in which our subsequent investigations would have to move. Our attention would have to be focused upon the Prieuré de Sion today.

What was the Prieuré's true *raison d'être*? If restoration of the Merovingian bloodline was the ultimate end, what were the means to be? Individuals such as Malraux and Juin were neither naïve idealists nor religious fanatics. This applied equally to the members of the Order whom we had met personally. How, then, did they propose to implement their objectives? The answer, quite patently, seemed to lie in areas such as mass psychology, political power and high finance. We were dealing with people active in the 'real world', and it was in terms of the 'real world' of the 1980s that we had to make sense of their centuries-old history.

But what *was* the Prieuré doing today? What traces could be found of its contemporary activity, of its involvement in current affairs? Who constituted the Order's membership? How powerful were they? What kind of resources could they command? If our hypothesis proved valid, how might they seek to turn to account the claim of a lineal descent from the Merovingians, and/or Jesus, and/or the Old Testament House of David? And what, in the modern world, might be the social and political repercussions of such a claim?

It seemed clear that the Prieuré was working to some kind of 'grand design' or 'master plan' for the future of France, ultimately for the future of Europe as a whole, and perhaps even beyond. This, certainly, had been the implication attending the various hints, suggestions and fragments of information which had come our way. Nor could we forget the flat, categorical, matter-of-fact way in which the man subsequently to become the Prieuré's Grand Master told us that the Order actually possessed the lost treasure of the Temple of Jerusalem. It would be returned to Israel, he said, 'when the time is right'. What might constitute time's 'rightness'? Only social and political factors, and perhaps a 'psychological climate'.

It was obvious that our research into the modern Prieuré would entail investigation in several directions simultaneously. First, we would have to recapitulate our research in religious history and biblical material, retracing our footsteps, re-examining and if possible augmenting our work in those fields. Previously, we had sought evidence attesting to a sacred bloodline. This time, we would have to concentrate primarily on the concept of Jesus as Messiah. We had observed that, in the Prieuré's own thinking, Messiahship seemed to enjoy a special relevance. It was impossible, for example, not to notice the insistence with which the Merovingian dynasty was repeatedly described in language usually reserved for Messianic figures. We would have to determine precisely what the idea of the 'Messiah' meant in Jesus's time, how it had altered in the ensuing centuries and how the ancient and modern ideas might conceivably be reconciled.

Secondly, we would have to try to establish how the concept of Messiahship could be applied in practice today. At a most basic level, we would have to satisfy ourselves that the concept could be in any way relevant to the twentieth century. This would entail a survey of the spiritual and psychological climate which characterises the modern world. We would have to confront certain apparently clichéd aspects of contemporary Western society – the crisis of meaning and the quest for spiritual values.

Finally, of course, we would be bound to pursue our own personal contacts with the Prieuré de Sion itself, with its Grand Master and with those members or associates whom we had identified or ourselves come to know. Here, it quickly became apparent, we would find ourselves amid quicksands of rapidly developing events, rapidly changing situations. We would have to determine some sort of truth behind bizarre claims and counter-claims. We would have to test new documentary evidence, uncover forgeries, thread our way through a maze of deliberately disseminated 'disinformation' – 'disinformation' generated by the obscure machinations of shadowy figures.

Gradually, we began to discern some extraordinary amalgams of possibility. We began to understand how an organisation such as the Prieuré de Sion might address itself to, and even capitalise upon, the current 'crisis of meaning'. And we learned that so apparently rarefied, ethereal and mystic a concept as 'Messiahship' could indeed figure in the practical world of twentieth-century society and politics.

ONE
The Messiah

I

Scholarship and Public Understanding

... This fell into my hands by chance a little while ago. Until
then I'd never had any intimation of what was being done
nowadays in the field of biblical research, or of the attacks
being launched by competent historians. It was a shock to me
– and a revelation! ... I learnt all sorts of facts that were
entirely new to me. That the Gospels, for example, were
written between the years 65 and 100. That means the Church
was founded, and was able to carry on, without them. Think
of it! More than sixty years after Christ's birth! It's as if
someone today wanted to write down Napoleon's words and
deeds without being able to consult a single written document,
only vague memories and anecdotes.[1]

Apart from the reference to Napoleon, the above quotation, to
judge from the letters and verbal declarations we received, might
have expressed, almost verbatim, the reaction of a contemporary
reader to *The Holy Blood and the Holy Grail* when it was
published in 1982. In fact, the words are from a novel, *Jean Barois*
by Roger Martin du Gard, published in 1912, and in that novel
they elicit the response:

... Before long all theologians of any intellectual standing will
have reached these conclusions. In fact, they'll be amazed that
nineteenth-century Catholics contrived to believe for so long
in the literal truth of those poetic legends.[2]

Yet even before the time of this fictional dialogue, set in the
1870s, Jesus and the origins of Christianity had begun to emerge as
a burgeoning industry for researchers, writers and publishers. In
the early sixteenth century, Pope Leo X is on record as declaring: 'It
has served us well, this myth of Christ.' As early as the 1740s,

scholars had deployed what we would now recognise as a valid historical methodology for questioning the veracity of scriptural accounts. Thus, between 1744 and 1767, Hermann Samuel Reimarus, a professor at Hamburg, had argued that Jesus was nothing more than a failed Judaic revolutionary whose body was removed from its tomb by his disciples. By the mid-nineteenth century, German biblical scholarship had truly come of age, and a dating of the Gospels had been established which – in its approach and in most of its conclusions – is still deemed valid. Today, no reputable historian or biblical scholar would deny that the earliest of the Gospels was composed at least a generation after the events it describes. The thrust of German research was eventually to culminate in a position summarised by Rudolf Bultmann of the University of Marburg, one of the most important, most famous and most esteemed of twentieth-century biblical commentators:

> I do indeed think that we can now know almost nothing concerning the life and personality of Jesus, since the early Christian sources show no interest in either, are moreover fragmentary and often legendary.[3]

Yet Bultmann remained a devout Christian. He did so by insisting on a crucial distinction between the Jesus of history and the Christ of faith. As long as this distinction was acknowledged, faith remained tenable. If the distinction were not acknowledged, faith would inevitably find itself eroded and embarrassed by the ineluctable facts of history.

This was the kind of conclusion to which nineteenth-century German biblical scholarship would eventually lead. At the same time, however, the bastion of traditional scriptural authority was also being challenged from other quarters. The controversial contentions of German research remained confined to a rarefied sphere of specialists: but in 1863 the French writer Ernest Renan caused a major international controversy with his celebrated best-seller *The Life of Jesus*. This work, which sought to strip Christianity of its supernatural trappings and present Jesus as 'an incomparable man', was perhaps the single most talked-about book of its age. Its impact on the public was enormous; and among the figures it most deeply influenced was Albert Schweitzer. Yet even Renan's treatment was to be regarded as saccharine and uncritically sentimental by the generation of Modernists who had begun to appear in the last quarter of the nineteenth century. And the majority of Modernists, it should be noted, were working within the framework of the Church – until, that is, they were officially condemned by Pope Pius X in 1907 and an anti-Modernist oath was introduced in 1910.

By this time, the findings of both German biblical scholarship and of the Roman Catholic Modernists had begun to find their way into the arts. Thus, in 1916, the Anglo-Irish novelist George Moore published his own fictionalised account of Jesus in *The Brook Kerith*. Moore caused considerable scandal by depicting Jesus as surviving the Crucifixion, and being nursed back to health by Joseph of Arimathea. In the years since *The Brook Kerith* was published, there have been numerous other fictionalised accounts of the Gospel story. In 1946, Robert Graves published his ambitious fictional portrait, *King Jesus*, in which Jesus again survives the Cross. And in 1954, Nikos Kazantzakis, the Nobel Prize-winning Greek author, caused an international rumpus with *The Last Temptation*. In contrast to the Jesus figures in Moore and Graves, Kazantzakis's protagonist does die on the Cross. Before he does so, however, he has a vision of what his life should and would have been had he not voluntarily submitted himself to his final sacrifice. In this vision – a kind of 'flash-forward' in fantasy – Jesus sees himself married to the Magdalene (for whom he has lusted all through the book) and fathering a family upon her.

These examples illustrate the extent to which biblical scholarship opened up new territory for the arts. Two hundred years ago, a novel dealing with scriptural material would have been unthinkable. Even poetry would not address such matters except in the more or less orthodox, more or less devotional form of *Paradise Lost*. By the twentieth century, however, Jesus and his world had become 'fair game', not for luridly sensational purposes, but as valid points of enquiry and exploration for serious, internationally acclaimed literary figures. Through their work, the fruits of biblical scholarship were disseminated to an ever-widening audience.

Biblical scholarship itself did not stand still. Jesus and the world of the New Testament continued to be addressed by professional historians and researchers who, with increasing rigour and fresh evidence at their disposal, sought to establish the facts surrounding that enigmatic individual of two thousand years ago. Many of these works were intended primarily for other experts in the field and attracted little popular attention. A few, however, were pitched to the general reading public and engendered considerable controversy. *The Passover Plot* (1963) by Dr Hugh Schonfield argued that Jesus staged his own mock crucifixion and did not die on the cross; the book became an international best-seller, with more than three million copies now in print. More recently, controversy was provoked by *Jesus the Magician*, in which Dr Morton Smith depicts his protagonist as a typical wonder-worker of the age, a figure of a kind that thronged the Middle East at the beginning of the Christian era. The Jesus of Morton Smith is not significantly different from, say, Apollonius of Tyana, or the prototype (assuming one existed) of the legendary figure of Simon Magus.

In addition to material devoted specifically to Jesus, there have been innumerable works on the origins of Christianity, the formation of the early Church and its roots in Old Testament Judaism. Here, Dr Schonfield has again played a prominent role with a series of works addressed to the background of the New Testament. And in 1979 Elaine Pagels attracted the world's attention, and an immense readership, with *The Gnostic Gospels* – a study of the Nag Hammadi Scrolls, discovered in Egypt in 1945, which offered a radical new interpretation of Christian teaching and tradition.

Biblical scholarship has made enormous advances during the last forty years, aided immensely by the discovery of new primary sources, material unavailable to researchers in the past. The most famous of these sources, of course, are the Dead Sea Scrolls, discovered in 1947 in the ruins of the ascetic Essene community of Qumran. In addition to such major discoveries, many parts of which have yet to be published, other sources have gradually been coming to light or, after long suppression, are being circulated and studied.

As a result, Jesus is no longer a shadowy figure existing in the simplistic, fairy-tale world of the Gospels. Palestine at the advent of the Christian era is no longer a nebulous place belonging more to myth than to history. On the contrary, we now know a great deal about Jesus's milieu, and far more than most practising Christians realise about Palestine in the first century – its sociology, its economy, its politics, its cultural and religious character, its historical actuality. Much of Jesus's world has emerged from the haze of conjecture, speculation and mythic hyperbole, and is clearer and better documented than, say, the world of King Arthur. And although Jesus himself remains to a significant degree elusive, it is as possible to deduce plausible information about him as it is to deduce such information about Arthur, or Robin Hood.

The Failure of Biblical Scholarship

Despite all this, the hopeful prophecy which we quoted at the beginning of this book has not been fulfilled. Theologians of intellectual standing have not – at least, not publicly – come to share those conclusions, nor to be amazed at the credulity of their nineteenth-century predecessors. In certain quarters, dogma is, if anything, more entrenched than ever. Despite the current problem of over-population, the Vatican can still impose its strictures on birth control and abortion – not on social or moral grounds, but on theological. A fire, caused by a bolt of lightning at York Minster, can still be regarded as evidence of divine wrath at the appointment of a contentious bishop. This bishop's ambiguous statements on aspects of Jesus's biography can still provoke outrage among people who refuse to believe anything but that their saviour was conceived by the Holy Spirit on a virgin. And in American communities, major works of literature can be banned from schools and libraries – or even, occasionally, burnt – for challenging traditional scriptural accounts, while a new current of fundamentalism can actually influence American politics through the support of millions eager to be raptured away to a heaven more or less interchangeable with Disneyland.

However unorthodox its presentation of Jesus, Kazantzakis's *The Last Temptation* is a passionately religious, passionately devotional, passionately Christian work. Nevertheless, the novel was banned in many countries, including the author's native Greece, and Kazantzakis himself was excommunicated. Among non-fiction works, Schonfield's *The Passover Plot*, despite immense sales, provoked much bitter hostility.

In 1983, David Rolfe, working for London Weekend Television and Channel 4, began work on a three-part television documentary entitled *Jesus: the Evidence*. The series took no position of its own, endorsed no particular point of view. It simply endeavoured to survey the field of New Testament studies and to assess the value of various theories proposed. Yet even before the project got under way, British pressure groups were lobbying to have the enterprise suppressed. When it was finished, in 1984, it had to be screened, in a private showing, to a number of Members of Parliament before it could be cleared for transmission. And although subsequent reviews found it thoroughly sane and quite uncontroversial, clerics of the Church of England publicly announced that they would be on standby alert to deal with any members of their congregation upset by the programmes.

Jesus: the Evidence had sought to bring some of the advances in New Testament scholarship to the attention of the lay public. Apart from *The Passover Plot*, virtually none of this scholarship has found its way into popular consciousness. A few works, such as

Jesus the Magician and *The Gnostic Gospels*, have been widely reviewed, discussed and distributed, but their readership has been largely confined to people with a particular interest in their subject matter. Most of the work done in recent years has impinged only on specialists. Much of it is also written specifically for specialists, being virtually impenetrable to the uninitiated reader.

So far as the general public is concerned, as well as the churches who minister to that public, the works cited above might never have been produced. George Moore's depiction of Jesus as having survived the Crucifixion followed on from a contention maintained not only by some of the oldest heresies, but also by the Koran, and thus widely accepted throughout Islam and the Islamic world. And yet the same claim, when promulgated by Robert Graves, then by Dr Schonfield in *The Passover Plot*, attracted as much scandal and incredulity as if it had never been broached before. In the field of New Testament studies, it is as if each new discovery, each new assertion, is swallowed up as quickly as it can be made. Each must constantly be presented anew, only to disappear again. Many people reacted to certain assertions in our own book as if *The Passover Plot*, or Graves's *King Jesus*, or Moore's *The Brook Kerith* – or, for that matter, the Koran itself – had never been written.

This is an extraordinary situation, perhaps unique in the entire spectrum of modern historical research. In every other sphere of historical enquiry, new material is acknowledged. It may be disputed. Attempts may be made to suppress it. Alternatively, it may be digested and assimilated. But at least people know what has already been discovered, what has already been said twenty or fifty or seventy years ago. There is some species of genuine advance, whereby old discoveries and contentions provide a basis for new discoveries and contentions, and a corpus of knowledge comes into being. Revolutionary theories may be accepted or discarded, but cognisance is at least taken of them and of what preceded them. A context exists. Cumulative contributions by successive generations of researchers create an increased and increasing understanding. Thus do we acquire our knowledge of history in general, as well as of specific epochs and events. Thus do we acquire a coherent image of such figures as King Arthur, Robin Hood or Jeanne d'Arc. These images are constantly growing, constantly mutating, constantly being augmented by new material as it becomes available.

So far as the general public is concerned, New Testament history offers a striking contrast. It remains static, unaffected by new developments, new discoveries, new findings. Each controversial assertion is treated as if it were being made for the first time. Thus the Bishop of Durham's theological pronouncements produce as much of a shock-horror reaction as if the Bishop's own acknowledged precursor, Archbishop Temple, had never lived, never presided over the Anglican Church between the wars and never made essentially similar pronouncements.

Each contribution in the field of biblical research is like a footprint in sand. Each is covered almost immediately and, so far as the general public is concerned, left virtually without trace. Each must constantly be made anew, only to be covered again.

Why should this be? Why should biblical scholarship, which is pertinent to so many lives, be thus immune to evolution and development? Why should the great mass of believing Christians in fact know less about the figure they worship than about historical figures of far less relevance? In the past, when such knowledge was inaccessible or dangerous to promulgate, there might have been some justification. The knowledge today is both accessible and safely promulgated. Yet the practising Christian remains as ignorant as his predecessors of centuries ago; and he subscribes essentially to the same simplistic accounts he heard when he himself was a child.

A fundamentalist might well assert that the situation bears witness to the resilience and tenacity of Christian faith. We do not find such an explanation satisfactory. The Christian faith may indeed be resilient and tenacious. History has proved it to be so. But we are not talking about faith – which must necessarily be an intensely private, intensely subjective affair. We are talking about documented historical facts.

In the wake of the television series mentioned above, a panel discussion on the subject was transmitted. A number of distinguished commentators, most of them ecclesiastics, were assembled to evaluate the programmes and their implications. During the course of this panel discussion, several of the contributors agreed on one telling point. In the last year, the same point has been echoed not only by the Bishop of Durham, but also by the Archbishop of Canterbury. It was also a focus of debate at a subsequent synod of the Church of England.

According to several participants, the prevailing ignorance of New Testament scholarship is in large part the fault of the churches themselves and of the ecclesiastical establishment. Anyone in the ministry, anyone training for the ministry, is, as a matter of course, confronted with the latest developments in biblical research. Any seminarian today will learn at least something of the Dead Sea Scrolls, of the Nag Hammadi Scrolls, of the history and evolution of New Testament studies, of the more controversial statements made by both theologians and historians. *Yet this knowledge has not been passed on to the laity.* In consequence, a gulf has opened between ecclesiastics and their congregations. Among themselves, ecclesiastics have become eminently sophisticated and erudite. They react to the latest discoveries with blasé aplomb, remaining unruffled by theological controversy. They may find contentions such as those we have made questionable, but not surprising or scandalous. Yet nothing of this sophistication has been transmitted to their flock. The flock receives virtually no historical background from its shepherd – who is believed to be the definitive authority in such matters. When, in consequence, such background is presented by writers like ourselves, rather than by the official shepherd, it can often produce a reaction amounting to trauma, or a personal crisis of faith. Either we become regarded as gratuitously destructive iconoclasts, or the shepherd himself becomes suspect for having withheld information. The overall effect is precisely the same as if there were an organised conspiracy of silence among churchmen.

This, then, is the situation at present. On the one hand, there is the ecclesiastical hierarchy, steeped in what has been written in the past, versed in all the latest aspects of biblical scholarship. On the other hand, there is the lay congregation, to whom biblical scholarship is totally unknown territory. The modern, more or less well-read cleric is acutely aware, for example, of the distinction between what is in the New Testament itself and what is an accretion of later tradition. He is aware of precisely how much – or, to be more accurate, how little – the scriptures actually say. He is aware of how much latitude, indeed, of how much necessity, there is for interpretation. For such a cleric, the contradictions between fact and faith, between history and theology, were personally confronted and resolved long ago. Such a cleric has long recognised that his personal belief is not the same thing as historical evidence, and he has effected some kind of personal reconciliation between the two – a reconciliation which, to a greater or lesser degree, manages to accommodate both. Such a cleric has generally 'heard it all before'. He is unlikely to be startled by the kind of evidence or hypothesis presented by us and by other writers. It will already have been familiar to him, and he will have formed his own conclusions long ago.

In contrast to the learned shepherd, the flock has not had

occasion either to familiarise itself with the evidence in question or to confront the inconsistencies between scriptural accounts and the actual historical backdrop. For the devout Christian, there has been no need to reconcile fact and faith, history and theology, simply because he has never had any reason to believe a distinction between them might exist. He may not even have thought consciously of Palestine two thousand years ago as a very real place, precisely situated in space and time, subject to a confused welter of social, psychological, political, economic and religious factors – the same factors that operate in any 'real' locality, past or present. On the contrary, the story in the Gospels is often utterly divorced from all historical context – a narrative of stark, timeless, mythic simplicity enacted in a sort of limbo, a never-never-land of long ago and far away. Jesus, for example, appears now in Galilee, now in Judaea; now in Jerusalem, or on the banks of the Jordan. For the modern Christian, however, there is often no awareness of the geographical and political relation between these places, how far they might be from each other, how long a journey from one to the other might take. The titles of various official functionaries are often meaningless. Romans and Jews mill confusingly in the background, like extras on a film set, and if one has any concrete image of them at all, it generally derives from one or another Hollywood spectacular – Pilate complete with Brooklynese accent.

For the lay congregation, scriptural accounts are regarded as literal history, a self-contained story no less true for being divorced from an historical context. Never having been taught otherwise by his spiritual mentors, many a devout believer has had no need to question the problems posed by such a context. When these problems are suddenly posed by a book such as ours, they will quite understandably assume the form of revelation, or of sacrilege. And we ourselves will instinctively be perceived as 'anti-Christian', as writers engaged in a fully fledged crusade which pits us, as militant adversaries, against the ecclesiastical establishment – as if we were personally bent on toppling the edifice of Christendom (and so naïve as to think such a feat possible).

Our Conclusions in Perspective

Needless to say, we harbour no such intentions. We are not engaged in any sort of crusade. We have no particular desire to make 'converts'. We certainly are not deliberately trying to shake people's faith. In *The Holy Blood and the Holy Grail*, our motivation was really quite simple. We had a story to tell, and the story seemed eminently worth the telling. We had been involved in an historical adventure as gripping as any detective tale or spy thriller. At the same time, the adventure had also proved immensely informative, uncovering vast tracts of our civilisation's past – and not just biblical – which we and our readers might not otherwise have had occasion to explore. It is a truism that a good story requires telling; it seems to have a life and momentum of its own, which demand expression. We wished to share our story, in much the same way that one might tug a friend's arm and call his or her attention to a striking landscape, or a spectacular sunset.

Our conclusions about Jesus were an integral part of our adventure. Indeed, the adventure itself led us to them. We simply invited our readers to witness the process whereby it had done so. 'These are the conclusions we reached,' we said in effect. 'They are *our* conclusions, based on our own research, our own predispositions, our own framework, our own lack of preconceptions. We are not trying to foist them upon you. If they make sense to you, well and good. If not, feel free to discard them and draw your own. In the meantime, we hope you found your sojourn with us interesting, entertaining and informative.' And yet it was inevitable, given our subject matter, that we should find ourselves caught in the inherent conflict between fact and faith. A simple example should serve to illustrate the complexities and the paradoxes of this conflict.

In 1520, Hernán Cortés, advancing on the ancient Mexican capital of Tenochtitlán, was regarded as a god by the Aztecs. Never having seen firearms or horses before, the Aztecs regarded these things not only as supernatural, but as confirmation of Cortés's divine status – of his identity as an avatar of their supreme god, Quetzalcoatl. Today, of course, it is understandable how such a misconception can have occurred. Even to a Western European at the time, it would have been comprehensible. It is quite clear that there was nothing in any way divine about Cortés. And yet it is equally clear that in the minds of those who believed in his divinity, he was indeed a god.

Let us suppose that a modern Mexican Indian, perhaps with vestiges of an Aztec heritage, asserts that he *believes* in Cortés's divinity. It might seem to us somewhat peculiar, but we could not presume to challenge his belief – especially if his background, his education, his upbringing, his culture had all conduced to foster it. Moreover, his 'faith' might entail something much more profound than a mere conviction of Cortés's divinity. He might assert that he experienced Cortés within him, that he communed personally with Cortés, that Cortés appeared to him in visions, that through Cortés he approached oneness with God or with the sacred. How could we possibly challenge such assertions? What a man experiences in the privacy of his psyche must of necessity remain inviolate and inviolable. And there are a great many people, quite sane, quite balanced, quite worthy of respect, who, in the privacy of their psyches, believe in things far stranger than the divinity of Hernán Cortés.

But the times in which Cortés lived, like the times in which Jesus lived, are documented. We know quite a bit about the historical context, the world in which both figures existed. This knowledge is not a matter of personal belief, but of simple historical fact. And if a man permits his personal belief to distort, alter or transform historical fact, he cannot expect others, whether or not they share his belief, to condone the process. The same principle obtains if a man permits his personal belief to derange dramatically the laws of probability and what we know of human nature. We could not, as we said, challenge a man who believed in Cortés's divinity, or who, in some manner or form 'experienced' Cortés within him. We could, however, challenge a man who asserted that, as a matter of historical fact, Cortés (like Quetzalcoatl) was born of an eagle and a serpent, or that Cortés was ordained to save the world, or that Cortés never died and now bides his time in some underground crypt awaiting a propitious moment to return and proclaim his sovereignty over Mexico. We could challenge a man who asserted that Cortés, even without his armour, was immune to spears and arrows, that he rode a horse through sea or sky, or that he used weapons which in reality were not invented until two centuries later.

It is not that established records of Cortés explicitly deny these things. They do not – for the simple reason that no such things were ever asserted about Cortés during his lifetime. But such things fly so flagrantly in the face of known history, so flagrantly in the face of human experience, so flagrantly in the face of simple probability, that they impose an inordinate strain upon credulity. As personal belief, they may be unimpugnable. But presented as historical fact, they rest on too improbable and too tenuous a basis.

Jesus poses a problem essentially analogous. We have no desire to challenge anyone's personal faith, anyone's personal belief. We are not dealing with the Christ or Christos of theology, the figure who enjoys a very real and very puissant existence in the psyches and consciences of the faithful. We are dealing with a different figure, someone who actually walked the sands of Palestine two thousand years ago, just as Cortés trod the stones of the Mexican desert in 1519. We are dealing, in short, with the Jesus of history – and history, however vague and uncertain it may sometimes be, will still often brazenly defy our wishes, our myths, our mental images, our preconceptions.

In order to do justice to the Jesus of history, one must effectively divest oneself of preconceptions – and especially of the preconceptions fostered by subsequent tradition. One must be prepared to contemplate biblical material as dispassionately as one might contemplate chronicles pertaining to Caesar, or Alexander – or Cortés. And one must refrain from *a priori* acts of belief.

Indeed, it can be argued that the wisdom of believing or disbelieving is itself questionable. 'Belief' may well be a dangerous word, implying, as it does, an act of faith which may often be unwarranted. People are prepared to kill all too readily in the name of belief. At the same time, to disbelieve is as much an act of faith, as much an unsubstantiated assumption, as belief. Disbelief – as exemplified by the militant atheist or rationalist, for instance – is in itself another form of belief. To say that one does not believe in telepathy, or in ghosts, or in God is as much an act of faith as believing in them.

It is preferable to think in terms of knowledge. Ultimately, the issue is quite simple. Either one knows something, immediately, directly and at first hand, or one does not. A man who touches a hot stove does not need to believe in pain. He knows pain; he experiences pain; pain is a reality that cannot be doubted. A man who receives an electric shock does not ask himself whether he believes in the form of energy known as electricity. He experiences something whose reality cannot be denied, whatever the term one attaches to it. But if one is dealing with anything other than empirical knowledge of this kind – if, in short, one does not personally *know* in the sense just explained – the only honest thing one can say is that one does not know. So far as the theological attributes accorded Jesus by Christian tradition are concerned, we simply do not know.

Within the general spectrum of 'things not known', virtually all things are possible. But on the basis of one's own experience, on the basis of human history and development, some of these are more possible than others, more or less likely, more or less probable than others. If one is honest, one can only acknowledge this situation – that all things are possible, but that some are more possible than others. It amounts to a simple balance of probabilities and plausibilities. What is more or less likely to have happened? What is more in accord with mankind's experience? In the absence of truly definitive knowledge about Jesus, it seems to us more likely, more probable, more in accord with our experience of humanity, that a man should have been married and tried to regain his rightful throne than that he should have been born of a virgin, walked on water and risen from his grave. And yet this conclusion, too, must, of necessity, remain tentative. It is a conclusion acknowledged as a more likely possibility, not embraced as a creed.

Interpretation in the Service of Belief

As we have said, much is known today about the world in which Jesus lived, the Palestine of two thousand years ago. But so far as Jesus himself, and the events surrounding his life, are concerned, there *is* an absence of definitive knowledge. The Gospels, indeed the whole of the Bible, are sketchy documents, which no responsible scholar would for a moment consider absolutely reliable as historical testimony. Given this situation, one must perforce hypothesise, if one is not to remain mute. Granted, one must not hypothesise wildly; one must confine one's speculation to the framework of known historical data and probabilities. Within this framework, however, it is perfectly valid, and indeed necessary, to speculate – to interpret the meagre, opaque and often contradictory evidence that does exist. Most biblical scholarship involves some degree of speculation. So, for that matter, do theology and the teachings of the churches. But while historical research speculates on the basis of historical fact, theology and clerical teachings speculate almost entirely on the scriptures themselves – often without any relation to historical fact.

People have argued, have slaughtered each other, have waged wars throughout the course of the last two thousand years over the way in which particular passages should be understood. In the coalescence of Christian tradition, there is one principle that has remained constant. In the past, when Church Fathers or other individuals were confronted with one of the various biblical ambiguities and contradictions, they *speculated* about its meaning. They attempted to *interpret* it. Once accepted, the conclusion of their speculation – that is, their interpretation – would become enshrined as dogma. Over the centuries, it then came to be regarded as established fact. Such conclusions are not fact at all. On the contrary, they are speculation and interpretation congealed into a tradition; and it is this tradition which is constantly mistaken for fact.

A single example should serve to illustrate the process. According to all four Gospels, Pilate affixes to Jesus's cross an inscription bearing the title 'King of the Jews'. Apart from this, the Gospels tell us virtually nothing. In John 6:15, there is a curious statement, that 'Jesus, who could see they were about to come and take him by force and make him king, escaped back to the hills by himself'.[4] And in John 19:21–22: 'So the Jewish chief priests said to Pilate, "You should not write 'King of the Jews', but 'This man said: I am King of the Jews.'"' Pilate answered, "What I have written, I have written."' But there is no elaboration or elucidation of these passages. We are given no real indication of whether the title was warranted or not, official or not, recognised or not. Nor are we given any indication of how, precisely, Pilate intended the appellation to be understood. What was his motivation? What was his action intended to achieve?

At some point in the past, it was *assumed*, on the basis of speculative interpretation, that Pilate must have intended the title mockingly. To have assumed otherwise would have been to raise a number of awkward questions. Today, most Christians blindly accept, as if it were a matter of established fact, that Pilate used the title in derision. But this is not established fact at all. If one reads the Gospels themselves, with no preconceptions whatever, there is nothing to suggest that the title was not used in all seriousness – was not perfectly legitimate and acknowledged as such by at least some of Jesus's contemporaries, including Pilate. So far as the Gospels themselves are concerned, Jesus may indeed have been King of the Jews – and/or been so regarded. It is only tradition that has persuaded people otherwise. To suggest that Jesus may actually have been King of the Jews is not, therefore, to stand at variance with the evidence. It is merely to stand at variance with a long established tradition – a long established system of beliefs based ultimately on someone's speculative interpretation. If anything stands at variance with the evidence, it is this system of beliefs. For in Matthew's account of Jesus's birth, the three 'wise men' ask, 'Where is the infant King of the Jews?' If Pilate intended the title to be derisive, what is one to make of the question of the magi? Did they, too, intend it as derisive? Surely not. Yet if they were referring to a legitimate title, why should not Pilate have been doing so as well?

The Gospels are documents of a stark, mythic simplicity. They depict a world stripped to certain bare essentials, a world of a timeless, archetypal, almost fairy-tale character. But Palestine, at the advent of the Christian era, was not a fairy-tale kingdom. On the contrary, it was an eminently real place, peopled by real individuals, such as one might find anywhere else in the world at any other time in history. Herod was not a king of obscure legend. He was a very real potentate, whose reign (37 to 4 B.C.) extends beyond its biblical context to overlap those of well known secular figures – of Julius Caesar, for instance, Cleopatra, Mark Antony, Augustus and other personages familiar to us from schoolbooks and even from Shakespeare. As we have said, Palestine in the first century, like any other place in the world, was subject to a complex welter of social, psychological, political, economic, cultural and religious factors. Numerous factions squabbled with each other and among themselves. Cabals manipulated and machinated behind the scenes. Various parties pursued conflicting objectives, often making tenuous alliances with each other for the sole purpose of expediency. Deals were clandestinely arranged. Vested interests jockeyed for power. The populace at large, like the populace elsewhere and at other times, veered between apathetic torpor and hysterical fanaticism, between abject fear and fervent conviction. Little, if any, of this is conveyed by the Gospels – only a residue of confusion. And yet these currents, these forces, are essential for any understanding of the historical Jesus – the Jesus who actually walked the soil of Palestine two thousand years ago – rather than the Christ of faith. It was this Jesus that we endeavoured to discern and comprehend more clearly. To make such an endeavour is not to declare oneself anti-Christian.

The Context

In the wake of *The Holy Blood and the Holy Grail*, when certain 'Christians' vehemently declared us to be anti-Christian, we could only shrug helplessly. We ourselves, it must be repeated, had no desire to assume the role of iconoclasts; we were simply caught in the conflict between fact and faith.

Nor, for that matter, did we regard the suggestions we made about Jesus as in any way shocking or outrageous. As the reader will have noted, virtually all the suggestions had been made before, most of them quite recently and in a well publicised way. Moreover, we were not alone. We were not concocting a cranky, hare-brained thesis calculated to produce an 'instant best-seller'. On the contrary, virtually all our suggestions were very much in the mainstream of contemporary biblical scholarship, and it was from precisely this scholarship that much of our research derived. We consulted the acknowledged experts in the field, many of whom were not known to the general public; and for the most part we did little more than synthesise their conclusions in a readily digestible fashion. These conclusions were already familiar enough to the ecclesiastical establishment, many of whom readily accepted them. What they had failed to do was pass them on to the laity.

In private discussions, we met churchmen of many denominations. Few expressed any hostility to the conclusions in our book. Certain of them took issue with us on one or another specific point, but most found our general thesis plausible, even in some cases probable, and in no way diminishing the stature of Jesus or the Christian faith. Among lay Christians, however, the same conclusions seemed to entail blasphemy, heresy, sacrilege and almost every other religious sin on the register. It was this discrepancy of reaction that we found particularly striking and instructive. Churchmen, whom one would expect to be most militant about the matter, responded with anything from sceptical but unsurprised indifference to outright endorsement. Their flock responded with anything from horrified disillusion to vociferous outrage. Nothing could have made so apparent the failure of the churches to keep their congregations abreast of developments in the field of biblical scholarship.

All the same, there are signs that the situation is slowly beginning to change. It may well be, of course, that these signs are misleading or illusory, and that the pendulum will once again swing back in favour of 'simple faith', with the fruits of historical scholarship continuing to be ignored or suppressed. In that respect, the contagion of American fundamentalism certainly augurs ill. Nevertheless, there are distinct signs of improvement in the air, so numerous as to amount, in their modest way, to a form of *Zeitgeist* – a spirit, or current, or movement, abroad in the world.

During the years of our research, numerous other publications were already in circulation, helping to create a favourable climate. In the 1970s, at least two novels, one of them a serious and well reviewed work of literature, postulated the discovery of Jesus's mummified body. Another popular novel called the Gospels into question by suggesting the existence of a new corpus of first-hand scriptural accounts – and this book was made into a television mini-series. In his monumental opus *Terra Nostra* – certainly one of the dozen or so most important novels to be published in any language since the Second World War – the respected Mexican novelist Carlos Fuentes depicted Jesus as surviving the Cross by means of a fraudulent crucifixion involving a substitute. At least one novel, *Magdalene* by Carolyn Slaughter, presented the Magadalene as Jesus's lover. And Liz Greene, drawing on some of our own research, wrote of a bloodline descended from Jesus in *The Dreamer of the Vine*, a novel about Nostradamus published in 1980.

So far as more academic scholarship was concerned, the Nag Hammadi Scrolls appeared for the first time in English translation in 1977, and within two years had inspired Elaine Pagels's bestseller *The Gnostic Gospels*. Morton Smith had disclosed his findings about the early church in *The Secret Gospel*, following it with his controversial portrait in *Jesus the Magician*. Haim Maccoby addressed himself to the historical Jesus in *Revolution in Judaea*, as did Geza Vermes in such works as *Jesus the Jew*. And Hugh Schonfield's on-going series of studies of first-century Palestine was appearing at regular intervals through the 1970s. On a theological level, a number of Anglican clerics provoked considerable controversy by questioning Jesus's divinity in a collection of essays, *The Myth of God Incarnate*. And it is also worth noting a curious, unsubstantiated but fascinating book, *The Jesus Scroll*, by an Australian writer, Donovan Joyce.

By 1982, then, when *The Holy Blood and the Holy Grail* appeared in print, the waters had already been disturbed by a fresh wave of material pertaining to the historical Jesus. True, many people still did not know the extent to which, for example, the Gospels contradict each other. Or that there are Gospels other than those in the New Testament, which were more or less arbitrarily excluded from the canon by councils composed of eminently mortal, eminently fallible men. Or that Jesus's divinity had been decided by vote at the Council of Nicaea, some three centuries after Jesus himself had lived. True, too, fundamentalism is still rabid in America. And, as we observed earlier, there are still people in Britain who can ascribe a fire caused by lightning in York to God's wrath at the appointment of a somewhat outspoken bishop – as if, amid the violence, hatred, prejudice, insensitivity and menace of the modern world, God had nothing more pressing on His mind, nothing better to do with His resources. And there are still people who can shout blasphemy or heresy and demand the same bishop's resignation when he makes so self-evident, common-sense a statement as that the Resurrection cannot be definitively 'proved'. Nevertheless, there is something 'in the air', of which the bishop himself is a manifestation.

It would be disingenuous on our part to pretend ignorance of our book's impact, both in sales and controversy. For the first time since Hugh Schonfield's *Passover Plot* in 1963, certain questions pertaining to the New Testament, to Jesus and to the origins of Christianity, were raised to the general reading public – to the so-called 'mass market', rather than to a cadre of academic specialists and theologians. And it became apparent that the general reading public was not only prepared, but positively eager, to listen.

Neither television nor the publishing establishment was blind to the possibilities. Since 1982, a number of new books have appeared. In 1983, *The Illusionist*, a novel by Anita Mason, offered a controversial but historically valid perspective on the coalescence of the early Church; it was short-listed for the Booker Prize, Britain's most prestigious literary award. In 1985, Anthony Burgess, perhaps even more controversially, explored much the same territory in *The Kingdom of the Wicked*. An incipient storm was provoked by Michele Roberts's novel *The Wild Girl*. Drawing, as we did, on evidence in the Nag Hammadi Scrolls, Michele Roberts depicts the Magdalene as Jesus's lover and as the mother of his child. On its paperback publication in 1985, *The Wild Girl* provoked dire fulminations not only from the expected pressure groups, but also from a would-be Torquemada in Parliament; and, until rather more sane judgments prevailed, the book was threatened with prosecution under Britain's antediluvian blasphemy law. In the meantime, Robert Graves's *King Jesus*, which makes assertions no less scandalous, was reissued for the first time since 1962, in a readily accessible paperback edition. (Graves's book, presumably, was too opaque for the self-appointed custodians of thought who objected to Michele Roberts. Or perhaps established literary figures enjoy a certain immunity from such cranky zeal. It might reasonably be argued that the single most inflammatory portrayal of Jesus anywhere is in D. H. Lawrence's *The Man Who Died*, published more than fifty years ago, a miniature masterpiece in which Jesus is depicted as having what used to be called 'sexual congress' with a priestess of Isis in an Egyptian temple. At the climactic moment, he declares, 'I am risen!').

Among biblical studies geared towards a non-specialist audience, two of Hugh Schonfield's books have been reissued, while a new one, *The Essene Odyssey*, appeared in 1985. The works of Morton Smith and Elaine Pagels have all been released in quality paperback editions. In television and cinema, there have been dramatisations (albeit glossy and uncontroversial) of the Siege of Masada and the dispute between Peter and Paul. More significantly, Karen Armstrong, a former nun, challenged established Christian tradition in an intelligent, well researched and lucidly presented series on Saint Paul, entitled *The First Christian*. As we have already noted, David Rolfe did likewise in his widely publicised series *Jesus: the Evidence*, which was followed by a book bearing the same title.[5] And in *The Sea of Faith*, Don Cupitt, Lecturer in Divinity and Dean of Emmanuel College, Cambridge, presented perhaps the most penetrating television study yet undertaken of Christianity today – a study containing statements far more contentious than those of the Bishop of Durham.

We would not presume to claim that *The Holy Blood and the Holy Grail* in itself necessarily influenced any of these works. Indeed, some of the individuals cited above would unquestionably find themselves at odds with certain of our conclusions. But we would like to think that the success of our book rendered both publishers and television producers more aware of the audience for material pertaining to the historical Jesus and the origins of Christianity – an audience whose appetite makes such books and films viable. The emergence of this audience constitutes an extremely significant new development. It also places a new and salutary responsibility on the churches, rendering increasingly untenable the kind of patronising censorship hitherto practised by churchmen with their congregrations. If, as in the past, shepherds withhold information from their flock, the flock will no longer acquiesce in the process. It will turn instead to books and television.

If we are correct in this assumption, we do have a basis for feeling gratified. Not, it must be repeated, because we are on a crusade. Not because we have a vested interest, personal or impersonal, in challenging, compromising or embarrassing the ecclesiastical establishment. But because we, too, live in the modern world. We are aware of, and affected by, the pressures of that world. We are vulnerable, like everyone else, to prejudice, and are conscious of how much havoc bigotry, the excesses of blind faith, and the tyranny which often accompanies it, can inflict on the world. It is to our benefit, as it is to everyone else's, that some measure of perspective should be restored.

2

Jesus as King of Israel

Once, when traversing the United States by plane, we were informed by the stewardess: 'We shall be landing momentarily in Chicago.' We quickly sought assurance that the aircraft would remain stationary long enough for us to get off. Words are imbued with a meaning which can often be affected by context, culture and history, all of which are subject to change. Our American colleagues do not understand the word 'momentarily' in the same way that we do. Some words and their meanings may achieve impressive longevity. 'Dog' remains dog through centuries of time and cultural change. (Though even so simple a word will conjure a variety of different images, depending upon the canine preferences of the reader.) But the word 'plane' could not possibly have conveyed to our eighteenth-century ancestors the meaning which it carries at the top of this page.

We must, necessarily, interpret language. We think we know what certain words mean, but the assumption can be dangerous. It is especially so when we try to impose our twentieth-century interpretation upon a word which once conveyed a subtly, or dramatically, different meaning in the past. Even more dangerous is it when we insist that a man of two thousand years ago meant what we mean in so contentiously abstract a sphere as religious faith.

Many of our contemporary attitudes to or beliefs about Jesus stem from interpretation – or misinterpretation – of biblical material. And biblical material is composed of words (themselves translations of other words) which attempt to convey ideas. Perhaps one of the most important of these ideas is that of Jesus as Messiah.

In the words of a much loved hymn, Jesus is described as 'prophet, priest and king'. And these appellations are all to be inferred when the Christian speaks of Jesus as Messiah. For most,

22

indeed, the title, applying uniquely as it now does to Jesus, also implies God. We must be cautious, though, in making the assumption that such words as 'king', 'prophet', or 'Messiah' still convey to us the meaning which they had at the time and in the world of Jesus.

We discussed evidence for Jesus as king in our previous book, but additional material must be presented and emphasised here. For to say that Jesus was a 'rightful king' means far more than it might imply in today's world – far more than just a legitimate inherited position as head, symbolic or otherwise, of a secular state. The 'nation of Israel' two thousand years ago was perceived primarily as a spiritual, rather than a secular, entity. It represented an extreme example of a theocracy – of a body politic organised essentially around religious principles. Not only were religion and the state virtually synonymous, as they might be today, for example, in Iran. The state itself was a manifestation of religion. Every other aspect of the culture was similarly absorbed within a religious framework. The very landscape was regarded as uniquely and especially favoured by God. Caves, valleys, mountains, rivers – all were invested with a profound reverential significance. Although social, political and economic factors were obviously important, the administrative machinery of government was geared ultimately towards creating a culture which earned God's endorsement and fulfilled what was deemed to be His will. Taxes levied by Rome or by local secular authorities might be grudged, but those claimed by the Temple were paid willingly, even eagerly. The people considered themselves 'God's chosen', and the king of such a people was regarded as something more than other kings – more even than the Emperor of Rome. He was a manifestation of God's will. He was an embodiment of God's divine plan for the people as a whole. He was a mouthpiece for God's intentions and wishes. He was ultimately as much an oracle, a high priest, a pope, a spiritual leader, as he was a king.

All of this, of course, in the context of the age, is what the term 'Messiah' would have signified. In a strictly literal translation 'Messiah' meant nothing more nor less than 'the anointed one'. In other words, it denoted the duly consecrated and divinely endorsed king. Every king of Israel was regarded as a Messiah. The term was habitually applied to David and to David's successors, from Solomon on. 'Every Jewish king of the House of David was known as Messiah, or Christ, and a regular way of referring to the High Priest was "the Priest Messiah" ...'[1]

Not only that. Around the time of Jesus's birth, a militant, armed opposition to Rome was organised and led by a man who also claimed the title of Messiah. He was recognised as such not only by his immediate followers, but also by a portion of the populace at large. His son, in A.D. 66, 'returned in the state of a king to Jerusalem' and, 'adorned with royal garments', visited the Temple to worship.[2]

Needless to say, there was nothing intrinsically divine about such figures. Indeed, to assert that any man was God, or even son of God, in a literal sense would have been, for Jesus and his contemporaries, blasphemous in the extreme. For Jesus and his contemporaries, the idea of a divine Messiah would have been utterly unthinkable.

But if the Messiah was not divine, he would certainly have had God's particular and unique blessing. He would have functioned as, so to speak, God's temporal viceroy, constituting the primary link between the Deity and ordinary humanity. Thus, although the term 'Messiah' simply meant 'the anointed one', or 'king', the concept of kingship it implied involved far more than concepts of kingship do today.

The status of the expected Messiah was augmented by the circumstances which obtained in Palestine at the period of Jesus's birth. This period – which we shall have occasion to discuss in more detail later – was known, for those living in it, as 'the Last Times', or 'the Last Days'. The nation was believed to have fallen into a phase of cataclysmic evil. The last dynasty of legitimate Judaic monarchs had been all but extinguished. Since 63 B.C., Israel herself had become a territory of the Roman Empire, forced to acknowledge a secular ruler who – in blasphemous affront to every tenet of Judaism – dared to proclaim himself a god. And the throne of the country was occupied by a puppet-king regarded as an iniquitous usurper. Herod, who reigned over Palestine at the time, could not even claim to be a Jew by birth. He was a native of Idumaea, the largely desert, and non-Judaic, region to the south.

At the beginning of his reign, Herod undertook to establish currency and legitimacy for himself. He repudiated his first wife and married a recognised Judaic princess, thereby seeking at least a form of legal sanction. In order to ingratiate himself with the populace, he rebuilt the Temple of Jerusalem on a hitherto unprecedented scale. He proclaimed himself a devout servant of the God of Israel. Such gestures failed dismally to ratify his authority. He remained reviled and hated by the people he ruled. Even his most generous acts were received with hostility and scorn, and this encouraged a natural predisposition towards tyranny and excess.

That such a man should be placed in the role of ruler over God's chosen was deemed a curse – an affliction visited by God upon His people, a punishment for transgression both past and present. Whatever social and political abuses Herod might perpetrate, these were seen merely as symptoms of a much more profound dilemma – the dilemma of a people who had been abandoned by their God. Throughout the Palestine of Jesus's time, there spread a yearning for a spiritual leader who would bring the nation back to God again, would effect a reconciliation with the divine. This spiritual leader, when he appeared, would be the rightful king – the 'Messiah'. As king, he would rescue his people. He would restore God's covenant with man. Aided by God, suffused by God, sanctioned and mandated by God, performing God's will, he would drive the Roman invaders from Palestine and establish his own righteous regime, as glorious as that ascribed by tradition to Solomon and David. The character of the Messiah is summed up by one historian of the period as:

> ... a charismatically endowed descendant of David whom the Jews ... believed would be raised up by God to break the yoke of the heathen and to reign over a restored kingdom of Israel to which all the Jews of the Exile would return.[3]

Christian tradition, of course, does not contest Jesus's claim to Messiahship. It contests only what Messiahship entailed, simply because this, for centuries, was not made sufficiently clear. To accept Jesus as a Messiah while denying his regal and political role is simply to ignore the facts – to ignore the historical context, to ignore what the word 'Messiah' meant and implied. Christians have regarded the Messiah as non-political – a wholly spiritual figure who posed no challenge to temporal authority, who had no secular or political aspirations himself, who beckoned his followers to a kingdom 'not of this world'. Biblical scholarship during the last two centuries, however, has rendered such an interpretation increasingly untenable. Few, if any, experts on the subject today would contest that the Messiah expected in Jesus's era was a largely political figure, intent on redeeming Israel from the Roman yoke. Judaism at the time acknowledged no distinction between religion and politics. To the extent that the rightful king was mandated and sanctioned by God, his political activity was mantled in a religious aura. To the extent that his religious function included freeing his people from bondage, his spiritual role was also political.

The Rightful King

The Gospels of Matthew and Luke state explicitly that Jesus was of royal blood – a genuine and legitimate king, the lineal descendant of Solomon and David. If this is true, it would have conferred upon him at least one important qualification for being the Messiah, or for being presented as such. He would have enjoyed a technically legal claim to the throne of his regal forebears – and perhaps, as had been suggested, *the* technically legal claim. It is evident that certain people, from radically diverse backgrounds and with radically diverse interests, are quite prepared to acknowledge the validity of this claim. As we noted, the three wise men come seeking 'the infant King of the Jews'. In Luke 23:3, Jesus is accused of '. . . inciting our people to revolt, opposing payment of the tribute to Caesar, and claiming to be Christ, a king'. In Matthew 21:9, on his triumphal entry into Jerusalem, Jesus is greeted by a multitude shouting 'Hosanna to the son of David'. There can be little question that, in this episode, Jesus is being hailed as king. Indeed, the Gospels of both Luke and John are explicit on the matter. In both of them, Jesus is hailed quite unequivocally as king. And in John 1:49, Jesus is told bluntly by Nathanael: 'You are the King of Israel!'

Finally, of course, there is the inscription 'King of the Jews', which Pilate orders affixed to the Cross. As we have already mentioned, Christian tradition ascribes this gesture on Pilate's part to derision. Yet even as an act of derision, it makes no sense whatever unless Jesus really *was* King of the Jews. If one is a tyrant and a bully, attempting to assert one's authority, to dominate people, to humble those in one's power, what does one accomplish by labelling a poor prophet a king? If, on the other hand, Jesus were a rightful king, then one would indeed assert one's authority by humbling him.

There is further evidence for Jesus's royal status in the Gospel narrative of Herod's Massacre of the Innocents (Matthew 2:3–14). Though highly questionable as the record of an actual historical event, this narrative attests to a very real anxiety on Herod's part about the birth of Jesus:

> When Herod heard this he was perturbed . . . He called together all the chief priests and scribes . . . and enquired of them where the Christ was to be born. 'At Bethlehem in Judaea', they told him, 'for this is what the prophet wrote . . .'[4]

However disliked Herod may have been, his position on the throne should in theory have been secure. Certainly, he cannot possibly have felt seriously menaced by rumours of a mystical or spiritual figure – a prophet or a teacher of the kind in which the Holy Land at the time abounded. If Herod felt threatened by a recently born child, it can only have been because of what the child intrinsically was – a rightful king, for example, with a claim to the throne which even Rome, in the interests of peace and stability, might recognise. Only a concrete, political challenge of this nature would suffice to explain Herod's anxiety. It is not the son of a poor carpenter whom the usurper fears, but the Messiah, the rightful anointed king – a figure who, by virtue of some inherent genealogical qualification, might rally popular support and, if not depose him, at least compromise him on specifically political grounds.

The Privileged Background

The image of Jesus as a 'poor carpenter' from Nazareth can be challenged at length. For the present, however, it is sufficient simply to note two points. The first of these is that the word generally translated as 'carpenter' does not, in the original Greek, mean merely a woodworker. The most accurate translation would be 'master', implying mastery of any art, craft or discipline. It would thus have been as applicable to a teacher, for example, as to a practitioner of any manual skill.[5] The second point is that Jesus was almost certainly not 'of Nazareth'. An overwhelming body of evidence indicates that Nazareth did not exist in biblical times. The town is unlikely to have appeared before the third century. 'Jesus of Nazareth', as most biblical scholars would now readily concur, is a mistranslation of the original Greek phrase 'Jesus the Nazarean'. This does not denote any locality. Rather, it refers to Jesus's membership in a specific group or sect with a specific religious and/or political orientation – the 'Nazarene Party', as certain modern experts call it.

There is notoriously little accurate information about Jesus's circumstances. But what there is clearly indicates that his family was well-to-do, and that his upbringing was of a kind available only to those with status and financial resources. All accounts, for example, depict him as a learned man – which was, one must remember, unusual in those largely illiterate times, when education was essentially an adjunct of class. Jesus is obviously literate and well educated. In the Gospels, he disputes knowledgeably with his elders about the Law, which presupposes some considerable degree of formal training. From his own statements, it is clear that he is word-perfect in his familiarity with the prophetic books of the Old Testament, can quote them at will, can move among them with the facility and expertise of a professional scholar. And if some of his entourage are apparently humble fishermen and artisans from Galilee, others are wealthy and influential people – Joseph of Arimathea, for example, and Nicodemus, and Joanna, the wife of Herod's steward. As we demonstrated in our previous book, moreover, the wedding at Cana – which may in fact have been Jesus's own wedding – was not a modest village affair, but a sumptuous ceremony of the gentry or aristocracy.[6] Even if the wedding were not Jesus's own, his presence, as well as his mother's, at such an occasion would patently suggest that they were members of the same social caste.

Public Recognition

Perhaps more significant than evidence of this kind is the simple fact that Jesus, on a number of crucial occasions in the Gospels, *acts* like a king, and does so quite deliberately. One of the most telling examples is his triumphal entry into Jerusalem on an ass. Biblical scholars concur that this incident – manifestly an important one in Jesus's career and calculated to attract maximum attention among his contemporaries – served a very specific purpose. It was intended, quite flamboyantly, to fulfil Old Testament prophecy. Indeed, in Matthew 21:4, it is made explicit that the procession was intended to fulfil the prophecy in Zechariah 9:9, which foretells the coming of the Messiah:

> Rejoice heart and soul, daughter of Zion!
> Shout with gladness, daughter of Jerusalem!
> See now, your king comes to you;
> he is victorious, he is triumphant,
> humble and riding on a donkey, ...

Given Jesus's familiarity with Old Testament teaching, there can be little question that he was aware of this prophecy. And being aware of this prophecy, he can hardly have fulfilled it unwittingly, or through 'sheer coincidence'. The entry into Jerusalem can only have been made with the calculated design of identifying himself, very specifically in the eyes of the populace, with the expected Messiah – in other words, with the rightful king, the 'anointed one'.

What is more, Jesus has indeed been anointed. The account

appears in garbled form in the New Testament. There has obviously been some attempt to alter and/or censor, but something of the truth can neverthless be teased out of the fragments that remain. Thus, both Matthew and Mark state unequivocally that a *royal* anointing occurred.[7] Both state that it involved 300 denarii of spikenard – the equivalent of perhaps £5,000 today. John states that the ritual was performed by Mary of Bethany, the sister of Lazarus. And he gives the game away by specifying that the ritual occurred on the day immediately preceding Jesus's triumphal entry into Jerusalem.[8]

And yet even before this there is evidence that Jesus was accorded some kind of official public recognition as Israel's Messiah, or rightful king. John the Baptist's ritual at the Jordan would certainly seem to have entailed something of the sort. It appears to have been roughly analogous to, say, the investiture of the Prince of Wales. Having been baptised by John, Jesus had the 'seal of approval' of an accepted and established prophet, a revered holy man – just as Saul, the first King of Israel, received a 'seal of approval' from the prophet Samuel. If John had been of the same family as Jesus, moreover, his 'seal of approval' would have carried the additional authority of a royal warrant.

One thing, at any rate, would seem to be clear, and this is that Jesus, after his baptism in the Jordan, undergoes a significant change. Prior to this ritual, he seems to have been incognito. Certainly there is no record of any public activity on his part, any behaviour that might attract attention. After his baptism, however, he moves suddenly towards the centre of the stage, not shrinking from the limelight, not shrinking from addressing large crowds, not shrinking from becoming the focus of public interest. What is more, his attitude seems to have been affected by his meeting with John at the Jordan. It is almost as if he has acquired something of John's own tempestuous wrath, John's own dire, apocalyptic menace, John's own threatening ultimata. In short, he begins to display precisely the comportment his contemporaries would have expected of their rightful king. Having been recognised and ratified as the Messiah, he now begins to act as a Messiah should.

The Effect of Jerusalem's Fall

The Gospels became depoliticised and responsibility for Jesus's crucifixion was transferred from the Roman administration to the Jews. In addressing ourselves to this process, we are not speculating. On the contrary, we are drawing upon the consensus of unbiased contemporary New Testament scholarship. And we are also drawing upon elementary common sense. Why, for example, should the same people who throng to welcome Jesus on his entry into Jerusalem clamour only days later for his death? Why should the same multitude who invoked blessings on the son of David rejoice in seeing him mortified and humiliated by the hated Roman oppressors? Why – assuming there to be any accuracy at all in the biblical account – should the very populace which revered Jesus suddenly do a complete turnabout and demand, at the cost of his life, that a figure such as Barabbas (whoever Barabbas was) should be spared? Such questions cannot be ignored. But neither the Gospels nor later Christian tradition attempt to answer them.

As we explained in our previous book, and as virtually all serious biblical scholars concur, the Gospels, in treating such issues as these, were either drastically rewritten or, more likely, distorted the events they describe – which would have taken place at least thirty years before they were composed. The Gospels date from the period after the Jewish revolt of A.D. 66 and the sack of Jerusalem by the Romans in A.D. 70. They date from a period of cataclysmic turmoil, when Palestine was ravaged by war, the Holy City and most sacred shrine of Judaism was destroyed, all records were scattered and people's memories of events were blurred or modified by more recent occurrences. The revolt of A.D. 66–73 was a watershed. Previous events were transformed in the light of it, often by means of the wisdom of hindsight. For the modern historian, the revolt warps all perspective: no testimony escapes being filtered through the dark, smoked glass of the upheaval.

But when Palestine erupted in A.D. 66, it was not a sudden or unexpected occurrence. On the contrary, the country had been smouldering for some time. The impending débâcle was 'in the air'. Before the decisive revolt, which provoked the full-scale Roman backlash, there had been numerous abortive insurrections extending back to Jesus's time and, indeed, well before. Since the beginning of the century, militant factions had become increasingly active, conducting a prolonged guerrilla war, raiding Roman supply caravans, attacking isolated contingents of Roman troops, harassing Roman garrisons, wreaking as much havoc as possible.

Evidence exists for Jesus's association with militant factions and for his own probable military activity. It is there, and it will not go away, however hard the authors of the Gospels have tried to disguise it – and however embarrassing it may be for later Christian tradition. But it would be a mistake, we think, to divorce such evidence from its context, as certain recent scholars have sought to do. It would be a mistake to regard Jesus simply as a freedom-fighter, an agitator, a revolutionary in the modern sense. An ordinary freedom-fighter or revolutionary – and there were a great many of them operating in the Holy Land at the time – might well have won popular support for his actions, but could not have been acclaimed as the Messiah. And there are enough fragments in the Gospels – the baptism in the Jordan, for instance, and the triumphal entry into Jerusalem – to indicate that Jesus did indeed enjoy that title, at least during the years of his ministry. If he was thus eligible for that title, there must have been something which qualified him – something which distinguished him from the numerous other leaders, both military and political, who at the time were themselves becoming thorns in the Roman side. In order to be accorded the title of Messiah, and acclaimed as such by the populace, Jesus would have had to possess some legitimate claim.

In contrast to a conventional revolutionary, Jesus must be seen as what the Gospels themselves acknowledge him to be – a claimant to the throne of David, a rightful king, whose sceptre, like David's, implied both spiritual and temporal sovereignty. And if he involved himself in military activity, he would simply have been discharging the martial duty expected of him as royal liberator. Armed resistance to Rome was implicit in the title and the status he had assumed.

3

Constantine as Messiah

The Messiah whom Jesus's contemporaries awaited was a variant of a familiar and long established principle. He was the specifically Judaic equivalent of the sacred priest-king. The principle underlying this figure obtained throughout the ancient world – not only in the classical cultures of the Mediterranean and the Middle East, but among the Celtic and Teutonic tribes of Europe and farther afield as well. Among other things, kingship functioned as a kind of conduit through which man was linked to his gods. And the social hierarchy culminating in the king was intended to mirror, on the terrestrial plane, the immutable order, coherence and stability to which the heavens seemed to bear witness.

Not infrequently, the priest-king was invested with a divine status of his own, becoming a god in his own right. Thus, for example, Egyptian pharaohs were deified, regarded as avatars of Osiris, Amon and/or Ra. In a somewhat similar fashion, Roman emperors promoted themselves to godhood, claiming lineal descent not only from demigods such as Hercules, but from none other than Jupiter himself. In Judaism, of course, the prevailing monotheism of the first century A.D. precluded any deification of the Messiah. Nevertheless, he was more than just royal. He was also sacred. If he was not a god himself, he was intimately linked to God, a manifestation of God's favour and God's will. He constituted the all-important connection between terrestrial and celestial order.

The principle of sacred kingship continues well into later Western history. Needless to say, it underpins the doctrine of 'divine right' as that doctrine gradually evolved. It also lies behind such developments as the medieval conviction that a monarch could heal by the laying on of hands. Not surprisingly, this latter aptitude, which so closely echoes that attributed to Jesus himself, was ascribed with particular emphasis to the Merovingians.

From the Merovingians to the Habsburgs, European dynasties regarded themselves, and were regarded by their subjects, as enjoying a unique mandate from 'on high'. Although this mandate was frequently enough abused, it nevertheless rested on an ultimately selfless foundation – on something originally intended to foster the common good, rather than to foster autocracy. Strictly speaking, the king was nothing more than a servant, a vessel, a vehicle, through which the divine will manifested itself. And to that extent, the king himself was deemed expendable.

In many ancient cultures, indeed, the king was ritually sacrificed after a stipulated period of time. The ritualised killing of the king is one of the most archaic and widespread rites of early civilised man. Albeit with certain symbolic variations, Jesus himself conforms to this pattern. And not only that. In ancient cultures across the globe, the sacrificed king's body became the object of a feast. His flesh was eaten and his blood was drunk. Thus did his subjects ingest and incorporate into themselves something of their dead ruler's virtue and power. A residue of this tradition is obvious enough in the Christian Communion service.

The Warrior Messiah

In the Europe of medieval Christendom, kings laid claim to 'divine right', but this right was conferred, ratified and legitimised only through the medium of the Church. From the eighth century onwards, the Church arrogated to itself the power to create kings. The Church, in other words, appropriated a prerogative previously reserved for God, and proceeded to install itself as God's mouthpiece. In accordance with Old Testament practice, it did so by anointing with oil. As in biblical times, the king became 'the anointed one', but only with the approbation of the Church.

For modern Christians, however, it would be surprising to find the Church according a secular ruler the other attributes ascribed by Jesus's contemporaries to their expected Messiah. It is difficult to imagine, for example, the Church acknowledging a secular ruler as a 'fully-fledged' priest-king in the traditional biblical sense. And yet that, precisely, is what the early Church did with the Emperor Constantine. In fact, it did more. Not only did it concur with Constantine's presentation of himself as Messiah. It also concurred with his presentation of himself as a specifically warlike Messiah –

a man who implemented God's will with the sword and whose triumphs bore testimony to God's favour. In other words, the Church recognised Constantine as successfully achieving what Jesus had signally failed to do.

Constantine, who presided unchallenged over the Roman Empire from A.D. 312 until his death in 337, is rightly regarded as a major pivot in the history and development of Christianity. But the position from which he is today assessed rests on precarious, even quaint, over-simplifications. According to popular tradition, Constantine had always been tolerant, if not sympathetic, towards Christianity – an intrinsically 'good man', even before he 'saw the light' definitively. In fact, Constantine's attitude towards Christianity seems to have been primarily a matter of expediency, for Christians by then were numerous in the Empire and he needed all the support he could muster against Maxentius, his rival for the imperial throne. In A.D. 312, Maxentius was killed and his army routed at the Battle of Milvian Bridge, leaving Constantine's claim to the throne unchallenged. Immediately before this crucial engagement, Constantine is said to have had a vision – later reinforced by a prophetic dream – of a luminous cross suspended in the sky. A sentence was allegedly inscribed across it: 'In Hoc Signo Vinces' ('By this sign you will conquer'). Tradition asserts that Constantine, in deference to this celestial portent, ordered the shields of his troops hastily emblazoned with the Christian monogram – the Greek letters *chi* and *rho*, the first two letters of the word 'Christos'. As a result, Constantine's victory over Maxentius came to represent a miraculous triumph of Christianity over paganism.

But tradition does not stop there. It also presents Constantine as a devout convert to Christianity. It credits him with 'Christianising the empire' and making Christianity the offical state religion of Rome. And by virtue of a document that purportedly 'came to light' in the eighth century, the so-called 'Donation of Constantine', he was believed to have conferred certain of his own secular powers upon the Pope. It was on the basis of this document that the Roman Church asserted its prerogative to create kings, as well as to establish itself as a temporal authority.

Saviour of the Church

We have already examined some of the traditions popularly associated with Constantine, and have endeavoured to disentangle the historical facts from a miasma of half-truths and legends.[1]

34

What emerged was a very different picture from the one generally portrayed. Since then, however, new material on Constantine has been forthcoming and this adds significant new dimensions to the picture. In consequence, it is necessary to look at that picture again.

It is true, certainly, that Constantine was tolerant towards Christianity. By the Edict of Milan, promulgated in 313, he forbade persecution of *all forms of monotheism* in the Empire. To the extent that this included Christianity, Constantine became in effect a saviour, redeeming the Christian congregations from centuries of imperial harassment. It is also true that he accorded certain privileges to the Roman Church, as well as to other religious institutions. He allowed high Church dignitaries to become part of the civil administration and, by doing so, paved the way for the Church's consolidation of secular power. He donated the Lateran Palace to the Bishop of Rome, and Rome was able to use it as a means of establishing supremacy over rival centres of Christian authority in Alexandria and Antioch. Finally, he presided over the Council of Nicaea in A.D. 325. At this council, the various divergent forms of Christianity were compelled to confront each other and, to whatever extent possible, reconcile their differences. As a result of Nicaea, Rome became the official centre of Christian orthodoxy, and any deviation from that orthodoxy became a heresy, rather than merely a difference of opinion or interpretation. At Nicaea, Jesus's divinity, and the precise nature of his divinity, were established by means of a vote.

It is fair to state that Christianity as we know it today derives ultimately not from Jesus's time, but from the Council of Nicaea. And to the extent that Nicaea was largely Constantine's handiwork, Christianity is indebted to him. But that is very different from saying that Constantine was a Christian, or that he 'Christianised the Empire'. Indeed, most of the popular traditions associated with Constantine can now be proved demonstrably erroneous.

The so-called 'Donation of Constantine', used by the Church in the eighth century to establish its authority in secular affairs, is now universally acknowledged as a blatant forgery – a forgery which, in a contemporary context, would be regarded as unequivocally criminal. Even the Church will today readily admit this, while remaining loath to relinquish many of the benefits obtained by the deception.

As for Constantine's 'conversion' – if that is the appropriate word – it does not appear to have been Christian at all, but conventionally pagan. He appears to have had some sort of vision, or dream, or perhaps both, in the precincts of a pagan temple to the

Gallic Apollo, either in the Vosges region or near Autun. There may also have been a second such experience immediately prior to the Battle of Milvian Bridge, at which Constantine defeated his rival for the imperial throne. According to a witness accompanying Constantine's army at the time, the vision was of the sun god – the deity worshipped by certain cults under the name of Sol Invictus, the 'Invincible Sun'. Just before his vision or visions, Constantine had been newly initiated into a Sol Invictus cult, which makes his experience perfectly plausible. And after the Battle of Milvian Bridge, the Roman Senate erected a triumphal arch in the Colosseum. According to the inscription on this arch, Constantine's victory was won 'through the prompting of the Deity'. But the Deity in question was not Jesus. It was Sol Invictus, the pagan sun god.[2]

Contrary to tradition, Constantine did not make Christianity the official state religion of Rome. The state religion of Rome under Constantine was, in fact, pagan sun worship, and Constantine, all his life, functioned as its chief priest. Indeed, his reign was hailed by his contemporaries as a 'sun emperorship', and Sol Invictus figured everywhere – including the imperial banners and the coinage of the realm. The image of Constantine as a fervent convert to Christianity is patently wrong. He was not even baptised until he lay on his deathbed. Nor can he be credited with the *chi rho* monogram. An inscription bearing this monogram was found in a tomb at Pompeii, dating from two and a half centuries before.[3]

The cult of Sol Invictus was Syrian in origin. It had been introduced to Rome a century before Constantine. Although it contained elements of Baal and Astarte worship, it was essentially monotheistic. In effect, it posited the sun god as the sum of all attributes of all other gods, and thus peacefully subsumed its potential rivals with no need to eradicate them. They could, in short, be accommodated, without any undue friction.

For Constantine, the cult of Sol Invictus was, quite simply, expedient. His primary, indeed obsessive, objective was unity – unity in politics, in religion and in territory. A state religion that included all others obviously conduced to this objective. And it was under the aegis, so to speak, of the Sol Invictus cult that Christianity proceeded to prosper.

Christian doctrine, as promulgated by Rome at the time, had much in common with the cult of Sol Invictus anyway; and thus it was able to flourish unmolested under the sun cult's umbrella of tolerance. Being essentially monotheistic, the cult of Sol Invictus paved the way for the monotheism of Christianity. At the same time, the early Church had no compunction about modifying its own tenets and dogma in order to capitalise on the opportunity afforded it. By an edict promulgated in 321, for example, Constantine ordered the law courts closed on 'the venerable day of the sun', decreeing that this be a day of rest. Christianity had hitherto held Saturday, the Jewish Sabbath, as sacred. Now, in accordance with Constantine's edict, it adopted Sunday as its sacred day. This not only brought it into harmony with the existing regime, but also enabled it to further dissociate itself from its Judaic origins. Until the fourth century, moreover, Jesus's birthday had been celebrated on 6 January. For the cult of Sol Invictus, however, the most symbolically important day of the year was 25 December – the festival of Natalis Invictus, the birth (or rebirth) of the sun, when the days began to grow perceptibly longer. In this respect, too, Christianity aligned itself with the regime and the established state religion. From that state religion, it plundered certain accoutrements as well. Thus the aureole of light crowning the head of the sun god became the Christian halo.

The cult of Sol Invictus also meshed conveniently with that of Mithras, a survival of the old Zoroastrian religion imported from Persia. Indeed, so close was Mithraism to the cult of Sol Invictus that the two are often confused. Both emphasised the status of the sun. Both held Sunday as sacred. Both celebrated a major birth festival on 25 December. In consequence, Christianity could also find lines of convergence with Mithraism – the more so as Mithraism stressed the immortality of the soul, a future judgment and the resurrection of the dead. The Christianity that coalesced and took shape in Constantine's time was in fact a hybrid, containing significant skeins of thought derived from Mithraism and from the sun cult. Christianity, as we now know it, is in many respects actually closer to those pagan systems of belief than it is to its own Judaic origins.

In the interests of unity, Constantine deliberately blurred distinctions between Christianity, Mithraism and Sol Invictus – deliberately chose not to see any points of contention between them. Thus he tolerated the deified Jesus as the earthly manifestation of Sol Invictus. Thus he would build a Christian church in one part of the city and, in another, erect statues of the Mother Goddess Cybele and of Sol Invictus, the sun god – the latter being in his own likeness, with his features. In such eclectic and ecumenical gestures, the emphasis on unity is again apparent. Faith, for Constantine, was a political matter; and any faith conducive to unity was treated with forbearance.

Yet Constantine was not simply a cynic. Like many soldierly rulers of his time – like many soldierly rulers since – he seems to have been both a superstitious man and one imbued with a very real sense of the sacred. In his relations with the divine, he appears to have hedged his bets – rather like the proverbial atheist who, on his deathbed, consents to receive the sacraments as a safeguard, 'just in case'. This led him to take quite seriously all the deities he sanctioned in his domains, to propitiate all of them, to accord all of them a measure of genuine veneration. If his personal god was Sol Invictus, and if his official stance towards Christianity was dictated by expediency and the desire for unity within the Empire, the fact remains that Constantine accorded the God of the Christians a certain unique deference – a deference of a distinctly novel kind.

It had long been a tradition for Roman emperors to claim descent from the gods, and on that basis to claim godhood for themselves as well. Thus, Diocletian had claimed a pedigree from Jupiter, Maximian a pedigree from Hercules. For Constantine, especially after he had given Christianity a mandate in his domains, it was advantageous to establish a new divine covenant, a new ratification from the sacred. This was all the more important, by virtue of the fact that he was, in some sense, a usurper – he had toppled a descendant of Hercules and needed some rival god's support for his own assertions of legitimacy.

In choosing a god for his sponsor or patron, Constantine turned – on a nominal level, at least – to the God of the Christians. He did *not*, it is important to note, turn to Jesus. The god Constantine acknowledged was God *the Father* – who, in those days prior to the Council of Nicaea, was not identical with the Son. His relation to Jesus was altogether more equivocal – and extremely illuminating.

The Denial of Jesus

In 1982, an important new book appeared on this subject, *Constantine versus Christ*, by Alistair Kee, senior lecturer in Religious Studies, University of Glasgow. Kee establishes, quite convincingly, that Jesus in effect played no part whatever in the religion of Constantine. Constantine chose the God of the Christians – God the Father – as his official patron, and simply ignored the Son completely. For Constantine, of course, God the Father would have entailed nothing more than new nomenclature for Sol Invictus, the sun god who already commanded his personal allegiance.

But if Constantine ignored Jesus, he certainly acknowledged the principle of Messiahship – in fact, he not only acknowledged it, he took the role of the Anointed One upon himself. For Constantine, in short, the Messiah was precisely what the Messiah had been for Jews in Palestine at the dawn of the Christian era – a ruler, a sovereign, a warrior leader like David and Solomon, who reigned wisely over a temporal realm, established unity in his domains, consolidated a nation and a people with divine sanction to support him. In Constantine's eyes, apparently, Jesus had attempted to be precisely these things. And Constantine saw himself as following, rather more successfully, in Jesus's footsteps – achieving what Jesus had failed to achieve. As Kee says: 'The religion of Constantine takes us back to the context of the Old Testament. It is as if the religion of Abraham ... is at last fulfilled not in Jesus but in Constantine'.[4] And: 'Constantine in his day was the fulfilment of the promise of God to send a king like David to save his people. It is this model, so powerful and so pre-Christian, that best describes Constantine's role'.[5]

Constantine's position was not so surprising in an essentially pagan potentate of warlike disposition. What is significant, as Kee points out, is that the Roman Church assented to the role Constantine arrogated for himself. The Roman Church of the time was quite prepared to concur with Constantine's conception of himself as a genuine Messiah, and a more successful Messiah than Jesus. It was also quite prepared to acknowledge that the Messiah was not a pacific, ethereal, lamb-like saviour, but a rightful and wrathful king, a political and military leader presiding not over any nebulous kingdom of heaven, but over very real terrestrial domains. In short, the Church recognised in Constantine precisely what Messiahship would have entailed for Jesus and his contemporaries. Thus, for example, Eusebius, Bishop of Caesarea, one of the leading theological figures of his day and a close personal associate of the Emperor, says: 'He grows strong in his model of monarchic rule, which the ruler of All has given to the race of man alone of those on earth'.[6] Indeed, Eusebius is quite explicit and quite emphatic about the importance of monarchy: 'Monarchy excels all other kinds of constitution and government. For rather do anarchy and civil war result from the alternative, a polyarchy based on equality. For which reason there is One God, not two or three or even more'.[7]

But Eusebius goes much further than this. In a personal address to the Emperor, he declares the Logos to be incarnate in Constantine. Indeed, he actually ascribes to Constantine a status and a virtue which should, in theory, be reserved for Jesus alone:

' ... most God-fearing sovereign, to whom alone of those who have yet been here since the start of time has the Universal All–Ruling God Himself given power to purify human life'.[8]

As Kee says, commenting on this address by Eusebius: 'Since the beginning of the world it is to Constantine *alone* that the power of salvation has been given. Christ is set aside, Christ is excluded and now Christ is formally denied.'[9] And: 'Constantine now stands alone as the saviour of the world. The scene is the fourth century, not the first. The world, spiritual and material, was not saved until Constantine.'[10]

Kee emphasises that there is no mention whatsoever of Jesus. The implications are unavoidable: ' ... it is clear that the life and death of Christ have no efficacy in this scheme of things ... the salvation of the world is now wrought by the events of the life of Constantine, symbolized by *his* saving sign'.[11]

The Final Destruction of the Historical Jesus

Why should the Roman Church in Constantine's time have adopted such a position, theologically so scandalous? For nearly three hundred years, Christians had defied the might of the Empire, had steadfastly refused to compromise their convictions, had allowed themselves to be martyred, had found solace in the prospect of a greater glory in heaven. Why now should they be prepared to recognise as Messiah precisely the imperial authority which, three centuries before, had crucified Jesus – and which continued to practise execution by crucifixion on rebels against the State?

One answer at least is obvious and simple. The Church, after all, was composed of human beings, who had suffered cruelly for their beliefs in the past. Now they had an opportunity for acceptance, for respectability, for an official place in the social structure – in exchange for certain compromises and relaxations in dogma. The transaction would have been difficult to refuse. After prolonged persecution, the prospect not only of a respite, but also of power, manifestly appeared worth the concessions.

There may well have been another, more subtle, reason underlying the Church's position. A secular power such as Constantine's, if aligned with the orthodoxy of the time, would have provided an effective bulwark against any attempt by Jesus's true heirs to assert their claim. If we were correct in our hypothesis of Jesus's marriage and children, or even if it were believed true at the time, it would do much to explain the agreed rapport between Constantine and the Roman Church. The existence, somewhere within the Empire or on its periphery, of a lineal descent from Jesus or his family would have represented a threat to the coalescing Church hierarchy – the propagators of specifically Pauline Christianity. And the best defence against a new Davidic Messiah, advancing with his legions, would have been an established Messiah already presiding over the Empire – a pro-Pauline Messiah, who had effectively pre-empted the claims of Judaic rivals.

All the same, it is extraordinary to find the Roman Church (1) acquiescing in Constantine's total indifference to Jesus; (2) deferring to Constantine's presentation of himself as the Messiah; and (3) acknowledging the definition of Messiahship – that is, a military and political figure – embodied by Constantine. On the other hand, perhaps, in the fourth century, it was not so extraordinary after all. Perhaps, in the fourth century, such attitudes were not as incongruous with Christian belief as they would appear today. Perhaps, in the fourth century, Christians recognised, far more clearly than their modern counterparts, how closely such attitudes conformed to the historical facts.

In Constantine's time, Christian tradition had not yet become immutable dogma. Many documents, subsequently lost or destroyed, were still in circulation and intact. Alternative interpretations were still prevalent. And the historical Jesus had not yet disappeared completely under the weight of later accretions. For the Church of the fourth century, there would almost certainly have been some rueful and grudging admission that Constantine was a Messiah who had succeeded where Jesus had failed, and that the Messiah as represented by both Constantine *and* Jesus was indeed a military and political figure – not a god, but a king with a mandate to govern.

It must be remembered that no complete version of the New Testament survives which pre-dates the reign of Constantine. The New Testament, as we know it today, is largely a product of Nicaea and other Church councils of the same epoch. But the Church Fathers who compiled the present New Testament were themselves aware of, and had access to, other, earlier and more historically reliable versions. These versions had not yet been officially rendered 'uncanonical'.

And yet even the New Testament as it is today bears witness, if one looks at it closely, to Jesus as a military and political Messiah – to Jesus, in other words, as a would-be precursor of Constantine. It is worth examining some of this testimony.

4

Jesus as Freedom-fighter

Later Christian tradition has emphasised the image of a meek, lamb-like saviour, who eschews violence and bids one turn the other cheek. As we have seen, however, the Messiah – for Constantine and the fourth-century Roman Church, as well as for Jesus and his contemporaries – was a very different figure: a stern martial leader and liberator, quite prepared to assert his right by force and, if necessary, to employ violence against his enemies. There is, of course, a solid enough basis for such an image in the Gospels themselves.

In A.D. 6, a few years after the death of Herod, Judaea was annexed and incorporated into the Roman Empire as a procuratorial province with Caesarea as its capital. A census was ordered for purposes of tax assessment. The Jewish High Priest of the time acceded to this and urged compliance from the populace. Almost immediately, however, a fierce nationalist resistance erupted, directed by a fiery prophet in the hills of Galilee. This man is known to history as Judas of Galilee, or Judas of Gamala. He is believed to have perished fairly early in the prolonged series of guerrilla activities he inaugurated against Rome. But the movement he created survived him, and its adherents became known as Zealots. The term appears to have first been used by Josephus, writing at least three-quarters of a century later, between A.D. 75 and 94. For Josephus, the Zealots acquired their name because they were 'zealous in good undertakings'. During the years of their operations, however, they were frequently referred to as Lestai ('Brigands') or as Sicarii ('Daggermen'), the name deriving from the *sica*, a small curved dagger especially favoured by the Zealots for political assassinations).

It must be stressed that the Zealots were not a religious sect or denomination. They were not a sub-division of Judaism,

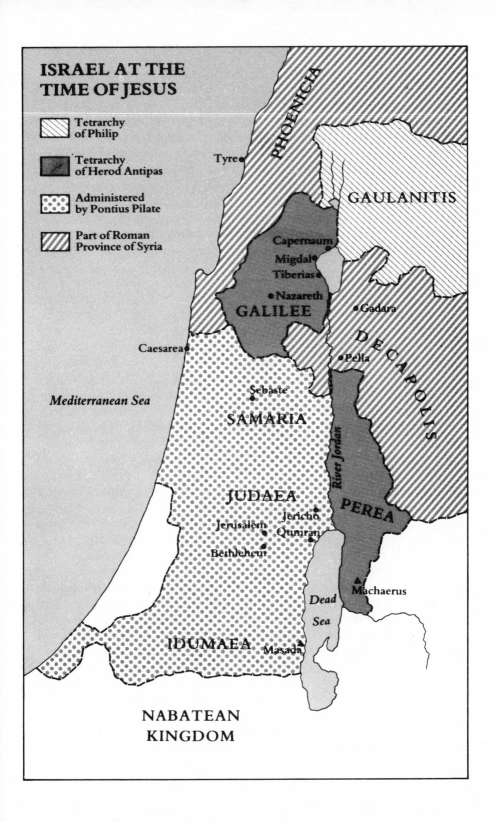

ISRAEL AT THE TIME OF JESUS

Tetrarchy
of Philip

Tetrarchy
of Herod Antipas

Administered
by Pontius Pilate

Part of Roman
Province of Syria

PHOENICIA

GAULANITIS

Tyre

Capernaum
Migdal
Tiberias
Nazareth

GALILEE

Gadara

DECAPOLIS

Caesarea

Pella

Mediterranean Sea

Sebaste

SAMARIA

River Jordan

JUDAEA

PEREA

Jerusalem
Bethlehem

Jericho
Qumran

Dead
Sea

Machaerus

IDUMAEA

Masada

NABATEAN
KINGDOM

propounding one or another theological position. They were not, in other words, like the Sadducees, Pharisees or Essenes. They may have obtained support, in manpower, money and material, from all three; but they themselves were essentially political in orientation. The Zealot position was straightforward enough. Rome was the enemy. No Jew should pay tribute to Rome. No Jew should acknowledge the Roman Emperor as his master. There was no master other than God. God had conferred a unique birthright on Israel, had concluded a covenant with David and Solomon. The patriotic and religious duty of every Jew was to fight for the reinstatement of this birthright, this covenant – the reinstatement of a rightful ruler presiding over the Kingdom of Israel.

In the name of these objectives, all means were sanctioned. When circumstances permitted, the Zealots engaged in large-scale conventional military operations. At other times, they waged an incessant guerrilla war, attacking isolated Roman garrisons, ambushing caravans, cutting supply routes. They did not shrink from assassination and, in so far as the technology of the epoch allowed, they employed techniques which today would be associated with terrorism. They were often ruthless. And they displayed the kind of fearlessness that only fanaticism confers. As Josephus says: 'They also do not value dying any kinds of death, nor indeed do they heed the deaths of their relations and friends, nor can any such fear make them call any man Lord . . .'[1]

To judge from what little evidence survives, there seems to have been a strong dynastic element involved in Zealot leadership. Two of the sons of Judas of Galilee were killed as Zealot commanders in their own right. Another son, or perhaps grandson, was responsible for seizing the fortress of Masada on the outbreak of the revolt in A.D. 66. And during the famous siege of Masada, which did not end until A.D. 73, the garrison of the citadel was commanded by a man named Eleazar, who was also descended from Judas of Galilee. Unfortunately, there are too few reliable records to indicate how centralised the authority of this family might have been over Zealot contingents throughout the Holy Land. It is impossible to gauge whether Zealot activity originated from a single headquarters, or whether it consisted of a multitude of groups operating independently. But certainly the family and descendants of Judas of Galilee seem to have been involved in many of the more ambitious, more co-ordinated, more professional Zealot enterprises.

The Zealots with Jesus

All through the centuries, theologians and biblical scholars have been plagued by problems of translation – or, to be more accurate, mistranslation. By the time a name, a word, a phrase, a sentence, a statement has passed from spoken Hebrew or Aramaic, to written Greek, to written Latin, and then to one or another modern language, it has often become utterly divorced from its original meaning. We have already commented on the corruption of 'Jesus the Nazarean' into 'Jesus of Nazareth'. A similar process of corruption can be discerned in a number of other New Testament names, including Jesus's own. 'Jesus', it must be remembered, is not Judaic, but Greek. Among his own people, Jesus would have been called 'Yeshua', which is simply the familiar biblical 'Joshua'.

The figure of Simon Zelotes, who appears in the Gospel of Luke and in the Acts of the Apostles, we have already discussed in our previous work, and there can scarcely be further need to belabour the obvious. Simon Zelotes is quite patently Simon the Zealot. In some more recent translations of the New Testament, he is named as such, making it explicit, even to lay readers, that Jesus included at least one Zealot – one political extremist – among his immediate followers. That this is still a source of embarrassment can be seen from the New English Bible, where Simon is introduced, with euphemistic caution, as 'Simon the Patriot'.

But whatever circumlocutions are conferred upon him, Simon would appear to be rather more obtrusive than some translators might wish. Thus, for example, in the King James versions of Matthew and Mark, there are references to 'Simon the Canaanite'. But while the sobriquet of 'Canaanite' might have meant something some two thousand years before, in Old Testament times, it makes no sense whatever in the context of the New Testament. Once again, there has been a corruption in the process of translation. In fact, the Aramaic word for Zealot was *qannai*, which was rendered into Greek as *kananaios*. 'Simon the Canaanite' thus becomes one and the same as 'Simon Zelotes' or 'Simon the Zealot', appearing in Matthew and Mark under the former designation and in Luke and in Acts under the latter.

In John's Gospel, there appears to be yet another Simon, Simon Bar Jonas. This is generally taken to refer to 'Simon, son of Jonas', even though the man's father is elsewhere identified as Zebedee. 'Bar Jonas' is, again, a mistranslation of another Aramaic word, *barjonna*, which, like *kananaios*, means 'outlaw', 'anarchist' or Zealot. Once again, it would seem clear that we are dealing with the same individual, whose militant nationalism it was deemed expedient to conceal.

Of all the Simons populating the New Testament, the most important is unquestionably Simon Peter, the most famous of Jesus's disciples and the one on whom Jesus allegedly founds his church. The Gospels themselves make it plain that he is not 'Simon Peter' but, rather, 'Simon *called* Peter'. 'Peter', in fact, is not a name but a nickname, another sobriquet. It simply means 'rock-like', implying 'tough'. (A modern equivalent would, indeed, be 'Rocky'.) If Peter is actually a 'tough' whose nickname means 'Rocky', is it not possible to equate him with the fierce individual known as Simon Zelotes or Simon the Canaanite – to equate him, that is, with Simon the Zealot? If Jesus's most important disciple, the one on whom he allegedly founds his church, was a Zealot, the implications become extremely interesting.

There is one more piece of the jigsaw to be inserted. In John's Gospel, Judas is identified as the son of Simon. In the synoptic Gospels, he is identified as Judas Iscariot. For centuries, baffled by Greek appellations, biblical commentators believed 'Judas Iscariot' to denote 'Judas of Kerioth'. But as the late Professor S. G. F. Brandon of Manchester University has convincingly argued, 'Judas Iscariot' now seems more likely to be a corruption of 'Judas the Sicarius' – or Zealot.[2]

A Militant Jesus

If Jesus numbered such figures as Simon the Zealot and Judas the Sicarius among his followers, those followers can hardly have been as placid and peaceable as later tradition maintains. On the contrary, they would seem to have been involved in precisely the kind of political and military activity from which Jesus, according to later tradition, is dissociated. But the Gospels themselves confirm that Jesus and his entourage, in keeping with what would have been expected of the Messiah, were militant nationalists who did not shrink from violence.

It is not necessary here to discuss the Crucifixion; it is sufficient to note that, whatever Jesus's association with the Zealots, he was certainly crucified by the Romans as a political revolutionary.[3] This much is stated by the Roman chronicler Tacitus, and thus constitutes the one sure assertion about Jesus to issue from a non-biblical, yet contemporary, source.[4] There is no question but that the Romans perceived Jesus as a military and political figure, and dealt with him strictly according to that perception. Crucifixion was a penalty reserved for transgressions against Roman law, and Rome would not have bothered to crucify a man preaching a purely spiritual message, or a message of peace. Jesus was not executed by the Jewish Sanhedrin – which could, with permission, stone to death a man who had trespassed against Judaic law[5] – but by the Roman administration. And the two men allegedly crucified with him are explicitly described as 'Lestai', Zealots. They are not, despite tradition, common criminals, but political revolutionaries – or 'freedom fighters'.

Jesus himself, in the Gospels, displays an aggressive militarism quite at odds with conventional images. Everyone is familiar with the famously awkward passage in which he announces that he has come not to bring peace, but a sword. In Luke 22:36, he instructs those of his followers who do not possess a sword to purchase one, even if it means selling their garments. When Jesus is arrested in Gethsemane, at least one of his followers is actually carrying a sword and uses it to lop off the ear of an attendant of the High Priest; in the Fourth Gospel, the man with the sword is specifically identified as Simon Peter. It is difficult to reconcile such references with the tradition of a mild, pacifist saviour.

We have already mentioned Jesus's triumphal entry into Jerusalem on an ass, to the accompaniment of a throng waving palm branches, spreading their cloaks in the road before him and invoking blessings on the son of David, the rightful king. This act, as noted above, had been foretold of the Messiah by the prophet Zechariah. For Jesus to perform an act long prophesied and expected of the rightful Messiah certainly reflects no diffidence on his part. He is quite brazenly staging a public spectacle – a spectacle for which he knew he would either have been stigmatised as an upstart and a blasphemer, or acknowledged as precisely what he claimed to be. Significantly enough he is acknowledged by a populace fully aware of the symbolism of his action; and even the more sceptical of modern biblical scholars regard this incident in the Gospels as historically authentic. But how could such an act not be fraught with political implications and consequences? It is an act of explicit challenge to Rome, an act of deliberate, militant provocation. The Messiah was regarded as a liberator. For Jesus to have been accepted as the Messiah, he must necessarily have been prepared to wield the liberator's sword.

That Jesus's entry into Jerusalem was fraught with political implications becomes evident in the Gospels a few days later. If the Old Testament had foretold the Messiah's entry into Jerusalem on an ass, it had also cited precedents for his cleansing and purifying of the Temple.[6] This, of course, is precisely what Jesus proceeds to do in his famous overturning of the moneychangers' tables. The incident can hardly have been a minor affair. Nor can it have avoided violence. A simple consideration of human nature is sufficient to reveal the consequences (unrecorded in the Gospels) of Jesus's behaviour. Neither moneychangers, nor bystanders, nor Jesus's own followers are likely to have stood idle, or engaged in theological debate, while loose coins rolled in all directions. Given the size and importance of the Temple, and the prominent role of the moneychangers, Jesus's overturning of their tables must have resulted in a full-scale riot. Nor can Jesus himself possibly have expected anything else. Here again he is adopting a course of confrontation, a course of deliberate challenge to established authority.

In these two prominent instances − perhaps the two most public acts of his career − Jesus behaves in a way which must provoke violence. It is in these two instances that the Gospels probably come closest to vouchsafing a portrait of the historical Jesus, a man who, in a flagrant, even flamboyant fashion stages public spectacles which implicitly assert his claim as Israel's foretold and rightful Messiah. And these spectacles are acts of calculated provocation, which reflect an undisguised militancy, an obvious preparedness to countenance force. What is more, both incidents make it clear that Jesus has a sizeable following. It clearly includes more than the original twelve disciples.

Corruption in the process of translation has tended to obscure more than names. Whether by accident or design, it has also served to conceal historical information of considerable importance. A single word may convey a wealth of historical background; and if the sense of such a word is altered, the revelation it offers will be lost. One of the most telling of such examples occurs in the account of Jesus's arrest in Gethsemane. It revolves around a single simple question: how many men came to arrest Jesus in the Garden? We have often posed this question in talks and lectures, and the answers from our audience have been fairly uniform. For most people, a mental image of the scene in Gethsemane exists in the mind, implanted, so to speak, by both the Gospel account and tradition. According to this image, somewhere between ten and thirty men come to arrest Jesus − a Jewish functionary or two, some representatives of the High Priest (one of whom has his ear injured by Simon Peter's sword), presumably a contingent of the Temple guard, perhaps one or more Roman officials and even

1 The Garden of Gethsemane, Jerusalem, where a cohort is said to have arrested Jesus.

2 The archaeological evidence that Pontius Pilate existed: an inscription found at Caeserea in 1961. He is styled 'Prefect' rather than 'Procurator'.

3 *Left*, the cliff-face below the buildings of the Dead Sea community at Qumran. In the centre is Cave 4, which contained the Dead Sea Scrolls.

4 *Above*, the remains of the Qumran community buildings, with the Dead Sea in the background.

5 *Below*, Qumran, looking towards the Judaean hills and Jerusalem. On the right are the ruins of the tower.

6–7 The Cathedral and early Christian burials at Santiago de Compostela, north-west Spain. It is argued that the fourth- and fifth-century graves beneath the floor of the Cathedral were placed close to the tomb of Priscillian of Ávila, who was martyred for his heretical teachings in A.D. 386.

8 Santa Maria de Bretoña, north-west Spain, centre of a Celtic Church bishopric from *c*.569 to the tenth century.

9 Kidron Valley, Jerusalem. The tomb on the left, with the two pillars, is probably that of James, brother of and successor to Jesus.

10 The twelfth-century Kilfenora Cross, Co. Clare. The figure on the left holds a familiar bishop's crozier, and that on the right the T-shaped staff of office traditionally carried by bishops of the Egyptian Church.

11–12 *Above left*, detail from an illustration of Anthony and Paul, Monastery of Anthony, Egypt, showing the Egyptian T-shaped staff. *Above right*, carving of St James, Portico of Glory, Santiago de Compostela, featuring the Egyptian staff.

13 *Below left*, cross shaft at Tighlagheany, Inishmore, Aran Islands. The rosette at the top is a characteristic Middle Eastern pattern.

14 *Below right*, Egyptian Church gravestone of the seventh or eighth century A.D. showing the rosette pattern.

15–16 *Above*, page from the seventh-century Celtic 'Book of Durrow'; *below left*, the *c.* seventh-century North Cross at Ahenny, Co. Tipperary. Both show the use of Egyptian-style interlaced patterns.

17 *Below right*, illustration from a twelfth-century Egyptian Church 'Bohairic' Gospel showing the interlaced pattern.

perhaps a small unit of Pilate's soldiery. Why do most modern readers tend to think in terms of ten to thirty men? No doubt because the phrase in the Authorised Version – 'a band of men' – is non-specific. Even in more recent translations of the Bible, the phrase is 'a number of men'. And yes, a 'band of men' or a 'number of men' does indeed suggest not much more than thirty.

Catholic readers, however, do not read the Authorised Version of the New Testament. Until recently, in accordance with strict Catholic dogma, they were obliged, on pain of punishment, to read the Vulgate. And in the Vulgate, as in certain more modern translations, the term used for those who come to arrest Jesus is correctly translated – and considerably more precise. Jesus, one learns, is arrested in Gethsemane not by an indeterminate 'number of men', but by a 'cohort'.[7] Is this a pedantic inconsistency, or does it reflect something more consequential?

If one goes back to the Greek, one will find the term *speiran*, a precise translation of 'cohort'. In modern English, the term 'cohort' is vague, implying a fairly large but still non-specific number. But for the writers and early translators of the Gospels, it was a very precise term, denoting a very exact figure. Just as modern armies are organised into companies, battalions, regiments, brigades and divisions, so the Roman Army was organised into centuries, cohorts and legions. A Roman legion was somewhat larger than a modern peacetime brigade in the British Army – six thousand troops. A cohort was one tenth of a legion – six hundred soldiers. If, that is, they were regular Roman soldiers. A cohort composed of auxiliaries, as those in the Holy Land were, would number at least five hundred troops,[8] and sometimes as many as two thousand – seven hundred and sixty infantry and one thousand two hundred and forty cavalry.

At this point, one must ask some simple, common-sense questions. Is it plausible that Pilate, or any other military governor in his situation, would have dispatched upwards of five or six hundred troops to Gethsemane for the sole purpose of arresting one man – a solitary prophet extolling love, who was attended by twelve disciples? The suggestion is patently preposterous. Not only would it have been a ridiculous example of 'overkill'. It would also have been an open invitation to civic disturbance. Unless, of course, such a disturbance already existed, and the cohort had been mustered to quell it.

One must imagine five or six hundred soldiers swarming into the Garden of Gethsemane. One must also bear in mind that Jesus, a short time before, had instructed his disciples to equip themselves with swords. And one must bear in mind, too, the striking off by Simon Peter of the ear of the High Priest's attendant. From these various details, a picture begins to emerge of something of considerable import occurring in Gethsemane that night – something on a larger scale than is generally envisaged, and something involving rather more than 'a band of men'. It would seem clear that there was a civil disturbance of substantial size in the 'Garden'. There may well have been fighting. But whether there was actual fighting or not, the situation was obviously perceived as a military threat by the Roman administration, who reacted to it with a large-scale military response.

Jesus's arrest in the Garden was clearly not a quiet affair in which a small 'band' of a dozen or two dozen men advanced, in furtive fashion, to arrest one prophet. Certain theologians have, on occasion, noted the anomaly of numbers. It has often caused them embarrassment. One writer, commenting on a cohort of troops in Gethsemane, declares, rather lamely, 'What a compliment to the power of Jesus!'

5

The Zadokite Movement of Qumran

Who exactly constituted Jesus's following? Who constituted the throngs which, on his entry into Jerusalem, acclaimed him as the son of David, the rightful king, the anointed one, the Messiah? Who, among the population of the Holy Land at the time, had a vested interest in seeing his enterprise succeed? From whom did his support derive?

It is clear that even the named and identified members of Jesus's following represent a broad and diverse spectrum. He seems to have elicited support from people of radically different social classes, radically different financial and educational backgrounds. As we have noted, there were a number of political extremists. There were also poor peasants from the hills of Galilee, and fishermen – perhaps poor, perhaps well-to-do – from the shores of Lake Galilee. There were wealthy women whose husbands occupied important official positions. There were important and influential citizens of Jerusalem, such as Nicodemus and Joseph of Arimathea. There were people who provided him with houses – such as that in Bethany – which were large and comfortable enough to accommodate, at the very least, his immediate entourage. There appears to have been a substantial number of 'rank and file' supporters scattered across the whole of both Galilee and Judaea. But where did these numerous individuals stand in relation to the context of first-century Judaism? What, if anything, distinguished them from 'the other Jews', sometimes hostile, sometimes sympathetic, milling around as supernumeraries in the background? How widespread was the preparedness to use force of arms, if necessary, to restore to Israel her rightful king?

The Sadducees and the Pharisees

The Holy Land, in Jesus's time, was literally swarming with

different religions, different sects and cults, a great number of them imported from abroad as a result of the Roman occupation. Roman rites – to Jupiter, for instance – were transplanted to Palestine, as well, of course, as the official worship of the emperor which constituted Rome's state religion. Religions, cults, sects and mystery schools from other parts of the Empire – notably from Greece, from Syria, from Egypt, from Mesopotamia and Asia Minor – also found their way to the Holy Land, struck roots and flourished. Thus, for example, worship of the Mother Goddess – as Egyptian Isis, as Phoenician Astarte, as Greek or Cypriot Aphrodite, as Mesopotamian Ishtar, as Cybele from Asia Minor – commanded the allegiance of many loyal followers. Then, too, there were residues of polytheistic Goddess-worship within the framework of Judaism itself, cults dedicated to the ancient Canaanite goddess Miriam or Rabath. In Galilee, Judaism had not even established itself until 120 B.C., and much pre-Judaic thought still survived. There were also forms of Judaism which the Jews themselves refused to acknowledge as such – the schismatic religion of the Samaritans, for instance, who insisted that *their* Judaism was the only true form. Finally, and to further compound the confusion, there were a number of differing schools or sects – and even, apparently, sects within sects – that constituted the Judaic orthodoxy of the time, if, indeed, any such orthodoxy can be said to have existed.[1] Among these, the Sadducees and the Pharisees are familiar, if only by name, to Christian tradition.

The Sadducees – or, at least, the main branch of the Sadducees – must be seen primarily in relation to the official priesthood, the Temple and the ritual sacrifice which worship in the Temple entailed. The Sadducees were the priestly caste. They furnished the Temple with its dignitaries and functionaries. They exercised an effective monopoly over Temple activities and Temple appointments. The whole of Sadducee thought was oriented towards the Temple, and when the Temple was destroyed during the revolt of A.D. 66, the official Sadducees ceased to exist. They exercised little, if any, influence on the subsequent evolution and development of Judaism.

For the rest, the Sadducees occupied many of the important civic and administrative positions in the land. Of necessity, this entailed an accommodation with Rome. And indeed, as long as their prerogatives in the priesthood and the Temple were left intact, the Sadducees were prepared to make such an accommodation. They resigned themselves to the Roman presence in their country, made their peace with the Roman authorities. In secular matters, they were worldly, sophisticated and cosmopolitan, adapting themselves to the Greco-Roman values, attitudes, manners and mores of the Empire. To this extent, their enemies at the time perceived them as collaborators. And although they emphasised purity and traditional observance in religion, their position in other spheres might justifiably be compared to that of, say, the Vichy regime in occupied France during the Second World War.

For the Pharisees, religion was rather more flexible, more subject to growth, modification and development, less exclusively vested in the Temple and its rites. For this reason, Pharisaic thought survived the fall of the Temple and provided the soil from which later Rabbinic Judaism eventually sprang. If the portrayal of the Sadducees in the Gospels is not without some historical justification, the portrayal of the Pharisees is often viciously distorted. No responsible biblical scholar today would deny that the Pharisees have been grievously slandered and maligned by Christian tradition. The greatest names in Judaic thought in Jesus's time – the famous teacher Hillel, for example – were Pharisees. According to most modern experts, Jesus himself was probably raised and trained in a Pharisaic context. Most of his teachings, most of the words ascribed to him, conform to the tenets of Pharisaic thinking. Indeed, some of his most famous pronouncements are paraphrases, even on occasion almost direct quotations, from Hillel. For example, Hillel declares: 'What is hateful to yourself, do not do to your neighbour.'

Jesus was perceived – justifiably, we maintain – as a threat to Rome, and was executed as such. He is also on record as defying the priesthood and challenging the institution of Temple worship. In consequence, the Sadducees – having yoked their interests to Rome and enjoying unique prerogatives in the Temple – would have reacted to Jesus precisely as they are described as doing in the Gospels. But the Pharisees would have provided him with some of his most loyal and fervent followers, and would have been among the first to regard him as the Messiah.

The Ascetic Essenes

The third major sub-division of Judaism at the time was that of the Essenes, about whom our knowledge is much more ambiguous, much less clearly defined. Until the middle of the twentieth century, most information about the Essenes derived from two contemporary historians, Pliny the Elder and Philo Judaeus, and from the late first-century Judaic commentator Josephus, who is often unreliable. With the discovery of the Dead Sea Scrolls, however, a corpus of Essene material was made available for the first time, and it is now possible to assess the Essenes on their own terms.

In both their life-style and their religious teachings, the Essenes were more rigorous and austere than either the Sadducees or the Pharisees. They were also much more mystically oriented, and had much in common with the various mystery schools prevalent in the Mediterranean world at the time. In contrast to other schools of Judaism, they seem to have subscribed to some form of reincarnation. They reflect both Egyptian and Greek influences, and have a number of points in common with the followers of Pythagoras. They encouraged an interest in healing and produced tracts on the therapeutic properties of herbs and stones. They were steeped in what today might be called 'esoteric studies', such as astrology, numerology and the various disciplines which subsequently coalesce into the Cabala. But whatever they assimilated from other cultures and traditions, they applied in a specifically Judaic context. Josephus at one point says of them: '[Some] undertake to foretell things to come, by reading the holy books and using several sorts of purifications, and being perpetually conversant in the discourses of the prophets . . .'[2]

For our purposes, one of the most important characteristics of the Essenes was their apocalyptic vision – their insistence that the Last Times were at hand and that the advent of the Messiah was imminent. Granted, expectation of the Messiah was rife throughout the Holy Land at the time. But, as Professor Frank Cross concludes: 'The Essenes proved to be the bearers, and in no small part the producers, of the apocalyptic tradition of Judaism.'[3] From the material that has come to light during our own century, it is clear that the Essenes were looser and more diffuse in their organisation, less centralised and less uniform than the Sadducees and the Pharisees. Not all Essenes subscribed to, or practised, precisely the same things. What they had in common was, again, an essentially mystical orientation – an insistence on a direct, first-hand, experiential knowledge of God, rather than a scrupulous adherence to dogma and law. Such knowledge, of course, renders superfluous the priest's role as interpreter, as intermediary between God and man. In consequence, the Essenes, like most mystical sects throughout history, were indifferent to, if not actively hostile towards, the established priesthood.

Despite recent discoveries pertaining to the Essenes, four long-standing misconceptions still cling to them. They are believed to have resided exclusively in isolated, monastic-style desert communities. They are believed to have been extremely few in number. They are believed to have been celibate. They are believed to have been non-violent, adhering scrupulously to an other-worldly pacifism.

Research since the discovery of the Dead Sea Scrolls has established each of these beliefs about the Essenes to be erroneous. The Essenes resided not only in remote desert communities, but also in urban centres, where they maintained houses not only for themselves, but also for wandering brethren from elsewhere and for other itinerants. Indeed, the network of Essene houses seems to have been both widespread and extremely efficient. Such houses were well integrated into the surrounding community, and rested on a solid basis of craft-work, commerce and trade. As this network of houses attests, the Essenes were rather more numerous than traditional accounts suggest. And, indeed, the sheer prevalence of Essene thought in the Holy Land at the time also bears witness to a congregation more numerous than a few conclaves of ascetics sequestered in the desert.

The notion that all the Essenes were celibate derives from Josephus. But even Josephus contradicts himself and declares, almost as an afterthought, that there *were* Essenes who married.[4] Neither in the Dead Sea Scrolls, nor in any other known Essene document, is there any mention of celibacy. On the contrary, among the Dead Sea Scrolls found at the community of Qumran, there are rules applying specifically to members of the sect who are married and have children. The graves of women and children have also been found in the nearby cemetery which borders the eastern walls of Qumran.

As for the Essenes' supposed non-violence, there is significant evidence to disprove it. After Jerusalem was razed by the Romans in A.D. 70, Israel's organised resistance was systematically extirpated, except for the fortress of Masada on the Dead Sea. Masada held out for two years. Only in A.D. 73, decimated by starvation and threatened by the Romans with a large-scale general assault, did the defenders of the citadel commit mass suicide.

The defenders of Masada are generally held to have been Zealots. Josephus, who was present at the siege, refers to them as Sicarii. For two years, they managed to hold at bay a Roman army, with experienced commanders, well-disciplined troops and extensive siege equipment. During the course of the action, they inflicted heavy casualties on their attackers and revealed themselves to be fierce and resourceful fighters – not amateurs, but professionals of a skill comparable to that of their Roman adversaries. In his account of the fall of the fortress, Josephus describes how two women and five children were the only survivors of the siege, having hidden 'in caverns underground'. From them, apparently, comes the report of the speech whereby the defenders were exhorted to their collective suicide. Not surprisingly, this speech is partly nationalistic in theme. In general, however, its tenor is explicitly religious. And the religious orientation it reflects is unmistakably Essene.[5]

The archaeological record further confirms our viewpoint. When Masada was excavated in the 1960s, certain documents were found identical to those discovered in the Essene community at Qumran. The Qumran community was not pacifist either. A forge for making weapons was found there.[6] And arrowheads and other debris excavated from the ruins indicate that Qumran, too, opposed the Romans by force of arms.

Jesus's teachings owe much to established Pharisaic thought. But they owe, if anything, even more to Essene tradition. There is little doubt that Jesus was steeped in Essene doctrine and practice – including, as Josephus says, that of 'being perpetually conversant in the discourses of the prophets'. He may even have been an Essene himself. He certainly seems, at some point prior to embarking on his public mission, to have undergone a form of Essene training. In this connection, it is worth noting the so-called 'Messianic Rule' of the Essenes found at Qumran. According to this rule, all male members of the community were obliged to wait until the age of twenty to marry and sire children; at the age of thirty, they were to be regarded as mature and initiated into the higher ranks of the sect.[7] Is it just chance that Jesus is said to be thirty years old when he embarks on his ministry?

The 'Sons of Zadok'

In addition to the Sadducees, Pharisees and Essenes, Judaism, in Jesus's time, included a number of smaller, less well-known splinter-groups and sects, two of which have begun to figure increasingly in biblical scholarship during the last two and a half decades. The first of them is the sect known as the 'Sons of Zadok', or Zadokites. The Zadokites, at first glance, would appear to have much in common with the Essenes, indeed to overlap with them. At least one eminent writer on the subject has maintained that Jesus and his followers were Zadokites,[8] though others insist on a distinction.[9]

The other important sub-sect to figure prominently in recent biblical scholarship has been familiar for a long time, but under a different name. It has traditionally been called 'the Early Church', or 'the Jerusalem Church'. Its members referred to themselves as Nazareans. Dr Hugh Schonfield uses the convenient appellation of 'the Nazarean Party'. This was composed specifically of Jesus's immediate followers.

The existence of sub-sects such as the Zadokites and the Nazareans has generated considerable confusion and uncertainty among biblical scholars. Jesus was unquestionably a Nazarean. He seems also to have been a Zadokite – but does this mean that the Nazareans and the Zadokites were one and the same? If so, what about the conventional Pharisaic aspects of his teachings? And what about the unmistakable traces of Essene training? Were the Nazareans and the Zadokites offshoots or sub-divisions of the Essenes? Were the Essenes themselves perhaps but one manifestation of a single, broader movement? Such questions have led to a bewildering muddle. This muddle, and the apparent contradictions inherent in it, have obscured a clear perception of Jesus's political and military activity. All the more so, because scholastic attempts to distinguish between the various religious denominations have deflected attention from the importance of the politically oriented Zealots.

In 1983, there appeared a new study of the issue by Dr Robert Eisenman, Chairman of the Department of Religious Studies at the University of California, Long Beach. Eisenman's work bears an unwieldy title – *Maccabees, Zadokites, Christians and Qumran.* But it does much to dispel the prevailing confusion and, in our opinion, constitutes one of the most important treatments of the subject to date. Although the specific evidence is complex, the conclusions are not only impressively convincing, but also beautifully simple. Indeed, Eisenman seems to have focused a searchlight on the underlying simplicity of what has hitherto seemed a complicated situation.

Working from original documents, and questioning the reliability of second-hand commentators such as Josephus, Eisenman traces the various names by which the members of the Qumran community – the authors of the Dead Sea Scrolls – referred to themselves. This leads him to conclude that the Sons of Light, the Sons of Truth, the Sons of Zadok, or Zaddikim (Zadokites), the Men of Melchizedek (the z-d-k ending reflecting a variation of

Zadok), the Ebionim (the Poor), the Hassidim (the Essenes) and the Nozrim (the Nazareans) are ultimately one and the same – not different groups, but different metaphors or appellations for essentially the same group, or the same movement.[10] The primary objective of this movement seems to have been oriented towards the dynastic legitimacy of the high priesthood. In the Old Testament, the High Priest of both David and Solomon is called Zadok, either as a personal name or as an official title. He is traditionally associated, very closely, with the Messiah, the anointed one, the rightful king. More specifically, he is associated with the *Davidic* Messiah.

As Eisenman demonstrates, the legitimacy of the high priesthood – of Zadok or of the Zadok – was resuscitated by the Maccabeans, the last dynasty of Judaic kings, who ruled Israel from the second century B.C. until Herodian times and the Roman occupation. (As we have already noted, Herod attempted to legitimise himself by marrying a Maccabean princess, then proceeded to murder her and her sons, thus extinguishing the Maccabean line.) It is ultimately to the Maccabean dynasty that Eisenman traces the movement which gains increasing momentum during the lifetime of Jesus and the years that follow. Eisenman also traces the Sadducees back to the same source, indicating that the term 'Sadducee' is in fact a variant, or perhaps a corruption, of 'Zadok' or 'Zaddikim'. In other words, the original Sadducees would have been a devout dynastic priesthood closely associated with at least the principle of an expected Davidic Messiah.

But with the accession of Herod, Eisenman argues, most Sadducees – the Sadducees whom we know as such from biblical sources and from Josephus – betrayed their original loyalties and aligned themselves with the usurper. This betrayal appears to have provoked a large-scale opposition – as it were, an alternative 'fundamentalist' priesthood, militantly at odds with the established one which had prostituted itself to an illegitimate king. On the one hand, then, there would have been the so-called 'Herodian Sadducees', who clung to their Temple privileges and prerogatives under Herod's reign and, after his death, accommodated themselves to the Roman administration. On the other hand, there would have been a 'true' or 'purist' Sadducee movement, consisting of Sadducees who wanted no part of such collaboration and remained loyal to the principle of a Davidic Messiah. It is these latter Sadducees who become known as Essenes, Zadokites or Zaddikim and the various other appellations that have hitherto confused researchers.

But this is not the whole of Eisenman's argument. On the contrary, it extends further to include the Zealots as well. The Zealots adopted or acquired their name to denote those who were 'zealous for the law'. This phrase is a clue, becoming a means whereby adherents of the same movement can be identified. It occurs in a number of quite precise and extremely crucial contexts, from the Maccabean regime on into the first century A.D. Thus the High Priest at the period of Judas Maccabeus (who died in 160 B.C.) is referred to as a Zaddik and described as being 'a zealot for the law'. Mattathias, father of Judas Maccabeus, commands 'everyone who has zeal for the law' to follow him and take a stand on the covenant.

Judas of Galilee, usually credited with founding the Zealots at the dawn of the Christian era, is also a 'zealot for the law – and is attended by a high priest called Zadok. And in the Acts of the Apostles (Acts 21:20), the Nazareans in Jerusalem – the so-called 'early Christians' – are again described, quite precisely, as being 'zealous for the law'. The Greek text is even more revealing. Here they are called 'zelotai of the law' – in other words, Zealots.[11]

What emerges is a kind of fundamentalist dynastic priesthood associated with the principle of a Davidic Messiah and extending from the second century B.C. through the period covered by the Gospels and the Acts of the Apostles. This priesthood is at war with the Romans. It is also at war with the 'Herodian' Sadducees. Depending on their activities at a given moment, and on the orientation of the chronicler, this priesthood is variously called Zealot, Essene, Zadokite and a number of other things – including, by their enemies, 'outlaw' and 'brigand'. The Essenes are not passive mystics. On the contrary, their vision, as Eisenman says, is 'violently apocalyptic', and constitutes a theological corollary to the violent action for which the Zealots are held responsible. A similar violence – both theological and political – can be discerned in the careers of John the Baptist and of Jesus. Indeed, Eisenman goes so far as to suggest that the families of Jesus and John the Baptist may even have been related to that of Judas of Galilee, leader of the Zealots at the time of Jesus's birth.[12]

If Eisenman is correct – and the evidence weighs heavily in his favour – then the confusion which has hitherto obtained is effectively dispelled. Essenes, Zadokites, Nazareans, Zealots and various other supposed groups emerge as no more than different designations – or, at most, different manifestations – of a single movement diffused throughout the Holy Land and well into Syria, from the second century B.C. on. The names which have previously

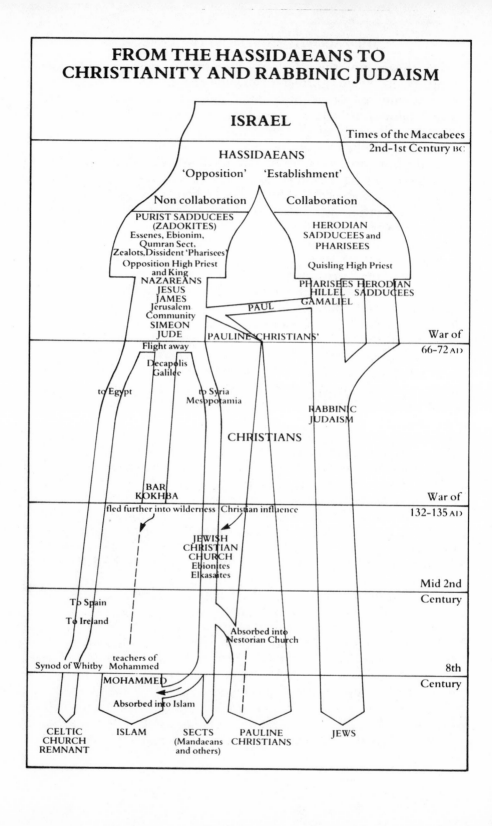

FROM THE HASSIDAEANS TO CHRISTIANITY AND RABBINIC JUDAISM

ISRAEL

Times of the Maccabees

2nd–1st Century BC

HASSIDAEANS

'Opposition'   'Establishment'

Non collaboration   Collaboration

PURIST SADDUCEES
(ZADOKITES)
Essenes, Ebionim,
Qumran Sect,
Zealots, Dissident 'Pharisees'

HERODIAN
SADDUCEES and
PHARISEES

Opposition High Priest
and King

Quisling High Priest

NAZAREANS
JESUS
JAMES
Jerusalem
Community
SIMEON
JUDE

PHARISEES HERODIAN
HILLEL   SADDUCEES
GAMALIEL

PAUL

PAULINE 'CHRISTIANS'

War of

66–72 AD

Flight away

Decapolis
Galilee

to Egypt

to Syria
Mesopotamia

RABBINIC
JUDAISM

CHRISTIANS

BAR
KOKHBA

War of

fled further into wilderness Christian influence

132–135 AD

JEWISH
CHRISTIAN
CHURCH
Ebionites
Elkasaites

Mid 2nd

To Spain

Century

To Ireland

Absorbed into
Nestorian Church

teachers of
Synod of Whitby Mohammed

8th

MOHAMMED

Century

Absorbed into Islam

CELTIC
CHURCH
REMNANT

ISLAM

SECTS
(Mandaeans
and others)

PAULINE
CHRISTIANS

JEWS

confused scholars would in effect have been like the variety of names used for, say, a contemporary political party or, at most, for the spectrum of groups and individuals which coalesced into a single movement – the French Resistance, during the German occupation. For Eisenman, there is no distinction at all between Zealots and Nazareans, Essenes and Zadokites. But even if there had been, the groups would still have been unified by their joint involvement in a single ambitious enterprise, a single overriding endeavour – to rid their land of the Roman occupation and reinstate the old Judaic monarchy together with its rightful priesthood. And if Jesus were the legitimate claimant of that monarchy, they would have been unified in their support of him, his family and his house.

The Nazareans or the Nazarean Party – the so-called (and misnamed) 'first Christians' or 'Early Church' – do not appear to have differed doctrinally from the groups generally known as Essene or Zadokite. If they differed at all, the differences would seem to have resided only in their membership – in specific individuals or personalities. We do not know the names of individual Zadokites or Essenes. We do know the names of those who constituted the Nazarean Party. They are people who either knew Jesus personally or apprenticed themselves, perhaps at second or third remove, to those who did. But apart from this, the Nazareans are indistinguishable from the broader movement of which they were part. The Nazarean Party must not therefore be seen as a separate unit, but rather as a nucleus – the equivalent of a general staff, a privy council or a cabinet.[13]

We must now look more closely at this cabinet – at its activities, its prominent personalities, its eventual fate – and at the process whereby circumstance, history and Saint Paul conspired to consign it to oblivion.

6

The Formation of Christianity

Apart from the Gospels themselves, the most important book of the New Testament is the Acts of the Apostles. Indeed, there are certain respects in which Acts, especially for the historian, may be even more significant.

The Gospels, as we have said before, are unreliable as historical documents. The first of them, Mark, was composed no earlier than the revolt of A.D. 66, and probably somewhat later.[1] All four Gospels hark back to a period long before their own composition – perhaps as long as sixty or seventy years. They pay scant attention to the historical backdrop, addressing themselves essentially to the figure of Jesus and his teaching. They are poetic and devotional works, rather than chronicles. Acts, by comparison, although extremely biased in its point of view, nevertheless reflects an endeavour to preserve an historical record, an account of 'what actually happened' in its historical context. It recounts a complex story in a more or less coherent fashion. It seems to have been subjected to considerably less editing than the Gospels. It reflects, often, a first-hand experience of the events it describes. And it was composed either only a short time after those events by someone who played a role in them, or more probably by someone with direct access to the testimony of an eyewitness.[2]

The period covered by the narrative in Acts begins shortly after the Crucifixion and ends somewhere between A.D. 64 and 67. According to most scholars, the narrative itself was composed between A.D. 70 and 95. It is thus, roughly speaking, contemporary with the earliest of the Gospels, if, indeed, it does not pre-date all four.

The author of Acts identifies himself as a man named Luke, and modern scholars concur that he is identical with the author of Luke's Gospel. Whether this Luke is the same as 'Luke the Doctor', who was with Paul in Rome while Paul was in prison (Colossians 4:14), is less certain, but most commentators are prepared to accept that he is.

Luke's account is primarily an account of Paul. It is quite clear that Luke knew Paul personally, in a way that neither he, nor the authors of the other Gospels, knew Jesus. It is from Luke that one learns of Paul's conversion and mission. At the same time, it is from Luke that one also learns a great deal about the Nazarean Party. Ultimately, Acts offers a more or less reliable historical account of Paul's dispute with the Nazarean Party, which would culminate in nothing less than the creation of an entirely new religion. It is thus worth summarising the historical background covered by the narrative in Acts.

John the Baptist appears to have been executed by Herod Antipas some time after A.D. 28, but no later than A.D. 35. Jesus's own crucifixion is variously dated between A.D. 30 and A.D. 36, and seems to have occurred after John's death. It cannot have been later than A.D. 36, because Pilate, in that year, was recalled to Rome.[3]

In A.D. 35, or early in 36, there occurred an uprising in Samaria, led by a Samaritan Messiah. This uprising was ruthlessly suppressed and many Samaritans, including the leaders, were exterminated in the process. At the same time, persecution of Jesus's immediate following seems to have intensified. In A.D. 36, for example, Stephen, usually hailed as Christianity's first martyr, was stoned to death in Jerusalem, and many Nazareans fled the city. By that time – possibly as little as a year and a half after Jesus's death – they must already have been widespread and numerous, because Paul, acting on behalf of the established Sadducee priesthood and armed with warrants from the High Priest, undertakes to hunt them out as far away as Damascus. In other words, there were already Nazarean enclaves in Syria, and these were regarded as enough of a threat to warrant extirpation. Syria, of course, was no part of Israel. Judaic authorities could assert themselves only as far north as Syria with the approval of the Roman administration. And for Rome to acquiesce in such witch-hunts must indicate that Rome herself felt threatened. If, moreover, at this early date, sizeable Nazarean enclaves existed as far distant as Syria, one cannot ignore the possibility that they had come into being prior to Jesus's death and were already established at the time of the Crucifixion.

By A.D. 38, Jesus was being openly proclaimed as the Messiah – not the Son of God but simply the rightful and anointed king – by Nazarean refugees, or perhaps established communities, as far away as Antioch. It was here, in the Syrian capital far to the north of Damascus, that the term 'Christian' was to be applied to them for the first time. Until then, they had simply been called Nazareans. And they continued to be called Nazareans elsewhere – especially in Jerusalem – for many years.

In A.D. 38, a centralised Nazarean authority was already well established in Jerusalem. By later Christian chroniclers, this administrative hierarchy was to become known as 'the Early Church'. Its most famous member was, of course, Peter. Its official head, however, conspicuously neglected by later tradition, was Jesus's brother Jacob, known subsequently as Saint James, or James the Just. By this time, the Magdalene, the Virgin and others of those closest to Jesus had disappeared, and there is no further mention of them in scriptural accounts. It is certainly reasonable to suppose that later assertions are accurate and that they sought refuge in exile. What is significant, however, is that it is not Peter, but Jesus's brother James who presides over the 'Church' in Jerusalem. Quite clearly, some principle of dynastic succession is at work. And it can hardly be coincidental that James is referred to as 'Zadok'.[4]

The Nazarean Party

Jesus himself, of course, had had no intention of creating a new religion. Neither had James and the Nazarean Party in Jerusalem. Like Jesus, they would have been horrified by the very idea, regarding it as the most appalling blasphemy. Like Jesus, they were, after all, devout Jews, working and preaching wholly within the context of established Judaic tradition. True, they were seeking certain renewed observances, certain reforms and certain political changes. They were also seeking to purge their religion of recently acquired alien elements and to restore it to what they deemed its original purity. But they would not have dreamed of creating a new system of belief which might become a rival of Judaism – and, worse still, its persecutor.

Nevertheless, it is clear that the Nazarean Party in Jerusalem was considered subversive, both by the Romans and by the official Sadducee establishment, for it was quickly in trouble with the authorities. As we have already noted, Stephen was stoned to death within a short time of the Crucifixion, and Saul of Tarsus was pursuing Nazareans in Damascus. Around A.D. 44, Peter, then John, then all the others were arrested, flogged and ordered not to speak the name of Jesus. In the same year, the disciple known as James, brother of John, was arrested and beheaded – a form of execution which only the Romans were allowed to perform. By the following year, guerrilla activity on the part of the Zealots had intensified to such a degree that Rome was obliged to take vigorous countermeasures. By A.D. 48–9, the Roman Governor of Judaea was seizing and crucifying both Zealots and Nazareans indiscriminately. Nevertheless, the disturbances increased. In A.D. 52, the Roman Legate of Syria – the immediate superior of the Governor of Judaea – had to intervene personally to prevent a full-scale insurrection.

In fact, the insurrection was simply delayed, not prevented. By A.D. 54–5, militant activity had again assumed epidemic proportions. The Sadducee High Priest, appointed by the Romans, was assassinated by the Zealots, and a major terrorist campaign was launched against other Sadducees who had aligned themselves with Rome. During A.D. 57–8, another Messiah appeared, said to have come from the Jewish community in Egypt. Having gained a substantial following in Judaea, he undertook to occupy Jerusalem by force of arms and drive the Romans from the Holy Land. Not surprisingly, this enterprise was violently thwarted, but the disturbances continued. At last, around A.D. 62–5, James, head of the Nazarean Party in Jerusalem, was seized and executed.

Once again, a dynastic principle of succession seems clearly to have obtained among the Nazareans. On James's death, his place was taken by an individual named Simeon, who is identified as a cousin of Jesus.[5] For a short time, Simeon kept the Nazarean administrative hierarchy in Jerusalem. But for him, as for everyone else in the capital, the course of events must now have been discerned as inevitable. Around A.D. 65, Simeon accordingly led the Nazareans out of the Holy City. They are said to have established their headquarters at the town of Pella, north of Jerusalem and on the east side of the Jordan.[6] Modern scholars have found proof that from here they continued to withdraw north-eastwards, groups of them eventually making their way to the vicinity of the Tigris–Euphrates basin, the region which now constitutes the border between Syria and Iraq. In this region, divorced from what had by now become the mainstream of developing Christianity, they continued to survive, and preserve their traditions, for centuries. There has been some speculation that Mohammed's father was a member of a Nazarean sect and that Mohammed himself was raised in Nazarean traditions. One of his wives is reported to have been Jewish and, by implication,

Nazarean. Certainly the treatment of Jesus in the Koran is essentially Nazarean in orientation.

Simeon's prudence in leaving Jerusalem was fully justified. In the spring of A.D. 66, serious fighting broke out in Caesarea. Shortly after, Roman troops ran amok in Jerusalem, murdering all Jews they could find, including women and children. In the wave of revulsion that followed, priests in the Temple were coerced into abolishing the official sacrifices to Rome and to the Emperor – an overt challenge which rendered open war inevitable. After a week of civil strife, Jerusalem itself was captured by the rebels. In the meantime, Zealot contingents commanded by a descendant of Judas of Galilee seized the fortress of Masada on the Dead Sea, exterminated the Roman garrison and prepared defensive installations that would withstand their enemies' siege until A.D. 73.

The Roman response was at first somewhat sluggish. A legion dispatched from Syria, and reinforced by auxiliaries, was repulsed from Jerusalem. Its retreat degenerated into a rout. Encouraged by this success, the rebels proceeded to organise a defensive network throughout the Holy Land. It is interesting to note that the commander of one region, extending from Jerusalem to the coast, is named as John the Essene[7] – another indication that the Essenes were not at all pacifist.

By A.D. 70, however, the situation was already hopeless. A massive Roman army besieged Jerusalem, utterly destroying the Temple and razing the city to the ground. It was to lie in ruins for another sixty-one years. Most of the inhabitants were killed or died of hunger. The majority of the survivors were sold as slaves. For three more years, Masada continued to hold out, but its fall was a foregone conclusion.

Paul as the First Heretic

It is against this turbulent background that Paul's career, chronicled in Acts, must be placed. Paul appears on the scene within a year or so of the Crucifixion. Under the name of Saul of Tarsus, a fanatical Sadducee or Sadducee instrument, he actively participates in attacks on the Nazarean Party in Jerusalem. Indeed, he participates so actively that he is apparently involved in the stoning to death of Stephen, officially regarded as the first Christian martyr (although Stephen would have seen himself, of course, as a pious Jew). Paul is quite explicit. He freely admits that he has persecuted his victims 'to the death'.

Shortly after Stephen's death, Paul (still Saul of Tarsus at this point), prompted by a sadistic fanatical fervour, embarks for Damascus, in Syria, to ferret out Nazareans there. He is accompanied by a band of men, presumably armed, and bears arrest warrants from the High Priest. As we have already noted, the High Priest's authority did not extend to Syria. For Paul to exercise a mandate there, he must have had the endorsement of the Roman administration, which indicates that Rome had a vested interest in eradicating Nazareans. In no other circumstances would she have tolerated militant vigilantes operating with impunity so far beyond their own domains.

The midday sun at the time appears to have acted more dramatically than it subsequently does with mad dogs and Englishmen. On the road, Paul undergoes something traumatic, which commentators have interpreted as anything from sunstroke, to an epileptic seizure, to a mystical experience. A 'light from heaven' allegedly knocks him from his horse and 'a voice', issuing from no perceptible source, demands of him: 'Saul, Saul, why are you persecuting me?' Saul asks the voice to identify itself. The voice replies: 'I am Jesus the Nazarean, and you are persecuting me.' It further instructs him to continue to Damascus, where he will be told what he must subsequently do. When this experience passes and Paul regains a semblance of his former consciousness, he finds he has been stricken temporarily blind. In Damascus, his sight is restored by a Nazarean.[8]

A modern psychologist would find nothing unusual in such an incident. It may indeed have been caused by sunstroke or by an epileptic seizure. It could also, as readily, be ascribed to hallucination, hysterical or psychotic reaction, or perhaps nothing more than a guilty conscience. Paul, however, interprets it as a visitation from Jesus, whom he never knew personally; and from this proceeds his conversion. He abandons his former appellation of Saul and becomes Paul. And from now on, he will be as fervently fanatical in his promulgation of Nazarean thought as he has hitherto been in trying to suppress it.

Around A.D. 39, Paul returns to Jerusalem. Here, according to Acts, he is officially admitted to the Nazarean Party. According to Paul himself, however, in his letter to the Galatians, his reception into the Nazarean Party was rather less than enthusiastic. He admits that they did not trust him and avoided him. But he is accorded some sort of grudging acceptance by 'James, the brother of the Lord', who dispatches him to Tarsus, to preach there. From Tarsus, Paul continues his missionary journey, which lasts some fourteen years and takes him across virtually the whole of the eastern Mediterranean world – not only throughout the Holy Land, but to Asia Minor as well, and across the sea to Greece. One would expect such energy to earn him the approval of the Nazarean hierarchy in Jerusalem. On the contrary, however, he has earned nothing but their displeasure. James and the Nazarean hierarchy send their own missionaries in his wake, to undo his preaching and compromise him with his own converts – for Paul, by now, is preaching something very different from what the Nazareans themselves, under Jesus's brother, have sanctioned. Harassed by James's emissaries, Paul at last returns to Jerusalem, where a full-scale dispute ensues. Eventually, after considerable friction, an uneasy agreement is concluded between James and Paul, but Paul, soon after, is arrested – or placed in protective custody. Taking advantage of his status as a Roman citizen, Paul demands that his case be heard by the Emperor personally and is sent as a prisoner to Rome. He is believed to have died there some time between A.D. 64 and 67.

In terms of miles covered and energy expended during his missionary travels, Paul's achievement is stupendous. There is no question that he acted with the dynamism of 'a man possessed'. Yet it is clear that things are not as straightforward as later Christian tradition would have one believe. According to that tradition, Paul is depicted as 'faithfully disseminating Jesus's message across the Romanised world of his time'. Why, then, should his relations with Jesus's own brother have been so awkwardly strained? Why should there have been such friction with the Nazareans in Jerusalem, some of whom had known Jesus personally and were certainly closer to him than Paul ever was? Why should Paul's preaching have so provoked the Nazarean hierarchy that they sent their own emissaries in his wake to discredit him? It would seem clear that Paul was doing something of which Jesus himself would have disapproved.

As we have said, neither Jesus nor the Nazarean hierarchy had any intention of creating a new religion. They were promulgating a specifically Judaic message for Judaic adherents. As Jesus himself says (Matthew 5:17): 'Do not imagine that I have come to abolish the Law or the Prophets. I have come not to abolish but to complete them.' For James and the Nazarean Party in Jerusalem, what matters is Jesus's teaching and his claim to Messiahship in the established context of the time – as rightful king and liberator. He is important less in himself than in what he says and what he represents. He is not intended, in his own person, to become an object of worship. He is certainly not intended to be regarded as divine.[9]

When James dispatches Paul and others on missionary expeditions, he desires them to convert people to Jesus's form of Judaism. The 'Nation of Israel', as Jesus, James and their contemporaries conceived it, was not just a geographical entity. It was also a community, which encompassed all Jews wherever they happened to reside. The process of conversion was intended to swell the ranks of the Nation of Israel. It is even possible that James saw this programme as a means of creating a reservoir of manpower, from which – as in the time of Judas Maccabeus – an army might be created. If organised revolt was simmering in the Holy Land, its chances of success would have been immensely augmented if it could be synchronised, say, with uprisings by Jewish communites across the length and breadth of the Roman Empire.

Paul either fails to see James's objectives or refuses to cooperate. In 2 Corinthians 11:3–4, he states explicitly that the Nazarean emissaries of James are promulgating *another Jesus*, a Jesus different from the one he is promulgating. Paul, in effect, betrays the commission entrusted to him by James and the Nazarean hierarchy. For Paul, Jesus's teachings and political status are less important than Jesus himself. Instead of making converts to Judaism, Paul makes converts to his own personal and 'pagan' cult of Jesus, while Judaism as such becomes incidental, if not irrelevant. What matters is simply a profession of faith in Jesus as a manifestation of God, and such a profession of faith is in itself sufficient to ensure salvation. The basic requirements for conversion to Judaism, such as circumcision, observance of the Sabbath and adherence to dietary laws, are abandoned in the process. Jesus, James and the Nazareans in Jerusalem advocated worship of God, in the strict Judaic sense. Paul replaces this with worship of Jesus *as* God. In Paul's hands, Jesus himself becomes an object of religious veneration – which Jesus himself, like his brother and the other Nazareans in Jerusalem, would have regarded as blasphemous.

The irreconcilability of Jesus and Paul raises questions of considerable contemporary relevance. How many 'Christians' today, for example, are aware of the discrepancy between the two men? And in what, for them, does 'Christianity' reside? In what Jesus taught? Or in what Paul taught? Except by sleight of logic and distortion of historical fact, the two positions cannot be harmonised.

The Cult of Paul

It is from Paul, and Paul alone, that a new religion begins to emerge – not a form of Judaism, but a rival and ultimately an adversary to Judaism. As Paul disseminates his own personal message, such Judaism as it contains undergoes a metamorphosis. It is fused with Greco-Roman thought, with pagan traditions, with elements from a number of mystery schools.

Once Paul's cult began to crystallise as a religion in itself, rather than a form of Judaism, it dictated certain priorities which had not obtained in Jesus's lifetime and which Jesus himself would unquestionably have deplored.[10] In the first place, it had to compete with already established religions in regions where it was trying to gain a foothold – with the religions of Syria, Phoenicia, Asia Minor, Greece, Egypt, the whole of the Mediterranean world and, beyond, the Roman Empire. In order to do this, Jesus had perforce to assume a degree of godhood comparable to that of the deities he now, posthumously, was intended to displace. Like many other such deities Tammuz, for example, the god of ancient Sumerian and Phoenician mystery teachings, had been born of a virgin, died with a wound in his side and, after three days, rose from his tomb, leaving it vacant with the rock at the entrance rolled aside. If Paul were to challenge successfully the adherents of Tammuz, Jesus would have to be able to match the older god, miracle for miracle. In consequence, certain aspects of the Tammuz story were grafted on to Jesus's biography. It is significant that Bethlehem was not only David's city, but also the ancient centre of a Tammuz cult, with a shrine that remained active well into biblical times.

One can trace numerous specific elements in the Gospels to their origin not in history, but in the traditions surrounding Tammuz, Osiris, Attis, Adonis, Dionysos and Zoroaster. Many of them, for example, were supposed to have been born of a god and a virgin. Mithraism exerted a particularly powerful influence on the coalescence of Christian tradition. It postulated an apocalypse, a day of judgment, a resurrection of the flesh and a second coming of Mithras himself, who would finally defeat the principle of evil. Mithras was said to have been born in a cave or a grotto, where shepherds attended him and regaled him with gifts. Baptism played a prominent role in Mithraic rites. So, too, did the communal meal. There is a passage in the Mithraic communion which is particularly interesting: 'He who shall not eat of my body nor drink of my blood so that he may be one with me and I with him, shall not be saved.'[11]

When Tertullian, one of the early Church Fathers, was confronted with this passage, he insisted it was the Devil, centuries in advance, parodying the Christian Communion in order to diminish the import of Jesus's words. If this was indeed the case, the Devil must also have been busy brainwashing Paul. As one modern commentator observes:

> Even with the comparatively slight knowledge we have of Mithraism and its liturgy, it is clear that many of Paul's phrases [in his letters] savour much more of the terminology of the Persian cult than that of the Gospels.[12]

But Christianity had not only to compete – to offer a god who could match his rivals miracle for miracle, wonder for wonder, supernatural occurrence for supernatural occurrence. It had also to make itself respectable and acceptable to a world which was, after all, part of the Roman Empire.

Intrinsically, it was not so at all. Jesus had been executed as a criminal for offences against Rome, in strict accordance with Roman law. His original followers would have been regarded as subversives, if not overt revolutionaries, actively dedicated to breaking Roman authority over Palestine. The Holy Land had long been a source of exasperation for Rome, and after the revolt of A.D. 66 Roman hostility towards Judaism intensified. No religion which contained vestiges of Judaic Messianic nationalism could hope to survive within the Roman imperium. In consequence, all traces of this Messianic nationalism had to be eradicated or transformed.

In order to diffuse itself through the Romanised world, Christianity transmuted itself – and, in the process, rewrote the historical circumstances from which it arose. It would not do to deify a rebel against Rome. It would not do to exalt a figure who had been executed by the Romans for crimes against the Empire. As a result, responsibility for Jesus's death was transferred to the Jews – not only to the Sadducee establishment, who undoubtedly had a hand in it, but to the people of the Holy Land in general, who were among Jesus's most fervent supporters. And Jesus himself had to be divorced from his historical context, turned into a non-political figure – an other-worldly, spiritual Messiah who posed no challenge whatever to Caesar. Thus, all trace of Jesus's political activity was de-emphasised, diluted or excised. And, so far as possible, all trace of his Jewishness was deliberately obscured, ignored or rendered irrelevant.

Simon Peter

The course and the eventual magnitude of Paul's ideological triumph over James and the Nazarean hierarchy can be gauged by the slowly shifting attitude of Simon Peter. Indeed, Simon Peter offers a kind of barometer of the situation. His personal position almost certainly mirrors that of numerous others who gravitated from James to Paul, from a form of Judaism to the increasingly autonomous new religion subsequently called Christianity.

In our previous book, we described Jesus's immediate entourage as consisting of two more or less distinct groups, 'adherents of the bloodline' and 'adherents of the message'. The 'adherents of the bloodline' would have constituted a relatively small circle of probably aristocratic or patrician caste, members of Jesus's own family and families related to it. For them, the primary concern would have been dynastic legitimacy – the installation on the throne of Israel of her rightful king and, when that failed, perpetuation of the royal bloodline intact. The 'adherents of the message' would have been considerably more numerous, constituting the 'rank and file' of the movement. Their priorities would have been quite different – more mundane, more limited in scope, more pragmatic. They would have responded primarily to Jesus's message, which, by its very nature, elicited emotions of, simultaneously, fear and hope. On the one hand, they would have been frightened by the urgency of the situation as Jesus describes it – the prospect of an imminent apocalypse, a day of judgment, the distribution of punishments and rewards. On the other hand, they would have been inspired by the promise that they, as loyal adherents of the Messiah, would be granted a unique recompense for their fidelity and for any suffering they had incurred. This joint appeal to fear and hope would have exercised a magnetic potency.

From what we know of him, Simon Peter would have been a typical 'adherent of the message'. He does not appear to have been a particularly well educated man. He seems to have little sense of the broader issues involved, political or theological. He is not privy to Jesus's inner council, and many decisions are made behind his back or above his head. As we have already noted, he may well have been a militant nationalist who did not shrink from violence. He may well have been a Zealot or a former Zealot – and may, in fact, be identical with Simon Zelotes.[13] For the whole of Jesus's public ministry, Simon Peter is at his master's side, almost as a kind of bodyguard – a function in keeping with his sobriquet of 'Rocky' or 'tough'. Although not conspicuously courageous, he is unswerving

72

in his devotion, at times almost abject. By the time Paul becomes active, James may be official head of the Nazarean Party in Jerusalem; but it is Simon Peter, whether by virtue of the mission entrusted to him by Jesus or by virtue of his own charisma, who wields the greatest influence and commands the most fervent allegiance.

At the beginning of Acts, Simon Peter is unquestionably aligned with James and the Nazarean hierarchy in Jerusalem. Gradually, however, he begins to gravitate towards Paul's position. By the end of Acts, his orientation has become entirely Pauline. Like James, Simon Peter is at first a devout Jew, who sees Jesus's teaching exclusively in a Judaic context. By the end of his career, he is, like Paul, preaching a trans-Judaic message to the Gentile world. Tradition anachronistically proclaims him as the first pope – the first ruler of the Church which was to enshrine Paul's triumph and constitute an edifice of Pauline thought.

In her novel *The Illusionist*, Anita Mason offers an impressive and poignant imaginative re-creation of the personal ordeal through which Simon Peter, and many others like him, must have passed. As a simple, untutored Galilean fisherman and bully, he must at first have taken Jesus's statements quite literally. Thus does one see him in the Gospels – loyal, but something of a yokel, and certainly not thinking in any very sophisticated religious or political terms. Jesus is attached to him, but can hardly be said to confide in him. As Anita Mason shows, Simon Peter must at first have been thoroughly convinced that the world would literally end with Jesus's death – that an apocalyptic holocaust would consume the whole of creation, that upheavals such as those recounted by Old Testament prophets would sweep the earth, that God would descend to pronounce stern judgment.

In the days immediately following the Crucifixion, Simon Peter must have been, as Anita Mason depicts him, increasingly puzzled – and more than a little alarmed – to find the world around him still intact. At the beginning of the period chronicled in Acts, his position has modified only slightly. Like many other Nazareans, he still expects the dissolution of creation. The apocalypse has been postponed, probably for obscure technical reasons unfathomable to mortals, but it has been postponed only temporarily. Simon Peter has no doubt whatever that it remains imminent and will occur in the course of his own lifetime. It is this conviction, this fervent hope, that constitutes his *raison d'être*.

But the years pass and nothing happens. Not only is there no apocalypse, no cosmic cataclysm. There is not even a significant change in the local situation. Roman officials are installed, then deposed. Puppet kings are placed on thrones, then removed. Civic disturbances increase, but prompted as much probably by impatience as by anything else. Everything continues more or less as it had before, and it becomes increasingly evident that Jesus's death has accomplished nothing. For a man like Simon Peter, this, of course, constitutes a terrifying prospect. He has committed himself definitively to a belief. After considerable dithering, he has pledged his life and his future to that belief, and now the validity of his belief has begun to appear more and more questionable. To Simon Peter, the burgeoning weight of doubt, the burgeoning suspicion that his commitment has been in vain, must, as Anita Mason depicts, have been an appalling psychological torment. It must have threatened him not only with disillusionment, but with a despair verging on the suicidal; and if he persists in disseminating the message, he does so almost somnambulistically, as a means of distracting himself from his uncertainties.

Paul, of course, offers Simon Peter an irresistible opportunity, a means of rescuing his commitment, of vindicating everything to which he has devoted himself. For Simon Peter, Paul's position is a viable alternative to despair. At first, of course, he sides with James in regarding Paul's work as highly suspect, if not blasphemous. Gradually, however, Paul's position becomes the only one whereby sense can be made of the situation. Paul's position, in short, provides Simon Peter with a viable explanation for why the world has not yet ended, why it may not for another thousand or two thousand years, while at the same time still justifying one's allegiance. Jesus becomes consubstantial with God. And if Jesus is consubstantial with God, the Kingdom of Heaven need not be something that will be inaugurated on earth in the immediate future, but something external – another realm, another dimension, in which one can expect a welcome and a reserved place on one's death. The apocalypse may have been postponed indefinitely, but there remains the assurance that it *will* eventually come, at the end of time; and, in the meanwhile, there are rewards to be reaped in heaven.

From this elaborate rationalisation, Simon Peter derives a new impetus, a new inspiration which enables him to continue his preaching and – according to traditional accounts – to go bravely to his martyrdom. By virtue of this supposed martyrdom, he does indeed become the rock on which a subsequent church – a Pauline church – is founded. And subsequent tradition, *a posteriori*, will proclaim Simon Peter the first Bishop of Rome and the founder of the papacy.

As we have said, Simon Peter's vicissitudes, as depicted by Anita Mason, cannot have been unique. On the contrary, there must have been many fervent followers of Jesus who conformed to a similar pattern – teetering on the brink of shattering disillusion, then finding a new justification in Paul. It is thus not difficult to understand why Paul's essentially 'pagan' cult should have been so persuasive, nor why it should subsequently have triumphed over the less comforting position of the Nazarean dynasty – of James and ultimately of Jesus himself. And with the fall of Jerusalem in A.D. 70, the Nazarean influence effectively disappeared from most of the Mediterranean world. Pauline thought would still continue to have rivals, of course. But none of them would be able to muster the authority, vested in dynastic succession, of James.

Judas Iscariot

In the course of its dissemination, Pauline thought revised much of the original story on which the Gospels are based. It inserted new material. It adapted itself to the world in which it was being promulgated. In the process, certain individuals were made to pay a price, if only in the eyes of posterity.

Simon Peter, of course, is the best known and probably the most popular of Jesus's original entourage – the one whom tradition has established as virtually synonymous with Christianity itself. In many ways, he is the most fully characterised of the disciples. And, in his weaknesses, he is the most endearingly human. But there is one other member of Jesus's first disciples who affords considerably more insight into what his master was really doing. His significance has been obscured by Pauline thought.

For nearly twenty centuries, the figure known as Judas Iscariot – Judas the Sicarius – has been accursed and despised, cast in the role of most heinous of villains. In relation to Jesus, popular tradition has imposed upon him one of the oldest and most archetypal of functions – that of the eternal adversary, the dark opposite, the embodiment of all the vices and iniquities that the hero is not. Symbolically speaking, Judas is the 'evil brother', the dark side of which Jesus is the light. In Judaeo-Christian tradition, the antithesis between them is another manifestation of the conflict dating back to Cain and Abel. One finds a similar conflict in other cultures, other mythologies, other cosmologies. In Egyptian myth, for example, the same duality is reflected by the eternal conflict between Set and Osiris. In Zoroastrian teaching – which, through its Mithraic vestiges, heavily influenced Christianity – it was dramatised by Ahura-Mazda or Ormus/Ormuzd and Ahriman. One can find parallel rivalries across the globe, from Aztec and Toltec beliefs in Mexico to the myths of India, China and Japan. And behind all of them lies the archetypal opposition between good and evil, light and darkness, creation and destruction, God and the Devil. If Jesus, in later Christian culture, becomes synonymous with God, Judas – dragging 'the Jews' in general with him – becomes the very embodiment of God's adversary.

Judas appears as a false friend who, for purely mercenary reasons, betrays his master and brings about his master's death. The picture is unmitigatedly black, and there are no exentuating circumstances. But a closer reading of the Gospels reveals a much more complex drama being enacted.

As we have seen, Jesus was steeped in Old Testament prophecies – especially those of Zechariah pertaining to the Messiah – and acted repeatedly in close adherence to them. Again and again, such prophecies dictate and determine his decisions, his attitudes, his course of action. Indeed, a large part of his public life and known history would seem to be little more than an embodiment and re-enactment of the prophecies. And, of course, the more of them he fulfils, the more substantial becomes his own Messianic claim. 'This took place to fulfil the prophecy' is a constant refrain throughout the New Testament – the refrain of a polemicist triumphantly presenting his proof.

For centuries, and despite contrary evidence in the Gospels themselves, Christian tradition claimed that the convergence between Jesus's life and Old Testament prophecy was 'coincidental' – not calculated on Jesus's part, but occurring spontaneously, in accordance with a divine plan. Today, however, such an assertion is wholly untenable. For modern scholars, there is no question but that Jesus was steeped in biblical teachings and especially those of the prophetic books. He is not conforming to their pattern by 'miraculous accident'. On the contrary, he is carefully, deliberately, often methodically and painstakingly modelling his career and his activities according to the statements of the prophets. He himself even says so. There has obviously been a conscious decision and determination on his part to make his life a fulfilment of prophetic utterance.

As we have seen, Zechariah's prophecies concerning the Messiah are of particular interest and relevance to Jesus. His triumphal entry into Jerusalem, for example, represents an attempt to conform to one of them. But Zechariah also prophesied that the

Messiah, descended from David, would be pierced and killed, and his followers scattered. And, in a somewhat opaque passage, the Messiah was equated with an allegorical 'good shepherd', who would be sold for the price of thirty shekels of silver.[14] From the Gospels, it is quite clear Jesus has determined that these prophecies, too, must be *made* to occur – not spontaneously, but by contrived design. In order to execute that design, a betrayer is necessary.

In all four Gospels, the Last Supper figures prominently. And in all four Gospels, Jesus announces publicly, to the assembled company, that he will be betrayed by one of them – because 'the time has come', because his 'hour is at hand' and also, quite explicitly, because 'the prophecy must be fulfilled'. In Mark and Luke, the betrayer is not named at the Last Supper itself. In Matthew and John, however, he is. In Matthew, for example, Judas openly asks, in front of all his comrades, 'Not I, Rabbi, surely?', and Jesus replies in the affirmative. In John's Gospel, Jesus, when asked to identify the man who will betray him, answers, 'It is true the one to whom I give the piece of bread that I shall dip in the dish.' Having dipped it, he then hands it brazenly to Judas, saying, 'What you are going to do, do quickly.' And John's Gospel, rather inconsistently, adds that no one else present knew precisely why Jesus said this to Judas.

The sequence, as it is described, inevitably raises questions. Why, most obviously, if Judas is identified as his master's betrayer, is he allowed to depart on his mission of treachery? Why is he not restrained – by Simon Peter, for example, who, only a short time later, is not only armed, but also sufficiently violent to attack an attendant of the high priest? Why are some other precautions not taken?

The answer to these questions is that Judas's mission is necessary. As Matthew declares, 'all this happened to fulfil the prophecies in scripture'. And again, a chapter later: 'The words of the prophet ... were then fulfilled. And they took the thirty pieces of silver, the sum at which the precious One was priced by the children of Israel ...'[15]

It is not that Judas is actually betraying Jesus. On the contrary, he has been deliberately selected by Jesus, probably to his own chagrin, to discharge a distasteful duty so that the drama of the Passion may enact itself in accordance with Old Testament prophecy. When Jesus proffers the dipped morsel, he is in fact imposing a task upon Judas. It is almost as if the man assigned the task has been chosen by lot, except that the drawing seems to have been fixed. And when Jesus orders Judas to do quickly what must be done, he is not making a statement of clairvoyant resignation, but issuing explicit instructions.

One thing clearly emerges from any close examination of the Last Supper. There has unquestionably been some kind of collusion between Jesus and Judas. The 'betrayal' cannot occur without such collusion, a voluntary participation on Jesus's part, a determination – not just a willingness – to be betrayed. In short, the whole business has been carefully planned, even though the other disciples seem not to have been privy to the arrangement. Judas alone appears to have enjoyed Jesus's confidence in the matter.

Doomed to be stigmatised and anathematised by posterity, Judas in fact proves to be as much a martyr, in his own way, as Jesus. For the Greek writer Nikos Kazantzakis, Judas's role is, if anything, even more difficult. In *The Last Temptation*, shortly before the Last Supper, the following dialogue occurs, in secret, between Jesus and Judas:

> 'I'm sorry, Judas, my brother,' Jesus said, 'but it is necessary.'
>
> 'I've asked you before, rabbi – is there no other way?'
>
> 'No, Judas, my brother. I too should have liked one. I too hoped and waited for one until now – but in vain. No, there is no other way. The end of the world is here. This world, this kingdom of the Devil, will be destroyed and the kingdom of heaven will come. I shall bring it. How? By dying. There is no other way. Do not quiver, Judas, my brother. In three days I shall rise again.'
>
> 'You tell me this in order to comfort me and make me able to betray you without rending my own heart. You say that I have the endurance – you say it in order to give me strength. No, the closer we come to that terrible moment ... no, rabbi, I won't be able to endure!'
>
> 'You will, Judas, my brother. God will give you the strength, as much as you lack, because it is necessary – it is necessary for me to be killed and for you to betray me. We two must save the world. Help me.'
>
> Judas bowed his head. After a moment he asked, 'If you had to betray your master, would you do it?'
>
> Jesus reflected for a long time. Finally he said, 'No, I'm afraid I wouldn't be able to. That is why God pitied me and gave me the easier task: to be crucified.'[16]

This dialogue, of course, is a fictional re-creation. Yet it is clear that something akin to what Kazantzakis depicts *must* have occurred in actuality. Commentators on the New Testament have long recognised how vital, how indispensable, Judas is to the entire mission of Jesus. Without Judas, the drama of the Passion cannot be enacted. As a result, Judas must be seen as something very different from the scurrilous villain of popular tradition. He emerges as precisely the opposite – a noble and tragic figure, reluctantly consenting to play an unpleasant, painful and oblig- atory role in a carefully pre-arranged script. As Jesus says of him: 'I have watched over them and not one is lost except the one who chose to be lost, and this was to fulfil the scriptures.'[17]

What remains indeterminate is whether Jesus was truly con- vinced that he himself had literally to die, or whether it was sufficient that he *appear* to die. As we discussed in our previous book, there is a substantial body of evidence in favour of the latter alternative. The truth, of course, is unlikely ever to be known. But it is certainly possible, at least, that he survived the Cross – if, indeed, it was he who was on it in the first place, rather than the substitute claimed by the Koran and by many early heresies.

But if it was intended that Jesus survive the Cross, or never perhaps be crucified at all, one cannot help wondering whether Judas was privy to the plan. Would he still have been in collusion with his master? Or did he go to his death in the anguished conviction that he was responsible for his master's?

Jude

As we have seen, Pauline thought appears to have altered dramati- cally the attitudes and orientation of Simon Peter. The traditions arising from Pauline thought blackened the name of Judas and obscured the role of Jesus's own brother, James, as head of the Nazarean hierarchy in Jerusalem. There is yet another figure whose importance, in the eyes of posterity, was to be distorted and diminished.

In the canon of the New Testament, there is a single letter from James, who identifies himself as 'the brother of the Lord'. There is also a letter from an individual named Jude, who identifies himself as 'a servant of Jesus Christ and brother of James'. It might seem from this at first that Jude, like James, was Jesus's brother.

In fact, modern biblical scholars concur that the letter ascribed to Jude is of too late a date to have been written by any contemporary of Jesus. It is believed to have been composed early in the second century, very likely by an individual who was indeed named Jude and who, together with his brother James, presided over the Nazarean party at the time. But according to the earliest Church historians, the James and Jude of the second century were the grandsons of another, older Jude, who *was* Jesus's brother.

The Gospels themselves make it clear that Jesus had a brother named Jude or Judah or Judas. Luke's Gospel and Acts both speak of a certain 'Judas of James', which is usually translated as 'Judas, son of James'. It is much more probable, however, that 'Judas of James' originally referred to 'Judas, brother of James'. If Luke is vague on the subject, Matthew and Mark are both quite explicit. Both of them speak of Jesus having four brothers – Joseph, Simon, James and Jude – as well as at least two sisters.[18] The context in which they are mentioned is curious. They are said to have reproved Jesus during his early days of preaching in Galilee. No reason for the reproof is suggested. Whatever it might have been, it was short-lived so far as James was concerned. Within a short time of Jesus's death, he had taken his brother's place, had assumed the presiding role in the Nazarean hierarchy in Jerusalem and had attained status as a holy man himself. There is abundant evidence to indicate that Jude followed suit.

And yet, curiously enough, there is no mention of Jude in Acts or in any other New Testament documents – at least not under that name. In fact, it is under another name that he must be sought. When found, he proves to have played an important role indeed.

7

The Brothers of Jesus

A number of seminal Essene and/or Zadokite texts speak not of one expected Messiah, but of two. According to these sources, the nation's identity and integrity rest on two parallel dynastic successions with numerous links between them. The two Messiahs are named specifically as the Messiah of Aaron and the Messiah of David.[1] The Messiah of David would be a royal figure, presiding over the secular administration of the new kingdom, which he would bring into being through his military prowess. The Messiah of Aaron, descended from Israel's first high priest in the Old Testament, would be a priestly figure, an 'Interpreter of the Law' who would preside over the people's spiritual life.

Ironically, this principle of a dual secular and spiritual authority would subsequently find expression in Western Europe through the Holy Roman Empire, wherein the emperor wielded a temporal sceptre and claimed descent from David while the pope exercised spiritual authority as interpreter of God's law. As we have repeatedly noted, however, politics and religion for Israel at the time were inextricably associated – were, in fact, essentially different manifestations of the same thing. In consequence, the Royal Messiah and the Priest Messiah would have had to be as closely linked as possible – which they were in Maccabean times, for example, when both were members of the same family. It would have been unthinkable to allow the kind of schisms between spiritual and temporal power that later characterised the Holy Roman Empire.

It can certainly be argued that the twin-Messiah theme appears in the New Testament, albeit in drastically modified and probably garbled form. Modern biblical scholars concur that among the most historically plausible incidents in the Gospels, among the incidents least likely to have been invented by later writers and editors, is Jesus's baptism in the Jordan by John. Certainly this is the single most crucial event in what we know of Jesus's public career prior to his triumphal entry into Jerusalem; and Christian tradition reinforces John's importance to the story. He is the pathfinder, the forerunner, the 'voice crying in the wilderness' who 'prepares the way'. Indeed, many of John's contemporaries were prepared to regard *him* as the Messiah. Luke reports that ' ... a feeling of expectancy had grown among the people, who were beginning to think that John might be the Christ'. And during the first three centuries A.D., there were certain Mandaean or Johannite sects, especially in the region of the Tigris–Euphrates basin, who honoured John, not Jesus, as their prophet. Indeed, one of these sects still exists. According to its thinking, John was 'the true prophet', while Jesus was 'a rebel, a heretic, who led men astray, betrayed secret doctrines'.

Biblical scholars have seen no reason to doubt Luke's assertion that John and Jesus were first cousins. It is now generally accepted that Jesus's mother was the sister of Elizabeth, the mother of John. But Luke also makes it plain that John the Baptist, through his mother, was descended from the priestly dynastic succession of Aaron – which would mean, of course, that Jesus was too. At the same time, Luke stresses Jesus's descent, through his father, from David. Thus, as a descendant of Aaron, John can lay claim to the title of Priest Messiah. Jesus, descended from both Aaron and David, can lay claim to the titles of Priest Messiah *and* Royal Messiah. This would seem to explain Luke's assertion in Acts (2:36) that God had made Jesus 'both Lord and Christ'.

The kinship between John and Jesus would have imparted an added prestige, plausibility and credibility to their respective roles. If, amidst the generally apocalyptic atmosphere of the time, devout Jews were anxiously awaiting the advent of two Messiahs – one royal from David, one priestly from Aaron – they would have had their eyes fixed on a limited number of families. If the anticipated figures appeared as first cousins, how much more striking and persuasive this would have been. Almost certainly, it would have been perceived as a sign, a portent, a palpable manifestation of God's hand.

If Jesus were the royal Messiah and John the priestly one, the baptism in the Jordan would have been all the more significant – the priestly Messiah conferring official status on his royal counterpart, who also, by the manifest workings of a divine plan, happened to be his close kin. The dual Messianic and familial threads would have reinforced each other. To the extent that spiritual and temporal functions were united in the same house, by the same blood, the union would be doubly consecrated, doubly sanctified, and the unity of the nation all the more hallowed. This, as we mentioned, was what had occurred during the Maccabean dynasty, Israel's last monarchy. And, as we noted, the movement of which Jesus and his followers seem to have been a part regarded the Maccabean regime as a prototype for their own aspirations.

If John *were* the Priest Messiah of Aaron, and Jesus the Royal Messiah of David, it is possible that Jesus, when John was executed by Herod Antipas, assumed both roles, incorporating the dead prophet's status and functions within himself. It may even have been that John, anticipating his imminent doom, ratified some such arrangement, perhaps in the ceremony at the Jordan. There would clearly seem to be some significance in the fact that only on John's decease does Jesus embark in earnest on his ministry. In any case, there is no question that Jesus's following included former devotees of John. And if Jesus incorporated in himself the double role of royal and priestly Messiah, he would indeed have been a figure worthy of such adherence.

Thomas the Twin

There are, however, other, even more provocative implications attending the principle of dual Messiahs. These implications involve not John the Baptist, but a much more elusive figure, whom later Christian tradition has been decidedly reluctant to accommodate. To do so would have entailed considerable embarrassment.

In all four Gospels, and in Acts, mention is made of the disciple known as Thomas. At the same time, however, little of consequence is ascribed to him. One learns virtually nothing about him. He is not in any way individualised from the rest of Jesus's following. He seems to function as a wholly peripheral supernumerary. Only in John's Gospel does he make one curious and profoundly interesting statement. When Jesus receives news that Lazarus is ill, Thomas urges everyone back to the sick man's home in Bethany, 'that we may die with him'. Apart from this, Thomas neither says nor does anything of note until after the Crucifixion. Then – in a passage of John's Gospel which is probably a later interpolation – he initially queries whether Jesus has indeed been resurrected in the flesh.

If one looks to sources other than the canonical scriptures, Thomas's role assumes larger proportions. According to Eusebius, the Church historian writing in the fourth century, Thomas migrated north-eastwards, evangelising among the Parthians[2] – the 'barbarian' people who occupied the region from the Tigris–Euphrates basin up through what is modern-day Iran. According to an apocryphal work dating from the third century, Thomas's mission takes him even further. He is said to die in India, pierced with lances; and the tomb in which he is buried is later found empty.[3] A similar tradition exists among a sect of Syrian Christians, who call themselves 'Christians of St Thomas'. According to them, they were converted by Thomas, who eventually died at Mylapore, near Madras.

If such accounts as these contain any veracity, Thomas emerges as one of the most active and influential of all the disciples. If Paul is Christianity's chief apostle to Western Europe, Thomas, almost single-handed, would seem to be responsible for its dissemination eastwards. What Thomas disseminated, however, was not Pauline Christianity. It was a form of Nazarean teaching, such as one would expect to emanate from James and the Nazarean hierarchy in Jerusalem.

But who exactly was Thomas? We know that Simon Peter and his brother Andrew, as well as the two sons of Zebedee, were fishermen from Galilee. We learn something of the backgrounds of various other disciples. About Thomas, however, we are told nothing. And the question becomes all the more pertinent because 'Thomas' is not a name at all. Just as 'Peter' is a nickname, meaning 'rocklike' or 'rocky', for a fisherman named Simon, so 'Thomas' is a sobriquet, the word being simply the Hebrew for 'twin'.

In the King James version of John's Gospel, there might at first seem to be some slight clarification. He is referred to there as 'Thomas Didymus' or 'Thomas called Didymus'. In fact, however, this only obscures the issue further – because the word 'didymus' also means 'twin'. When translated, 'Thomas Didymus' yields the redundancy of 'Twin Twin'. 'Thomas called Didymus' becomes even more grotesque – 'Twin called Twin'. Nor do more recent translations, which speak of 'Thomas called the Twin', offer any greater illumination. Once again, we are left with an absurdity – 'the Twin called the Twin'.

What is it that is being so clumsily concealed here? What was Thomas's real name? And whose twin was he?

These questions are partially answered, quite explicitly, by the apocryphal Gospel of Thomas, a very early work dating probably from the end of the first century. Here, Thomas is identified as 'Judas Thomas', which translates as 'Judas the Twin'. In another, slightly later apocryphal work, the Acts of Thomas, the issue is further clarified. Here, too, Thomas is named specifically as Judas Thomas. And when Jesus appears to a young man, ' . . . he saw the Lord Jesus in the likeness of the Apostle Judas Thomas . . . the Lord said to him: "I am not Judas who is also Thomas, I am his brother." '[4]

The Apocryphal Testimony

Modern biblical scholars concur that the churches which evolved in Syria, in Asia Minor and in Egypt embodied a form of 'Christianity' no less valid than Rome's, different from Rome's though it was. Indeed, it can be argued that the churches in such places were heir to a 'purer' tradition than Rome's, because it was not diluted and distorted by Pauline thought; it was something closer to what Jesus himself, James and the original Nazarean hierarchy would have propagated. Certainly the Church in Egypt, to take but one example, possessed texts at least as old and as authoritative as those in the canonical New Testament – texts which the compilers of the canonical New Testament chose deliberately to exclude. This point is stressed by Professor Helmut Koester of Harvard University Divinity School, who argues that in the ' . . . vast treasure of non-canonical gospel literature there are at least some writings which have not found their rightful place in the history of this literary genre'.[5] Among these writings, Professor Koester cites specifically the Gospel of Thomas. When interviewed in the television series *Jesus: the Evidence*, Professor Koester was quite unequivocal in his assertions. On the basis of the most recent evidence, there could be little doubt that Judas Thomas was indeed Jesus's brother – the brother mentioned in the Gospels as Jude.

If Judas Thomas, or Jude the Twin, were indeed Jesus's twin brother, what would have been his status among his contemporaries? In the Acts of Thomas, there is the following quotation: 'Twin brother of Christ, apostle of the Most High and fellow initiate into the hidden word of Christ, who dost receive his secret sayings . . .'[6] And again, even more explicitly, in an invocation to the Holy Ghost (which, significantly enough, is feminine): 'Come Holy Spirit . . . Holy Dove that bearest the twin young. Come, Hidden Mother . . .'[7]

In a fragment from another apocryphal work, Jesus, approaching Simon Peter and Judas Thomas, addresses them 'in the Hebrew language'. There seems to have been some obfuscation, perhaps deliberate, in the translation of the original Coptic text, but what Jesus appears to say is: 'Greetings, my venerable guardian Peter. Greetings, Thomas [Twin], my second Messiah.'[8]

From such references as these, the figure of Judas Thomas emerges not only as Jesus's twin brother Jude. He also emerges as an acknowledged Messiah in his own right.

Cult of the Twins

The suggestion that Jesus had a twin brother was one of the most persistent and tenacious of the ancient 'heresies'. Nor did it ever completely disappear, despite repeated attempts to extirpate it. During the Renaissance, for example, it surfaced repeatedly, albeit in somewhat garbled form. It is conspicuous in certain of Leonardo da Vinci's works, especially 'The Last Supper'.[9] The theme recurs in subsequent painters, including Poussin. It also figures prominently today in the work of Michel Tournier, one of the most esteemed voices in contemporary French culture and probably the single most important novelist France has produced since Proust. And in the decorations commissioned by Bérenger Saunière for the church at Rennes-le-Château, both Mary and Joseph are depicted, one on each side of the altar, holding a Christ-child.

To most contemporary Christians, of course, and even to most contemporary agnostics, the suggestion that Jesus had a twin brother will seem at best far-fetched, at worst blasphemous. But it is important, indeed vital, to bear one crucial fact in mind. The texts in which Judas Thomas appears as Jesus's twin were at one time widely used by Christian congregations, not only in Egypt and Syria, but also, as we shall see, as far away as Spain and, it seems, Ireland. They were accepted works of scripture, as legitimate as the canonical Gospels of the New Testament, or the Acts of the Apostles. This can only mean that, at the time, *the idea of a twin was perfectly acceptable to devout Christians*. There were, in short, pious men and women who not only failed to find it blasphemous, but regarded it as an integral part of their belief – as integral, say, as Peter's role is to the Church of Rome.

At this point, it is worth digressing briefly into wholly speculative territory – territory which will yield no proof one way or the other, but which warrants at least passing consideration. In the ancient world, the processes of human procreation were not understood as we understand them today. In many respects, ancient understanding of these processes was less than ours. It is doubtful, for example, if the biological factors involved in the birth of twins were fully, or even adequately, appreciated. For this simple, self-evident reason, the birth of twins, and especially identical twins, would have seemed to the ancients nothing short of miraculous – a phenomenon attesting to some intervention of divine origin. The theme of twin brothers is among the most resonant, and among the earliest, of all cultural/religious motifs. From the dawn of recorded history, the Mediterranean world in particular had made a cult of the Dioscuri, the Divine Twins. Under the names of Castor and Pollux, these twins had played an extremely important role in the formulation and evolution of Greek mythical thought. Romulus and Remus were revered as the pair from whom the foundation of Rome derived. By its very nature, the birth of twins became an event which partook of the mythic, which linked man with some of his oldest and most potent mythic images and ultimately with his gods. Although such twins, as we have seen, were often arch-enemies, they need not have been. Often, they complemented each other peaceably to form a single unity.

Thus, for example, Edessa, now Urfa in Turkey, had long been a centre of the twin cult, worshipping the pair under the names of Momim and Aziz. This pair was supplanted by Jesus and Judas Thomas, and Edessa became a centre for the new cult of the twin Messiahs. It is in Edessa that the Acts of Thomas is believed to have been written. It was also in Edessa that the oldest known church was built, then destroyed in A.D. 201. And there is persuasive evidence that Judas Thomas visited the town personally and brought his teachings directly to the established king, Abgar.

The Jews of Jesus's time were waiting in anguished anticipation for the advent of the Messiah – and, so far as many of them were concerned, for the advent of two Messiahs. Because Messiahship was regarded as something dynastic, something in part dependent upon a bloodline, people's attention, as we observed before, would have been focused on a relatively small network of interlinked families who could claim descent from both David and Aaron. If a pair of twins were born into one of these families, would it not have seemed significant indeed – a divine sign, a portent, a confirmation of expectations? Would not a royal and a priestly Messiah, both issuing simultaneously from the same family, have seemed an eloquent testimony of God's favour?

The Descendants of Jesus's Family

In *The Holy Blood and the Holy Grail*, we spoke at length about the likelihood of a blood descent from Jesus. Might there also have been a descent from Jesus's family? Established sources concur that there indeed was. Thus, for example, the historian Julius Africanus, who lived between A.D. 160 and 240 and maintained close links with the royal house of Edessa, writes:

> Herod, who had no drop of Israelitish blood in his veins and was stung by the consciousness of his base origins, burnt the registers of their families ... A few careful people had private records of their own, having either remembered the names or recovered them from copies, and took pride in preserving the memory of their aristocratic origin. These included the people ... known as *Desposyni* [i.e. the Master's People] because of their relationship to the saviour's family.[10]

Two quite different events, occurring some seventy years apart, appear to have been garbled or telescoped in this passage. On the one hand, there would appear to have been Jesus's own aristocratic and royal pedigree, which, as we have discussed, Herod, as a usurper, deemed a threat to his legitimacy. Among other things, this would have engendered the tradition of Herod's Massacre of the Innocents. On the other hand, it has been argued that the burning of genealogies to which Julius Africanus refers was perpetrated not by Herod, but by the Romans after the revolt of A.D. 66. They, quite as much as Herod, would have been threatened by the survival of a legitimate royal bloodline, around which the rebellious Jews might have rallied.

According to Paul's own statements, he himself had been married and, at the time of his conversion, was a widower.[11] Certainly there was no prohibition against marriage and paternity, either in Jesus's immediate entourage or in the so-called 'Early Church'. According to Clement of Alexandria, the disciple Philip, as well as Simon Peter, had married and sired families.[12] And in Corinthians, Paul seems clearly to indicate that Jesus's own brothers were married: 'Have we not every right to eat and drink? And the right to take a Christian woman round with us, like all the other apostles and the brothers of the Lord ...?'

There is no specific mention of a descent from James, but James is described repeatedly as a fervent adherent of the law, and one of the dictates of the law was to marry, be fruitful and multiply. Although no reference to them exists among surviving documents, it is certainly reasonable to assume that James sired children. In Jude's – or Judas Thomas's – case, there is confirmation of a bloodline. As we noted earlier, the Nazarean hierarchy, at the beginning of the second century, was directed by two brothers, James and Jude, who are specifically identified as grandsons of Jesus's brother. According to Eusebius, quoting a still earlier authority:

> ... there still survived of the Lord's family the grandsons of Jude, who was said to be His brother, humanly speaking. These were informed against as being of David's line and brought ... before Domitian Caesar ... Domitian asked them whether they were descended from David, and they admitted it ...[13]

Eusbeius reports that the Desposyni – the descendants of Jesus's family and possibly of Jesus himself – survived to become leaders of various Christian churches, according, it would seem, to a strict dynastic succession. Eusebius traces them to the time of the Emperor Trajan, A.D. 98–117. A modern Roman Catholic authority recounts a story which brings them up to the fourth century – the time of Constantine. In A.D. 318, the then Bishop of Rome (now known as Pope Sylvester) is said to have met personally with eight Desposyni leaders – each of whom presided over a branch of the Church – at the Lateran Palace. They are reported to have requested (1) that the confirmation of Christian bishops of Jerusalem, Antioch, Ephesus and Alexandria be revoked; (2) that these bishoprics be conferred instead on members of the Desposyni; and (3) that Christian churches 'resume' sending money to the Desposyni Church in Jerusalem, which was to be regarded as the definitive Mother Church.[14]

Not surprisingly, the Bishop of Rome rejected these requests, stating that the Mother Church was now Rome and that Rome had authority to appoint her own bishops. This is said to have been the last contact between the Judaeo-Christian Nazareans and the coalescing orthodoxy based on Pauline thought. From then on, Nazarean tradition is generally believed to have disappeared. In fact, however, it did no such thing.

8

The Survival of Nazarean Teaching

After the revolt of A.D. 66 and the fall of Masada eight years later, the politically oriented Messianic movement embodied by Jesus, his brothers and his immediate followers was seriously disrupted. But although its thrust had been effectively blunted, it could still muster enough adherents to create large-scale upheaval in the Holy Land. Thus, between A.D. 132 and 135, Palestine again rose in revolt. The leader of this insurrection was one Simeon bar Kokhba. There is evidence to suggest that he was descended from Judas of Galilee, leader of the Zealots a century and a quarter before, and from the Zealot commanders at the capture and subsequent siege of Masada. Dr Robert Eisenman, whom we cited earlier, believes there may well have been close links between Simeon's family and the descendants of Jesus's – if, indeed, they were not one and the same. Once again, the principle of dynastic succession is worthy of note.

When he embarked on his rebellion, Simeon turned to the now well established Pauline 'Christians' for support. This is hardly surprising. As we have already suggested, Jesus's brother James, and the other members of the Nazarean hierarchy in Jerusalem, seem to have regarded their evangelising as a form of recruitment – a means whereby an army for the nation of Israel might be created. For Simeon bar Kokhba, it would have been perfectly natural to expect the adherents of an earlier Messiah – the rightful king dedicated to freeing his country from the Roman yoke – to aid him in just such an enterprise. But the Pauline 'Christians' had by now evolved their own doctrine of a non-political, wholly spiritual Messiah. Angered by what must have seemed a monstrous betrayal, or a display of contemptible cowardice, Simeon turned upon them and persecuted them as traitors.

Simeon's revolt, like the one which preceded it sixty-six years before, was ruthlessly suppressed, but not before the Holy Land had once again been ravaged. Once again, Jerusalem was razed. When it was rebuilt, Jews were forbidden to return to it or establish residence within its precincts. The survivors of Simeon's army fled, some north into Syria and Mesopotamia, some south into Egypt. And it was in these places that Nazarean tradition was to continue.

In the wake of Simeon's revolt, the adherents of the old Nazarean hierarchy would have found themselves under increasing pressure from three quarters. So far as Rome was concerned, they were, of course, rebellious outlaws, to be hounded, harried and ruthlessly extirpated. By this time, too, they had begun to engender antipathy among Jews. Although the old collaborationist Sadducee priestly establishment of Herod's and Jesus's time had disappeared, a new form of Judaism had begun to coalesce, oriented towards rabbinical teaching. This rabbinical Judaism, the progenitor of Judaism in its modern form, had, in its disillusionment, repudiated the Messianic movement, repudiated ambitious political enterprises and – to ensure its own survival – entrenched itself behind the cultivation of learning, scholarship and ritual observance. For rabbinical Judaism, militant activity was perceived as more than just an embarrassment. It was also a threat, which might 'rock the boat' and provoke another disastrous onslaught of Roman wrath and retribution. The Pauline 'Christians' adopted a similar attitude. They, too, were intent on their own survival and, to ensure it, on propitiating Rome. For them, too, military and political activity had to be scrupulously avoided. Moreover, they had their own doctrines by now of who Jesus was and what the term 'Messiah' meant. They were not prepared to have these doctrines shaken, even by descendants of Jesus or his family.

In consequence, the adherents of the old Nazarean hierarchy – of Jesus and his brothers – found themselves squeezed between diverse factions and relegated increasingly beyond the pale of recorded Western history. It amounted, in effect, to a kind of 'exile from history'. Although they had formerly represented the true repository of Judaism, and although they provided Christianity with the very focus of its worship, they had now been disowned by Jews and Christians alike. And their very definition of the Messiah had been hi-jacked and twisted into something radically different. It is probably one of the cruellest ironies in the evolution and development of any major world religion.

By the second century, Nazarean thought was already being branded as a form of heresy. Thus, indeed, would many 'Christians' regard it today. But the very word 'heresy' is consistently misused, and must be restored to its correct perspective. Among modern believers, it is generally assumed that once upon a time there was a 'pure' form of Christianity preached by Paul, from which various 'deviations' – that is, 'heresies' – subsequently occurred. In reality, nothing could be further from the truth. If anything, the first real 'heresy' was Paul's. Paul's preaching and Pauline thought constituted the 'deviation', while Nazarean tradition – which Paul defied and which Pauline thought supplanted – was the closest thing to a 'pure' Christianity that ever existed. But once Pauline thought had consolidated its own position, it automatically became the 'established orthodoxy', and from that point on anything that clashed with it became, by definition, a 'heresy'. The absurdity of applying this label to Nazarean thought – an absurdity comparable to calling Marx an 'heretical Marxist' or Freud an 'heretical Freudian' – was conveniently overlooked.

Despite being repudiated, condemned and persecuted, Nazarean teachings continued to survive, for much longer than is generally suspected. During the subsequent centuries, those teachings would surface under a bewildering variety of names. Earlier writers often employed the term Ebionite. Several scholars today refer to them as Zadokite, a name which appears periodically in the teachings themselves. Other researchers use the designation Judaeo-Christian, which is in fact confusing, misleading and self-contradictory. On the basis of the evangelising role of Judas Thomas, Dr Herman Koester speaks of a Thomasine tradition, in contrast to the Pauline tradition of what we today call Christianity. There were also, of course, later accretions, later developments and modifications, later amalgamations with other doctrines, and these engendered a plethora of additional names – Gnostic, Manichaean, Sabean, Mandaean, Nestorian, Elkasaite. For our purposes, and for the sake of simplicity, it will be easiest to retain the term 'Nazarean'. It will no longer imply a specific body of individuals, however. Rather, it will denote a general mode of thought, an orientation – an orientation towards Jesus and his teachings which derives ultimately from the original Nazarean position, as articulated by Jesus himself, then propagated by James, Jude or Judas Thomas and their immediate entourage. This orientation can be characterised by certain basic attitudes, chief among which are (1) a continued and strict adherence to the tenets of Judaic law; (2) a recognition of Jesus as Messiah in the original Judaic sense of the word; (3) a repudiation of the Virgin Birth and an insistence on Jesus having been born by natural processes, without any divine intervention; and (4) a militant hostility towards Paul and the edifice of Pauline thought. Where these attitudes appear together, one can discern vestiges of the original Nazarean position – the position of Jesus himself, of James, Jude and the hierarchy in Jerusalem.

Thus Justin Martyr, writing around A.D. 150, speaks of those who regard Jesus as having been the Messiah, yet at the same time still a man. They adhere to Judaic law in such matters as circumcision, observance of the Sabbath and dietary restrictions. And they are shunned by gentile – i.e., Pauline – Christians.[1]

Approximately half a century later, Irenaeus, Bishop of Lyons, issued his violent and dogmatic attack on the prevalent heresies of the time, *Adversus haereses*. Irenaeus was the voice of the coalescing orthodoxy, and his labelling of heresies, as well as his selection of canonical works, was to leave an indelible imprint on the Church of Rome. In his opus, Irenaeus fulminates against a group whom he calls the 'Ebionites' – a term used by the writers of the Qumran texts to describe themselves, which can be translated as, simply, 'the Poor'. According to Irenaeus, the Ebionites insist that Jesus was man, not God, and was not born of a virgin. They claim that he became the Messiah only at the time of his baptism – that is, his anointment or coronation. They use only the Gospel of Matthew and, like Jesus himself, as well as the Essenes or Zadokites of two centuries before, expound upon the prophetic books of the Old Testament. They adhere scrupulously to Judaic law. They reject the Pauline letters, and 'they reject the apostle Paul, calling him an apostate from the Law'.[2]

A century later, in Constantine's time, Nazarean teaching was still thriving and being disseminated. As we have already noted, the Bishop of Rome, in A.D. 318, is reported to have had a meeting with Nazarean or Desposyni leaders directly descended from Jesus's family. At the same time, the Church historian Eusebius was attacking the Nazareans (whom he, like Irenaeus, calls Ebionites) for being heretical. They held that ' . . . the epistles of the Apostle [Paul] ought to be rejected altogether, calling him a renegade from the Law; and using only the "Gospel of the Hebrews", they treated the rest with scant respect'.[3]

A hundred years later, in the late fourth or early fifth century, another Church writer, Epiphanius, launched a fresh attack on what he called heresies. He uses the terms 'Ebionite' and 'Nazarean' interchangeably. Like Irenaeus, Epiphanius condemns the Ebionites or Nazareans for denying the Virgin Birth, teaching that Jesus was a man born of men, declaring that Jesus became Messiah only on his baptism and using alternative versions of the

Acts of the Apostles. They are 'not ashamed', Epiphanius writes indignantly, to denounce Paul, believing him to be *pseudapostolo-rum* – a 'false apostle'.[4]

In one Nazarean text, Paul is called 'the enemy'. The text maintains insistently that Jesus's rightful heir was his brother James, and takes great pains to argue that Simon Peter never in fact 'defected' to Pauline thought. Simon Peter is quoted as issuing a warning against any authority other than the Nazarean hierarchy: 'Wherefore observe the greatest caution, that you believe no teacher, unless he brings from Jerusalem the testimonial of James the Lord's brother ...'[5]

In the 1960s, a medievalist scholar, Professor Schlomo Pines, found in a collection of Arabic manuscripts, dating from the tenth century and held in a library in Istanbul, a number of lengthy and detailed verbatim quotes from an earlier, fifth- or sixth-century, text, which the Arab writer ascribes to '*al-nasara*' – the Nazareans. The earlier text is believed to have been written originally in Syriac and to have been found at a Christian monastery in Khuzistan, south-west Iran, near the Iraqi border. It appears to reflect a tradition dating, without a break, back to the original Nazarean hierarchy which fled Jerusalem immediately prior to the revolt of A.D. 66. Again, Jesus is stated to be a man, not a god, and any suggestion of his divinity is rejected. The importance of Judaic law is again stressed. Paul is castigated and his followers are said to 'have abandoned the religion of Christ and turned towards the religious doctrines of the Romans'. The Gospels are dismissed as unreliable, second-hand accounts which contain only 'something – but little – of the sayings, the precepts of Christ and information concerning him'. But this is not all. The tenth–century Arab document goes on to assert that the sect from whom the Nazarean text issued is still in existence, and is regarded as an élite amongst Christians.[6]

One of the primary repositories of Nazarean tradition was the 'heresy' now known as Nestorian Christianity. It took its name from an individual named Nestorius, who, in 428, was appointed Patriarch of Constantinople. Like the Bishop of Durham more recently, Nestorius lost no time in making his position clear. In the same year that he assumed his appointment, he stated bluntly: 'Let no one call Mary the mother of God. For Mary was but human.'[7] Needless to say, this immediately provoked a scandal. Three years later, Nestorius was condemned and excommunicated. The letter informing him of the sentence pronounced upon him was headed derisively: 'The Holy Synod to Nestorius the new Jew.'

In 435, Nestorius was exiled to the Egyptian desert, but his influence remained undiminished. The Persian Church became Nestorian in its orientation.[8] And when, in 451, Nestorius was officially classified as a heretic, the Egyptian Church, while not agreeing with him, refused to accept the ruling. It, too, split with the Roman orthodoxy and eventually coalesced into the Coptic Church. In the meantime, Nestorian thought not only continued to survive elsewhere, but displayed an astonishing tenacity. By the twentieth century, it was still active, maintaining a theological school at Nisibis in northern Mesopotamia. More recently, the official Patriarch and many of his followers emigrated to San Francisco, where the Nestorian Church exists today.

But if the Nestorian Church provided one vehicle whereby Nazarean thought survived into a later epoch, there were also others. We had encountered suggestions, in Prieuré de Sion sources, that certain of its early members, and of their offshoot, the Knights Templar, had established contact with certain Essene/Zadokite/Nazarean sects still in existence during the time of the Crusades, more than a thousand years after Jesus's era. Although not implausible, these suggestions were not substantiated by any solid evidence, and we had therefore been reluctant to accord them credence. The matter seemed to lie beyond the pale of any definitive confirmation.

Shortly after the publication of *The Holy Blood and the Holy Grail*, however, we received a letter from Dr Hugh Schonfield, author of *The Passover Plot* and a number of other important works on the origins of Christianity. In the course of subsequent meetings with him, what Dr Schonfield had to tell us was startling indeed. Some time previously, he had discovered a system of cryptography – he called it the 'Atbash Cipher' – which had been used to conceal certain names in Essene/Zadokite/Nazarean texts. This system of coding figured, for example, in a number of the scrolls found at Qumran.

In *Secrets of the Dead Sea Scrolls*, Dr Schonfield offers a detailed explanation of how precisely the Atbash Cipher works.[9] In his most recent book, *The Essene Odyssey*, he describes how, after reading our book in 1982, he became intrigued by the mysterious principle allegedly worshipped by the Knights Templar under the name of 'Baphomet'. Dr Schonfield applied the cryptographic principles of the Atbash Cipher to 'Baphomet'. The enigmatic word 'decoded' itself perfectly into 'Sophia' – Greek for 'wisdom'.[10]

This could hardly have been coincidence. On the contrary, it proved, beyond any doubt, that the Templars were familiar with

THE ANCIENT ATBASH
ALPHABETICAL CIPHER.

א = ת

ב = שׁ

ג = ר

ד = ק

ה = צ

ו = פ

ז = ע

ח = ס

ט = נ

י = מ

כ = ל

the Atbash Cipher and employed it in their own obscure, heterodox rites. But how could the Templars, operating in the early twelfth century, have acquired such familiarity with a cryptographic system dating from a thousand years before, whose practitioners had apparently long vanished from the stage of history? There is only one really plausible explanation. It would seem obvious that at least some of those practitioners had not in fact vanished at all, but still existed at the time of the Crusades. And it would seem obvious that the Templars had established contact with them. From the Templars' use of the Atbash Cipher, it is probable that some form of Nazarean or neo-Nazarean sect had continued to survive in the Middle East as late as the twelfth century, and had made its teachings available to the West.

The Nazareans of Egypt

So far, we have traced the migration and survival of Nazarean thought north-eastwards from the Holy Land, to Syria, Asia Minor, Turkey, Persia, parts of southern Russia and of the Indian subcontinent – the regions which tradition, and Dr Koester, believe to have been evangelised by Judas Thomas, Jesus's twin brother. But these regions – divorced, for the most part, from the mainstream of developing Western ideas – were not the only refuge for Nazarean thought. It was also transmitted south-westwards, into Egypt and along the coast of North Africa, where it would come into much more direct contact with the coalescing orthodoxy of Rome – and, despite Rome's attempts to suppress it, exercise a more discernible influence on the evolution of Christianity in Western Europe.

Since Old Testament times, there had been constant traffic, in ideas as well as in commodities, between Palestine and Egypt. In Jesus's epoch, Alexandria was the most eclectic, ecumenical and tolerant city in the whole of the Roman Empire – the single most important crossroads of the Mediterranean's trade-routes and, as such, a kind of central clearing-house not only for goods, but for modes of thought as well. Mystery schools descended from ancient Egypt cohabited amicably with Greek mystery schools, with Hellenistic philosophy, with religious teachings from Palestine and Syria, with skeins of Zoroastrian and Mithraic tradition, with sects and cults from every quarter of the Mediterreanean, even with offshoots of Hinduism and Buddhism imported from as far away as India. The great library of Alexandria was the most famous and most comprehensive in the known world and made the city a natural centre of study.

Not surprisingly, Alexandria provided a natural haven for Jews from the Holy Land – for commercial reasons during periods of stability, as a refuge in times of upheaval and war. Indeed, it is estimated that as much as one-third of Alexandria's population in the first century was Jewish. According to the Gospels, Jesus and his family, fleeing Herod's persecution, sought safety in Egypt, where there would have been no dearth of sympathetic supporters, like-minded in orientation. And in fact, under the name of 'Therapeutae', Philo speaks of a Judaic sect or enclave whose attitudes and practices are identical with those of the Essenes or Zadokites in the Holy Land – identical, in other words, with those of Jesus's subsequent following. And after both of the major revolts in Palestine – that of 66–74 and that of 132–5 – substantial numbers of defeated Judaic militants are reported to have fled to Alexandria.[11]

If Judas Thomas did not travel to Egypt himself, Nazarean teaching of the kind he propagated in Syria unquestionably did. It was in Egypt that the Gospel of Thomas was first found – along with the wealth of other Gnostic Thomasine or Nazarean documents in the corpus of Nag Hammadi scrolls. Nazarean thought left an ineradicable imprint on the development of Egyptian Christianity. Even so esteemed a Church Father as Clement of Alexandria was actually, in many respects, closer to original Nazarean doctrine than he was to the Pauline orthodoxy of Rome. The so-called 'heresies' which, in Syria and points north-eastwards, served as repositories for Nazarean thought also existed in Egypt. Other 'heresies' – that of Arius who saw Jesus as man, not God, for example – arose there and also reflected Nazarean influence.

In the fifth century, the Pauline orthodoxy of Rome was still attempting to impose its hegemony over Egypt. The great library of Alexandria was burnt by 'Christians' in A.D. 411. The last great Neo-Platonic philosopher, a woman, Hypatia, was stoned to death as she returned from a lecture at the library – again by 'Christians' – in A.D. 415. Nevertheless, the heterodox character of Egyptian Christianity continued to survive. In 435, as we have already mentioned, Nestorius was removed from his position in Constantinople and exiled to the Egyptian desert. And in 451, the Egyptian Church refused to accept the growing authority of Rome.

Ultimately, however, Egyptian Christianity's most lasting effect was less its simple perpetuation of Nazarean thought than its development of an administrative system for housing and transmitting that thought. This system was monasticism.[12] If Rome, during the time of Constantine, began to assume the characteristics of the old Herodian Sadducee priesthood, Egyptian Christianity beyond the city centres diverged increasingly towards the kind of framework that had served the Zadokites or Essenes of Jesus's time. It seems clear that the Egyptian monastic system, with its network of desert communities, was closely modelled on prototypes such as Qumran.

The first Qumran-style desert community was established by Pachomius around 320 – at precisely the time that the Pauline orthodoxy of Rome was gaining official sanction for itself from Constantine. Pachomius's monastery quickly generated a number of offshoots. By the time of his death in 346, there were several thousand monks scattered about the Egyptian desert, and the principles underlying the monastic system were being transmitted elsewhere. Perhaps the most famous exemplar of Egyptian monasticism is Saint Antony. It is significant that both Antony and Pachomius avoided ordination. The point is that the monastic system was not just a spontaneous occurrence. It represented a form of opposition to the rigidly hierarchical structures of Rome.

It is true, of course, that there were Pauline bishops of Alexandria. But despite the nominally Roman superstructure, the real thrust of Egyptian Christianity was opposed to the Pauline ecclesiastical hierarchy and administration of Rome, and found its truest expression through the monastic system. In effect, the monasteries came to represent a kind of alternative administrative structure, which owed nothing to – and often clashed directly with – Rome. They became repositories for a parallel, and often specifically Nazarean, tradition.

While Rome aspired ever more ambitiously to a new imperial ideal, the Egyptian monasteries prided themselves on a much purer, much more faithful and accurate record of Jesus himself, his kin and his teachings. And while the Roman Church organised itself into an elaborate chequerboard of dioceses or bishoprics, presided over by bishops and archbishops, the monastic system in Egypt allowed for a much looser, much more flexible development – as well as for greater emphasis on learning. Although the abbot of a monastery exercised a certain administrative authority over his flock, he was ultimately no 'higher' spiritually than they. Unlike the bishop or the archbishop, the abbot had no special prerogatives conferred on him by God, nor did he wield any civic power. He was elected by his brethren for a purely utilitarian purpose, but in God's eyes he remained just another humble seeker. The monastic system was essentially non-hierarchical. And while the hierarchy of the Roman Church dictated the texts which were to become the canonical New Testament, the monasteries in Egypt embraced a much more diverse body of teaching, exemplified by the Gospel of Thomas and by the other texts found at Nag Hammadi.[13]

The Spanish Heresy of Priscillian

From Syria and from Egypt, Nazarean tradition began to diffuse itself even further afield. Most Mediterranean trade with both Gaul and Spain was Syrian controlled. Ships from Alexandria sailed daily for the Atlantic coast of Europe. It is hardly surprising, therefore, that substantial vestiges of Nazarean thought found their way to this coast. By the time that Pauline Christianity, moving overland from Rome, arrived, they had already consolidated themselves.

Probably the single most important figure in the development of early Spanish Christianity was the late fourth-century teacher Priscillian of Ávila. Born into a high-ranking family, Priscillian remained a layman, never receiving ordination from Rome.

Although it began in southern Spain, his movement quickly spread west and north, eventually establishing its most tenacious roots in Galicia, which was to become its heartland. In its location there, on the Atlantic coast of north-western Spain, it appears to have received a constantly renewed nourishment and impetus through the maritime trade routes from Egypt and the eastern Mediterranean. Gradually, it filtered across the Pyrenees into Gaul and became the dominant form of Christianity in Aquitaine. At the same time, Priscillian made an active attempt to acquire material that lay outside the province of the Roman Church. Thus one of his leading disciples, a woman named Egeria, embarked, between 381 and 384, on a special journey to the Middle East. She sought out uncanonical texts. She visited Edessa, the centre of Thomasine teaching. She undertook an extended tour of the Mesopotamian churches with their Nazarean and Nestorian orientation.[14] The importance of this must not be minimised. It indicates the means whereby a form of Christianity which entirely circumvented the Pauline orthodoxy of Rome began to establish itself in Western Europe.

Priscillian's own teaching was characterised by a marked strain of Nestorian thought, as well as by skeins of Gnostic Manichaeanism. At the same time, he also drew heavily on a strictly Judaic body of material, including numerology and other forms of early Cabalism – which, as we noted previously, were firmly rooted in Essene/Zadokite/Nazarean sources. Priscillian seems, too, to have demanded adherence to at least certain tenets of Judaic law. In contrast to Pauline Christianity, he observed the Sabbath on Saturday. He denied the Trinity. And he used a great many books of specifically Nazarean orientation, among them the Acts of Thomas. Like his precursors in Egypt, Syria and Asia Minor, Priscillian taught that Judas Thomas was Jesus's twin brother.[15]

In 386, Priscillian and at least five of his disciples became the first heretics to be executed. The sentence was carried out at Trier, but Priscillian's body was carried back to Spain and buried in Galicia. He was celebrated there as a martyr, and his grave became a shrine, a sacred site, a pilgrimage centre. At least one authority on the subject, Professor Henry Chadwick of Oxford, argues that the shrine of Santiago de Compostela is in fact Priscillian's grave.[16]

Santiago de Compostela bears testimony to how effectively Nazarean tradition established itself in Spain. As we have seen, the Pauline Church of Rome found Jesus's brother James something of an embarrassment, and went out of its way, whenever possible, to circumvent him and his role. Only one fragmentary letter of his survives in the canonical New Testament. Apart from this, he figures only briefly, in passing, in the Gospels and as a peripheral background character in Acts. Yet Santiago de Compostela – the Church of Saint James at Compostela – became, with the exception of Rome itself, the single most important shrine and pilgrimage centre in medieval Christendom. It was from Santiago that the Reconquista – the crusade to reconquer Spain from the Moors – was launched. Indeed, Santiago spawned its own military chivalric order, the Order of Santiago, modelled on the Knights Templar and Hospitaller.

According to Spanish tradition of the seventh century, Saint James actually visited Spain and preached there. It was also claimed that his body, after his death, was brought from Jerusalem to Santiago and buried there. Both of these assertions, though questionable, attest to the kind of currency James enjoyed in what is usually regarded as a purely Pauline sphere of influence. Santiago de Compostela can legitimately be regarded as a shrine to the survival of Nazarean thought, in implicit defiance of Rome.

In the early ninth century, human bones were exhumed at Santiago. At the time, they were believed to be the bones of James. Much more recent excavations, between 1946 and 1959, uncovered a number of fourth- and fifth-century graves. The tombs faced east, towards Jerusalem – as Nazareans did when they prayed. It is now believed that the graves are those of early Spanish Christians, placed in proximity to the mausoleum of some established holy man. As we have said, at least one modern authority maintains that the mausoleum in question is Priscillian's, and this is widely accepted by the local populace as well. In fact the major pilgrimage route to Santiago is said to be that by which Priscillian's body was brought back for burial from Trier.[17]

The Celtic Church of Ireland

Ultimately, however, Spain was a stepping-stone in the transmission and survival of Nazarean tradition, which continued its migration northwards, along the Atlantic perimeter of the Roman Church's authority, until between the mid-fifth and the mid-seventh centuries it found its fullest European expression in the Celtic Church of Ireland.

For the first few centuries of the Christian era, Ireland was largely isolated from the rest of Europe. Geography and topography effectively ensured Ireland's immunity from the Teutonic invasions – from the Saxons, for example, who were to overrun England and pit Wotan and the Germanic pantheon against a still fledgling Christianity. Insulated by the Irish Sea, Ireland remained a refuge, a haven. During the peak (or nadir) of the so-called 'Dark Ages', it became the true centre of learning for the whole of Europe. While the continent, and even England, were wracked by turmoil and conflict, Ireland existed as a bastion of study, of culture, of civilisation. Scholars in flight from upheaval elsewhere congregated there. Vast quantities of manuscripts were transported there for safe-keeping and copying. With their extensive libraries, Irish monasteries attracted students from all over the world. Although missionary work was certainly undertaken, learning enjoyed a still higher priority. Christians gravitated to Ireland not to impose their creed on others, but to immerse themselves in the teachings of the past – and to discover, in the seclusion and peace of the island, their own inner communion with their God, independent of hierarchical priesthoods. Ecclesiastics from all over the Christian world trained in Ireland. So, too, did members of various noble and royal houses. In the mid-seventh century, Dagobert II, one of the central figures in the mystery of Rennes-le-Château, was raised and educated at the monastery of Slane, just north of what is now Dublin.

During this period, Ireland's contact with Rome was often difficult and tenuous. She was never entirely cut off, as nineteenth-century religious historians sometimes claimed when trying to explain the heterodox character of the Celtic Church. On the contrary, the orientation of the Celtic Church was voluntary and deliberate, not a consequence of enforced isolation and ignorance. But Rome, separated from Ireland by a continent in upheaval, had little means of implementing her decrees or ensuring their enforcement. Ireland remained free to absorb ideas which came to her, like her trade, from almost every quarter of the known world. Commerce with Ireland was entirely by sea; and this maritime traffic derived not only from England and Gaul, but also from Spain and North Africa, as well as the eastern Mediterranean.

It is not known when Christianity first established itself in Ireland – or, for that matter, anywhere else in the British Isles. According to the sixth-century chronicler Gildas, there were 'Christians' in England during the time of the Emperor Tiberius, who died in A.D. 37. This cannot be verified and seems somewhat early but, given the constant maritime traffic, not altogether impossible. In any case, one or another form of 'Christianity' must have reached Britain within a few years of the time specified by Gildas.

By A.D. 200, the Church historian Tertullian makes it clear that there is some kind of well-established Christian community in Britain — not only in Romanised England, but also in regions 'unapproachable to the Romans'. This is unlikely to mean Scotland. Almost certainly, it means Wales and, quite possibly, Ireland. In any case, by 314, a century or so later, there were three British bishops at the Council of Arles, attesting to some kind of organised congregation. At the Council of Arminium forty-five years later, there were four British bishops, one of whom apparently paid his own way — which would seem to indicate some degree of prosperity. By this time, too, it was also being alleged that some of the original apostles had travelled to Britain.

By the early fifth century, certainly, Christianity had already established itself in Ireland. So, too, had the Pelagian heresy which, among other things, queried the doctrine of original sin and credited man with a greater degree of free will than Roman orthodoxy would allow. In about 431, Palladius became Ireland's first bishop. A year later, Palladius was followed by the Northumbrian monk known today as Saint Patrick. Palladius had presided over an already organised congregation, probably along Ireland's south-eastern coast. Patrick's evangelical work is believed to have been chiefly in the north of the country, which was still largely pagan. It is interesting that Patrick's activity seems to have been dictated as much by personal disillusion or disappointment as by religious fervour. His ecclesiastical superiors had deemed him unfit to be a priest.[18] Does this reflect mistrust of Patrick's competence? Or of his thinking?

There is certainly evidence that Patrick was 'tainted' by the Arian heresy — which, among other things, insisted that Jesus had been born mortal, by mortal means.[19] Unfortunately, there is no indication of the precise degree to which Patrick embraced Arian thought. It is significant, however, that nowhere in what survives of his writings and teachings is there any mention whatever of the Virgin Birth — a glaring omission for an evangelist in the circumstances. Nor does Patrick appear to have accepted the pronouncements of the Church Fathers or the canons of the councils. Indeed, he seems to have resisted mediation of any kind, whether by angels, saints or a priestly hierarchy. He appeals solely to scripture for his authority.

In the wake of recent archaeological discoveries, there is now little question that Celtic Christianity, as it evolved between Patrick's time and the Synod of Whitby in the mid-seventh century, owed little to Rome. For the most part, it effectively circumvented Rome, drawing its primary impetus and orientation

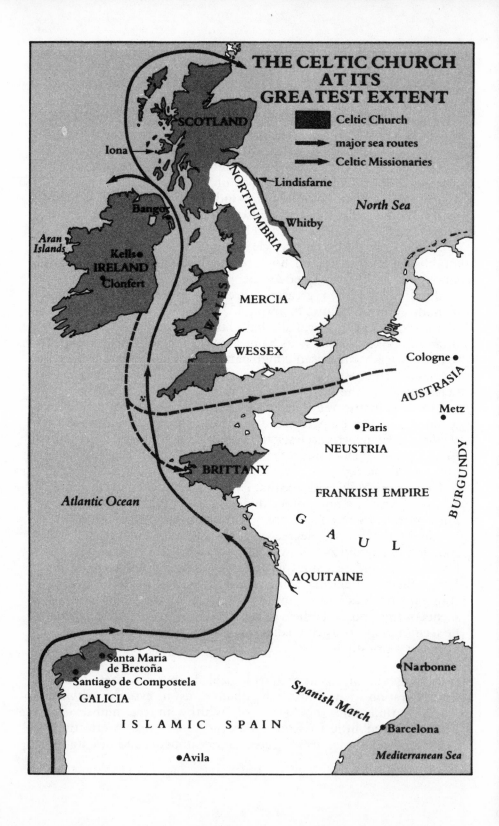

THE CELTIC CHURCH
AT ITS
GREATEST EXTENT

■ Celtic Church

→ major sea routes

→ Celtic Missionaries

SCOTLAND

Iona

Lindisfarne

North Sea

NORTHUMBRIA

Whitby

Bangor

Aran
Islands

Kells

IRELAND

Clonfert

WALES

MERCIA

WESSEX

Cologne ●

AUSTRASIA

Metz ●

● Paris

NEUSTRIA

BRITTANY

BURGUNDY

FRANKISH EMPIRE

Atlantic Ocean

G   A   U   L

AQUITAINE

Santa Maria
de Bretoña

Santiago de Compostela

GALICIA

● Narbonne

Spanish March

I S L A M I C   S P A I N

● Barcelona

Mediterranean Sea

● Avila

from Egypt, Syria and the Mediterranean world. In some cases, this impetus was filtered through Spain. Thus, for example, Priscillianist texts were used in Ireland, despite their heretical status in Rome's eyes.[20] And from at least 569 the Celtic Church had its own See, the bishopric of Bretoña, centred upon Santa Maria de Bretoña near Mondoñedo in Galicia,[21] the region of north-western Spain whose later capital was at Santiago de Compostela, and which had remained most loyal to Priscillianist teaching. But if some of the Celtic Church's impetus derived from Spain, much of it derived directly from much older sources. In the words of the Swedish writer Nils Aberg: 'We are compelled ... to assume a direct long-distance influence between the Mediterranean world and Ireland.'[22]

Irish monks are known to have visited Egypt. There are even travel journals, containing descriptions of the Pyramids, for example, and precise instructions on how to make one's way to the Holy Land. At the same time, an Irish martyrology records that seven Egyptian monks were buried at Disert Ulidh in Ulster. An Egyptian influence is discernible in Irish place-names for townlands and parishes – Desertmartin near Londonderry, for instance, or Desert Oenghus in Limerick. There are no deserts as such in Ireland. It is now believed that such names were used for monastic communities modelled on genuine desert prototypes in Egypt.[23]

The evidence of Irish contact with Egypt is too extensive to review in detail. A few examples will suffice to illustrate the point. Thus a portion of the Irish text known as the 'Salthair na Rann' is an eleventh- or twelfth-century copy of the 'Book of Adam and Eve', composed in Egypt in the fifth century and not known to have found its way to any other European country.[24] Unmistakably Egyptian motifs and decorations have been found in Irish books and manuscripts. The liturgy of the Celtic Church contained discernible Egyptian and Syrian elements. Episodes in an Irish 'Lives of the Saints' derive directly from an Alexandrian source. Masses and prayers from apocryphal works used in Egypt were also used in Ireland. The Celtic Church celebrated the feast days of the Virgin at the same time as the Egyptian Church, rather than at the time decreed by Rome. Glass chalices, identical to chalices used in Egypt, have been found in County Waterford. The fifth-century 'bell of Saint Patrick' is a clear imitation of bells used in Egypt. There are numerous additional examples of this kind, which thirteen centuries of Romanised Pauline orthodoxy have not been able to eradicate.[25]

If Celtic Christianity drew heavily on Egypt, it also drew heavily on the more explicitly heretical traditions of Syria, Asia Minor and Mesopotamia. We have already discussed how Nestorian thought served as a repository for certain Nazarean traditions. As early as 430 – the time of Saint Patrick – a book explaining the teachings of Nestorius was being circulated in the West. Nestorius himself had studied at the theological school of Antioch, where his mentor was a man known as Theodore of Mopsuestia. At the Fifth Ecumenical Council in 553, Theodore and all his works were officially anathematised and declared heretical. In consequence, most of his teachings have long since vanished. And yet much of what we know of him today comes from Ireland. One of his major scriptural commentaries survives only in an old Irish manuscript.[26] Additional material from Theodore turns up in other Irish manuscripts, dating from the eighth century, the ninth century and, in one case, from the late tenth century – more than four hundred years after Theodore was condemned. It has been suggested that Theodore's works were translated and brought to Ireland by no less a figure than Saint Columban.[27]

The non-Roman, Eastern influence on the Celtic Church manifested itself most obviously in Irish monasticism. Like the Egyptian Church, the Celtic Church was organised less around the diocese than around the abbey or monastery. So great was the prestige of such institutions that a so-called 'mitred abbot' in Ireland was accorded unusually high official status – a status equal, in the ecclesiastical hierarchy, to that of a bishop. Indeed, it was not uncommon for Irish abbots actually to have bishops under their jurisdiction.

Irish monasteries were organised in close adherence to those in Egypt, Syria and elsewhere in the Mediterranean world outside Rome's sphere of influence. In many cases, the physical lay-out and arrangement of the monastic community were identical. The Irish 'Rule of the Anchorites' is essentially similar to the rules which regulated anchoritic practice in Egypt, Syria and the Holy Land. And like monks in the Middle East, Irish monks, under the auspices of the Celtic Church, appear to have married.

As we have said, Ireland, between the fifth and the seventh centuries, was a centre of learning and scholarship. With the possible exception of Rome, there was no comparable place in Europe. Indeed, in many respects, Ireland was equalled only by Byzantium. In Ireland, as in the Middle East, learning and scholarship were an integral component of the monastic system, and Irish libraries became depositories for material from all over the known world. During the early seventh century, Irish monasteries exercised a virtual monopoly on the teaching of Greek. Many pagan writers were studied as well. Nor did the Celtic Church repudiate Ireland's own pre-Christian cultural heritage. Bardic tradition, for example, found a refuge in the Celtic Church and was thereby preserved. Saint Columban himself, after becoming a monk, lived and studied with a bard in Leinster. Later, he championed the cause of the bards when their schools and teachings came under attack.

In its organisation, then, in its use of certain texts, in many of its outward aspects, the Celtic Church circumvented the Church of Rome and functioned as a repository for elements of Nazarean tradition transmitted from Egypt, Syria and Asia Minor. But what was the doctrinal position of the Celtic Church? Where did it stand in relation to Rome? Was it indeed a form of heresy, which Rome, for reasons of her own, dared not openly stigmatise as such? And what basis was there for the seventh-century maxim that 'the Celtic Church brings love while the Roman Church brings law'?

In 664, the Synod of Whitby effectively dissolved the Celtic Church, and Ireland was brought into the Roman fold. At Whitby, the Celtic Church relinquished its last claim to autonomy and independence. From then on, Christianity in Ireland was determined and defined by Rome, and any compromising documents would have been destroyed or sequestered. In the aftermath of Whitby, Rome's was the only voice to speak about whatever differences had previously existed between the two churches.

According to that official voice, the differences were minimal enough, and easily reconcilable. They are said to have disagreed on the ceremony of ordination for a bishop, Rome requiring at least three other bishops to be present while the Celtic Church required only one – a plausible enough position, given the difficulties Ireland posed to travel at the time and the small number of bishops in the country anyway. They are said to have disagreed about the calendar cycles whereby the dating of Easter was fixed each year. They are said to have disagreed about the shape of the clerical tonsure, Rome insisting on a variation of the tonsure familiar today while prelates of the Celtic Church shaved the entire frontal section of the head, from the temples to the middle of the scalp, and left long hair hanging behind – the stereotyped modern image of the Druid. Finally, they are said to have disagreed about technicalities in the baptismal service. The Celtic Church apparently deemed one immersion sufficient, while Rome demanded three. And Rome insisted that the ritual occur in a consecrated church – which, given the relatively few churches in the country at the time and their tendency to be congregated in certain areas, was not always possible in Ireland.

Trifling though they may appear, these are the conventionally cited points of contention between the Celtic and Roman churches. And yet the two were so different in so many other crucial respects that one cannot but suspect something else to have been involved – something which the four issues listed above served to mask for posterity.

Indeed, later commentators have been understandably suspicious. John McNeill, for example, asserts that the ' ... issue between Romans and Celts went far deeper than the recorded exchange of arguments indicates'.[28] He concludes that the ' ... ultimate issue was that of Celtic ecclesiastical autonomy against integration within the Roman ecclesiastical system'.[29] In fact, the ultimate issue was even more profound and more wide ranging in its implications.

A closer examination of the Celtic Church reveals a much greater deviation from Rome than is generally acknowledged or even known. The Celtic Church, for example, had its own ordination rite for priests, and this differed markedly from Rome's. It had its own liturgy and Mass, both of which incorporated distinctly Eastern, non-Roman elements. It even had its own translation of the Bible – a translation which Rome deemed unacceptable. In flagrant contravention of the Nicene Creed, the Celtic Church seems consistently to have glossed over belief in the Trinity, even on occasion to have queried it. Later clerics of the Celtic Church seem to have followed Saint Patrick in circumventing the Virgin Birth. And as late as 754, nearly a century after the Synod of Whitby, there were complaints to the pope that Irish missionaries 'ignored the canons of the Church, rejected the writings of the fathers and despised the authority of the synods'.[30]

But there is more still. For Rome, the Old Testament had become increasingly incidental and the Mosaic Law superfluous; Jesus was believed effectively to have abrogated the Mosaic Law. In the Celtic Church, the Old Testament continued to enjoy a status equal to the New. And whenever Patrick consecrated a church, he was said to have left in it both the Gospels *and* a copy of the Mosaic Law. Mosaic Law was actively propagated as a major component of Celtic Christianity. Usury was forbidden, as it was not by Rome. Sexual relations were prohibited during the time of a woman's menstruation. Women were deemed unclean during and immediately after childbirth. Marriage laws adhered strictly to the tenets of the Old Testament.

The Judaic Sabbath was observed. The Judaic Passover was officially celebrated. The killing of animals for food was performed in accordance with Judaic requirements. And surviving missals and other documents of the Celtic Church prove to be riddled with excerpts from Judaic apocryphal books and additional texts which had long and rigorously been forbidden by Rome. Indeed, so marked was the Judaic orientation of the Celtic Church that it is on record as having been explicitly accused of Judaism, and its adherents of being Jews.[31]

Not surprisingly, no document survives – or, at any rate, has been allowed to come to light – which indicates that the Celtic Church might have differed significantly from Rome in its attitude towards Jesus. After the Synod of Whitby, all such evidence would obviously have been suppressed or destroyed. But, given the Judaic character of the Celtic Church, it is reasonably safe to suppose that attitudes towards Jesus were, at very least, extremely questionable in Roman eyes. In almost every other respect, certainly, the Celtic Church appears to have been something more than simply a repository for Nazarean thought – as Nestorian Christianity was, for example. The Celtic Church appears to have *been* Nazarean, in a purer, less diluted way than any other comparable institution of its time.

Rome's Quiet Invasion

By Roman standards, the Celtic Church was indubitably heretical. Certainly other forms of Christianity elsewhere were branded as such for far lesser deviations from Pauline orthodoxy. Why was the Celtic Church not so branded? Probably because Rome had no alternative if she hoped to establish her dominion over Ireland at all. To brand the Celtic Church heretical would have been tantamount to a declaration of war; and in the event of such a war, Rome would have had no prospect whatever of victory. She had no army of her own. And the secular armies which established her hegemony for her on the continent were in no position to undertake a full-scale military campaign against Ireland. In effect, there was no apparatus, military or political, whereby Rome could have imposed herself forcibly on Ireland. Any attempt at forcible conquest – by the word or by the sword – could easily have been neutralised or repelled. Nor was there any centralised political authority in Ireland itself – a 'strong man', for example, who could have done Rome's work for her. It was thus impossible to make the kind of pact that had been made with Clovis in France.

Given these factors, any attempt to brand the Celtic Church heretical would only have entailed the complete loss of Ireland. In consequence, Rome had recourse to diplomacy and negotiation. Instead of being coerced or bludgeoned into submission, the Celtic Church was simply subsumed. The process was not unlike that whereby, today, a large corporation might swallow up its smaller competitors. As a result, Ireland was spared the kind of violence with which Rome established her sovereignty elsewhere.

By virtue of this, there does not appear to have been in Ireland any large-scale persecution of heretics. Nor does there seem to have been any wholesale burning of books and manuscripts. Most of the Celtic Church's sacred texts apparently continued in use for a time, after which they were gradually and quietly consigned to the libraries of orthodox Irish abbeys and monasteries. The implications of this are potentially significant.

As we have noted, the Celtic Church drew upon a broad spectrum of texts beyond Rome's sphere of influence – Nazarean texts, Nestorian texts, Priscillianist texts, Gnostic and Manichaean texts, books of both Judaic and 'Christian' apocrypha. In one instance, the Book of Cerne, a prayer is found ultimately deriving from a work in the corpus found at Nag Hammadi.[32] Other works are unique to Ireland, having survived only there. Still others are named, are known to have been in circulation, but have never been seen. Hundreds of such works are known to have been destroyed by the Vikings during their raids on the Irish coast. But others are known to have been preserved. A number are reported to have been smuggled out of Ireland during the period of the Viking depredations, and brought to safety in Welsh monasteries. It is thus possible that there exists today, in some archive, library or monastery in Ireland or Wales, a corpus of material comparable in value to the texts found at Nag Hammadi, or to the Dead Sea Scrolls.[33]

9

The Last Days

During childhood, one is often encouraged to believe that Christianity appeared suddenly, as a coherent, comprehensive, fully
developed and immutable edifice of thought, issuing directly from
Jesus and organised around him by his associates. One is encouraged to imagine that Christian doctrine was formulated as neatly,
as definitively and as unimpugnably as a Newtonian law. Indeed,
one is encouraged to think of the world – at least the world of the
Middle East – as having discovered an entirely new religion all at
once, in a single moment of awareness, rather as Newton is
depicted discovering the law of gravity through an apple falling on
his head. And one is encouraged to imagine Paul disseminating the
new religion rather as Coke or Pepsi might be marketed to the
Third World – a single swig, and the natives are hooked. Many
people, if they think about the matter at all, continue to carry such
ideas into their adult lives.

Certainly, there have been schools of thought and systems of
belief which arose, to some extent at least, in such a fashion.
Specific schools of Islam, for example, are largely the same today as
when they were first promulgated. Specific schools of Buddhism
descend in a somewhat similar fashion from the first-hand teachings of the Buddha. In our own age, there are individuals who
revere and evangelise Marx and/or Lenin as if their teachings were
immutable, as if the world had not changed since they lived – and
as if it had indeed been accurately reflected in their doctrines.

But no one at all conversant with the historical facts would
dream of making such a claim on behalf of Christianity. No one
would dispute that what we today call Christianity – in all its
manifold and often irreconcilable forms – is the result of a
prolonged, gradual, often haphazard process involving much trial
and error, much uncertainty, much schism, much compromise,

much improvisation, much *a posteriori* accretion – and a great deal of historical accident. At every turn in the coalescence of Christianity, there are random factors, arbitrary elements, distortions and modifications dictated by chance or by simple social and political expediency.

Some pious Christians, no doubt, would assert that this process nevertheless reflects a divine plan – a pattern designed and shaped by some hand greater than man's. And indeed, the very vagaries, vicissitudes, false starts, cul-de-sacs and erratic progressions can be interpreted as testimony to such a plan. It might even be argued that only a superhuman power could have extracted anything approaching coherence from the welter of human confusion.

We do not presume either to endorse or to repudiate such assertions. We claim no such insight into the designs of Providence, or the cosmos, or whatever other principle might be responsible for shaping the course of human history. But we remain acutely aware of how much an historical accident Christianity actually is, of how easily chance or circumstance could have altered its development, or even have thwarted it completely. Had things fallen out only slightly differently, the edifice now called Christianity would never have mutated beyond a particular school of Judaism. Had things fallen out only slightly differently in another direction, there might have been two or more millennia based on the teachings of Pythagoras, or Plato, or Hillel, or Apollonius of Tyana, or any of the other wise men, prophets, sages and teachers of the ancient world. The balance was always a precarious one. It could have been tipped in any of a number of alternative ways by the historical equivalent of a feather, and what we now call Christianity could well have evolved along, say, Arian lines, or Manichaean lines, or Nestorian lines, or the lines of various other 'heresies' – or even not at all. The triumph of Roman Christianity was as much a 'near-run thing' as Wellington, in that famous phrase, described his victory at Waterloo to have been.

Of all the numerous factors which converged to ensure the coalescence, development and survival of Christianity, there is one which, in our opinion, is absolutely crucial. This factor is the psychological climate, the ambience or milieu from which Jesus arose, and which enabled him to make the impact he did during his lifetime. For Jesus was very much the product of a specific epoch in his people's history. We have alluded to that epoch before, if only in passing. To Jesus and his contemporaries, it was known as the Last Days, or the Last Times.

Messiahs had been predicted, and had appeared, prior to Jesus.

As we noted, David was a Messiah. So was Solomon. So were the descendants of their line who subsequently occupied the throne of Israel down to the Maccabees. So, too, were members of the priestly line of Zadok claiming descent from Aaron. What made the Messianic expectation of Jesus's time unique was that it became inextricably linked with a form of apocalyptic hysteria.

The Holy Land in Jesus's time was passing through an acute crisis of meaning. Existing repositories of faith were being challenged and proving invalid, inadequate, untrustworthy. John the Baptist was exhorting men to repent because the day of judgment was imminent, and across the Judaic world men were convinced that indeed it was. There was a concurrent mood of fear, both for the world and for oneself, and a concurrent desire to save, if not the world generally, then at least oneself. There was a concurrent anguish of guilt, of breast-beating for past mistakes. There was disillusion with the prevailing material values imported from Greece and Rome. Accusations of decadence, of immorality, of corruption, of moral lassitude and depravity were broadcast wholesale, together with threats of divine wrath and divine retribution. Latter-day prophets appeared, repeating the pronouncements of earlier prophets whose words, dating from centuries before, were interpreted as having contemporary relevance. Amidst this dire rhetoric, a general sense of collapse obtained – prevailing laws, prevailing codes, prevailing hierarchies of value seemed to be in a state of disintegration. Social and political institutions were in disarray. Terrorism was gaining a more and more frightening momentum. And beneath the surface of increasing turbulence there was a desperate quest for meaning, which led to a renewed longing for the spiritual. How could God be made to keep His promise and send a Messiah to deliver His people?

Capitalising on the renewed longing for the spiritual, religious fundamentalism reasserted its uncompromising claims, aligned with powerful social and political forces. A new premium was set on the ancient Mosaic Law – not only as a religious principle, but also as an adhesive binding the social fabric into a coherent order. Along with such fundamentalism, there was a proliferation of mysticism. New ways of establishing contact with God were desperately sought. Sects and cults of a bewildering spectrum and diversity appeared, often as if overnight, and flourished. Esoterica – magic, astrology, divination, other forms of the 'occult' – enjoyed a booming business, generally on the most superficial of levels. Miracles were routinely expected from magi, prophets and religious teachers. Humanity lived in the ever darkening shadow of an impending, climactic, millennial event. And, increasingly, humanity longed for a genuine spiritual leader, embodying some divine mandate or sanction, to guide it and ensure salvation.

The mechanisms underlying the situation were simple enough. For Jesus and his contemporaries, God was assumed not only to possess the attributes of goodness, omnipotence, omniscience and jealousy, as described in the Old Testament. He was also assumed to be especially disposed towards the people of Israel – to regard them with a very particular favour. They, after all, were His chosen people. He had made a unique covenant with them. Their exalted status in His eyes was beyond question. And yet it was increasingly impossible to ignore the fact that the people of Israel were in a wretched situation, bereft of their rightful monarchy, saddled with a tyrannical usurper. They had been subjected to the hardship and humiliation of an alien occupying army and administration riding roughshod over their country, their values, their culture, their religion, their heritage.

If God were indeed all-powerful, how could one make sense of Israel's misfortune? If God were indeed all-powerful, how could one explain His permitting His Temple to be defiled? How could one explain His letting His own authority be challenged by a secular ruler in Rome who presumed to arrogate divinity to himself? There were ultimately only two possible explanations. Either God was not all-powerful after all – a suggestion which would have been not only inadmissible, but also unthinkable. Or Israel's misfortune was occurring, if not through God's active will, at least with His tacit consent. It seemed obvious at the time that, whatever God's favour towards His people, this favour was being withheld or withdrawn. Israel, in short, was being abandoned by her God.

Why? It was inconceivable that God would have broken his covenant. If the covenant had been broken, the fault could only be man's. The logical conclusions were inescapable. Man had transgressed. Man had incurred God's displeasure. God, in His wrath, was punishing man accordingly.

This was not, in the context of the time, a matter of complicated theology. One had only to look around to see the state of the world in which one lived. It remained only for religious teachers to draw the obvious parallels with ancient prophecies. The general situation conformed to the prophets' accounts of the period just prior to the end of the world. It seemed obvious, therefore, that God was preparing to end the world – either in exasperation at a failed experiment, or in order to create a new and better world for those who had remained loyal to Him.

Such conclusions brought overwhelming emotional forces to the surface. There was, of course, fear — fear both for the future of the world and for oneself. A sense of guilt was also, of course, fostered, for wrongs both real and imagined. Guilt in turn engendered a longing to atone, to repent — either to avert the general cataclysm or, if that were not possible, at least to save oneself, to ensure one's own salvation.

It was from this turbulent welter of emotions that the Messianic movement of Jesus's time derived its impetus. And this impetus invested the movement with an element of self-fulfilling prophecy. Belief in the imminent end of the world helped to provoke the revolt of A.D. 66. And with the revolt of A.D. 66, with the destruction of the Temple, the sack of Jerusalem, the dispersal of the city's populace and the near extermination of Judaism in the Holy Land, the world did indeed end — at least so far as Jews at the time were concerned.

On the other hand, the survival of a small and loyal elect had been forecast. By shifting their original ground and embracing the idea of a purely spiritual Messiah, Paul and his adherents were able to see themselves as this elect. And by seeing themselves as an elect whose survival had been promised by God, they proceeded, over the subsequent centuries, to transform themselves into what they imagined themselves to be.

TWO

The Quest for Meaning

10

The Activation of Symbol

Different as our modern world may be from the world of two thousand years ago, it is astonishing how much our own epoch has in common with what Jesus and his contemporaries regarded as the Last Times. We may, today, be technologically more adept and endowed with considerably more knowledge. But, regrettably, we do not appear to be any wiser, any more intelligent or any closer to our gods. Indeed, we no longer even know their names.

We are once again living through an acute crisis of meaning, an uncertainty about our direction and our goals. The various systems, programmes and ideologies which, less than a century ago, seemed to promise so much have all, to one degree or another, proved hollow. As in Jesus's time, there is a pervasive awareness that something is disastrously wrong. Each new terrorist outrage, each new air crash, each new natural disaster produces a frisson of panic. The profound and rapid changes in our civilisation, the dissatisfaction at our systems of government, the increasing use of indiscriminate murder and terrorism as means of political protest – all have fostered a sense of general collapse, a wholesale disintegration of values. Society feels itself 'held to ransom'. Often and increasingly, by the bomber and the hijacker, it is. 'What does it all mean?' we ask. And, disillusioned by materialism's failure to answer the question, we seek, as in Jesus's time, a response in another dimension – a spiritual one.

In Islam, in Judaism, in other religions as well as Christianity, a new fundamentalism is flourishing. Prophets and preachers inveigh against decadence, immorality, corruption, moral dereliction. On the one hand, there are calls for renewed discipline and a return to the more rigorous codes of the past. On the other hand, mysticism is once again a booming business. Sects, cults, disciplines and therapies proliferate, command immense followings, draw in stag-

119

gering sums of money and enjoy the support of powerful political interests.

As in Jesus's time, we live, quite palpably, in the shadow of an impending apocalyptic event. Militant fundamentalists can proclaim that the end of the world is imminent. Even for people who have no personal reason to anticipate the intervention of divine wrath, the threat of a semi-senile finger on the nuclear button is quite real. We are all helpless hostages to a reality we no longer fully control, to the spectre of a destruction we are individually powerless to avert. And beneath the general anxiety, the maddening sense of impotence, the disillusionment with inept or irresponsible politicians, there is a profound longing for a genuine spiritual leader, an 'all-wise' and 'all-gentle' figure who will understand, will take charge and – without of course violating established democratic freedoms – assume the role of guide, conferring meaning once again on lives which have grown increasingly empty.

There have been, of course, other such periods in Western history, not to mention world history, during the last two millennia. The characteristics of the Last Times might seem equally applicable to the eleventh century, when Western Europe seethed on the eve of the Crusades, or to the early sixteenth century, when a conjunction of constellations in the heavens was held to portend an imminent apocalypse and, though the world itself remained more or less intact, the Catholic hegemony of Europe gave way to the Protestant Reformation. A century later, as the year 1666 approached, there was another wave of hysteria. Christians anticipated the imminent arrival of the Antichrist, who was presumed to measure time in strict accordance with the Gregorian calendar. Concurrent with this, Jews from Russia, the Ukraine, Persia and the Ottoman Empire to Holland and the Atlantic coast sought to see the prophesied Messiah in the self-styled prophet Sabbatai Zevi – now held to be one of the greatest embarrassments in Judaic history. Nor are these the only instances of Messianic hysteria in Western history. Very often, millennial thinking has gone hand in hand with revolution. In both the French and Russian Revolutions, many people, on both sides, contrived to see an apocalypse of cosmic, as well as social, proportions. Upheaval in the social order was interpreted, depending on one's politics and caste, as either a blessing or a curse bearing God's signature.

In certain respects, then, our age is not unique in its parallels to the Last Times of the first century. But in other respects it is. Mass movements based on self-proclaimed prophecy tend, with disquieting consistency, to become self-fulfilling prophecy. As we have seen, Jesus's contemporaries were convinced that the end of the world was at hand. Acting on this conviction, they inadvertently proceeded to bring about the end of the world – if not of the world *in toto*, at least of their world. In a similar fashion, the apocalyptic hysteria of the early sixteenth century precipitated the end of a world. So, too, did the movements culminating in the French and Russian revolutions. What distinguishes our culture from such antecedents is that we possess the power, quite literally, to bring about the end of the world – not just a metaphorical world, nor a world confined to a specific region or group of people, but the world as a physical whole. When an American president begins to think in terms of Armageddon, one is obliged to take the matter seriously. Not, certainly, because the president in question is endowed with an insight that the rest of us lack. Nor because he is any more privy than the rest of us to divine plans or blueprints of Providence. Nor because his idiosyncratic religious views warrant respect. But simply because we are humiliatingly at his mercy; and it is perfectly possible, technologically, for him to precipitate an Armageddon, while fobbing responsibility for it on to God.

The Last Times, or the apocalypse, can function as an immensely potent symbol, striking some of the deepest chords in the human psyche, eliciting a response on a massive scale. But such symbols, precisely because of the power inherent in them, will often be appropriated by small groups of people, deliberately manipulated and used to exploit others. What is more, such symbols, all through history, have displayed a disquieting tendency to break free from those who seek to control them and to run amok, becoming what the French writer Michel Tournier calls 'diabols'. According to Tournier, a 'diabol' is a symbol which has become autonomous, a law or a principle unto itself, a Frankenstein's monster on the loose, enslaving – if not destroying – the very people it was meant to serve. Symbols can be dangerous; and, as Tournier says, he who sins by symbols will often be punished by symbols.

It is in this sobering context that today's Messianic religion, with its doctrine of a new Last Days, must be placed. It is *to* this context that twenty centuries of Messianic expectation, however erratic and/or diluted, have led. For Messianic religion works primarily through the activation and utilisation of symbols. So do many other individuals, groups and institutions. So, too, if we understand it correctly, does that elusive semi-secret society which figured so prominently in our previous book, the Prieuré de Sion.

The crucial question, of course, is *what kind of meaning* is being conferred by the use of certain symbols – what stands to be gained, what lost, and by whom. What, for example, might be the repercussions of a proved blood descent from Jesus or his family, and how might these repercussions be turned to account? How have other principles, invested with a potent symbolic import, been utilised and made to function earlier in our century? In order to do justice to the matter, it is worth surveying the connections, during the last hundred years or so, between the quest for meaning, the religious impulse, the shaping of values, and political power.

II

The Loss of Faith

Jesus, quoting Deuteronomy, asserted that man does not live by bread alone. More recently, psychologists such as C. G. Jung have maintained that there are internal, non-material needs as profound, as urgent, as elementary as the need for food, for shelter, for procreation. It could probably be argued that such internal needs constitute a more valid justification than 'reason' for distinguishing humanity from the animal kingdom. One of the most basic of these internal needs is the need for meaning, the need to find some purpose for our lives. Human dignity rests on the assumption that human life is in some way significant. We are more prepared to endure pain, deprivation, anguish and all manner of ills, if they serve some purpose, than we are to endure the inconsequential. We would rather suffer than be of no importance.

Traditionally, and whether justifiably or not, the task of defining meaning and purpose has been discharged – sometimes more, sometimes less effectively – by religion. Even the concept of the state (which in the form of nationalism assumed religious proportions of its own) was still held to exist in an essentially religious framework. The state, secular though it might be, could still be rationalised as a political unit reflecting a divine mandate, or a guarantee of certain God-given rights, or the actualisation of certain laws rooted ultimately in religious soil. Even the French Revolution, which at first undertook to abolish organised religion completely, perpetrated its excesses in the name of 'the rights of man', and these rested ultimately on a religious foundation. And in the end Robespierre, while still repudiating the Church and any conventional anthropomorphic deity, nevertheless proceeded to establish his 'Cult of the Supreme Being'.

Since the late nineteenth century and the early twentieth there has been a bewildering proliferation of fields of human knowledge.

These fields have become more and more specialised, and they have continued to multiply. This has dictated an orientation towards reality radically different from that of our predecessors. The names most often associated with the new orientation are, of course, Marx, Darwin and Freud – though one could cite numerous other thinkers in sociology, psychology and the sciences. Since Darwin, the sciences have assumed an authority in the popular mind such as they had never previously enjoyed. Prior to the mid-nineteenth century, sociology did not exist as a discipline at all, and psychology had no such status until even more recently. What is more, each such discipline or field of knowledge continues to spawn new sub-disciplines and sub-fields. In the process, the all-embracing framework once provided by religion has been inexorably eroded.

For Isaac Newton, a century and a half before Darwin, science was not separate from religion but, on the contrary, an aspect of religion, and ultimately subservient to it. For Newton, science was a means of discovering and revealing the Deity's perfect design. It was integrated with philosophy, inseparable from philosophy. It was one of a multitude of activities working in concert with each other to illuminate man's place in the cosmos, as well as the laws according to which both man and the cosmos functioned. Newton would never have dreamed of, still less sanctioned, a science that was autonomous, a law unto itself. But the science of Darwin's time became precisely that, divorcing itself from the context in which it had previously existed and establishing itself as a rival absolute, an alternative repository of meaning. As a result, religion and science were no longer working in concert, but rather stood opposed to each other, and humanity was increasingly forced to choose between them. Thus, Darwinian science came to represent a major threat not only to the theological claims of religion, but also to religion's functional utility – its capacity to 'hold things together', to confer purpose and meaning.

A similar process occurred in the fields now labelled sociology, and psychology. They, too, became progressively more dissociated from the context, ultimately religious, in which they had previously been embedded. They, too, established themselves as rival absolutes, alternative repositories of meaning. They, too, proceeded to challenge the status of religion and to proffer different, often conflicting, hierarchies of value. The arts, too, asserted their independence. From ancient times, the arts had been inextricably associated with man's religious impulse and religious rituals. From Babylonian images believed to be inhabited by the gods, through Renaissance painting, to the music of Bach and Handel, the arts had been, in effect, apprenticed to religion. The root of 'culture', after all, is the same as that for 'cult' – *colere*, 'to worship'. In the nineteenth century, however, culture proceeded to make a cult of itself – a cult which sought to supplant established religion and to become a new absolute. This was exemplified by the doctrine of '*l'art pour l'art*, 'art for art's sake'. It is reflected in the aesthetics of figures such as Flaubert, Joyce and Thomas Mann, who explicitly compare the artist to God and draw an analogy between the word (small 'w') as an instrument of creation and the Word (capital 'W'), or Logos. It achieved an apotheosis with the Wagnerian productions at Bayreuth, where art became a religious ritual or festival supplanting religion itself. To attend *The Ring* at Bayreuth offered nothing less than a mystical experience – not only for an educated élite, but for minds such as Adolf Hitler's as well:

> When I hear Wagner, it seems to me that I hear rhythms of a bygone world. I imagine to myself that one day science will discover, in the waves set in motion by *The Rhinegold*, secret mutual relations connected with the order of the world. The observation of the world perceived by the senses precedes the knowledge given by exact science as well as by philosophy.[1]

The Betrayal of Faith

By the eve of the First World War, Western society found itself in an unprecedented situation. In the past, there had been one all-pervasive absolute, one all-pervasive repository of meaning which encompassed all others. Now, there was a multitude of conflicting and irreconcilable absolutes, each of which made its own claim to be a repository of meaning, to hold the answers to the most important questions, to be the definitive hope for the future. Each asserted its supremacy over the others. Each sought to become a religion in itself and to activate the religious impulse in man. Not surprisingly, the human intelligence, forced to assess this welter of conflicting claims, was baffled. How could one choose between them? Where was one to commit oneself, without commitment seeming arbitrary? One inevitable conclusion, which characterises our own century, was that it was pointless to commit oneself to anything except self-interest.

The magnitude of this crisis was not immediately apparent. The period prior to the First World War was a period of ebullient optimism – probably the most deeply, and certainly the most complacently, optimistic period Western culture had ever experienced. The future seemed to be unequivocally rosy. The newly opened fields of knowledge seemed to promise genuinely fertile territory for exploration, which would bring only benefits to mankind. Art, science, psychology and sociology were regarded as valuable conduits for the improvement of the human condition; and through them the virtues inherent in progress, culture, civilisation and unbridled capital expansion were expected to produce a true Utopia. Such was the attitude reflected by the most popular writers of the day, H. G. Wells and Jules Verne. For both Wells and Verne, the perfectibility of mankind was only a matter of time and fine tuning.

In effect, progress, culture and civilisation became, in the period prior to 1914, a form of religion in themselves. They provided their own, seemingly viable, context for the erupting conflict of absolutes, and appeared to offer a medium for its reconciliation and resolution. In their name, everything could be accommodated and vindicated. And to the extent that they did indeed 'hold things together' and furnish humanity with a sense of meaning, purpose and justification, they *can* be said to have performed the traditional function of a religion.

The war itself, of course, not only shattered this new 'religion' but made it seem, in retrospect, cruelly and bitterly deceptive. Progress, culture and civilisation seemed to have betrayed the faith reposed in them. Science, which had seemed to offer new prospects for the betterment of human life, instead produced new and more terrifying means of destroying it. For the generation who served through the Great War, science became virtually synonymous with such developments as the submarine, aerial bombardment and, most hideous of all, poison gas. Progress occurred primarily in the sphere of destruction. Culture and civilisation, instead of humanising society by their influence and converting it to peaceful beneficial activity, had effectively led to the bloodiest and most insane war ever experienced. The very sanity of its leaders was called seriously into question. The religion of progress, culture and civilisation was negated by what appeared, to those living at the time, the consummation of a long dormant European death-wish.

A religion is only as viable as the maturity of its adherents. The First World War established that technological development had outstripped psychological maturity. Technologically, we had advanced into a new age. Mentally, we were still living in the eighteenth century, if not earlier. In consequence, technology was like a live grenade in the hands of a child. This discrepancy has continued up to the present, if anything growing even more marked. Society has not grown appreciably more mature, but the grenade in its hands has grown still more dangerous.

The period following the First World War was a period of profound and bitter disillusion. The conflict of absolutes, far from being resolved, erupted anew and loomed inescapably, in all its stark disorienting reality. Society became increasingly paralysed, unable to choose between the various, mutually exclusive claims of more and more specialised fields of knowledge. In the wake of the trauma that had just occurred, none seemed reliable or worthy of respect. Having once been betrayed, we had lost our capacity for trust – except perhaps in what was least relevant. We could, for example, accept atomic theory on trust; but atomic theory did not offer much guidance to the problems of living, or to the crystallisation of values. By the end of the 1920s, mushrooming inflation and the Stock Market crash had rendered even money unstable and unreliable. The result was a lapse into nihilism – a belief in nothing, only a feverish quest for distraction from the void that represented the future. The world immediately following the First World War is now known as the world of the 'Lost Generation'.

The situation was compounded and intensified by another factor, which had not been noticed at first and which had occurred in the wake of the proliferation of specialised knowledge. As science, sociology and psychology consolidated their respective positions, they began to challenge four of the most important premises underlying Western society – time, space, causality and personality. Conventional or traditional conceptions of both time and space were called increasingly into question. Psychology, for example, had destabilised external measurements by insisting on the importance of internal time and internal space. Time was no longer confined exclusively to the calendar and the clock, space no longer to the ruler and the map. Each had its own internal continuum as well. In consequence, external measurements began to emerge not as definitive truths, but as mere conveniences, which were ultimately arbitrary, inventions of the human intellect. And even the validity of such conveniences was challenged by Einstein's Theory of Relativity. Time and space now become fluid, mercurial, uncertain, ultimately relative.

So, too, did the cherished principle of causality. Psychology had established the impossibility of quantifying or simplifying human motivation, insisting on an ambivalence in human behaviour which defied logical equations of cause and effect. Indeterminacy, unpredictability, random elements, unforeseen mutations and what are popularly called 'quantum leaps' began increasingly to enter scientific thinking. And, of course, if time and space were wholly relative, the temporal and spatial basis on which causality rested was effectively neutralised. This new instability of causality radiated to other, more practical, spheres. Morality, for example, rested, to a significant extent, on the concepts of punishment and reward. Punishment and reward rested, in turn, on cause and effect. With cause and effect compromised, the underlying laws governing punishment and reward became ever more bendable. Punishment no longer followed ineluctably from transgression, nor reward from virtue. On the contrary, one could hope to evade the punishment one deserved and reap rewards one did not.

If time, space and causality had previously constituted three of the most important pillars of Western thought, personality had constituted a fourth. Since Aristotle's time, character had been thought of as a more or less fixed quality, the individual as a unique entity. Now, the individual character or personality found itself suddenly confronted with the traumatic awareness of its own instability – if not, indeed, its non-existence. Sociology was presenting personality not as something fixed and unique, but as an accretion, a layering of conditioned reflexes governed almost exclusively by environment and heredity. Science was offering support for these claims. And psychology, by positing the existence of the unconscious, was administering a *coup de grace* to personality as it had been conceived in the past. Dreams, previously regarded as something issuing from external sources, as something peripheral to one's identity, were now declared to be as much an expression of one's self as waking consciousness. Madness was no longer a random occurrence, nor even a disease in the conventional sense, but rather a potentiality carried within every human being. We were forced increasingly to recognise that we contained many selves, many impulses, many dimensions within us, not all of which could be reconciled with one another. If we existed at all, we were both more and other than what we had thought ourselves to be. As a consequence of increased knowledge, we became even more of a mystery to ourselves.

As time, space, causality and personality became ever more untenable as fixed and immutable principles, so, too, did the world in which we lived. Belief in anything, even in oneself, became increasingly impossible. Life became increasingly bereft of meaning, devoid of significance – a wholly random phenomenon, lived for no particular purpose. Everywhere, there obtained the statement which has now become a cliché: 'It's all relative.'

The distinguished Austrian novelist Robert Musil described the age as characterised by 'a relativity of perspective verging on epistemological panic'. The phrase is extremely apt. The West did indeed exist in a state of panic about knowledge and meaning, the two primary issues to which the branch of philosophy called epistemology addresses itself. Beneath the frenzied self-indulgence of the era of the Charleston and the flapper, there lurked a sense of desperation, an often frantic terror at the absence of meaning, the uncertainty of all knowledge, the impossibility of saying definitively *what* or even *that* one knew. Meaning and knowledge became as relative, as mutable, as provisional as everything else.

12

Substitute Faiths: Soviet Russia and Nazi Germany

It is the state of uncertainty and despair that is most susceptible to the awakening of the religious impulse. It is into just such a vacuum that religion, offering a new sense of meaning and coherence, can most effectively introduce its claims. The period immediately following the First World War cried out for interpreters. People wanted desperately to know 'what it had all been for', 'what it had meant'. But organised religion made no serious attempt to confront the problem, nor to answer the needs of the time. It simply tried to pretend that nothing had happened, and attempted to continue as it had done for centuries before – as a social, political and cultural institution, rather than as an interpreter conferring new meaning. By the 1920s, therefore, organised religion was largely discredited, regarded as inadequate to fill the void that had opened in Western society.

And with the failure of organised religion to offer any solutions to the crisis of meaning, society, understandably enough, looked elsewhere. As a result, two new principles emerged and began to assume the all-encompassing status of a religion. In fact, these principles were to become the religions – or at any rate the ersatz religions – of the 1930s.

The Religion of Lenin and Stalin

The first of the new religions was socialism, particularly in its Marxist-Leninist form, as exemplified by the Soviet Union at the time and the Communist Party. Marxist thought had been around for some three-quarters of a century, and socialism for still longer. But in the heady aftermath of the Russian Revolution the doctrine assumed the status of a creed, and in the West it supplied intellectuals and idealists with the cause they needed. On its behalf, in Spain, many of them died. In England many of them spied.

Marxist-Leninist doctrine officially repudiates all religion. Yet there are formal and functional parallels between Marxist-Leninism and organised religion which are generally acknowledged and too obvious to require discussion here. At the same time, it is not generally known how much Soviet doctrine undertook, as a matter of calculated policy, not just to assume the form and function of a religion, but actually to become one. Lenin, after all, was an extremely shrewd manipulator, with a penetrating understanding of the psyche's needs. He recognised the necessity of adapting his system to man's religious impulse, however cynical he himself may have been about it.

In this respect, as in many others, it can be argued that Lenin's thought owes more to Bakunin than to Marx. In its organisation, in its techniques for recruitment, in its means of eliciting loyalty from its adherents, in its Messianic urgency, Lenin's revolutionary party structure derives directly from Bakunin, as Lenin himself acknowledges in his notebooks. But for Bakunin, revolution was more than a social and political phenomenon. It was ultimately cosmic, theological, religious in character. Having spent more than twenty years working his way up through the ranks of Freemasonry, Bakunin had acquired a metaphysical philosophical framework for his social and political ideas. Bakunin was a self-proclaimed Satanist. According to one commentator, he saw Satan 'as the spiritual head of revolutionaries, the true author of human liberation'.[1] Satan was not only the supreme rebel, but also the supreme freedom-fighter against the tyrannical God of Judaism and Christianity. The established institutions of church and state were instruments of the oppressive Judaeo-Christian God, and according to Bakunin it was a moral and theological obligation to oppose them. Although Lenin himself never explicitly indulged in any such cosmological conceptions, there is no question that he recognised their utility. Bakunin and Lenin 'were both apocalyptic zealots, while their Marxist rivals ... were – in comparison – Pharisees'.[2] In Lenin's hands, accordingly, Bolshevism sought to become something considerably more than a political party or a political movement. It sought to become nothing less than a secular religion and, as such, to minister to the need for meaning. To further this objective, it did not hesitate to equip itself with all the accoutrements of a religious faith.

Stalin, perhaps with even greater cynicism, made a point of retaining these accoutrements. Stalin had trained as a priest in a theological seminary in Tiflis. He is also known to have lived for a time – in 1899 or 1900 – with the family of one of the twentieth century's more influential 'magi' and spiritual teachers or gurus, G. I. Gurdjieff.[3] From sources such as these, Stalin learned not only to recognise the religious impulse, but also how to activate and manipulate it. In consequence, it is not especially surprising to find him devising what amount, quite unmistakably, to religious rituals. The following liturgical text, with its responsory-style choruses, is more than just a parody of a religious rite. It is intended to *be* a religious rite in itself:

> In departing from us, Comrade Lenin enjoined on us to hold high and keep pure the great calling of Member of the Party.
> – WE VOW TO THEE, COMRADE LENIN, THAT WE WILL HONOURABLY FULFIL THIS THY COMMANDMENT.
> In departing from us, Comrade Lenin enjoined on us to guard the unity of the Party ...
> – WE VOW TO THEE, COMRADE LENIN, THAT WE WILL HONOURABLY FULFIL THIS THY COMMANDMENT.
> In departing from us, Comrade Lenin enjoined on us to guard and strengthen the dicatorship of the Proletariat ...
> – WE VOW TO THEE, COMRADE LENIN, THAT WE WILL HONOURABLY FULFIL THIS THY COMMANDMENT ...[4]

Stalin systematically undertook to wring as much religious significance as possible from Lenin's death. Accordingly, Lenin's body was laid in state in the Hall of Columns in the House of Trade Unions. For four days, it was kept on display there, while tens of thousands queued in sub-zero temperatures for an opportunity to walk past the coffin. Other Bolshevik leaders were astounded by this outpouring of unabashed religious emotion.

At the second All-Union Congress of Soviets, it was decided to elevate Lenin to a status approximating to godhood. The anniversary of his death was established as a day of national mourning. His statue was erected in every important city of the Soviet Union. His body was embalmed and placed in a stone structure of specifically religious design, reminiscent of the stepped pyramids of ancient Assyria and Babylon. Even today, Lenin's body (or a convincing wax effigy of it) lies on display in Red Square, the modern equivalent of a medieval pilgrimage centre. The reverence the corpse receives is comparable to that accorded Christian relics, and Lenin's tomb might be compared to that of Santiago de Compostela. All of this is markedly incongruous with a rationalist, wholly secular system of belief which declares itself to be not only atheistic, but also hostile to all forms of religion – and the 'cult of personality'.

The mystique attached to Communist Party membership, especially during the 1930s, was similarly essentially religious in nature – or, at any rate, ersatz religious. Admission into the Party was as portentous, as ritualistic, as fraught with evocative resonance as initiation into an ancient mystery school, or into Freemasonry. In children, particularly, the religious impulse was often deliberately activated, then systematically channelled into Party interests. Thus, admission into the Pioneers at the age of nine was the great event of a child's life, a fully-fledged *rite de passage*, analogous to, say, First Communion – and possessing a vitality and intensified significance that First Communion had long ceased to enjoy. Amid various quasi-liturgical vows and pledges, the new Pioneer was given, as a sacred talisman, a red handkerchief. This piece of cloth was declared to be his most precious possession. He was instructed to guard it, revere it, preserve it from the touch of anyone else's hand. It embodied, he was told, the blood of revolutionary martyrs. To posit blood symbolically latent in a piece of cloth is not significantly different from positing blood more or less symbolically latent in wine. The premise is essentially a religious one, and the young Pioneer's red handkerchief was intended to function very much like a crucifix, or a rosary, or some other such familiar religious talisman.

In its attempt to consolidate its position both within the Soviet Union and elsewhere, the Communist Party of the 1930s exalted Marxist-Leninist doctrine to religious status. Although it claimed to have abolished religion, it sought in fact merely to replace one religion with another. And yet any religion must appeal to, and elicit a response from, something more than the intellect alone. To use the clichéd phrase, it must win hearts and minds alike, catering for profound emotional needs, as well as making logical humanistic sense. It must confront the irrational dimension in man, providing answers to questions arising from that irrational dimension; and it must at least acknowledge, and if possible accommodate, such themes as the longing for love, the fear of death, the anguish of loneliness.

There is a crucial distinction between a religion on the one hand and, on the other, a philosophy or an ideology. Notwithstanding its aspirations, Marxist-Leninist doctrine has never truly been more than a philosophy or an ideology. In its abstraction, in its emotional sterility, it has failed to do justice to man's internal needs – neither acknowledging the validity of those needs, nor ministering to them. To this extent, Marxist-Leninst doctrine has been psychologically naïve. It assumed, quite simplistically, that internal needs could be assuaged by a full belly and a creed of logical consistency. In consequence, it offered bread and a theory about the production, economic value and distribution of bread. It also offered History, capitalised, as a lofty absolute in itself. And it offered the concept of the People.

Once again, however, man does not live by bread alone, nor by theories about bread. Principles such as job alienation, the relation between labour and capital, the dialectic, even the class struggle and the unequal distribution of wealth elicit no visceral response, offer no satisfaction for man's less tangible, less well defined, but no less pervasive and obsessive forms of hunger – his hunger for 'peace of mind', for emotional and spiritual fulfilment, for an understanding of his place in the cosmos, for answers to questions that lie beyond the pale of sociology and economics, beyond the pale of materialism generally. At the same time, the concept of History as an absolute is inadequate to encompass human yearning for, and sense of, the sacred or the divine.

In addressing itself to the problem of meaning, Marxist-Leninist doctrine offered only provisional solutions. Purpose and direction were established only for a given place at a given moment, subject to permutation and change. But the religious impulse seeks something more durable. It is not in relation to social or economic issues, but to such mysteries as time, death, loneliness, love and conscience that the need for meaning is most acute. And it is precisely these *mysteries* – mystery being the real province of religion – that the ersatz religion of Marxist-Leninism has most signally failed to confront or even acknowledge. To that extent, it has proved increasingly inadequate to humanity's inner needs.

It is not therefore surprising that organised religion tenaciously persists within the Soviet imperium, despite official disapprobation, persecution and ambitious programmes of 'indoctrination' designed to neutralise it. In countries such as Poland and Czechoslovakia, the Church poses an increasing challenge to the regime, precisely because it ministers to deeper needs than the regime will recognise. And within the Soviet Union itself, the Politburo is not only plagued by a stubbornly unquenchable Christianity, but also threatened by a major upsurgence of Islam. Whether religion is 'the opiate of the people' or not, addiction cannot be cured simply by stifling the source of supply and leaving society to wrestle unaided with the agonies of withdrawal.

Adolf Hitler as High Priest

The second primary religion, or ersatz religion, of the 1930s was the spectrum of totalitarian movements now collectively called Fascism. It Italy, the original form of Fascism, as promulgated by Mussolini, never in fact achieved the status of a religion, remaining, even more, perhaps, than Marxist-Leninism, a political philosophy, an ideology. The traditional role of religion was for the most part left to the Church. As a partial result of this, Italian Fascism, especially when compared with developments elsewhere, proved a relatively hollow affair.

In Spain, Franco's variant of Fascism took pains to align itself closely with the Church and thus arrogated a form of divine mandate for itself. In consequence, it possessed a much greater energy, a much greater dynamism, than its Italian counterpart – and the unique cruelty of which only religious fanaticism is capable. In many respects, at least from a distance of nearly half a century, there is something almost laughable about Mussolini. Franco, with the hold he established over Spain and the Spanish people, is an altogether more sinister figure.

But the supreme example of a right-wing totalitarianism achieving the status of a religion is Nazi Germany. Unlike Fascism in Italy, Nazism was not just a philosophy or an ideology. Unlike the Spanish variant of Fascism, Nazism did not align itself with vested religious interests. On the contrary, it undertook, quite systematically, to supplant all such interests and establish itself as an entirely new religion.

It has now been forty years since the end of the Second World War. These years have witnessed an endless stream of historical commentary, exposition and explication about the phenomenon of Adolf Hitler, the Nazi Party and the Third Reich. And still the questions remain; still the mysteries remain. How could a civilised and cultured people – a people who gave the world Goethe and Beethoven, Kant and Hegel, Bach and Heine – follow so perverse a pied piper and plunge *en masse* into so monstrous, so demonic an orgy of destruction? Writers have sought to answer this question in a variety of ways. Nazism has been explained as a social phenomenon, a cultural phenomenon, a political phenomenon, an economic phenomenon. It has been blamed on the Versailles Treaty, on fiscal depression, on runaway inflation, on a loss of national self-respect, on the rise of Communism, on a collapse of the middle class, on a welter of other things.

Certainly all these items, and many others, played a vital part.

Certainly, too, they are all interrelated. But the most crucial element in any understanding of Nazism is the extent to which it deliberately activated the religious impulse in the German people. It elicited an emotional as well as a cerebral response, uniting, in its own depraved fashion, both hearts and minds. It became a fully-fledged religion and, as such, it redeemed post-First World War Germany from the purgatory of meaninglessness. It was the religious dimension of Nazism that inspired the dynamism, the hysterical fanaticism, the demonic energy and ferocity which so transcended the parallel totalitarian movements in Italy and Spain. One could plausibly argue that the Third Reich was the first state in Western history since ancient Rome to be based ultimately not on social, economic or political principles, but on religious principles, on magical principles. And its self-styled Leader was not so much a politician, nor even a demagogue, as a shaman.

The rise of the Third Reich did not simply and more or less accidentally 'happen' as a result of one man's venomous charisma. On the contrary, it was carefully contrived and meticulously orchestrated. With a frightening degree of self-awareness and psychological sophistication, the Nazi Party undertook to activate and, manipulate the religious impulse in the German people, to address itself to the question of meaning in a religious sense. Nazi Germany offered a cosmology, as well as a philosophy and an ideology. It appealed to the heart, to the nervous system, to the unconscious, as well as to the intellect. In order to do so, it employed many of religion's most ancient techniques – elaborate ceremonial, chanting, rhythmic repetition, incantatory oratory, colour and light. The notorious Nuremberg rallies were not political rallies of the kind that occur in the West today but cunningly stage-managed theatre of the kind, for example, that formed an integral component of Greek religious festivals. Everything – the colours of the uniforms and flags, the placement of the spectators, the nocturnal hour, the use of spotlights and floodlights, the sense of timing – was precisely calculated. The film-clips depict people intoxicating themselves, chanting themselves into a state of rapture and ecstasy using the mantra 'Sieg Heil!' and doting on the Führer as if he were a deity. The faces of the crowd are stamped with a mindless beatitude, a vacuous, enthralled stupefaction perfectly interchangeable with the faces at a revivalist church meeting. It is not a question of persuasive rhetoric. In fact, Hitler's rhetoric is quite unpersuasive. More often than not, it is banal, childish, repetitious, devoid of substance. But his delivery has a venomous energy, a rhythmic pulse to it as hypnotic as a drumbeat; and this, combined with the contagion of mass emotion, with the pressure of thousands of people packed together in a confined area, with a deliberately ecclesiastical form of pageantry and spectacle inflated to Wagnerian proportions, produces a mass hysteria, an essentially religious fervour. What one witnesses at Hitler's rallies is an 'alteration of consciousness' such as psychologists generally associate with a mystical experience. And Hitler himself becomes a black Messiah, acting as a receptacle for the religious energy he has evoked. In the words of one commentator, 'It was not long before the German people began to see Hitler as a Messiah of Germany. Public meetings – especially the Nuremberg rally – took on a religious atmosphere. All stagings were designed to create a supernatural and religious atmosphere.'[5]

Nor were Germans at the time oblivious of the religious dimension of what Hitler was doing. On the contrary, they were not only aware of it, but in some cases actually welcomed it. Thus the Mayor of Hamburg is on record as saying, 'We need no priests. We can communicate direct to God through Adolf Hitler.'[6] And in April, 1937, a conclave of German Christians declared, 'Hitler's word is God's Law, the decrees and laws which represent it possess divine authority.'[7]

One of the most valuable sources of information on Hitler's own thinking is a man named Herman Rauschning. Rauschning was one of the earliest adherents to the Nazi Party, joining in 1926. He soon became one of Hitler's most trusted colleagues and confidants, and was made President of the Danzig Senate in 1933. By 1935, however, he had become genuinely alarmed at what was happening in Germany, and he fled, first to Switzerland, then to'the United States. Deeming it essential to warn the world about the Third Reich, he published, in the years immediately prior to the war, two books in which he recounted much of Hitler's own conversation. From numerous extracts in Rauschning, it is apparent that Hitler knew full well what he was doing, and that the activation of the religious impulse in the German people was part of a meticulously calculated design. Paraphrasing Hitler, Rauschning says, 'He had made the masses fanatic, he explained, in order to fashion them into instruments of his policy. He had awakened the masses. He had lifted them out of themselves, and had *given them meaning and a function* [our italics].'[8]

He then quotes Hitler directly:

> At a mass meeting ... thought is eliminated. And because this is the state of mind I require, because it secures to me the best

sounding-board for my speeches I order everyone to attend the meetings, where they become part of the mass whether they like it or not, 'intellectuals' and bourgeois as well as workers. I mingle the people. I speak to them only as a mass.[9]

And further, as Hitler himself writes in *Mein Kampf*:

In all these cases one deals with the problem of influencing the freedom of the human will. And that is true especially of meetings where there are men whose wills are opposed to the speaker and who must be brought around to a new way of thinking. In the morning and during the day it seems that the power of the human will rebels with its strongest energy against any attempt to impose upon it the will or opinion of another. On the other hand, in the evening it easily succumbs to the domination of a stronger will ... The mysterious artificial dimness of the Catholic churches also serves this purpose, the burning candles, the incense ... [10]

Hitler acknowledged that he employed religious techniques. He also acknowledged, at least in part, where he had acquired them. 'I learned above all from the Jesuits. So did Lenin, for that matter, if I remember rightly.'[11] And, after one of his characteristic attacks on Freemasonry, he adds:

[Their] hierarchical organisation and the initiation through symbolic rites, that is to say without bothering the brains but by working on the imagination through magic and the symbols of a cult – all this is the dangerous element and the element I have taken over. Don't you see that our party must be of this character? ... An Order, that is what it has to be – an Order, the hierarchical Order of a secular priesthood.[12]

Nazism did not just adopt the accoutrements of a religion. It quite literally *became* a religion in its substance as well. Some of this substance derived from Richard Wagner, who, in the nineteenth century, had extolled the uniquely sacred quality of Germanic blood and, in the words of one commentator, 'passionately believed in the theatre as a temple of Germanic art where mystic rites might redeem' the German people and the German soul.

But Wagner was only one of a number of influences which converged to form the vision of National Socialism. Hitler also drew upon the philosopher Friedrich Nietzsche, much of whose thought he misappropriated, divorced from its true context and twisted to suit his own ends. Nietzsche was not alive to protest.

When the Nazi hierarchy sought to plunder the works of the poet Stefan George in the same way, George was alive, and did object, with scathing vehemence. As a gesture of repudiation and contempt, he promptly went into exile in Switzerland – but not before planting the seeds of the German resistance to Hitler in one of his closest disciples, the young Count Claus von Stauffenberg, who was later to engineer the 1944 bomb plot against the Führer.

Hitler and his entourage were also influenced by a number of small occult groups and secret societies – the so-called Order of the New Templars, for example, the Germanenorden, or Germanic Order, and the Thulegesellschaft, or Thule Society – which were active between the late 1870s and the period following the First World War.[13] In the teachings of these groups, one finds a militant hostility to Christianity and an insistence on old Germanic paganism.

The extent to which Hitler himself was personally associated with occult groups has never been definitively established, and is never likely to be. But he certainly knew people who were so associated, and the membership of these groups consistently overlaps with that of the early Nazi Party. Rudolph Hess and Alfred Rosenberg, for example, are known to have been involved in the Thulegesellschaft. *Mein Kampf* is dedicated to Dietrich Eckart, a minor and demented poet who was one of the leading figures not only in the Thulegesellschaft but in other such organisations as well.

What, then, was the nature of Hitler's new religion? How did it manage to win back the hearts and minds lost by the traditional Church? According to a commentator of the late 1930s, 'The totalitarian National Socialist *Weltanschauung* is a pagan faith that cannot but regard Christianity as alien and antagonistic.'[14]

In 1938 Dr Arthur Frey, head of the Swiss Evangelical Press Service, published a book which remains one of the most profound explorations of National Socialism as a religion. It is true, of course, that Frey, as a Christian, had his own vested interests to protect and his own axe to grind, but his observations are none the less pertinent. According to Frey, the Third Reich was aiming to be 'not only a state but also a religious community, i.e., a church'.[15] And 'The Führer is not only a secular Kaiser, who carries out in the state the task of government; he is at the same time the Messiah who is able to announce a millennial kingdom.'[16]

This assessment is no exaggeration. In fact, it is echoed almost verbatim by Baldur von Schirach, the director of the Hitler Youth and the man in charge of educating a generation of young

Germans: ' ... the service of Germany appears to us to be genuine and sincere service of God; the banner of the Third Reich appears to us to be His banner; and the Führer of the people is the saviour whom He sent to rescue us.'[17] As for Christianity in Germany, Hitler himself said:

> What can we do? Just what the Catholic Church did when it forced its beliefs on the heathen: preserve what can be preserved, and change its meaning. We shall take the road back: Easter is no longer resurrection but the eternal renewal of our people. Christmas is the birth of *our* saviour ... Do you think these liberal priests, who have no longer a belief, only an office, will refuse to preach *our* God in their churches?[18]

Dr Frey sums up the creed of National Socialism as follows: 'To German Faith the "blood" is holy ... In the course of the centuries ... the creative secret of inherited blood gives itself the form of the race.'[19]

The importance of blood is illustrated by the Nazi ceremony which, according to the French writer Michel Tournier, amounts to 'an insemination of flags'. In this ceremony, the original Nazi flag – stained with the blood of those who marched under it when Hitler first attempted to seize power in 1923 – was preserved and ritually produced. Other, new flags were touched to it, so that it might transmit – as if by a grotesque form of sexual magic – something of its own sacred quality. In the following passage, one of Tournier's characters describes the ceremony:

> You know what happened: the volley of shots, which killed sixteen of Hitler's escorts; Goering seriously wounded; Hitler dragged to the ground by the dying Scheubner-Richter and escaping with a dislocated shoulder. Then the Führer's imprisonment in the fortress at Landsberg, where he wrote *Mein Kampf*. But all that is of minor importance. As far as Germany was concerned, man was irrelevant from then on. The only thing that counted that day in Munich, November 9, 1923, was the conspirators' swastika flag that fell among the sixteen bodies and was stained and consecrated with their blood. Henceforward the flag of blood – *die Blutfahne* – was the most sacred relic of the Nazi Party. Ever since 1933, it has been exhibited twice a year: once on November 9, when the march on the Feldherrnhalle at Munich is re-enacted, as in a medieval passion play; but above all in September, at the annual Party rally in Nuremberg which marks the peak of

Nazi ritual. Then the *Blutfahne*, like a sire fertilising an infinity of females, is brought into contact with new standards seeking insemination. I have been present ... and I can tell you that when he performs the nuptial rite of the flags, the Führer makes the same movement as the cattle breeder guiding the bull's penis into the cow's vagina with his own hand. Then whole armies march past in which each man is a flag-bearer and which are simply armies of flags: a vast sea, heaving and undulating in the wind, of standards, ensigns, banners, emblems and oriflammes. At night the cressets complete the apotheosis, for the light of the torches illuminates the flag-poles, the bunting and the bronze statues, and relegates into the shadows of the earth the great mass of men, doomed to darkness. Finally, when the Führer steps on the monumental altar, a hundred and fifty searchlights suddenly spring alight, raising over the Zeppelinwiese a cathedral of pillars a thousand feet high to attest the sidereal significance of the mystery being celebrated.[20]

This ceremony of 'insemination of the flags' was only one of a number of feasts, festivals and commemorations whereby the Nazis revised and adapted the Christian calendar to their own, specifically pagan ends: ' ... we celebrate festivals of the sun, of the year, of growth, of harvest, where these have not been destroyed by a religion that is foreign to the world, hostile to the earth'.[21] A most important such rite was an ancient Indo-Germanic festival of the young sun god. At special SS-run boys' training academies, the Yule festival was celebrated, not as the birth of Christ, but as the rising from his ashes of the 'Sun Child' at the winter solstice. There is no need to belabour either the religious or the specifically pagan character of such rituals. What they involve is essentially a twentieth-century variant of the old Sol Invictus cult, to which Constantine had subscribed some 1,600 years before. The only real difference was that, for National Socialism, even the sun, in some unquantifiable way, was uniquely Germanic.

If Hitler was the Messiah of a new religion, his priesthood was the élite black-clad *Schutzstaffel*, or SS. Hitler spoke of Heinrich Himmler, commander-in-chief of the SS, as 'my Ignatius Loyola' – implying thereby a parallel between the SS and the Jesuits. In many respects, the SS was indeed modelled on the Jesuits, and made deliberate use of Jesuit techniques in such spheres as psychological conditioning and education. But the Jesuits themselves had derived much of their structure and organisation from the still older military-religious-chivalric orders like the Knights Templar and the Teutonic Knights (*Deutschritter*). Himmler himself conceived of the SS as an Order in precisely this sense, and saw it, quite specifically, as a reconstituted *Deutschritter* – a modern equivalent of the white-mantled knights with black crosses who, seven hundred years before, had spearheaded an earlier Germanic *Drang nach Osten* ('drive to the East') into Russia.

The original, pre-war, SS was indeed as strictly recruited, organised and ritualised as the medieval *Deutschritter*. The elaborate and mystical induction ceremony was designed to be reminiscent of chivalric investiture. Candidates for admission had to produce a family tree showing pure 'Aryan' blood for at least two and half centuries – or, in the case of prospective officers, three centuries. Each candidate had to undergo a religious-style novitiate before he was accepted into the Order. From Freemasonry, the SS learned the importance of ritualistic insignia, so that hierarchical rings and daggers figured prominently. Runes were also accorded a special significance. On the sleeves of every SS tunic, there was a runic inscription embroidered in silver braid. And the emblem of the organisation itself, the twin S's in the form of two jagged lightning-flashes, was described as the so-called '*Sig*'-rune, the 'rune of power', allegedly used by ancient Germanic tribes to denote the lightning-bolt of the storm god – Thor or Donar according to some accounts, Odin or Wotan according to others.

Himmler introduced into the organisation ever broadening dimensions of crankiness. SS weddings had less in common with Christian marriage than with pagan nuptial feasts. According to Himmler, children conceived in a graveyard were imbued with the spirit of the dead who lay there. In consequence, SS personnel were encouraged to sire their offspring on tombstones – tombstones of noble 'Aryans', needless to say. Cemeteries which research had proved to house the bones of the appropriate Nordic types were duly recommended, and lists of them were regularly published in the official SS newspaper.[22]

Around himself, Himmler planned an inner cadre of high priests, a conclave of twelve SS *Obergruppenführer* (the SS equivalent of a lieutenant-general), who were to constitute his own personal 'Knights of the Round Table'. This quasi-mystical circle of thirteen members – the number deliberately reminiscent of occult covens, as well, of course, as of Jesus and his disciples – was to have its headquarters at the small town of Wewelsburg, near Paderborn in what is now West Germany. Although the work of construction was not completed before the end of the war, Wewelsburg was intended to become the SS's official capital, its cult centre. It was described as the '*Mittelpunkt der Welt*' – the 'mid-point of the world'.[23]

At the centre of Wewelsburg was a castle within which, it was planned, each of the thirteen presiding high dignitaries would have a room of his own, decorated in the style of a specific historical period – the period, according to most commentators, corresponding to his own supposed previous incarnation. In the great North Tower, the thirteen 'knights' were to meet at ritualised intervals. Below, in the precise centre of the crypt beneath the tower, would burn a sacred fire, reached by three steps, and about the walls stood twelve stone pedestals, the true planned use for which is unknown. These numbers of three and twelve find constant repetition in the architecture of the rebuilding project. Symbolism was crucial: around the castle, and centred upon the crypt, the planned town was to radiate out in meticulously plotted concentric circles.

Himmler himself spoke frequently of geomancy, 'earth magic', and ley lines, and he liked to fantasise about Wewelsburg as an occult 'power centre' similar (as he imagined it) to Stonehenge. The official journal of the *Ahnenerbe* – the 'research bureau', so to speak, of the SS – used often to publish articles devoted to such subjects.

It is interesting that none of the 'occult' aspects of Nazi Germany found its way into the copious evidence and documentation of the Nuremberg Trials. Why? Were the Allied prosecutors unaware of it at the time? Did they dismiss it as irrelevant or incidental? In fact, neither. The prosecutors were only too aware of it. And far from under-estimating it, they actually feared its potency – feared the psychological and spiritual implications in the West if it became publicly known that a twentieth-century state had established itself and attained the power it had on the basis of such principles. According to the late Airey Neave, one of the Nuremberg prosecutors, the ritualistic and occult aspects of the Third Reich were therefore deliberately ruled to be inadmissable evidence.[24] The rationale for this was that a clever defence attorney, appealing to Western rationality, might be able to claim diminished responsibility on grounds of insanity for the war criminals he represented.

We have dwelt at such length on the religious aspects of Hitler's Germany because it is precisely those aspects that are most relevant to the quest for meaning today. Post-war Western culture has accustomed itself to thinking of National Socialism simply as an extremist political party, and of the Third Reich as a state governed by a small conclave of madmen. Mad they may well have been, but that is not the point. The point is that they were able to transmit their madness and transmute it into a form of Messianic energy. Nazism, as we said before, was not merely a political philosophy or ideology which 'duped' the German people. It was a religion, which exercised the hold it did precisely because it performed the traditional religious function of imparting meaning and coherence to a world in which those essentials were apparently lacking.

It is in this respect that the Third Reich offers perhaps its most pertinent object lesson today, and its most dire warning. Many people at present, disillusioned with materialism, advocate a state based ultimately on spiritual principles. This appears to be one objective of the Prieuré de Sion. In theory, it is a valid enough objective, and not one with which too many responsible individuals would be disposed to quarrel. But the Third Reich demonstrates that a state based on spiritual principles need not, for that reason, be intrinsically laudable or desirable. If the 'spiritual' principles are distorted, the potential for destruction is, if anything, greater than that of materialism. 'Spirit', running amok, is far more dangerous than mere matter. 'Holy war' can be the most unholy war of all, whether it be waged by Islamic fundamentalists in the Middle East or Christian fundamentalists in America.

13

The Post-War Crisis and Social Desperation

In his perverse way, Hitler gave the German people a new sense of meaning, conferring a new religion upon them and thereby redeeming them from uncertainty – from the 'relativity of perspective verging on epistemological panic' cited above. In the process, ironically and paradoxically, he gave the rest of the world a new sense of meaning as well. Because of Hitler and the Third Reich, the world made sense, if only for a time.

The First World War had been an insane war. What made it particularly terrible was that the madness was both rampant and as diffuse and all-pervasive as a cloud of poison gas. There were no real heroes or villains. Everyone was to blame and no one was to blame; everyone wanted it and no one wanted it; and, once under way, the whole thing had a grim juggernaut momentum of its own, which no one was able to control. The madness in the First World War was essentially formless, and that which lacks form cannot be opposed. The only possible solution was attrition and exhaustion.

In contrast, the Second World War made sense. Not only was it a sane war; it was perhaps the most sane war to have been fought in modern history. It was sane, so far as the Allied powers were concerned, precisely because Germany had effectively incarnated in itself the burden of humanity's collective madness. By taking upon its own shoulders mankind's capacity for horror, for outrage, for atrocity, for bestiality, Germany, paradoxically, redeemed the rest of the Western world into sanity. It took Auschwitz and Belsen to teach us the meaning of evil – not as an abstract theological proposition, but as a concrete reality. It took Auschwitz and Belsen to teach us the acts we were capable of, and to make us want to repudiate them. Unlike the war of 1914–18, the war against the Third Reich became a legitimate crusade, in the name of decency, humanity, civilisation.

To that extent, Germany conferred a renewed sense of meaning not only on her own deluded people, but, more validly, on the rest of the Western world as well. There was no question of where the evil lay. And it *was* evil, not just stupidity, not even conventional tyranny such as might have been associated with the Kaiser, or Napoleon, or even Stalin. In short, the world's collective madness, by being embodied in a specific people, acquired form; and once endowed with form, it could be opposed. The act of opposing it restored a lapsed hierarchy of values.

Unfortunately, the West did not learn from the experience as well as it might have done. By dismissing the Third Reich as a social, political and economic phenomenon, historians failed to recognise or acknowledge the psychological needs which, when exploited by Hitler and his clique, had engendered it. And the West has continued to ignore the reality and importance of those needs. The issue has never really been honestly confronted. In consequence, it continues to lurk in the background, on the threshold of consciousness, in a subliminal form. Nazi Germany had, it seemed, exemplified the irrational. As a result, Western society came to distrust the irrational, to repudiate all manifestations of it – except for those few hours, rigorously circumscribed and contained, allocated to church on Sunday. There was even an attempt to de-mystify the church service, with simple, updated versions of the Prayer Book and the Bible. Because Hitler had proved a false prophet, Western society came to distrust all prophets. Because the Third Reich had promulgated its own warped absolutes, Western society came to distrust all absolutes. Eventually, the distrust of absolutes would culminate, once again, in an all-pervasive relativity of perspective.

This was not immediately apparent. In the years following 1945, it was still possible to cling to the values which had obtained during the crusade – decency, humanity and civilisation. These were now aligned with a new faith in material progress. It had been, after all, material resources which had defeated Hitler, and such resources could therefore be perceived as forces of 'goodness'. In conjunction with decency, humanity and civilisation, they seemed to represent something in which one could genuinely believe. Thus, in the late 1940s, the atom bomb was regarded as an instrument of peace, rather than a potential threat.

This faith in progress served to carry the West into a short-lived epoch of materialistic complacency, best exemplified perhaps by the 'grey flannel suit' mentality of the Eisenhower administration and by Macmillan's 'You've never had it so good'. The most salient characteristic of the new epoch was the proliferation of what is now called the 'consumer society'. But the values, such as they were, which sustained the 'consumer society' were ultimately provisional values – the implicit equivalent of Detroit's 'planned obsolescence'. They were not promulgated as any form of absolute. They did not presume to answer the basic questions of meaning. The great ideal of the age was implicit in the catch-phrase of 'normality' – which, in practice, amounted to mere uniformity. Anything 'abnormal', any stirring of deeper internal needs – religious yearnings or experiences, nervous breakdowns, neuroses, even simple deviation from convention – was stigmatised, regarded as a pathological condition.

The closest approximation to meaning and purpose offered by the period was the so-called 'Cold War'. For men such as Senator Joseph McCarthy, meaning and purpose for the West consisted of maintaining a 'bulwark against Communism'. In other words, the West was to define itself essentially by virtue of its opposite, without fully comprehending what that opposite was. In consequence, Communism became more or less synonymous with the age's most grievous aberration, 'abnormality'. In retrospect, it all seems quaint and naïve. But it was also dangerously hollow. It is not enough to know what one stands against. One must know what one stands *for*. To define oneself as simply the bulwark against something whose nature is unclear – this is a tenuous and shifting foundation on which to build a society and give it meaning. And yet it was proffered as the only available underpinning for the new faith of consumer-oriented materialism. There was no positive creative energy at work in post-war Western culture, nothing to impart an all-encompassing order and coherence.

By the mid-1960s, the West was in disarray, and its values (such as they were) had become increasingly discredited. Nationalist movements across the world had begun to impinge significantly on popular consciousness and to challenge the assumption that Western society was 'the best there is'. The assassinations of John and Robert Kennedy and of Martin Luther King traumatised not just America, but the entire Western world, by revealing the precarious nature of existing structures. A generation of youth revolted, defying the preconceptions of their elders, proclaiming their disillusion with materialism and flaunting 'abnormality' as a source of pride. 'Abnormality' ceased to be 'abnormality', becoming instead 'originality', 'creativity', 'self-expression'. And social upheavals, from the Civil Rights and anti-Vietnam movements in the States to the 1968 student uprising in Paris, definitively exposed the fragility and hollowness of materialistic consumerism. The faith of the post-war world proved to have little more substance than the Emperor's new clothes.

Now, as during the period between the two world wars, Western society again hovers in a limbo of uncertainty. Once again, 'everything is relative'. Once again, there is no positive direction, only a nebulous notion that one must somehow 'muddle through' and survive; and these have become goals in themselves. Once again, there is a crisis of meaning. And the sense of underlying panic is of course intensified by three factors which had not previously figured in calculations for the future. One of these is the impending threat of over-population, which looms progressively larger with each passing decade. The second is the threatened destruction of a habitable environment by over-industrialisation and pollution. The third is the spectre of nuclear holocaust. These three issues cast a terrible shadow over our lives, a shadow whose pall effectively blurs, if not eclipses, our belief in the future, still more our coherent vision of the future. And without a belief in the future, we are forced all the more painfully into an increasingly feverish present. Having thus been forced back upon the present, we have begun increasingly to question it. And the present cannot acquit itself satisfactorily in the face of such interrogation.

The result of this process has been a new quest for meaning – for something that will, in effect, perform the function of a religion, imparting purpose and direction. Organised religion has made little serious effort to rise to the occasion and fill the vacuum. On a social level, it is vigorous enough, and one can only applaud its humanitarian and charitable activities. But such activities do not minister to our internal needs. So far as these are concerned, organised religion seems for the most part to have capitulated and abandoned the field.

In some cases, it has remained inert, static, refusing to grow, refusing to adapt and render itself relevant to the age, refusing to assume responsibility for offering guiding principles appropriate to contemporary problems. Thus, for example, the Anglican Church, already in a sorry enough condition, wastes time and energy harrying Freemasons and bogs itself down in tortuous quibbles about the ordination of women – precisely when there are so many more valid things it could be doing, and when Freemasons and ordained women could only help it to do them. But if the Anglican Church is stagnant, the Roman Catholic Church, under Pope John Paul II, has been positively retrogressive. During the last few years, Rome has displayed a blinkered obliviousness, attempting to entrench itself behind outmoded values which are not only inapplicable to the contemporary world, but which impose an ever more onerous strain on credibility and thus authority. To promulgate obsolescent dogma, while studiously ignoring questions pertaining to the role of women, to birth control and abortion, to the prospect of over-population, is to abdicate responsibility. In effect, the Church is no longer ministering to her congregation, no longer discharging her obligations to her flock, no longer providing for their needs. On the contrary, she is subordinating their needs to her needs – to her programme for self-preservation and survival. To that extent, she is not only rendering her flock ever more vulnerable. She is also embarking on a course of self-destruction, of institutional suicide.

Confronted by this situation, Western society, not surprisingly, has begun to turn elsewhere, to look for alternatives – alternatives which, more effectively than organised religion, fulfil the need for meaning in contemporary society. The nature of some of these alternatives attests to the desperation of the search.

14

Trust and Power

One of the primary components of any functional religion is trust. A valid religion must serve as a viable repository for trust. And it must be able creatively to convert that trust into the basis of its authority. Only through the element of trust can a religion discharge its responsibility for conferring meaning.

We have an instinctive need to trust, both individually and collectively – a need to confide in someone or something certain aspects of our own most internalised nature. In the most intimately personal sphere, we seek to repose our trust in family, friends, spouse or sexual partner, psychoanalyst, chaplain, father confessor or fortune-teller. But the need for trust extends to more impersonal spheres as well – to institutions to which we are accountable or which exercise one or another sort of sway over our lives. Companies, armies, governments, educational and religious structures are all repositories of trust. And the company director, the military commander, the head of state, the educator and the religious leader must be able to accommodate the trust not just of one individual, nor even of a few, but of many.

The nature of the responsibility or the authority entrusted to such figures will, of course, vary. A politician, for example, may be entrusted with authority to shape a man's destiny by, say, sending him off to war; but he will not necessarily be entrusted with the burden of a guilty conscience. A religion, when it is taken seriously, will be endowed with a broader spectrum of trust than any other institution, its authority extending not only to social and cultural spheres, but also to our inner life – our sense of guilt, for example, our most secret yearnings and impulses, our uncertainties, our deepest fears and, ultimately, our need for meaning. Unlike a political leader, the priest or the minister can offer the catharsis of the confessional, whether it be in the form of a ritualised sacrament, as in the Roman Catholic Church, or in the more informal framework of other denominations.

What we tend to forget is that the conferring of trust is not a passive process. We tend, without thinking about the matter, to speak of 'an act of trust', and this, precisely, is what conferring trust entails – *an act*. Conferring trust is an active, not a passive process. Something is actively given by one party and received by another.

There is an instrinsic, inescapable correlation between trust and power. It is as if trust, in the very process of being confided, undergoes the equivalent of a chemical change. In consequence, what begins as trust when it leaves the donor becomes converted into power in the hands of the recipient. If one actively trusts an individual, one is giving that individual a degree of power over oneself. If twenty people perform a similar act of conferring trust upon the same individual his power increases proportionately. When eighty million Germans actively conferred their trust upon Adolf Hitler, they were endowing him with enormous power. Indeed, Hitler's power – or the power of the Ayatollah Khomeini, or that of any other demagogue – can be defined as simply the trust actively reposed in him by a multitude of people. It is impossible to escape this transaction between trust and power.

Three key questions naturally arise. The first is how trust, in a given situation, is acquired. Is it genuinely earned? Or is it obtained by some other means – by deception, for example, or by extortion? Certain of the 'great men' of history, such as, say, Abraham Lincoln, inspire a kind of respectful affection and are deemed (rightly or wrongly) to have earned the trust reposed in them. Others, such as Bismarck, unquestionably acquired trust by more dubious means.

The second key question is the nature of the trust involved in a given situation. How far does it extend? Among public figures who receive the trust of large numbers of people are military commanders, politicians and religious leaders. Usually, the nature of the trust reposed in each will be quite different. A devout Catholic, however patriotic he might be, would still not regard his head of state as he would the Pope. On the other hand, there are occasional instances – Hitler, for example, or Khomeini – when many different kinds of trust are fused, so to speak, into one. The result – in Hitler's case, in the Ayatollah's or, a century ago, in the Mahdi's – will usually produce a figure of Messianic proportions.

The third key question, of course, is what precisely the recipient of trust does with the power of which he finds himself the beneficiary. Does he employ it to reciprocate and benefit those who conferred it upon him, or does he exploit them as mere pawns in some ambitious game of his own? In Gandhi's case, or in Martin Luther King's, trust, when converted into power, was deployed very differently from the way in which Stalin deployed it.

The contemporary quest for meaning entails a quest for someone or something worthy of receiving the broadest spectrum of trust – a quest, in other words, for a religious principle. To the extent that organised or institutionalised religion fails to provide meaning, it fails to inspire trust; and to the extent that it fails to inspire trust, it becomes increasingly powerless. This, of course, is the situation that obtains for organised religion today. In consequence, the degree of trust it receives has been diminished, with doctors, psychiatrists, politicians and various other repositories of trust claiming ever larger slices of the pie.

The medieval papacy, or the Anglican Church in the seventeenth century, or the faith of the Puritan founding fathers in America all wielded a very real power, which encompassed all aspects of people's lives, from matters of personal conscience to large-scale affairs of state. In part because of past abuses, the power of their modern equivalents is entirely nominal or symbolic, if it exists at all. As a result, God has become more and more powerful over less and less, so that one is increasingly unsure what exactly His supposed 'omnipotence' refers to. Police, courts and governments can lop off ears and limbs, imprison and torture, confiscate property, impose death sentences – not in God's name, but in that of the criminal code, the party, the state or even some such vague formula as 'national security'. God, meanwhile, is reduced to tossing an occasional petulant thunderbolt at a hapless cathedral.

The Plundering of Trust

What are some of the means whereby individuals and/or institutions acquire the trust of those who constitute their following? It is not possible, of course, in the context of this book, to undertake even a cursory, still less a comprehensive, survey. But certain specific techniques are worth noting because of the way in which they can be used to activate the religious impulse.

One such technique is the calculated use of intimidation and fear. The mechanism is familiar enough and needs little elaboration. A generalised adversary is posited – Satan, for example, the Antichrist, Communism, Fascism. This adversary is then made to appear more and more pervasive, more and more monstrous in its proportions, more and more threatening to all that one holds dear – the family, the quality of life, the homeland. Having generated sufficient panic, one need only offer oneself or one's own institutions as a bulwark, a rampart, a refuge, a haven of safety. The so-called 'lessons of history' should have taught us by now to see through such devices. And yet their continued efficacy is demonstrated by even a casual glance at today's world. We live in a world of labels and slogans, most of which denote either a supposed dire adversary or a supposed bastion of salvation from it.

At the same time, there are more subtle stratagems. Politicians, for example, will often make appeals to reason or common sense – or what often purports to be reason or common sense. They will also, as everyone knows, be profligate in making promises. Such promises are pitched specifically to people's expectations and needs, and often have little or no likelihood of fulfilment. But by making such a promise, one is implicitly acknowledging these expectations and needs. And this recognition, frequently enough, is in itself sufficient. The promise need not necessarily be kept. Indeed, it is generally accepted as liable to breakage, and one will not usually be called to account for breaking it. The recognition of needs and expectations which it implies is deemed an adequate token of good intent. So disillusioned have we become that a mere token of good intent will not only appease us, but furnish us with a repository of trust.

It is a truism today that modern politics relies heavily on the media. What this means in practice is that modern politics depends on its ability to use the media's potential for advertising. During the last quarter of a century, it has become increasingly apparent that the acquisition of trust is very much a matter of promotion, publicity and public relations. Politics, policies and politicians are now presented in the same fashion as commodities. In other words, they must be 'sold'. To this end, all the techniques of advertising are skilfully deployed, including numerous techniques of psychological manipulation.

There is, of course, a risk in reducing politics to the level of advertising. Recent studies have revealed that television viewers equipped with remote-control sets tend to switch channels, or shut off sound, during commercial breaks. This has engendered a degree of alarm in the advertising industry, and various 'countermeasures' are supposedly being discussed. Yet surely the inevitable conclusion of such studies is that viewers find much television advertising dull, inane or even downright offensive. Most educated consumers – and most consumers today *are* educated – are rather more sophisticated than the advertising industry believes them to be. Nor are they as readily seduced, cajoled or persuaded. On the contrary, they are much more cynical; and if they buy a particular product, it is unlikely to be because they are genuinely convinced by the claims of advertising. To conduct politics on the level of advertising is to foster a similar cynicism about politics. People may cast votes out of laziness, out of curiosity, out of a desire for novelty. But the power and the mandate accrued in this way will be very different from the power and the mandate based on trust.

On the other hand, it must be admitted that the techniques of advertising have produced some notable, if questionable, successes. Not all of these successes have been political in nature. In the United States, as we shall see, religion, too, is now being marketed like hairspray, deodorant or chewing gum. Salvation is hawked on television as if it were a species of spiritual fluoride, guaranteed to guard against moral decay. One can be saved by mail-order, or by a visit to a drive-in church. Such developments elicit not only some degree of trust. They also elicit vast sums of money. Later in this book, we will attempt to determine how effectively they discharge the function of conferring meaning – to determine, that is, whether they qualify as a religion in any valid sense, or whether they are something else.

Ritual and Consciousness

If man has an innate desire to trust, he also has an innate propensity to doubt, to mobilise his intellect and his critical faculties in the service of scepticism. Thus does he assert his individuality, his sense of his own uniqueness. Through the centuries, religion has sought to neutralise man's tendency towards scepticism by, so to speak, anaesthetising the intellect, lulling it or even stunning it into submission. To this end, an assault will often be launched upon the senses. Light, colour, sound, scent will be deployed with an intensity that effectively usurps awareness of any other reality. Flickering candles, for example, a dazzling array of colours, chants, repetition, rhythmic effects, the smoke of incense will all be utilised, quite deliberately, to create a general atmosphere of 'otherness', a dimension divorced from the mundane world, a quality of 'enchantment'. And some of these techniques operate very subtly indeed. Research has established, for instance, that if a recurring drumbeat is synchronised with the beat of the heart, then accelerated, the beat of the heart will follow it. Thus – as certain pop stars have recognised at least since the 1960s – is excitement induced.

All of this, of course, is ritual. Its function is to create a state of mind essentially similar to trance, or to light hypnosis. In such a state, the individual's self-awareness is mesmerised into quiescence. He can then be absorbed into something greater – the congregation or the mob, the idea, the atmosphere, the values being promulgated. Very often, this sensation of liberation from oneself, of being subsumed by some other entity, conduces to an excitement so intense it amounts to ecstasy. In its psychological dynamic, if not necessarily in its content, such ecstasy has much in common with what is called the 'religious experience', or the 'mystical experience'. This, of course, is what can be discerned at work in evangelical meetings, for example, when people enter a state of rapture and begin 'speaking in tongues', or break down in tears, or collapse in epileptic-like seizures. It is what sects or cults in almost all religions practise. In a more structured, directed, regulated and stage-managed form, it is what characterised the Nuremberg rallies of the Third Reich. In a less structured, much more unpredictable form, it is what occurs at many rock concerts. One need only think of the effect initially produced by Elvis Presley, the Beatles or the Rolling Stones – the solid sheets of scream, the beatific rapture, the frenzy, the ecstatic swoons.

Such states of mind involve a temporary transformation, if not indeed eclipse, of consciousness. The rock star, like Adolf Hitler, is functioning as a shaman, inducing a form of religious experience in his audience. He is, in effect, a manifestation of the traditional pied piper. And like the pied piper, he can employ his power for good or ill. At the beginning of the tale, the pied piper is a positive figure, who exorcises the village of Hamelin of its rats by luring them after him into the river. But by the end of the story, he is demonic, luring not rats but the village's children to their death. Hitler exemplifies the latter version of the tale. Most rock stars aspire to exemplify the former – although, as at the Rolling Stones' concert at Altamont, California, in 1969, the aspiration may backfire, and the would-be sorcerer may lose control of what he has 'conjured up'.

An assault on the intellect and the senses can induce a state of religious ecstasy. In certain Islamic sects, the names of God are rhythmically recited over and over again until they become devoid of significance, mere sounds which envelop consciousness. Such an effect can be produced by any rhythmic chant, whether it be 'Jesus saves', or 'Peace now', or 'All you need is love', or 'Here we go, here we go, here we go' – or 'Sieg Heil'. The state of mind that ensues might be described as a state of 'porousness', whereby data is assimilated, and emotional responses stirred, without being filtered through the critical apparatus of the intellect. The surrender of this critical apparatus – the temporary self-abandonment or self-abdication involved in relinquishing it – is one particularly dramatic example of the act of trust. In the state of mind just described, trust is *actively* given and received, and the transaction is discernible not only to those involved in it, but to a detached onlooker as well.

It was just such an alteration of consciousness that the shaman in a 'primitive society' sought to induce; and the more effectively he induced it, the more profoundly he would be revered. In later cultures, priests of all religions sought to induce the same alteration of consciousness, and they continue to do so today. So do certain ideologues and demagogues. So does the military.

The value of such a state is that it turns the mind temporarily into a *tabula rasa*, a blank slate. All previous programming is, for the moment, erased. This may not be of any particular significance to the rock star, but it is to the religious, political or military leader. For him, it is an opportunity to insert, as it were, a 'new programme', which will leave the individual, to one degree or another, transformed. This new programme may constitute what is commonly called a religious conversion. It may also constitute a form of brainwashing.

The next question, of course, is the nature of the 'new programme' inserted. For the military, the 'new programme' consists of a code of behaviour, a series of reflexive responses and reactions, a limited number of attitudes in a rigorously circumscribed sphere. For the political or the religious leader, the 'new programme' is intended to be much more comprehensive. In some cases, it will include an answer – more or less viable, more or less practicable – to the need for meaning. In other cases, it will offer only a distraction from that need.

Archetype and Myth

There is one other technique worth noting, which, through the centuries, has been used to elicit trust and confront – or pretend to confront – the need for meaning. This technique is as old as ritual, but it is much more subtle than ritual. For that reason, it has been of especial value not only to religious and political institutions, but also to such organisations as Freemasonry, the various 'Rosicrucian' bodies – and the Prieuré de Sion. It entails the use of symbols in a fashion which – to borrow Jungian terminology – might be described as the 'activation and manipulation of archetypes'.

It is impossible in this work to present, even in abbreviated form, an outline of Jung's thought. For our purposes, it will be sufficient to establish the nature and function of what Jung called 'archetypes'. According to Jung, an 'archetype' is a certain elemental experience, or pattern of experience, common to all mankind – an experience, or pattern of experience, which men have shared from time immemorial. Thus defined, archetypes and archetypal patterns are familiar enough. Indeed, we tend nowadays to take most of them for granted. They would include such events as birth, puberty, sexual initiation, death, the traumas of war, the cycle of the seasons, as well as more abstract concepts – of fear and desire, the yearning for a 'spiritual home' and, of course, the very quest for meaning which we have been discussing.

Because such archetypes form the basis of the most elemental and primeval facets of human nature, their significance often defies the resources of language. Language is a product of the intellect and of rationality; archetypes and archetypal patterns extend beyond the intellect and rationality. In consequence, they generally find expression most directly by means of symbols, because a symbol does not address itself to the intellect alone, evoking resonances from deeper levels of the psyche – from what the psychologist calls 'the unconscious'. For this very reason, symbols have always been of paramount importance not only to the priest and the religious leader, but also to the artist, to the poet and painter – especially when he is functioning in a priestly capacity.

There are, of course, many levels of symbol. Every individual has his own personal symbols, for example – images associated with his own unique and intimate experience. Thus, one may regard a particular flower or a particular stone as a kind of talisman; one may preserve a memento of a loved one; one may retain a sporting trophy as emblematic of a triumph or an achievement. There are also more generalised cultural and national symbols – the old fleur-de-lis of France, the Cross of Lorraine adopted by Charles de Gaulle for the Free French forces during the Second World War, the Nazi swastika, the bald eagle associated with the United States. Or specific individuals can function as collective symbols. Thus, for instance, Jeanne d'Arc is often depicted as embodying some essential quality of France, King Arthur of England, El Cid of Spain.

Archetypal symbols have an even broader frame of reference. They pertain not to a specific individual, but to mankind as a whole. The phoenix, for example, with its connotations of death and rebirth, is a typical archetypal symbol. So, too, is the unicorn, traditionally associated with virginal purity and mystical initiation. The Paradise of Christian tradition, the Valhalla of the ancient Teutonic tribes, the Isles of the Blessed in Celtic legend and the Elysian Fields of the Greeks are symbols for essentially the same archetype, or the same archetypal yearning. Archetypal patterns are also frequently symbolised by anthropomorphic figures – the hero, the wanderer, the persecuted maiden, the *femme fatale*, the lovers united in death, the warring brothers or twins, the dying and reviving god, the wise old woman, the hermit in the forest or the desert, the sacred fool touched by god, the lost or dispossessed king. Such figures embody principles of universal relevance, applicable to all cultures and all ages. Sometimes they will appear in disguise, adopting the superficial characteristics of a given era while remaining, beneath their external trappings, essentially the same. Thus, for example, the noble outlaw, as depicted in Arthur Penn's film *Bonnie and Clyde*, is a twentieth-century equivalent of a much earlier figure – Robin Hood. Thus Kojak, 'cleaning up' Manhattan, is a modern variation of Wyatt Earp 'cleaning up' Dodge City; and Wyatt Earp, in turn, is an extension of the medieval knight-errant. The modern knight-errant no longer rides a horse. He drives a car. But the basic pattern of his activities is essentially the same as it was centuries ago. And the modern city is now the jungle, the danger-fraught frontier, the perilous enchanted forest, where monsters – human or otherwise – lurk in ambush and menace stalks every dark byway. Having destroyed the frontiers and the forests of the past, we have proceeded to create new ones in the very heart of our civilisation. But behind the accoutrements of a given age, there lies something perennial – an archetypal symbol or image which, so to speak, 'reincarnates' itself through the centuries.

Symbols can function either separately or in conjunction with other symbols. A religious ceremony, for example, often involves a multitude of symbols, which operate in concert, producing an ensemble of effects. When symbols are organised into a coherent narrative, or story-line, they can become what is called a 'myth'. The word 'myth' should not be used in the once fashionable sense of 'fiction' or 'fantasy'. On the contrary, it implies something altogether more complex and more profound. Myths were not devised simply to entertain and amuse, but to explain things – to account for reality. For the peoples of the ancient world – the Babylonians and Egyptians, Celts and Teutons, Greeks and Romans – myth was synonymous with religion and, like the Catholic Church of the Middle Ages, encompassed what today we classify as science, psychology, philosophy, history, the entire spectrum of human knowledge. On this basis, myth can be defined as *any* systematic attempt to explain or account for reality, past or present. By such a definition, any system of beliefs – Christianity, Darwinism, Marxism, psychology, atomic theory – can be classed as a myth, and the word implies no disparagement, no diminution. All systems of belief evolve and develop for the same purpose – to elucidate 'the order of things', to make sense of the world.

Classical mythology was the science, psychology and philosophy of its day, and we are being naïve if we think the science, psychology and philosophy of our own day are not similarly forms of myth and will not be regarded as such at some time in the future.

Like the symbols which compose it, a myth, depending on which aspects of it are emphasised, can be personal, archetypal or anything in between – national, for example, or tribal. Personal myth is self-explanatory. Every man has his own account, implicit or explicit, of reality. Every man has experiences or adventures which, especially in memory, assume mythic proportions – incidents from childhood, for example, old love affairs, escapades in school. The stuff of nostalgia is also very often the stuff of myth. Distance, in both time and space, is often a crucial factor in the myth-making process. We all, then, mythologise our own past – our childhood, parents, the figures who shaped our lives long ago. We also tend to mythologise things, places and individuals from whom we are separated, by geographical distance, by enforced estrangement or by death. Everyone is familiar with the kind of status that absent friends or loved ones come to assume in the mind. They are often reduced to a stark simplicity, complexities falling away so that one remembers only certain prominent features which elicit a powerful emotional response. On a collective level, figures such as John F. Kennedy and Marilyn Monroe had a mythic status even when they were alive. By virtue of their deaths, they were radically transformed, and their mythic status was inflated, intensified.

Most collective myths have both an archetypal and a purely tribal aspect. Either of these can be emphasised at the expense of the other, and the myth itself then becomes either archetypal or tribal. An archetypal myth, like the archetypal symbols it embodies, reflects certain universal constants of human experience. Whatever its origin in a specific time or place, an archetypal myth will transcend such factors and refer to something shared by humanity as a whole. The unique quality and virtue of archetypal myth is that it can be used to bring people together by stressing what they have in common. The archetypal aspects of Christianity – the principle of a saviour, for example, divine or otherwise, who martyrs himself in order to confer some spiritual bounty on his people – can elicit a response from Christians and non-Christians alike. And indeed, it was precisely through an emphasis on such archetypal aspects that Christianity, in the hands of its missionaries, was able to establish itself in societies as alien as sixteenth-century Mexico and Japan.

Tribal myths, in contrast, emphasise not what men have in common, but what divides them. Tribal myths do not pertain to the universal and shared aspects of human experience. On the contrary, they serve to extol and exalt a specific tribe, culture, people, nation or ideology – necessarily at the expense of other tribes, cultures, peoples, nations and ideologies. Instead of leading inwards towards self-confrontation and self-recognition, tribal myths point outwards, towards self-glorification and self-aggrandisement. Such myths derive their impetus and energy from insecurity, from blindness, from prejudice – and from the wilful creation of a scapegoat. Because they lack an internal core, they must manufacture an external adversary with whom to contend – an adversary who must be inflated to sustain the weight and burden of everything one wishes to repudiate and project elsewhere. Tribal myths reflect a deep-rooted uncertainty about inner identity. They define an external identity by means of contrast and negation. White thus becomes identified as everything that is not black, and vice versa. Everything that the enemy is, one is not. Everything that the enemy is not, one is.

All through history, religions have availed themselves of both tribal and archetypal myths. Or, rather, they have used essentially the same myth, and emphasised either its tribal or its archetypal aspects – to elicit trust and, in reciprocation, to confer meaning, or at least a semblance of meaning. The meaning conferred by archetypal myth can often be both valid and viable – as, for instance, when the Church assumes the archetypal status of 'mother' and performs the maternal role of healing, reconciling, providing shelter, solace and compassion. In contrast, the semblance of meaning purveyed by tribal myth is, more often than not, spurious – not so much meaning as a distraction or diversion from an absence of meaning. During the Crusades, for example, or during its wars with Protestantism, the Catholic Church emphasised the tribal aspects of its doctrine, defining itself primarily by means of its declared adversary, by projecting the 'infidel' or the 'heretic' as scapegoat. What the Church offered in these instances was not meaning but, at best, a palliative for its lack of meaning – and, at worst, a mere licence for atrocity, conquest and plunder. When a religion operates on this level of tribal myth, it ceases to be a religion at all and becomes an ersatz religion.

The Last Times as Archetype

One of the most powerfully resonant of all symbolic and mythic motifs is that of the apocalypse. It occurs frequently in the history of most of the world's major religions, and is used in a variety of ways. Sometimes it is employed archetypally – to induce, as a preliminary to judgment, soul-searching and self-assessment, whether of an individual or of a culture. Sometimes it is produced as an explanation for assorted ills, real, imagined or anticipated. Sometimes it is deployed to intimidate people, to play upon their guilt, break down resistance and extort trust. Sometimes it is utilised in a crudely tribal fashion, as an instrument for creating a self-styled élite of the 'saved' as opposed to the mass of the 'damned'. Sometimes it is even made to serve as an excuse for persecuting the supposedly 'damned'.

In Part One we discussed how the archetype of apocalypse was exploited during the Last Days of the first century – during the lifetimes of Jesus and his brothers – and how potent such an archetype can be when activated and manipulated. As we shall see, that potency is of considerable relevance to the contemporary world. If man's need for meaning today can be answered only by the archetype of imminent apocalypse, and if that apocalypse is to be taken literally, then the implications are grave indeed.

The Secret Society as Archetype

A second archetype worthy of note is what might be called the cabal, or the 'invisible junta', or, to give it its most popular name, the secret society. These can be found across the world, in every culture, in every age. Usually, the secret society is characterised as a conclave of puppet-masters, a clandestine circle of individuals working for good or ill 'behind the scenes', manipulating others, orchestrating events, applying pressure, pulling strings, 'making things happen'. In Judaic esoteric tradition, for example, there are the dozen or so (the number varies) wise men or 'men of virtue', who remain unknown to the multitude, who are scattered across the world and whose righteousness so pleases God that it is the sole factor persuading Him to keep the cosmos intact. In other words, they, by their power, hold reality together. In certain forms of Buddhism, as well as in Theosophy and Anthroposophy, a similar function is performed by the so-called 'Secret Masters', endowed with a supernatural wisdom and power, who reincarnate from epoch to epoch and are said to reside in some mystical city hidden in the Himalayas.

These, of course, are extreme versions of the theme. Less extreme versions can be found within religious institutions themselves. Every priesthood, for example, is a cabal or a secret society, more or less organised. And every priesthood has its own inner, still more secret, priesthood. Thus, for instance, there is the inner order of the Jesuits, the mysterious hierarchy which directs the Jesuits as a whole and is reputedly privy to some puissant secret. Until very recently, the most imposing example of the cabal within Catholicism was the Holy Office – that is, the Inquisition. Today, the mystique attached both to the inner order of the Jesuits and to the Holy Office has been, at least to some extent, appropriated by Opus Dei, the powerful but shadowy organisation which now controls Vatican Radio, which possesses immense investments in land and business throughout the Western world, and which maintains a network of schools whose drastic principles of education were the subject of a BBC exposé. Then, too, there are occasions – the election of a new pope, for instance – when the Curia itself assumes the role of a cabal.

The element of the cabal associated with the Knights Templar is perhaps the primary source of the fascination they still exercise for many people even today, nearly eight centuries after their dissolution. The psychological power of the cabal as archetype is illustrated by the original 'Rosicrucians' of the early seventeenth century. They – whoever 'they' were – announced their 'invisible' existence through the publication of inflammatory tracts and pamphlets. Their historical existence as an organisation has never been satisfactorily established. Yet the belief in their existence was enough to engender a wave of hysteria throughout Europe – and, as Frances Yates has argued, to play a vital role in the development of seventeenth-century thought, culture and political institutions. Then, too, of course, there is Freemasonry, probably the supreme example of the archetypal cabal during the eighteenth and nineteenth centuries. Not only did Freemasonry function as a cabal to outsiders. Within the craft's own ranks, the hierarchy – especially when it culminated in 'unknown superiors' – formed a cabal inside a cabal, an enigmatic pyramid whose apex was swathed in shadows.

The archetype of the cabal plays a particularly important role in contemporary Western society. It appears wherever modern man seeks to find a clandestine conspiracy, for good or ill – in the Mafia, in Freemasonry (again), in governments and political parties, in the activities of international terrorism, in the institutions of high finance, in organisations such as the Trilateral Commission and the Bilderburg. It is particularly obvious in the modern intelligence agency. MI5 and MI6, the CIA and KGB, are evocative merely in their initials. They are true secret societies, in the strict sense of the term. But the mystique of the cabal with which they are mantled increases both their secrecy and their influence. The modern intelligence agency has become a kind of 'bogeyman', the mere mention of which can frighten or manipulate whole groups of people as if they were children.

From these examples, certain characteristics of the cabal as archetype emerge. Above all, a cabal is organised, is secret and is at very least believed to be powerful. Whether it is powerful in reality or not is ultimately beside the point. It can become powerful simply by virtue of people's belief in its power. Some cabals – the intelligence agencies, for example – unquestionably wield a very real power, which is augmented by people's beliefs about them. Other cabals may have no power at all apart from what is ascribed to them – but that, in itself, may give them considerable power. In the early nineteenth century, certain figures – Charles Nodier, for example, alleged Grand Master of the Prieuré de Sion at the time, and Filippo Buonarroti, a master conspirator who was much admired by such men as Bakunin – made a point of inventing, and disseminating information about, a number of wholly fictitious secret societies. So convincing was this information that perfectly innocent people found themselves being harried and persecuted for alleged membership of clandestine organisations that did not exist. Confronted by such persecution, the victims, as a means of self-defence, began to form themselves into a real secret society which conformed to the blueprint of the fictitious one. Thus the myth would sire a reality. Such is the *practical* power of an archetype set in motion.

Obviously, the cabal can be perceived as sinister, or laudable, or both, depending on the degree to which its objects coincide with one's own. In either case, it will still exercise a certain fascination, and will usually elicit some sort of emotional response as well. If one happens to be 'on the same side' as the cabal, its existence, or even its supposed existence, can be immensely reassuring. If one happens to be 'on the opposite side', it will elicit, if anything, an even stronger reaction, because it then caters to one's paranoia – and paranoia about cabals and conspiracies has become one of the psychological and cultural fashions of our age. (Not that such paranoia is always without foundation. On the contrary, we have learned only too well this century how much can be accomplished by a small, well-organised conclave working behind the scenes; and we are justifiably mistrustful of any concentration of power in the hands of such conclaves – especially when we do not know what they are doing with it.)

And yet, even if the cabal is perceived as hostile, there is, often, still an element of reassurance in it. Why? In part because it is more consoling to think that complications and upheavals in human affairs, at least, are created by human beings rather than by factors beyond human control. Belief in a cabal is a device for reassuring oneself that certain occurrences are not random, but ordered – and ordered by a human intelligence. This renders such occurrences comprehensible and potentially controllable. If a cabal can be implicated in a sequence of events, there is always the hope, however tenuous, of being able to break the cabal's power – or of joining it and exercising some of that power oneself. Finally, belief in the power of the cabal is an implicit assertion of human dignity – an often unconscious but necessary affirmation that man is not totally helpless, but is responsible, at least in some measure, for his own destiny.

In part, this book is about a cabal – the Prieuré de Sion. What makes the Prieuré significant, and what distinguishes it from many other contemporary cabals, is its profound understanding, and utilisation, of precisely the mechanisms we have been describing. Insofar as we, in our researches, have come to know the Prieuré, we have encountered an organisation which, in full consciousness of what it is doing – and, indeed, as a matter of calculated policy – activates, manipulates and exploits archetypes. Not only does it traffic in familiar and traditional archetypes – buried treasure, the lost king, the sacredness of a bloodline, a portentous secret transmitted through the centuries. It also, quite deliberately, uses itself as an archetype. It seeks to orchestrate and regulate outsiders' perceptions of itself as an archetypal cabal – if not, indeed, *the* archetypal cabal. Thus, while the nature and extent of its social, political and economic power may remain carefully veiled, its psychological influence can be both discernible and substantial. It can convey the impression of being what it wishes people to think it is, because it understands the dynamics whereby such impressions are conveyed. As will become apparent, we are thus dealing with an organisation of extraordinary psychological subtlety and sophistication.

15

The Artist as Priest, the King as Symbol

For the past century and more, organised religion has suffered increasingly severe blows to its credibility. But the religious sense – of 'the sacred', of 'the numinous', of a coherent pattern transcending one's personal experience – remains, for a great many people, essentially intact. The traditional custodians of 'the spiritual' may have been compromised or have compromised themselves. We may even have become self-conscious about using that word except in inverted commas. And yet, for a great many people, 'the spiritual' remains a reality, even if organised religion no longer speaks on its behalf.

There is an entire facet of twentieth-century thought and culture which reflects an aspiration towards meaning and the 'spiritual' *outside* the context and framework of institutionalised religion. Thus, for example, Einstein, following in the footsteps of Newton, attempted to reconcile his own monumental and disorienting discoveries with a serene sense of the divine. Thus, more and more individuals, recognising the bankruptcy of prevailing systems, have sought one or another valid means of synthesis for reintegrating a fragmented reality.

One examplar of this process is C. G. Jung, who, placed in perspective, can be seen not only as a psychologist, but also as a philosopher, even a prophet. Jung's overriding concerns were ultimately religious in nature. His concentration on universal experience and his use of the crucial instrument of synthesis, rather than analysis, springs from his desire to re-assemble the world, to imbue it again with meaning. What is more, he sought to do so not in purely theoretical (or theological) terms, but in terms which might be *directly experienced* rather than merely accepted as articles of faith – and which, translated into psychological dynamics, might be practically viable not just on Sundays, but throughout the individual's life.

Unlike Freud, Jung did not see psychology and religion as incompatible. On the contrary, he saw them as complementary, each aiding the other to generate a renewed sense of meaning and coherence. And Jung understood religion in its broadest, most profound and most valid sense – not as a mere edifice of conceptual dogma, not as any one particular denomination or creed, but as something encompassing all of them, a basic element in the make-up of the human psyche. In consequence, Jung proceeded to synthesise, to compare and establish common sources, common denominators, common psychological dynamics, shared patterns – not only in the world's major religions, but in much of man's other activity as well. The result was something that could indeed function as a viable religious principle for the modern age – a mode of thought and understanding which did indeed confer meaning, while at the same time fostering tolerance, flexibility and humanity.

Thus, the Jesus of history is incidental to Jung, while the Jesus of faith – the Jesus who exists as a psychological reality within the believer – becomes an archetype; and such episodes as, say, the temptation in the wilderness, or the 'harrowing of hell', or the Resurrection become components of an archetypal pattern which is shared by all humanity. Temptation, descent to the underworld and triumphant emergence from it are themes that occur in every culture, every religion, every mythology. By virtue of these themes, Jesus is brought into harmony with other archetypal figures across the globe. They partake of him and he of them, and all of them come to embody certain enduring, universal truths. At the same time, Jesus as archetype is also, quite literally, within each individual, just as Christianity claims. Everyone in his personal life can experience temptation. Everyone can experience death, either literally or in the metaphorical sense of descent into the depths of one's own psyche – into the hell that all individuals carry somewhere within them. Everyone can experience a form of rebirth and renewal. To the extent that we share his experience, we do indeed become one with Jesus and Jesus one with us. Nor is there any conflict with historical fact.

During much of his lifetime, and in the years immediately following his death in 1961, Jung was held suspect by the orthodox, largely Freudian psychological establishment, who regarded him as a 'mystic' and dismissed him accordingly. Today he is widely regarded as having made one of the most original, and most valuable, contributions to twentieth-century thought. He has also pointed the way for others, in fields as diverse as anthropology, psychology and comparative religion, who have followed in his footsteps to seek a reconciliation between psychology and religion, between personal experience and the deeply rooted sense of the sacred. It is indicative that Don Cupitt, addressing the crisis confronting organised religion in the late twentieth century, says of Jung that 'we shall all probably have to follow him'.

The Repository of the Sacred

But Jungian thought and its offshoots are by no means the only valid attempts to establish meaning in the contemporary world. One finds a similar process at work in the arts, among many of the leading cultural figures of the century, who have maintained the artist's traditional responsibility in addressing the question of meaning, in endeavouring to synthesise, in seeking to weld disparate fragments together into a coherent reality. In some cases, the artist has done so spontaneously, in others, as part of a carefully calculated programme. Thus, for example, in the mid-nineteenth century, Flaubert castigated organised religion for abdicating its responsibility, for failing to function any longer as a repository of meaning and of 'the sacred'. To redress this failure, he methodically undertook to establish the artist as a new species of priest, to invest the artist with the responsibility of conferring meaning. Art, for Flaubert personally, had always been a repository for meaning and 'the sacred'. Now, however, it was to be so deliberately, as part of a conscious policy adopted by the artist. At the same time that Flaubert was enunciating these principles in his letters, Richard Wagner, in Germany, was enunciating the same principles publicly. And in Russia, figures such as Dostoevsky and Tolstoy were proceeding to act upon them.

Flaubert today may be dismissed as the voice of an anachronistic aestheticism. Nevertheless, many of the greatest names in twentieth-century literature – Joyce, Proust, Kafka, Thomas Mann, to cite but four examples – have followed in his footsteps and openly acknowledged their debt to him. Nor can it be contested that the arts have indeed sought to perform a religious function, to serve as a repository for 'the sacred', to confer meaning, to synthesise, weld together and make sense of a fragmented reality. In some cases – the mystical Catholic poetry of Paul Claudel, for instance – a specific denominational position is explicit. In others, such as Tolstoy's, there is a broadly 'Christian' orientation which defies denominational categories, but which is none the less deeply religious. There are other works – by D. H.

Lawrence, by Patrick White, by some of the contemporary Latin American writers – which are not even necessarily Christian, yet which manifest a profound religious sense and an essentially religious vision. And though Joyce, Proust and Thomas Mann are not usually thought of as 'religious writers' at all, they none the less address themselves to the questions generally regarded as organised religion's territorial prerogative. All of the examples cited seek to confront and resolve the problem of meaning. And they do so by means of a 'spiritual' orientation which can only be described as religious.

Since the 1880s, much has been made of the books that comprise the 'Wisdom Tradition of the East' – books such as the *Bhagavadgita*, the *Ramayana*, the *Mahabharata*, and the *Tao tē ching*. Would-be European and American mystics have often asked why there is no comparable tradition in the West. In actuality, there is, and it resides in our cultural heritage. The *Ramayana* and the *Mahabharata* are both epic poems. The *Bhagavadgita* is a cross between an epic poem and a dramatic poem. None of them is significantly different from works such as *The Divine Comedy*, *Paradise Lost* or Goethe's *Faust*. And if they differ from, say, the plays of Shakespeare or Pushkin, the novels of Tolstoy or Hermann Broch, the difference is essentially one of literary form or genre, not of content or vision. Similarly, the *Tao tē ching* consists of a series of short mystical lyrics. Their Western equivalents would be the mystical verse of Yeats, of Eliot, of Stefan George, or, most particularly, of Rilke's *Sonnets to Orpheus*.

The West does indeed have its 'wisdom tradition', a tradition that is constantly growing, constantly evolving and developing. If this body of material has become divorced from organised religion, that is primarily a consequence of organised religion's narrowness and inadequacy. The depiction of Jesus in a book such as Kazantzakis's *Last Temptation* is ultimately more deeply religious, and more deeply 'Christian', than the bowdlerised portrait generally purveyed by the churches. In that respect, one can see Flaubert's objective as having been fulfilled. The arts have indeed become a repository for the sacred, and for meaning.

That Western society often fails to perceive this is its own shortcoming and its own loss. It is the result primarily of laziness. In the industrialised West, a major work of serious literature is proverbially unlikely to become a best-seller. Occasionally, if it wins some prestigious prize, causes controversy or can be associated with a highly publicised film or television production, it will do well commercially. Even then, however, it will still be regarded primarily as a form of entertainment or diversion; and if it is considered 'too difficult' – if, that is, it imposes demands on the reader's concentration – it will be doomed. Western society did not always treat its literature so cavalierly. As late as the nineteenth century, Goethe, Byron, Pushkin and Victor Hugo were best-sellers in their own lifetimes, devoured by millions, shaping the values and attitudes of their society. And today, in other parts of the world supposedly 'less developed' than our own, the arts are taken seriously, and permitted to perform the religious function of conferring meaning.

In 1968, Gabriel García Márquez published *One Hundred Years of Solitude*. On the book's translation into English, it was immediately hailed as 'a modern classic', one of the 'truly great' novels of the twentieth century – and promptly appropriated by the academic establishment, where it has generated a dissertation industry of its own. Until its author won the Nobel Prize in 1982, however, both he and the book remained largely unknown to the 'general reader'. Despite the Nobel Prize, both, sadly, may still be so. Many Western readers, who will readily slog through a thousand pages of Gurdjieff, or Rudolf Steiner, or disquisitions on Eastern thought, in search of meaning or 'self-improvement', put García Márquez aside as being 'too difficult'. And yet in Latin America itself, *One Hundred Years of Solitude* was voraciously read and devoured by every literate level of society in Caracas at the time, or Santiago, or Mexico City. It sold on a scale equalled only by the Bible. It was cited and quoted in bars, in pool halls, in the street. Incidents from it were referred to as if they were common knowledge. People were as familiar with it as, in Britain or the States, they might be with the latest developments in *Dynasty* or *Dallas*.

Granted, such a book would obviously, to some degree, speak more immediately to those whose world it directly reflected. But this alone hardly explains why British and American readers should find it 'difficult'. Or why, as a point of reference and comparison, one should have to cite *Dallas* and *Dynasty* – why, in other words, no work of English or American literature, classic or contemporary, enjoys in its milieu a comparable shared familiarity. In the course of a lecture, we once had occasion to put these questions to a visitor from Latin America. His reply was revealing. 'Because we *study* our literature,' he said proudly. 'We study it the way people in Europe, a few centuries ago, studied Luther's first translation of the Bible. Not study it academically. But as a guide to living and understanding. Books like that help us to make sense of the modern world and of our lives. We turn to them for meaning, the way people once turned to the Bible.'

The respect accorded significant literature in Latin America is reflected by the status accorded those who create it. Latin American writers have consistently been charged with important political responsibilities. Pablo Neruda, the Nobel Prize winning poet, was a close personal friend and advisor to President Salvador Allende in Chile. The Mexican novelist Carlos Fuentes has served as his country's ambassador to France. Sergio Ramírez, currently vice-president of Nicaragua, is also a distinguished novelist. In Peru, the novelist Mario Vargas Llosa was invited to become his country's president.

The best the British government has managed to do in this respect is Jeffrey Archer. For Ronald Reagan, the nearest approximation would appear to be the mind, or lack thereof, behind *Rambo*.

The Archetypal Aspect of Monarchy

Both Jungian thought, then, and the arts are spheres in which the traditional religious function of seeking, finding or perhaps creating meaning is still being performed. At the same time, however, both Jungian thought and the arts remain circumscribed spheres of interest and activity. For a number of reasons, too complex to be adequately explored here, neither impinges significantly on the populace at large; and to that extent, neither can provide the kind of all-encompassing 'umbrella' for society as a whole that organised religion once did.

But are there any other positive principles, with a wider currency, at work in contemporary culture? Are there any established – that is, 'ready made' – institutions, for example, that are genuinely archetypal, that impinge even if only subliminally on the collective consciousness and thereby function, at least in some measure, as a repository for meaning? In some of its aspects, at least, monarchy can be seen as such an institution.

At its worst, as exemplified by numerous autocratic regimes of the past, monarchy can be synonymous with tyranny. At its best, however, monarchy can indeed be seen as a repository of meaning – which, albeit in a circumscribed way, *does* perform at least a semi-religious function. Certainly monarchy rests on an archetypal basis. Kingship in itself is an archetype. Royalty, by its very nature, is the stuff of fairy-tale, and fairy-tale is a manifestation of myth – myth as defined above, a creative attempt to account for reality.

Whatever the form of government under which one lives, the psyche, from childhood on, will still be populated by kings and queens, princes and princesses. However 'republican' one may be, such figures are part of a collective cultural heritage, with a psychic validity of their own. In the absence of genuine dynastic royalty, we will endeavour to create a surrogate royalty from, say, film stars, pop singers – or, in the United States, from families like the Kennedys. Yet such surrogates are always pale imitations of the originals on which, deliberately or otherwise, they are based. Despite one's fantasies to the contrary, one instinctively recognises that the cinematic image one sees is ultimately celluloid. And the regal status of families like the Kennedys inevitably becomes tarnished by the tawdriness of politics.

On the eve of the First World War, the President of the Third French Republic complained that he, as President, in his top hat and frock coat, elicited no respect from his people, whereas any minor Balkan princeling, visiting Paris in gold braid and ostrich plumes, could have the population lining the streets to watch the pageant of his passage. In other words, the French President astutely recognised the intrinsic appeal of monarchy and of spectacle, and the extent to which the French people were starved of both. His recognition of the unprepossessing figure he cut, in his drab civilian garb, beside the majesty and splendour of other heads of state, was not a matter of petty personal vanity. It was, rather, a matter of national self-esteem. If Frenchmen were ashamed to be Frenchmen because their head of state looked paltry and pathetic, there were genuine grounds for concern.

Some sixty-five years before, a French president had confronted precisely the same dilemma, and had acted upon it. In December 1848, Louis Napoleon – the nephew of Napoleon I – was elected President of the Second Republic, a position which entailed distinctly limited powers. He, too, found himself eclipsed by the pomp and grandeur of other European rulers. Accordingly, on 2 December 1851, Louis Napoleon staged a *coup d'état* whereby he effectively took over the government and radically redefined in his favour the powers of the presidency. He then took an unprecedented step. He submitted what he had done to the approval of the French people in the form of a plebiscite. By an overwhelming majority, they endorsed him. A year later, on 2 December 1852, Louis Napoleon, capitalising on his illustrious uncle's name, proclaimed himself Emperor of the French – and submitted this act, too, to a plebiscite of the populace. In effect, Louis Napoleon asked the French people which (all other things being equal) they preferred – the egalitarian mystique of a republic, or the hierarchical pomp and grandeur of an empire. The French people emphatically chose the second, and Louis Napoleon, under the title of Napoleon III, assumed the throne of a new imperium which was to make France the cultural capital of the world.

At the time that Louis Napoleon became an emperor, the chief model for a successful revolutionary republic was, of course, the United States of America. The United States had, after all, staged an effective revolution more than a decade before France did; and unlike the one in France, the revolution in America had not culminated in the excesses of a Reign of Terror or the rise of a new dictator. But the United States was not created as a republic of the kind implied by that word today. Most of the men responsible for creating it were staunch Freemasons, and the new nation was originally conceived as the ideal hieratic political structure postulated by certain rites of Freemasonry. The state as a whole was seen as an extension, and a macrocosm, of the Lodge. Moreover, the same men who framed the Declaration of Independence were themselves at first incapable of imagining anything other than a monarchy. Americans tend to forget that George Washington, having led the original thirteen colonies to independence, as a matter of course and with virtually unanimous approval, was offered the status of king.

Granted, the world has changed dramatically since the eve of the First World War, more radically still since the times of Napoleon III and of George Washington. But the appeal exercised by royalty is self-evident. One need only note the way in which, for example, the Prince and Princess of Wales are regarded abroad. They may be harried by the media; they may become objects of gossip and lurid speculation; they may be treated like show-business celebrities. And yet, in some intangible way, they command and elicit a respect, verging almost on a kind of awe, which even the most acclaimed film idol or pop star does not. This effect extends even to America, where republican principles are firmly enshrined in the Constitution and the 'inequality' implicit in the very idea of royalty is supposedly inimical. In *The Times* of Friday, 8 November 1985, Michael Binyon wrote of the hysteria attending the imminent visit of the Prince and Princess of Wales to Washington:

> ... Americans have an ambiguous attitude to monarchy. Made up of people whose ancestors fled European tyrannies, reared on a tradition of equality and free republican spirit, the United States still feels a lack of symbol at the centre, a living focus for

its traditions and values. It has a flag, of course, and the presidency. But the flag cannot satisfy all the patriotic sentiment. And the presidency, being politically partisan, cannot impartially unify and represent the nation as well as a monarch.

And, further:

Many Americans would dismiss the idea that they hanker for the old European symbols. But they often do. Mrs Jacqueline Kennedy brought something of that to the White House, and Nixon tried to dress up the White House guards in ceremonial uniforms, with pompoms and tassles. They looked so laughably silly that the plan was quickly dropped. But ceremony is sought in the person of the President ...

who, Mr Binyon might have added, has sought increasingly over the last thirty-five or so years to assume a regal demeanour and regal trappings, and, by hobnobbing with royalty, has endeavoured to flaunt a reflected lustre. But the very nature of the American presidency militates against a regal status. Not only, as Mr Binyon suggests, because it is politically partisan. Nor because certain recent holders of the office have brought discredit upon it; there have been enough monarchs who did little enough credit to their thrones. Ultimately, the American presidency cannot achieve the same resonance as royalty because royalty implies continuity and duration; and neither continuity nor duration can be reconciled with a four- or, at most, eight-year tenure of office. Underlying the concept of royalty is the principle of a dynasty, which spans and symbolically conquers time. In its capacity to transcend and thus, so to speak, neutralise time, a dynasty performs the same function as, say, the Church. It bears witness to certain enduring values, an on-going sense of purpose and identity, which are not liable to be revised or even overturned at the next election. It embodies, in a way that no mere government as such possibly can, the mystical connotations of such terms as 'Mother Russia', 'the German Fatherland', 'la belle France'. These connotations lie in a sphere beyond politics – a sphere that verges on the religious.

In 1981, the wedding of the Prince and Princess of Wales elicited an extraordinary outpouring of popular loyalty and enthusiasm – an outpouring from precisely 'the People' on whose alleged behalf not only Marxism, but even American-style republicanism, condemns royalty. The essential point is that this outpouring occurred specifically in response to the ritual of a royal marriage, and all that such a marriage implies – offspring, the continuation of a line, the perpetuation of a dynasty and of the values embodied by that dynasty, values equated with Britain herself. Something archetypally timeless was being celebrated – the crystallisation in the present of a particular order or coherence dating from the distant past, and the promise of its prolongation into the future. Everything about the ceremony – the age-old setting, the coaches, the uniforms, even the words spoken – served to accentuate the 'timelessness' of the moment. By virtue of this 'timelessness', time itself, and everything inherently threatening about both the present and the future, was temporarily annulled.

For the majority of those who thronged to it in 1981, the royal wedding, consciously or unconsciously, represented a bastion of stability in an otherwise terrifyingly volatile world. Amidst a plummeting pound, political disillusionment, social unrest, racial friction, rising unemployment, new incursions by microchip technology, strikes, parliamentary recriminations and other manifestations of turbulent change, monarchy – by the promise of renewing and perpetuating itself through marriage – constituted a bulwark. It functioned as a principle of duration and continuity. Both duration and continuity are important aspects of meaning. To the extent that it reflects duration and continuity, monarchy can serve as a repository of meaning.

In order to maintain its status in the contemporary world, monarchy must keep up with the times. It cannot, of course, be the kind of institution still extolled by certain royalist factions on the continent. It cannot involve, either explicitly or implicitly, any principle of 'divine right'. It cannot entail a rigid social hierarchy of the sort that often obtained in the past. It cannot advocate a return to an *ancien régime*-style despotism or absolutism. It cannot even sully itself with the degraded processes of politics and government. But a constitutional monarchy, such as that in Britain or Spain, Holland or Belgium, Denmark or Sweden, is a different matter, and can serve a very real creative function.

The essence of such a monarchy is that it rests on the basis espoused by the Prieuré de Sion and ascribed to the old Merovingian dynasty of France. For the Merovingians, the king ruled but did not govern. In other words, he was ultimately a symbolic figure. To the extent that he remained unsoiled by the tawdry business of politics and government, his symbolic status remained pristine. As one of the Prieuré de Sion's writers declares in an article, 'The king *is.*' In other words, his currency resides in what he embodies as a symbol, rather than in anything he does, or in any real power he might or might not exercise. The most potent symbols always exert an intangible authority, which can only be compromised by the more tangible forms of power. Thus the papacy, during the centuries that it enjoyed a temporal sovereignty, became increasingly discredited – to such an unseemly degree that there were at several points two or more popes shamelessly jostling each other for the throne of Saint Peter. Only when it renounced its claim to temporal sovereignty did the papacy regain a measure of respect.

And yet, by very virtue of its official powerlessness, a constitutional monarchy such as Britain's does exert a very real, albeit intangible, influence. By virtue of a single statement, the Prince of Wales can create banner headlines, elicit the gleeful support of the populace, turn the architectural establishment on its head and scupper plans for a proposed extension to the National Gallery. Simply by expressing an interest, he can impart a new and, in our opinion, deserved legitimacy to Jungian psychology and certain forms of complementary medicine. Even if it is misquoted or irresponsibly reported, his concern about inner-city decay and the disenchantment of a generation of youth can impart new momentum to the will to redress such matters.

The intangible authority wielded by monarchy can extend beyond such issues. During the German occupation of Denmark in the Second World War, all Danish Jews were ordered to wear yellow stars on their coats, thus facilitating the process of identification and deportation to concentration camps. In contemptuous defiance of the power occupying his country, King Christian took to wearing a yellow star himself, as a gesture of sympathy and solidarity with his Jewish subjects. In support of their king, thousands of non-Jewish Danes followed suit. The effect of the gesture was more than symbolic. Anti-semitism and denunciations of Jews dwindled and countless lives were saved.

A more recent example of monarchical authority occurred in 1981. On 23 February of that year, certain contingents of the Civil Guard stormed into the Cortès, the Spanish House of Parliament, and, in conjunction with a few high-ranking officers commanding garrisons across the country, attempted to stage a military coup. The consequences might have been ugly indeed had not King Juan Carlos appeared on television and issued a regal appeal to cease and desist. As king, he was able to issue his appeal from a position above politics, above the ideological opposition of Left and Right. As the embodiment of a principle of continuity, he was able to speak for Spain as a whole, not for any specific faction. If not for her monarch, Spain might have lapsed into another civil war as

18 The remains of the ancient stronghold of Megiddo, roughly
15 miles south-east of Haifa, Israel. According to Christian
Fundamentalists it is here that the final battle against the Antichrist
– Armageddon – will take place.

19 *Left*, the 'Cathedral of Light' designed by Albert Speer for the Nazi Party festival at Nuremberg.

20 *Above*, Hitler as a Grail Knight. These posters were issued in autumn, 1936, and withdrawn shortly afterwards.

21 The crypt beneath the north tower at Himmler's castle, planned as
the 'cult centre' of the SS, at Wewelsburg. Three steps lead down to the
centre of the floor, where a sacred flame marking the exact centre of the
entire planned complex was to burn. The castle was to represent 'the
middle of the world'.

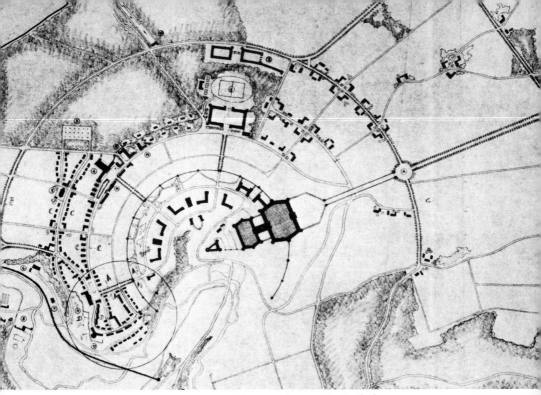

22–3 Projected constructions at Wewelsburg: *above*, 1941; *below*, 1944. In both plans the town radiates out from the centre of the north tower. The road forms a haft to the spearhead, with the triangular castle at the extreme tip.

24 *The Last Supper*, fresco by Leonardo da Vinci. Note the curious similarity between the depiction of Jesus, in the centre, and the figure shown second from the left, in profile. Can this be explained by the argument that Leonardo subscribed to a Renaissance version of the old belief that Jesus had a twin brother, Thomas?

25–6 Lenin's tomb, Red Square, Moscow: *above*, the first, temporary, structure used from January to July 1924; *below*, the third and final structure, dating from 1930. The stepped pyramid design remains an important feature, deliberately evoking the religious architecture of the ancient world.

costly and appalling as the one fought in the late 1930s – or, equally disturbing, a right-wing military dictatorship as pernicious as Franco's, or General Pinochet's in Chile, or, until the Falklands War, that of the military junta in Argentina.

There is one important aspect of monarchy which is largely neglected today and, for the moment, seems unlikely to be resurrected. But it is worthy of note because it might conceivably come to the fore again in future, and because it would appear to play at least some role in the thinking of the Prieuré de Sion. This aspect is dynastic marriage.

Today, of course, the very concept of dynastic marriage – of marriage for political reasons – seems repellent, a distasteful residue of feudal thinking. For centuries, the idea has prevailed in the West that marriage should rest entirely on a basis of romantic love. We ourselves would not dream of impugning romantic love. And yet it is obvious enough that people today, whatever their lofty sentiments on the matter, *do* marry for all sorts of other reasons. They marry out of loneliness. They marry for security. They marry for the sake of expediency, in order, for example, to confer citizenship or residency status on a partner. They marry for money, for status and prestige. None of these reasons is particularly lofty, yet all of them are tacitly condoned, even accepted. Should one therefore sneer at the idea of two people marrying – as they often did among royal and aristocratic houses of the past – in order to bring two nations closer together, or in order to prevent a war? If a high-level marriage could bring peace to, say, Lebanon, would it be reprehensible?

From the beginning of recorded history until the twentieth century, dynastic alliances were not only the norm, but also one of the cornerstones of international politics. It is only during the last seventy-five years or so that the West has come to spurn a political principle which had previously obtained for some thirty or forty centuries. From ancient Egypt and from Old Testament times to Europe on the brink of the First World War, marriage, as much as today's more accepted forms of diplomacy, served to create bonds between disparate peoples, disparate nations and cultures. Granted, these bonds were often fragile and often failed to sustain the unity they were intended to forge. Even the closest network of dynastic ties failed to prevent the catastrophe of 1914. Despite such failures, however, the principle has succeeded at least as often as other forms of diplomacy. It remains something which cannot be altogether discounted, even today.

Let us consider a purely hypothetical example. Let us suppose that, at some time in the mid to late twenty-first century, the heir or heiress to the British throne marries the heir or heiress to the throne of Spain. In effect, the result of such an alliance would be a United Kingdom of Great Britain and Spain. This does not, of course, imply a return to autocracy, for the king, in accordance with the tenets of constitutional monarchy, would rule but not govern. Nor does it mean that Britain and Spain would be coerced into an artificial unity. On the contrary, both countries would remain as independent as they are today, and power would be exercised by the British Parliament and the Spanish Cortès. Nevertheless, a very special relationship would have been forged between the two nations – a relationship analogous in some ways to that, say, between Britain and Australia, where the Queen's nominal authority is still officially recognised as long as it is not exercised politically.

Would Spain or the United Kingdom object to such an arrangement? It seems unlikely. On the basis of the adulation the present Prince and Princess of Wales receive, it is probably safe to say that most of the nations of Europe would be thoroughly delighted to claim the couple's descendants as their own – provided, of course, that this did not entail any compromise of their values, culture, constitutional independence, heritage or tradition. The royal weddings of 1981 and 1986 were international media events, fairy-tales in which the whole of Western Europe, and, indeed, the world, participated. What would be the effect of a similar event involving not one royal dynasty, but two?

16

Towards an Embrace of Armageddon

For those prepared to acquaint themselves with it, the thinking of C. G. Jung and his successors could offer a partial repository of meaning by integrating psychology and religion – by redefining the limits of both, by expanding the parameters of both and thus by vitalising both. For those prepared to approach them as something more than entertainment or an esoteric cult in themselves – prepared, that is, to approach them as 'instruments of vision' and to 'study' them the way people in the sixteenth century studied Luther's translation of the Bible – the arts, too, could offer a repository of meaning. So too if it rested on certain crucial premises, could monarchy, on a much broader, much more accessible scale. Ultimately, however, any repository of meaning will be only as valid or invalid as individuals themselves choose to make it. Christianity, for example, is only as vital, as effective, as relevant, as comprehensive, as functionally archetypal as its congregations will allow it to be. If one expects and demands a genuine sense of meaning, that can frequently be obtained. If one expects and demands something else, however, one will get something else.

The current proliferation of sects, cults, disciplines, therapies and programmes of one sort or another bears witness to the urgency of the modern quest for meaning. What was previously sought in church, or in organised religion, is now sought in the columns at the back of *Time Out* or *The Village Voice*. Very often, the need for meaning manifests itself in any number of superficial symptoms – loneliness, guilt, self-alienation, a sense of inadequacy, a lack of direction or motivation, depression, apathy, sexual uncertainties, crises of identity. But though superficial, such symptoms can be so disturbing that many people will seek their urgent alleviation, while neglecting the underlying cause. And many of the sects, cults, disciplines, therapies and programmes to which they

179

turn in their desperation address themselves primarily, if not entirely, to symptoms, functioning not as repositories of meaning, but simply as tranquillisers.

There have always, of course, been sects, cults and mystery schools, some deeply sincere in their aspirations and psychologically valid in their dynamics, others spurious in one or the other, or both. There has also always been, in man's relation to his gods and his search for meaning, a tendency to seek a short cut – to find some means of avoiding the work, the energy, the psychic investment, the sacrifices entailed. In the past, such attempts to find a short cut were invariably deemed suspect. Now, however, under the aegis of a consumer society, they have acquired an unprecedented legitimacy. Consumerism has rendered the short cut respectable in virtually every sphere. Any short cut is a marketable commodity.

On a mundane level, this manifests itself in the welter of products designed to save time, save work, save energy. It is evident in fast-food chains, in frozen dinners, in 'instant' coffee and anything else that can be made similarly 'instant'. The 1960s labelled such commodities 'plastic', and spurned them. 'Plastic' became synonymous with shoddiness. It implied something inharmonious with a living and evolving universe. It denoted the ersatz. But there is a psychological or 'spiritual' equivalent of the 'plastic' which the poet Stefan George, at the beginning of this century, diagnosed as *das Leichte* – 'the facile'. It is rampant today among the sects and cults that thrive in Western society, filling the 'therapy and growth' columns of magazines. Pre-packaged 'self-realisation' programmes, boil-in-the-bag white light, quick-frozen or freeze-dried 'enlightenment' – such are the promises offered by organisations which, in exchange, extort millions of pounds or dollars from their followers. 'Major breakthroughs' are propagated, whereby – in the course of a weekend of yelling, weeping, peering cross-eyed at the end of one's nose, making substitutional love to pillows or letting oneself be insulted – the problems of a lifetime can be summarily exorcised. The wisdom and understanding which ordinarily require years of experience are, if certain advertisements are to be believed, dispensed like pills, to be downed at a gulp with a glass of cola and a ham sandwich. The promises are always exorbitant, implicitly or explicitly – self-confidence and self-assurance, success (whatever that means), health, wealth, the romantic partner of one's dreams, assorted powers (from mind-reading to turning invisible at will), ultimately union with the cosmos. And, of course, through these things, a prospect of meaning.

Many such activities and the organisations which promote them are quite harmless – as harmless, at any rate, as going to the cinema, attending a football game or various other ways of spending money. Some may, in certain respects, actually be beneficial, provided what they have to teach is kept in perspective. But there are others that are rather more sinister. For years now, newspapers and television have been reporting stories of 'brainwashing', psychic manipulation and bullying, kidnapping, forced marriage, sundry forms of 'voodoo', reprisals exacted against would-be defectors, even on occasion ritual murder. One of the most dramatic examples occurred in Jonestown, Guyana, a settlement founded in South America by the self-styled 'Reverend' Jim Jones and the congregation of his 'People's Temple'. There, on 18 November 1978, with Jones and his followers threatened by Congressional investigation, three American journalists and an American Congressman were shot to death, while nine hundred people committed mass suicide by drinking fruit juice laced with cyanide.[1] The so-called 'Jonestown Massacre' illustrates the kind of power a sect or cult can wield over its members as a corollary of the trust they repose in it – and as an adjunct of its ability to confer either meaning or a semblance of meaning.

Another short cut to meaning – another ersatz religion, that is, or another manifestation of *das Leichte* – was the drug culture of the 1960s and some of its more recent offshoots. One cannot ignore the fact that psychedelic drugs have had a legitimate place in many religious traditions or that they have proved valuable and illuminating to many artists and thinkers in the West. But to use such drugs as they were used in the 1960s – as tickets, so to speak, to 'instant Nirvana' – is indeed another manifestation of 'the facile'. At their worst, and especially when the rituals attending them are appropriated in the name of a sect or cult, they can be truly frightening. Perhaps the most notorious instance of a drug-based sect or cult would be the 'psychedelic satanism' of Charles Manson and the dupes who constituted his 'Family'. As Manson's group illustrates, there is often a very precarious border between a guru on the one hand and a Führer on the other, between a disciple on the one hand and, on the other, a slave.[2]

The spectrum of so-called 'esoterica' – magic in its various forms, astrology, alchemy, symbolic systems for divination such as Tarot or the I Ching, physical or mental disciplines such as yoga and the Cabala – has existed for as long as organised religion itself, if not indeed longer. It has, of course, been fashionable, for at least three centuries, to scoff at esoterica. Among scientists and churchmen today, it is fashionable to deplore the eagerness with which the esoteric is often embraced. One even periodically hears self-proclaimed 'moral reformers' muttering darkly of 'witchcraft' and 'paganism'. But the resurgence of esoterica in our own age is not just a fad, a passing trend. It is symptomatic of a profound malaise, and a very genuine need. It attests to how grievously organised religion, science and the programmes of 'moral reformers' have failed to answer that need. And it bears witness, once again, to the urgency of the search for meaning in contemporary society. But esoterica, too, are all too often reduced to the facile. Sun-sign columns, do-it-yourself witchcraft manuals and other forms of 'occultism for the masses' are equally manifestations of *das Leichte*.

During the last quarter of a century, many people have also turned to Eastern thought – to Hinduism, Buddhism and Taoism. Granted, westerners have been looking eastwards for at least two centuries now, and many of them have found there truths more profound and more viable than those of Judaeo-Christian tradition. But during the last quarter of a century, increasing numbers of lost individuals have turned to Eastern thought in the same way that they have turned to esoterica. They have accepted facile, bastardised, pre-packaged forms of it, embraced any self-styled master or guru who offered an attractively presented variant, blindly committed themselves to an ashram or some other obligatory life-style with a docile, uncritical passivity – and with expectations so exorbitant as to be ludicrous. Speaking of the generation of Western youth who flocked to India in search of enlightenment, the Indian writer Gita Mehta observes: 'Never before had the Void been pursued with such optimism and such razzle dazzle. Everyone suspected that whatever America wanted, America got. Why not Nirvana?'[3] And again: ' ... the seduction lay in the chaos. They thought they were simple. We thought they were neon. They thought we were profound. We knew we were provincial. Everybody thought everybody else was ridiculously exotic and everybody got it wrong.'[4]

The Fundamentalists

Among the questionable alternatives to religion embraced by contemporary society – among the various ersatz religions, that is – one must include the kind of fundamentalist teaching promulgated by certain sects and churches in Britain, in South Africa and in the United States. Like all ersatz religions, these teachings eschew responsibility for everything a genuine religion entails and offer something else – something potentially dangerous – as a palliative.

Granted, Christianity, like most other religions, has in the past had its fanatics, espousing over-simplified dicta and prohibitions, more intent on coercing conformity from their neighbours than on crystallising their own sense of meaning. Indeed, it could well be argued that the social, cultural and political history of religion, at least in the West, is to some degree the history of such imposition. Judaism, at various points in the past, and Islam, in the past and today as well, are equally guilty. But it is disturbing to see the same phenomenon developing in the West on as broad a scale as that which obtains today. It has taken us a great many centuries, and cost a great deal of bloodshed, to learn a measure of tolerance. That we can feel shame at such aberrations as the Inquisition, or the witch-trials of the Middle Ages, the Renaissance and the Counter-Reformation, attests to some genuine advance in learning, some genuine education on the level where education truly matters – in values and attitudes. It bodes ill when such gains are threatened by a return to fundamentalist simplicities – by a return, in other words, to the use of religion as mere tribal myth.

In the past, fundamentalist simplicity has often served as a refuge for oppressed minorities, or even for an occupied country. Sometimes is has assumed a violent and aggressive form – that of Polish Catholicism, for example, when, during the nineteenth century, Poland lay prostrate beneath the alien yoke of Lutheran Germany and Orthodox Russia. Sometimes, and probably more often, it has provided a consolation for the helpless, counselling resignation while at the same time proffering hope. In this capacity, fundamentalist teaching performed a genuinely therapeutic role for nineteenth-century Jewish ghettos in Eastern Europe, or for black communities in the American South.

What is occurring today, however, is the embrace of fundamentalist simplicities not by an oppressed and persecuted minority, but by some of the wealthiest, most comfortable, most powerful and, theoretically, best educated people in the world. This in effect nullifies much of what Western culture has so painstakingly learned – not only in purely academic spheres such as biblical study and evolutionary theory, but also in the more relevant and ultimately more important spheres of humanity and tolerance. Not since the excesses of seventeenth-century Puritanism – Cromwell's Protectorate in Britain, the witch-trials in New England as well as in Western Europe – has religious fanaticism and bigotry been allied in the West with wealth and power on so large a scale. Except, of course, for the Third Reich.

Modern fundamentalism in America derives ultimately from seventeenth-century Puritanism, with its concept of an 'elect' who enjoyed a special 'covenant' with God. This 'elect', of course, included the men now honoured as the 'Founding Fathers' of the United States. But the more immediate roots of modern fundamentalism lie in the fractured and free-associative history expounded by certain nineteenth-century theological propagandists. In 1840, for example, a London phrenologist disarmingly named John Wilson published a book entitled *Our Israelitish Origin*. According to Wilson, God had faithfully fulfilled His pledge to sustain the seed of Abraham. Driven into exile by the Assyrians, the Israelites, Wilson asserted, had become the Scythians, who in turn were the ancestors of the Saxons. Through this kind of demented logic, Wilson eventually concluded that the English were in fact the lineal descendants of the Tribe of Ephraim. An important piece of evidence in his feat of historical detection was the derivation of the word 'Saxon' – based apparently on the assumption that the ancient Hebrews and Scythians spoke English – from 'Isaac's sons'.[5] It would all be charmingly dotty, if not for the fact that Wilson's claims are still being promulgated by fundamentalist textbooks today.

In 1842, Wilson published a second book, *The Millennium* – in which, not surprisingly perhaps, his reasoning led him to the conclusion that the Second Coming was at hand. Jesus's 'return engagement' was imminent, he argued, and this event would be followed by the establishment of a species of what we would now term a thousand-year Reich. First, of course, there would be the Antichrist, and the world would lapse into a period of chaos. But the Antichrist, menacing though he (or it) be, was doomed *a priori* to defeat. European civilisation was so great, Wilson had earlier argued, that it could only be the product of a new 'chosen people', whom God, in adherence to His covenant, would never abandon.[6] During the ensuing hundred and forty years, this assertion of supremacy was to be eagerly embraced by Afrikaans settlers in South Africa, who, even today, regard it as a major cornerstone of apartheid.

Wilson was followed by other writers of much the same ilk. In 1861, for example, a certain Reverend Glover endeavoured to associate the British lion with the lion of the Tribe of Judah. Serenely undeterred by self-contradiction, he then echoed Wilson in equating England with the Tribe of Ephraim, but equated the

Welsh and the Scots with that of Manassah.[7] In 1870, Edward Hine of Manchester published *The English Nation Identified with the Lost House of Israel by Twenty-seven Identifications*. Four years later, a revised edition of the book was issued, Hine having added another twenty 'identifications' to make a total of forty-seven. For Hine, Britain was no longer associated with one or two of ancient Israel's lost ten tribes, but with all of them. Unaware apparently that the 'Tuatha de Danann' of Irish tradition meant simply the people of the goddess Danu, Hine construed the name as some sort of Gaelic transliteration for the Tribe of Dan[8] – a solecism still asserted by fundamentalists today. Further confirmation for this contention seemed to be provided by the frequency with which 'Dun' – a variant of 'Dan', according to Hine – occurred among Irish place-names. In reality, 'Dun' meant nothing more than a fortified dwelling-place – of which, needless to say, there were many in Ireland.

Like Wilson, Hine anticipated an imminent Second Coming: 'Armageddon looms in the distance. This is the time when almost the entire world will be gathered to battle against us, and for which we have to be prepared.'[9]

It must be remembered, of course, that the ideas of men such as Wilson, Glover and Hine were very much products of the Victorian era. Granted, even in the context of their time, most people would have found them ridiculous. But they would have seemed slightly less so than they do today; and they did, after all, harmonise with the prevailing mood of complacency and self-congratulation. The British Empire was then approaching the zenith of its grandeur, the halcyon period of the Pax Britannica. The entire world acknowledged the magnitude of British achievement. There was really nothing to challenge the conviction that civilisation, under Britain's benign aegis, had attained a point just marginally short of perfection; and this lent itself to interpretation as God's seal of approval, or even the workings of His divine plan.

Needless to say, the subsequent erosion of Britain's overseas imperium constituted an incommodious embarrassment for the successors of Wilson, Glover and Hine, one of whom, speaking in 1969, declared, rather poignantly (if not altogether lucidly): 'We cannot now talk glibly of the identity mark, that we possess the gates of our enemies. We cannot talk proudly that one of the marks of Israel is that we are the wealthiest of nations, who lend but never borrow; we cannot really talk with great emphasis of *Great Britain*.'[10] But there is, of course, an explanation for this: ' ... the measure of our fall into disgrace and abject conditions is the measure of our departure from Almighty God'.[11]

If Britain had fallen from grace, however, America had not. Stressing its British – that is, white Anglo-Saxon Protestant – origins, Hine had already identified America with the Tribe of Manassah. By the end of the First World War, the thinking of men such as Hine, rather like the influenza epidemic of the same period, had found its way across the Atlantic. The deterioration of British exports is by no means a modern phenomenon.

Modern American fundamentalism rests on premises that are often startling in their anachronism, their credulity and their naïvety. The Bible is held to be immutable as it stands, the indisputable and unalterable word of God, as if councils such as Nicaea had never occurred, and as if there were not alternative gospels. Nothing has ever been, or can ever be, added to it or subtracted from it. In its existing form, it contains all the knowledge necessary for individual salvation. In this respect, of course, fundamentalism has much in common with other Christian sects, especially of an evangelical character. But there are certain premises which are specifically fundamentalist.

The first of these is that the United States and the United Kingdom today are to be identified – sometimes symbolically but more often quite literally – with the scattered 'remnants' of ancient Israel. Modern Judaism is believed to derive from the biblical Tribe of Judah, but the descendants of the remaining tribes are deemed to be the white Anglo-Saxon Protestants of Britain and America – and their kindred abroad, in places such as South Africa. These are the new 'elect', the new 'chosen people'.

The second underlying premise of modern fundamentalism is that biblical prophecy is of cardinal importance. Certain specific works are repeatedly cited, notably the Book of Revelation (dating from the late first or early second century A.D.) and the 'classical' prophecies of the Old Testament (dating from between the eighth and fifth centuries B.C.). These works, it is believed, were composed in large part to predict events in the modern world – events 'scheduled' to occur in our own time. Despite numerous documented blunders by Old Testament prophets about their own epoch, they are held to be infallible prognosticators about ours. Even their dire fulminations against each other are lifted out of the original historical context and deemed applicable today. And yet it is worth remembering at least something of the historical context which fundamentalists so cavalierly ignore. Ancient Israel, after all, was a loose-knit, ill-defined and often ungovernable political entity smaller than the county of Yorkshire, or the state of New Jersey – and with a bare fraction of the population of either. It occupied an inconsequential fragment of what, even then, was the known world. And yet the records of its internal wranglings are regarded as an infallible guide to the late twentieth century, in virtually every sphere, from personal conduct to foreign relations. It is rather as if the vision of the future propounded by one member of a Yorkshire council, or the New Jersey legislature, in 1986 were to be used, quite literally, as a means of explaining friction between, say, Canada and China, or even between earth colonies in space, in the fiftieth or sixtieth century.

The third premise underlying modern fundamentalism involves the specific message of certain prophecies. This message, of course, is that the apocalypse is imminent. For the fundamentalist, the world has entered the Last Days, just as it was believed to have done in Jesus's time. The Antichrist will shortly appear (if he has not already done so) and wreak assorted kinds of havoc. A period of 'tribulation' will ensue, culminating in the epic Battle of Armageddon, and the world will be utterly destroyed in some kind of holocaust. After this débâcle, the Second Coming will occur – Jesus will descend in glory from the heavens, the dead will rise from their graves and the new Kingdom will be inaugurated. Needless to say, only the 'elect' or the 'saved' will be granted residence permits.

This, in general, is the prospect envisaged by fundamentalist preachers. At given points here and there, certain of them become more specific. Thus, for example, the Antichrist is often identified with the Soviet Union – the 'evil empire' castigated by Ronald Reagan. One of the wealthiest and most powerful fundamentalist organisations, however, identifies the menacing ten-crowned 'Beast' of the Book of Revelation – that is, the Antichrist – quite precisely as the EEC with its ten member nations.[12] (That they are now twelve is presumably some new, pernicious and devious stratagem on the part of the 'Beast'.) It is predicted that the nations of the EEC will wage war against the United States and the United Kingdom, will defeat them and will then enslave them. Britain and America will become satellites of a new world power based in Europe, and this power will embark on the Third World War[13] – presumably against the Soviet Union. Biblical prophecies are invoked to forecast that the war will last two and a half years and cost the lives of two-thirds of the population of Britain and America, all in order to bring people around to God's way of thinking. 'In this fearful, awesome atomic age, World War III will *start* with nuclear devastation, unleashed on London, Birmingham, Manchester, Liverpool, New York, Washington, Philadelphia, Detroit, Chicago, Pittsburg without warning!'[14] Curiously enough, the major cities on America's West Coast, which would surely seem to qualify as the modern world's Sodom and Gomorrah, are exempted from this catalogue of destructive retribution. But then again, as the Old Testament prophets never mentioned any of the cities in question, there is probably a greater margin for error on the part of the modern interpreter. It was inconsiderate of Jeremiah not to have said anything about Hollywood, thus leaving its residents uncertain of their fate.

At the end of the Third World War, the climactic Battle of Armageddon will be fought somewhere in the Middle East. The Antichrist will appear again – or perhaps it is a different Antichrist – and contend against the forces of God. Since the game has been fixed in advance, God's forces, commanded by Jesus in the role of field-marshal, will naturally emerge triumphant – but the whole affair will have been messy in the extreme. However, if one repents *now*, if one allows oneself to be 'saved' and especially if one makes a financial contribution to the church, one will be spared all the carnage and removed to a place of safety until the turmoil has been resolved. In a variation on this theme, certain fundamentalist preachers speak of a moment in the present generation when the faithful will be 'raptured away'.[15] Without warning, all true believers will suddenly evaporate, dematerialise, disappear in the flicker of an eyelid from their offices, their homes, their golf-courses, their cars (left careering driverless across streets and motorways), and will rocket upwards to a personal interview with Jesus. From a position of shelter amidst his celestial entourage, they will be permitted detachedly to watch the unfolding cataclysm as if it were a football match.

It is, of course, easy enough to scoff at such convictions, compared with which the beliefs of many so-called 'primitive societies' appear downright sophisticated. And yet an extra-ordinary and ever increasing number of people in America today take them quite seriously, and are not only resigned to an imminent apocalypse, but actually, in some sense, look forward to it, in expectation of a blissful eternity in the millennial Kingdom of the Second Coming. Among this number, it has been suggested, is the President of the United States. In an article which appeared both in the Washington *Post* and in the *Guardian*, for example, Ronnie Dugger, a prominent American journalist, writes: ' ... Americans could fairly wonder if their president ... is personally predisposed by fundamentalist theology to expect some kind of Armageddon beginning with a nuclear war in the Middle East'.[16] And, further: 'If a crisis arises in the Middle East and threatens to become a nuclear confrontation, might President Reagan be predisposed to believe that he sees Armageddon coming and that this is the will of God?'[17]

According to the President himself, certain unspecified and unidentified 'theologians' have told him that at no previous occasion in world history were 'so many prophecies coming together'.[18] In a television interview during his campaign for his party's nomination in 1980, he said: 'We may be the generation that sees Armageddon.'[19] During the same campaign, in an address to prominent New York Jews, he is quoted as saying: 'Israel is the only stable democracy we can rely on in a spot where Armageddon could come.'[20]

In 1983, the President stated that when he read the Old Testament prophets and 'the signs foretelling Armageddon', it was difficult for him to avoid pondering the likelihood of the battle occurring in the present generation. Certainly, he added, the ancient prophets had precisely described the times now being experienced by the contemporary world.[21] According to the Washington *Times*, James Mills, a California politician, recalls a conversation in which the President spoke at length about Armageddon. After quoting from the prophecies of Ezekiel, he is reported to have said: 'Everything's falling into place. It can't be long now.'[22]

In a letter to us, dated March 1986, Ronnie Dugger declares: ' ... I am now convinced that his Armageddon ideology lies at the root of his foreign and military-nuclear policies toward the Soviet Union.' Dugger's conclusion, ironically, was anticipated by Jerry Falwell, one of the most prominent fundamentalist preachers, and president of America's self-styled 'Moral Majority' (now absorbed by the 'Liberty Federation'), which played an important role in Reagan's election campaigns: 'Reagan is a fine man. He believes what the Moral Majority believes, what God tells us.'[23] When questioned by an interviewer on whether the President endorsed biblical prophecy as a guide to the future, Falwell replied: 'Yes, he does. He told me, back in the campaign ... "Jerry, I sometimes believe we're headed very fast for Armageddon right now."'[24]

The President is not alone in appearing to think in terms of an approaching Armageddon. At Harvard University, Casper Weinberger was asked if he expected the end of the world and, if so, whether by man's hand or God's. Weinberger replied that he was familiar with biblical prophecy, '... and yes, I believe the world is going to end – by an act of God, I hope – but every day I think that time is running out'.[25] The American writer Christopher Reed reports that Weinberger actually stated where he thought Arma-

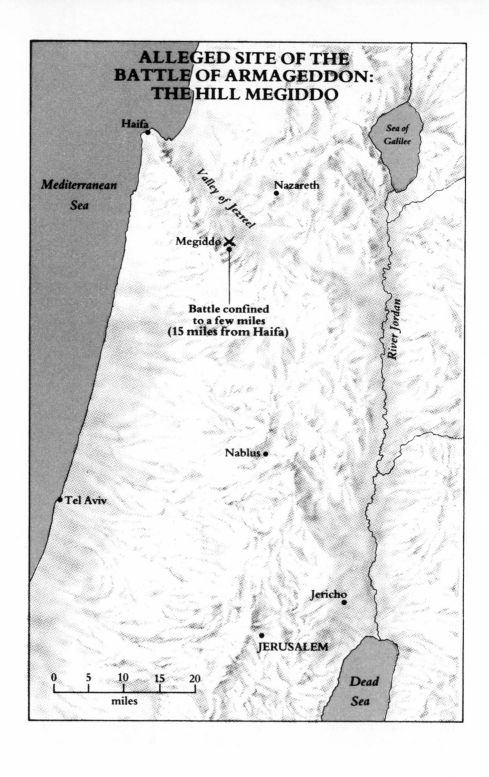

ALLEGED SITE OF THE
BATTLE OF ARMAGEDDON:
THE HILL MEGIDDO

Haifa

Mediterranean
Sea

Sea of
Galilee

Valley of Jezreel

Nazareth

Megiddo ✗

Battle confined
to a few miles
(15 miles from Haifa)

River Jordan

Nablus

Tel Aviv

Jericho

JERUSALEM

0   5   10   15   20
miles

Dead
Sea

geddon would occur. He named the hill of Megiddo, some fifteen miles south-east of Haifa, in Israel[26] – though he did not clarify how a conflict of such cosmic proportions could be confined to so circumscribed an area. Unless he envisages Ronald Reagan and Mikhail Gorbachov duelling in single combat with laser-swords out of *Star Wars*.

Another apparent adherent of apocalyptic thinking would seem to be James Watt, former Secretary of the Interior in Reagan's cabinet and noted for making statements comparable in finesse to a dropped drawer of silverware. To a White House committee, Watt declared: 'I do not know how many future generations we can count on before the Lord returns.'[27] And Simon Winchester, in the *Sunday Times*, reports a conversation with a senior aide to an American senator, who is quoted as saying: 'Dozens of young men and women on Capitol Hill, in the Pentagon, in the various departments of government, insist that we are the generation who will be lucky enough to see Christ return.'[28] Admiral James Watkins, Chief of United States Naval Operations, has, in public speeches, blamed Lebanese suicide-bombings on 'the forces of Antichrist', while General John Vessey, Head of the Joint Chiefs of Staff, urges young men to 'enlist in God's Army'. At a breakfast meeting, he is reported to have got so carried away by Messianic fervour as to have begun leading cheers of 'Hurrah for God!'[29]

Again, all this would be laughable if it were not so ominous. The underlying premises of fundamentalism all conduce to make mass self-immolation morally and theologically acceptable, even desirable. The Muslim fundamentalist in Lebanon, whom Admiral Watkins brands an agent of the Antichrist, is thoroughly convinced that, in destroying his enemies along with himself, he is striking a blow against his version of 'Satan' – and, in the process, earning an express ticket to Paradise. The Christian fundamentalist is convinced of exactly the same thing, from a diametrically opposed point of view. Each is a mirror image of the other and each, when backed into a corner, will react in the same way. But if a man has his finger on a nuclear button, his act of self-immolation in the name of his God will drag the whole of humanity with him.

Even apart from Armageddon, the prevailing image for the fundamentalist is the image of war, rationalised and justified as a crusade. Among the casualties already incurred in this war have been books. If the printed word can serve to convey the will of God, it can also, the fundamentalist believes, convey the will of God's adversary. In consequence, the last few years have witnessed a new wave of censorship in the United States. In communities in more than thirty American states, major works of both fiction and non-fiction have been banned – not only from schools, school curricula and school libraries, but from public libraries as well, so that not even adults have access to them. All of this is part of what the fundamentalist 'Liberty Federation', formerly the 'Moral Majority', describes as its crusade against the 'religion of secular humanism'. In theory, the only grounds for acting against a book are supposed to be obscenity, pornography or 'unsuitability for minors'. In practice, books have been condemned for sexual explicitness (even in biology texts), for the depiction of 'unorthodox family arrangements', for unflattering representations of American authority, for criticism of business and corporate ethics, for questionable political ideas and for 'speculation about Christ'. The list of works to have come under attack includes *Slaughterhouse-Five* by Kurt Vonnegut, *Soul on Ice* by Eldridge Cleaver, *The Naked Ape* by Desmond Morris, *The Bell Jar* by Sylvia Plath, *Goodbye Columbus* and *Portnoy's Complaint* by Philip Roth, *Jaws* by Peter Benchley, *The Abortion* and other novels by Richard Brautigan, *Manchild in the Promised Land* by Claude Brown, *Kramer vs. Kramer* by Avery Corman, *The Godfather* by Mario Puzo, *Catch-22* by Joseph Heller, *1984* by George Orwell, *Brave New World* by Aldous Huxley, *The Grapes of Wrath* by John Steinbeck, *The Art of Loving* by Erich Fromm, *The Electric Kool-Aid Acid Test* by Tom Wolfe, *Lord of the Flies* by William Golding, *A Farewell to Arms* by Ernest Hemingway, *The Catcher in the Rye* by J. D. Salinger, established nineteenth-century classics by Mark Twain, Robert Louis Stevenson, Nathaniel Hawthorne and Edgar Allan Poe, and (most perplexingly) *One Day in the Life of Ivan Denisovich* by Aleksandr Solzhenitsyn – not to mention *The American Heritage Dictionary* and *The Dictionary of American Slang*.

As we have said, fundamentalists see themselves as engaged in a war against the Antichrist, whom they usually regard as embodied by Communism and the Soviet Union. And yet, paradoxically, the consequences of many fundamentalist policies tend to further precisely the objectives of the very 'Antichrist' they purport to oppose. By advocating American isolationism, for example, and by issuing dire pronouncements about the EEC, fundamentalism is in effect seeking to alienate the United States from her most important allies, driving a wedge into NATO. By proscribing books such as those listed above, fundamentalism is in effect alienating America herself from her own cultural heritage and her own most intelligent citizens – if not, indeed, from intelligence in general. No calculated programme could possibly be more congenial to the aims of the KGB. One could reasonably argue that fundamentalism is in fact doing the KGB's work for it.

The Absurdity of Apocalypse

Despite two thousand years of having 'been saved', the world today is not an appreciably safer, saner or more humane place than it was in Jesus's time, nor is man appreciably more responsible or mature. To say so is not, of course, to asperse Christianity or its validity on the level of individual faith. On the level of historical fact, however, there can be little dispute that Jesus, as 'saviour', has proved a signal failure. That, naturally, is hardly his fault, for he had no intention of functioning as 'saviour' in the sense subsequently ascribed to him. But for two thousand years, people have foisted an impossible expectation upon him and sought rationalisations to explain his incapacity to fulfil it. Someone or something has been sought to shoulder the blame for their disappointment.

In this respect, very little has changed, very few 'lessons of history' have been learned, and the mentality which obtained during the Last Days of the first century is as vigorous as ever. Now, as then, it is impossible to ignore the realisation that something is grievously amiss. Now, as then, there is the instinctive assumption that, since God cannot possibly be to blame, humanity must be. In consequence, now, as then, there is a pervasive sense of guilt. But the guilt is transferred, projected on to others whose values and attitudes differ from one's own and can therefore safely be labelled 'sinful'. It is *other people* who are to blame, not oneself. And it is not the world that one seeks to 'save', nor other people's souls, but one's own. The rest of humanity is complacently abandoned to suffer the fate which the guilty conscience secretly fears for itself. 'To hell with the wicked,' one proclaims as a watchword, 'but not me.'

We spoke earlier about the distinction between tribal and archetypal myths. We discussed how archetypal myths lead one inwards towards self-confrontation and a recognition of what men share, while tribal myths, by manufacturing a scapegoat to serve as 'adversary', lead one outwards towards self-aggrandisement, self-glorification, conflict and an emphasis on differences. Any myth, as we said, can itself become either tribal or archetypal, depending on which aspects of it are stressed and on the way in which it is used. In its essential character, the mythology of Christianity is archetypal. It is in this archetypal dimension that Christianity's most profound validity ultimately lies. Whether one subscribes to Jesus's divinity or not, his story, as it is related in his teachings, in the Gospels and in the Acts of the Apostles, is a reservoir of archetypal implications. On this level, Christianity has much to teach – about the nature and meaning of sacrifice, about the relation of humanity to its gods, about personal integrity, about the loneliness of the visionary, about the incompatibility of spiritual aspirations with the mundane world, about decency, charity, forgiveness, humanity and a host of other values which represent or reflect man at his best. When these aspects of Christianity are emphasised – as they are, to take but one example, by a woman such as Mother Theresa – Christianity itself becomes archetypal, something that addresses and encompasses the whole of humankind. It becomes a genuine religion in the strict sense of that word, conferring meaning on the welter of experience, fostering understanding, leading not only to knowledge but to a very real wisdom – wisdom about oneself, about others, about the world.

On the other hand, it is equally possible to emphasise the tribal aspects of Christianity – the elements that encourage an autocratic impulse to impose one's values on others, that encourage an élite conviction of one's own superiority, that encourage a sense of self-righteousness, sanctimoniousness and complacency. This is the orientation of American fundamentalism and its kindred beliefs abroad. Fundamentalism rests not on the acknowledged Christian virtues of charity, forgiveness and understanding, but on war – on an imaginary epic conflict between the self-styled 'forces of God' and those of His adversary. Reality is reduced to a simple matter of 'us' and 'them'. The creed defines itself by virtue of its opposite, defines its adherents by everything and everyone that they are not. Whatever seems opposed to certain basic tenets – not of Jesus usually, but of the congregation and its own idiosyncratic interpretations of scripture – is, *ipso facto*, damned.

By dint of this process, Christianity is in effect drained of its universal applicability. It becomes, instead, merely a ratification of something much more parochial. Christianity is in effect made synonymous with the values of Middle America; God is perceived as a patron of, say, Peoria, Illinois, and such places come to be seen as blueprints, so to speak, for Paradise. Dostoevsky's famous parable of the Grand Inquisitor becomes, if anything, even more apt than when *The Brothers Karamazov* was written just over a century ago. Were Jesus indeed to return, to appear on the streets of Peoria and begin preaching, he would immediately be arrested as (among other things) unAmerican and subversive. Even if he were recognised and identified, he would have to be bundled away, muzzled and suppressed. There is no question that, at very least, he would be an acute embarrassment to the creed promulgated in his name. As a social, cultural and political institution, that creed could not risk being compromised by his presence, or, more likely, publicly repudiated by him.

But although there is much about modern fundamentalism that Jesus himself – the historical Jesus *or* the Jesus of faith – would find horrifying, appalling, downright blasphemous and positively immoral by his own tenets, there is one thing, at any rate, that he would recognise and find familiar. This is the Messianic anticipation, the apocalyptic hysteria reminiscent of the Last Days in which he lived. Thus, in an almost quaintly simplistic fashion – a fashion two thousand years old and long left behind by historical developments – do a great many modern Americans seek to impart meaning to the contemporary world. The mere fact that they can do so reflects the paucity of other alternatives, other principles for imparting coherence to a reality which seems to be running out of control.

As we have noted, apocalyptic hysteria can perform a functional role, imparting a governing myth to an epoch and some sort of meaning to an otherwise fragmented reality. Certainly it has done so in the past, with – depending on circumstances – greater or lesser efficacy. But we cannot afford to let it become the governing myth of our epoch, because, as we also noted before, humanity today is perfectly capable of creating its own apocalypse, its own Armageddon, and of passing responsibility for the débâcle on to God. If the hysteria of American fundamentalism is allowed to become a self-fulfilling prophecy, adopted or embraced as high up as the White House, the result could well be, quite literally, the end of the world – not in a rapturous return of long-dead Zadokites skipping hand-in-hand through Elysian fields, but in the slow breathless agony of a nuclear winter. That we, as authors, can actually write of such a prospect without feeling ourselves over-dramatic is a measure of the extent to which humanity as a whole has come to accept, even to expect, the possibility of mass suicide. If that is the only meaning to be found in the modern age, humanity is indeed bankrupt, and God – however He may be conceived denominationally – has simply been wasting His time.

And yet one must be more precise. It is not, ultimately, a question of 'humanity destroying itself'. 'Humanity' has no desire to do any such thing. If 'mankind' is destroyed, it will not be by 'man', but by a handful of specific individuals whose power, derived from the trust reposed in them, has been mishandled and abused. The Arabs, 'en masse', do not wish to destroy Israel, nor did the Israelis, 'en masse', wish to occupy Lebanon. The Argentinians did not collectively decide to invade the Falkland Islands, nor the Russians Afghanistan, nor the Americans to wage war in Vietnam. Nor, for that matter, do the Americans 'en masse' stand behind every act of Ronald Reagan, the Russians behind every act of Mikhail Gorbachov, the British behind every act of Margaret Thatcher, the French behind every act of François Mitterrand. It is not ultimately 'humanity', but a frighteningly small conclave of political figures – some more or less 'democratically elected', some not – who wield the authority of life and death over the entire planet. Some of them are intelligent and responsible, but some are unimaginative, insensitive, even positively stupid. Some are manifestly incompetent. Some are arguably insane, to one or another degree. Yet it is they who, with a signature appended to a document, or even with a single spoken word, can send individuals into battle, can determine people's nationalities, can dictate the circumstances in which one lives, can pronounce where one can go or cannot go, what one can do or cannot do. It is they who, for example, by drawing a line on a paper map, can conjure a 'frontier' into being, a barrier as restrictive and insurmountable as any physical wall. They can even order the construction of a physical wall to mark the fictitious 'frontiers' they have invented. And it is they, not 'humanity' who, if there is indeed to be an apocalypse, will bring it about.

There is, needless to say, something monstrously absurd about this situation. There is something intrinsically *wrong*, in the most profound moral sense of the word, about such people, and so small a number of people, being allowed not just to represent but actually to determine the future of 'mankind' – especially when they have so consistently failed to demonstrate their aptitude or qualification for that task. At the same time, there is hardly likely to be any change in the existing state of affairs. Many regimes, past and present, do not allow the luxury of choice; and even where choice has existed, it has often existed only between different forms of mediocrity. In the Western 'democracies', we have come increasingly to accept our helplessness, rather as we accept the vicissitudes of climate. The more remote and inaccessible government becomes, the more it assumes the inexorable character of a force of nature. One acquiesces, grumbling, in a drought in meaning and in 'spirit' just as one acquiesces in a drought caused by weather.

But where one is fortunate enough to enjoy at least some voice in the matter, one should not, by silence, sanction ineptitude. Even droughts (or famines) caused by weather can be assuaged, as demonstrated by, say, Bob Geldof's 'Live-Aid' crusade – a valid crusade, preached on behalf of what humanity as a whole shares, rather than on tribal differences and scapegoat adversaries. If we can muster the energy exemplified by 'Live-Aid' to cope with the enormity of a 'natural disaster', are we not capable of mobilising a similar effort to cope with the disasters we, by our own negligence, have created in our own affairs? This does not, of course, mean 'revolutions', strikes, marches, petitions or other 'mass movements' based essentially on slogans – slogans as hollow as the political rhetoric they purport to oppose. It means assuming personal responsibility for the creation and dissemination of meaning.

Most political and religious leaders today are themselves frightened, uncertain, lacking their own sense of meaning. Many of them can offer only facile substitutes for meaning to their followers. If we accept such substitutes uncritically, we will remain trapped in our own helplessness. If trust is granted in too careless and too profligate a fashion, it will be betrayed, and power will be aggrandised at the expense of those who, through their trust, conferred it. It is time individuals assumed the responsibility of creating meaning for themselves, from within themselves, not passively accepting second-hand surrogates. The more we come to make our own decisions, the less latitude there will be for others to make them for us.

At the same time, we, as authors, recognise that such exhortations have been made 'from time immemorial', and have not served to change anything. We are not so naïve as to think our own exhortations might fare any more successfully. Society will continue to desire its realities, and the meaning of its realities, to be pre-fabricated. Society will continue to seek short cuts. Society will continue to avail itself of one or another 'crutch'. This being the case, it is a matter of choosing one's 'crutches' wisely. What remains to be established is the kind of crutch – assuming there to be one – that the Prieuré de Sion might have to offer.

THREE
The Cabal

17

Fragments in the Post

Even while *The Holy Blood and the Holy Grail* was in production, new information was forthcoming – information which could be included only as last-minute notes in the book, or not included at all. Some of this information derived from the Prieuré de Sion's own sources, particularly from a series of pamphlets by the Marquis Philippe de Chérisey. Some of it derived from our own research. Some of it was contributed by other individuals who, being privy to our project, had undertaken enquiries of their own and offered their conclusions to us.

After publication, the influx of information began to assume torrential proportions. Material issuing from the Prieuré de Sion became markedly more focused, less diffuse. Our own research, of course, continued. And some of our readers were quick to offer such data as they happened to possess. Indeed, the sheer quantity of mail surprised us and we were delighted by its general tenor. The bulk of it was intelligent, reasoned and thoughtful; and there were letters which contained genuinely new and valuable fragments of evidence, culled from a multitude of diverse sources.

Needless to say, however, the publication also inaugurated an unscheduled silly season, and some of the more eccentric letters we received might well merit a book of their own. At least a dozen self-proclaimed Messiahs hastened to contact us, for reasons which none of them satisfactorily clarified. One of them staged a sullen sit-in in our publisher's offices. Another sent us a photograph of himself apparently suspended in mid-air and clinging to a football post – 'to keep from drifting away'. A third enclosed a genealogy intended to establish his descent not only from Jesus, but from Robin Hood as well. 'I'm the person you're looking for,' several of them declared, although we were unaware that we had been looking for anyone. Still others, engaged in the perennial game of

'Spot the Antichrist', pronounced us to be his avatar(s). Some fulminated imprecations, charging us not only with blasphemy, but also with responsibility for assorted social and moral ills, from unemployment to nudist beaches. Some demanded, either courteously or bumptiously, one or another kind of 'rightful due' – a share of some imagined 'treasure', a percentage of our royalties or, in one instance, simply an unspecified 'piece of the action'. Some requested official acknowledgment from us, or recognition, or certification or stamp of approval. Amidst the importunities of candidates for Messiahship, it was refreshing to receive one letter from God himself, who wrote to us from an English coastal town. His mundane name, he informed us, was Ian. Although a little ragged in his spelling, he was commendably restrained – and, on the whole, rather more congenial than certain public figures who aspire to godhood under one or another altruistic guise.

In addition to the self-proclaimed Messiahs, there were numerous correspondents claiming a Merovingian pedigree, usually on the basis of a surname derived or derivable from something French – or, in one case, on the basis of an illegible eighteenth-century parchment which eventually proved to be a document ratifying someone's commission in the army of Louis XV. Some of these neo-Merovingians also demanded a share of whatever 'treasure' might be involved, declaring it to be rightfully theirs, and one insisted that we help him promulgate his claim to the French throne. Others merely requested an introduction to the Prieuré de Sion and its Grand Master, Pierre Plantard de Saint-Clair.

We were also badgered by treasure-hunters and by occultists. The former had been thronging the vicinity of Rennes-le-Château with all manner of equipment, from metal detectors down to spades. To our knowledge, they found nothing but holes in the ground, and some of them undoubtedly created new ones. Several people wrote to us, or contacted us through intermediaries, to announce that they had discovered a cave. Given the fact that the region is a veritable honeycomb of caves, abandoned mines and subterranean passages, such discoveries afforded circumscribed grounds for triumph.

On one occasion, we were ourselves exploring the overgrown ruins of some ancient buildings, perhaps fragments of a Roman or even pre-Roman temple, which lay in a particularly inaccessible part of the area. We had paused to brew a cup of coffee on a small solid-fuel burner. Suddenly, from the steep forested slope of the hill below, we heard a ferocious crashing in the undergrowth, drawing steadily nearer. It proved to be two elderly yet fit gentlemen, one of them wielding a vicious machete and holding in front of him an ancient brass compass which might have been part of the kit issue for the Maginot Line. Glancing at us perfunctorily, they passed and continued briskly upwards into the forest, hacking their way through the welter of vegetation, intent not on mere ruins but on something else – bearings, presumably, which they hoped would lead to some sort of 'treasure'. Later that afternoon, we encountered them again. This time they paused to chat. They had indeed, they confirmed, spent years slogging through the surrounding mountains and forests in search of 'treasure'. They had used all sorts of equipment, including metal detectors and walkie-talkies. They had crawled hundreds of yards down ancient Roman mine-passages, constantly threatened by the collapse of a roof in places no more than two feet high. They had braved precipices, crevices and sheer cliffs. They had rummaged their way through innumerable caves. To date, their endeavour had led them to nothing more dramatic than the bones of a goat in the rubble of an old mine. Although they cheerfully admitted this, they remained undeterred, and soon set off again on their tenacious quest.

As for the occultists, they refused to believe that we were not privy to some arcane mystical secret which we had deliberately withheld from our readers, scattering only a few portentous clues here and there for the 'initiated'. Then, too, there was a letter from one self-styled 'magician' who – declaring he had learned his craft from a certain illustrious mentor (whose name meant nothing to us) – offered, on the basis of our commendable enterprise, to accept us as his apprentices. A week later, we received a letter from this man's illustrious mentor, who asked if he could become our apprentice. Had we endeavoured to establish our own cult, coven or secret society, there would have been no shortage of recruits.

There were, too, numerous people who, quite inexplicably, persisted in confronting us with the Shroud of Turin. 'What about the Shroud of Turin?' we were asked repeatedly. (What indeed?) Or, 'How does the Shroud of Turin affect your thesis?' It was extraordinary how frequently this *non sequitur* occurred. It is true, of course, that one of us was associated with David Rolfe's award-winning film on the Shroud, *The Silent Witness*, and wrote the screenplay for it. It is true, too, that the evidence suggests the Shroud to have been, at one time, in the possession of the Knights Templar. But apart from this, the Shroud had no bearing whatever on our material. Whatever it proves or disproves is still, at present, undecided. And whatever it might ultimately be found to prove or disprove has no relevance to Jesus's political activity, or to the possibility of a bloodline descended from him.

There were also letters which defied classification. One example came from a woman in the United States who had seen the phrase 'Et in Arcadia Ego' flashed on her television screen – a trailer for the American transmission of *Brideshead Revisited*. Our correspondent was convinced that, by means of subliminal messages on the airwaves, the Prieuré de Sion were launching an attempt to brainwash Western civilisation.

On the whole, however, this kind of thing was an exception to the rule. Most of the letters we received were lucid, serious and, even when critical of us, still well reasoned. And not a few of them contributed genuinely valuable snippets of information.

The Holy Blood and the Holy Grail also seemed to spawn a modest cottage industry for publishers on the subject of Rennes-le-Château. Within a few weeks of our book's appearance, a slim but glossy and lavishly illustrated volume was rushed into print in France. Entitled *Rennes-le-Château: capitale secrète de l'histoire de France*, this work was published in an edition of 200,000 copies and sold on news-stands, like a magazine. A number of individuals associated with the Prieuré de Sion had a hand in its production. According to some statements, the arrangement of photographs in the work constituted a ciphered message. If so, no one as yet appears to have deciphered it.

In English, there appeared a slender volume entitled *The Holy Grail Revealed*, whose blurb proclaimed it to be a 'scathing rebuttal' of our work. In fact, it neither scathed nor rebutted. On the contrary, it merely suggested, rather tentatively, that the Grail might be a concrete object of some kind – perhaps a strange artefact or 'power source' created by some 'ancient, long-forgotten technology' which had been brought to earth by a spaceship.

A somewhat similar approach was adopted in *The Sign of the Dove* by Elizabeth van Buren, who presented herself as something of a neo-Zoroastrian and our book as a gloss on the cosmic battle between light and darkness. Jesus, the Merovingian Dynasty and its descendants were portrayed as conscious agents of the forces of light. The headquarters of these forces apparently lay ultimately in some trans-galactic sphere. The mythical sea-creature called a 'quinotaurus', which figures in legends about the Merovingians, was, according to Elizabeth van Buren, 'almost certainly an extra-terrestrial astronaut who had touched down in one of the oceans of this globe'.

In another slender volume, *Rebirth of a Planet*, Ruth Leedy displayed a different preoccupation. Her book was sent to us with a printed form letter announcing that the recipient – in this case, ourselves – had been 'carefully selected' to help end 'the greatest and most pernicious cover-up of our time'. This cover-up consisted of a conspiracy, on the part of established authorities, to conceal the truth of the so-called 'Hollow Earth Theory'. In her text, the authoress argued that we, in our own book, could be seen – if one read 'between the lines' – as proponents of the theory in question. Much of her logic derived from a close critical analysis of the poem by Jehan l'Ascuiz which we used as the dedication for *The Holy Blood and the Holy Grail*.

Finally, in an opulently produced work entitled *Genisis* (*sic*), David Wood combined some rigorous geometric calculation with numerology, Egyptian mythology, skeins of sundry esoteric traditions and Platonic references to Atlantis. Using these as if they were a Rorschach test, he proceeded to adduce evidence that Rennes-le-Château bore witness to the historical existence of Atlantis, as well as a species of 'super-race' – extra-terrestrial – from which mankind was descended.

For our part, we were baffled by the apparent compulsion that seemed to drive so many people into the nether realms of science fiction. So far as we were concerned, the mysteries with which we were dealing lay wholly within the sphere of human history. The fact that there was no documented explanation for some of them did not sanction a quantum leap of faith into some other dimension. Certainly we have never encountered any evidence in our research to suggest the involvement of anything or anyone other than man. That so many people want so urgently to believe in the intervention of something superhuman – whether galactic visitors or secret masters in the Himalayas – seems, in our opinion, further testimony of the contemporary crisis in meaning. As organised religion and its dogmatic conceptions of God continue to lose credibility, individuals begin to seek a 'higher intelligence' elsewhere – across the galaxy, if need be. It is as if, feeling abandoned by the deities of the past, they were impelled out of sheer panic to fabricate a new form of reassurance that 'we are not alone'. It is precisely this kind of 're-channelling' of the religious impulse into science fiction that accounts for the popularity of such films as *Star Wars*, with its mystical, quasi-Taoist 'Force', and *Close Encounters of the Third Kind*. Once again, people look outwards for solutions, when they should be looking within themselves.

An Invisible Editor

As we have said, a number of the letters we received contained fragments of genuine consequence. Our investigation of some of these fragments led us, on occasion, into intriguing territory, albeit of a highly specialised nature. Not surprisingly, however, the most provocative body of new material was to come from the Prieuré de Sion itself, or from sources directly or indirectly associated with that Order.

Towards the latter part of 1981, for example, we received several packets of documents from the Marquis de Chérisey, a close friend and associate of the Grand Master of the Prieuré de Sion. Some of Chérisey's material was of purely historical interest, referring to specific events or personages cited in the book we had just finished. But there were other items of a more contemporary character and a more immediate relevance. One of these items referred specifically to the parchments allegedly found by Bérenger Saunière in the church of Rennes-le-Château in 1891. We had heard conflicting stories about what became of these documents, but all of them were too vague to be checked. Although it subsequently became clear that Chérisey had not seen them personally, he at least offered what appeared to be some tangible clues. According to Chérisey, the clues in question were confided to him by an aged aristocrat, Henri, Comte de Lenoncourt. Speaking of Saunière's discovery, Lenoncourt is reported by Chérisey as saying:

> Saunière found it – and never parted with it. His niece, Madame James of Montazels, inherited it in February, 1917. In 1965, she sold it to the International League of Antiquarian Booksellers. She was not to know that one of the two respectable lawyers was Captain Ronald Stansmore of the British Intelligence Service and the other was Sir Thomas Frazer, the 'eminence grise' of Buckingham [*sic*]. The parchments of Blanche de Castille are presently in a strongbox of Lloyds Bank Europe Limited. Since the article in the *Daily Express*, a paper with a circulation of 3,000,000, nobody in Britain is unaware of the demand for the recognition of Merovingian rights made in 1955 and 1956 by Sir Alexander Aikman, Sir John Montague Brocklebank, Major Hugh Murchison Clowes and nineteen other men in the office of P. F. J. Freeman, Notary by Royal Appointment.[1]

As our research developed, all these names were to assume an increasingly large significance. It also later became apparent that

Chérisey (or Lenoncourt) had got some of his data, and at least one name, muddled. Nevertheless, he had provided us with something tangible to pursue, even if its full relevance was not immediately clear. He also provided us with something even more intriguing, and more perplexing.

In 1979, when we had first met Pierre Plantard de Saint-Clair, the rendezvous had been arranged by a researcher for the BBC, a journalist who lived in Paris named Jania Macgillivray. At our first encounter with the representatives of the Prieuré de Sion, Jania had been present. She was also present during the filming of our programme for the BBC's *Chronicle*, transmitted in the autumn of 1979 as *The Shadow of the Templars*.

During the late summer of 1979, while *The Shadow of the Templars* was still being edited, Jania had written an article from her own point of view. With a somewhat sceptical but intrigued journalistic detachment, she described her role as intermediary and conducted her own independent interviews with such representatives of the Prieuré de Sion as would speak to her. One copy of her article she submitted to a press agency, who passed it on to a French magazine, *Bonne Soirée*, for translation into French and possible publication. Another copy, in the original English version, was sent to us care of our BBC producer – who, for reasons best known to himself, never forwarded it to us. In consequence, we did not know what Jania had said, or even that she had written an article, until the Marquis de Chérisey sent us a French translation of it in 1981. The French text proved to be astonishing. We contacted Jania and were able to confirm what we already suspected – that a hand other than hers had been at work.

For the first eleven of the article's twelve pages, the French text – though it included a number of brief additions – conformed more or less to what Jania had written in English. But the last page was not Jania's at all. According to the title page, the English version had been translated into French by one Robert Suffert – whom, despite much effort, we have so far been unable to trace. Both *Bonne Soirée* and the press agency, as well as Jania, denied having any record or knowledge of him. It is not even clear whether Suffert actually exists, or whether his name is a pseudonym – perhaps for the Marquis de Chérisey himself. Nor is it clear whether the alterations to Jania's text were made by Suffert or by someone else. In any case, the last page of Jania's article had been the work of an entirely strange hand. Neither we nor she have been able to establish when a perfectly innocent article submitted to a French magazine can have been thus doctored.

One major point of interest in the doctored text pertained to a question which had perplexed us for some time – namely, the identity of the Prieuré de Sion's Grand Master between 1963 and 1981. According to the Prieuré's own statements and documents, Jean Cocteau had presided as Grand Master from 1918 until his death in 1963. In 1981, Pierre Plantard de Saint-Clair had been elected Grand Master, and this was reported in the French press at the time. But who had presided in between – during the crucial period, that is, when word of the Prieuré's existence and many of its own documents were being 'leaked' piecemeal to the public? In 1979, we had been told that the Grand Master was an influential French belle lettrist and ecclesiastic, the Abbé François Ducaud-Bourget. This suggestion raised all sorts of perplexing questions and contradictions, particularly as Ducaud-Bourget himself had denied any such involvement, both to us and to an interviewer from *Bonne Soirée*. And the Marquis de Chérisey, in a letter to us, stated that Ducaud-Bourget had not been elected 'by a full quorum', and had subsequently disqualified himself anyway.

The interpolated last page of Jania's article partially answered the question of the Prieuré de Sion's Grand Mastership between 1963 and 1981:

> It is not known who is the present Grand Master, though it is believed that, since Cocteau's death, power has been exercised by a triumvirate consisting of Gaylord Freeman, Pierre Plantard and Antonio Merzagora.

According to the elusive translator and editor of Jania's article, then, there had in effect been no single Grand Master during the eighteen years that so interested us. On the contrary, the Grand Master's responsibilities had apparently been discharged by three people. At the time, the names of Gaylord Freeman and Antonio Merzagora meant nothing to us. Merzagora's still doesn't. Gaylord Freeman's name, however, was soon to assume paramount significance.

Perhaps the most important addition to the doctored text of Jania's article was a quote from an individual cited only as 'Lord Blackford'. Jania had never interviewed him, never met him, never even heard of him. As amended, however, her text stated that she had done all three:

> A few years ago, I was able to have an interview with one of the 121 high-ranking members of the Prieuré de Sion, the Honourable Lord Blackford.

In the statement ascribed to him which follows, Blackford appears unusually knowledgeable, as well as unusually forthcoming, about the Prieuré de Sion. He even hints at a potentially major schism within the Order dating from 1955 or 1956:

> An association called the Prieuré de Sion was indeed constituted in France around 1956, with specific objectives. It had a legal existence, it was registered in the *Journal officiel*, it was dissolved after the events in France of 1958, when Plantard de Saint-Clair was Secretary General of the Committees for Public Safety. This new organisation of 1956 reflected an internal crisis in the venerable Sionis Prioratus, founded around 1099 in Jerusalem. It was the reforms of Jean Cocteau in 1955 which caused the creation [of the new organisation] by denying members of the Order their anonymity. At that time, all members were compelled to furnish a birth certificate and a notarised signature. A necessity perhaps ... but an infringement of freedom.

When we first read this statement, in 1981, Blackford's name, like Antonio Merzagora's and Gaylord Freeman's, was wholly unknown to us. Nor, at the time, was the significance of his assertion apparent. But both Blackford and the words ascribed to him were soon to become relevant indeed.

Conversation with M. Plantard

While working on our book, we had not revealed any of its content to those representatives of the Prieuré de Sion with whom we had contact. We could not anticipate their reaction, but had every reason to believe it would not be entirely sympathetic. We might, for all we knew, have divulged things the Prieuré did not want divulged; we might even have upset some timetable to which the Order had implied it was working.

Once the book was finished, however, we were naturally enough curious to see what the Prieuré's response would be. We even jokingly wondered whether M. Plantard, M. Chérisey or some of the other individuals named as possible blood descendants of Jesus might attempt some sort of legal action. On what basis? For libel? Could it be construed as libellous to suggest of a person that he is descended from Jesus? If nothing else, we might create some sort of weird legal precedent. And, in the process, make 'Merovingian' a household word.

Our first reactions from the Prieuré were not just ambiguous, but surprisingly uncoordinated. In 1979, when we had first met M. Plantard, our contact had been the writer Jean-Luc Chaumeil – who was not, as he himself declared, a member of the Order. By the time our book appeared, M. Chaumeil was no longer on the scene, and the role of the Prieuré's ambassador was now being discharged by another writer, Louis Vazart. M. Vazart visited a friend of ours in Paris. Stating that he was conveying M. Plantard's views, he declared M. Plantard to be 'pleased'. But while M. Vazart was thus endorsing the book, we received a signally rude letter from M. Chérisey and a haughtily irate one from M. Plantard. The latter was particularly disturbed by the fact that we had got his coat-of-arms wrong. We had reproduced the motto on his coat-of-arms as 'Et in Arcadia Ego'. In fact, M. Plantard pointed out, those words should have been followed by three dots: 'Et in Arcadia Ego ... '. On one level, of course, this objection could be construed as petty. On another level, however, it offered us an intriguing clue. With three dots after it, the enigmatic phrase became, as M. Plantard stated, the beginning of a sentence.

We were not, of course, prepared to censor, amend or adjust our book in accordance with the Prieuré de Sion's dictates. On the other hand, we had no objections to M. Plantard calling our attention to any errors we might have made regarding the Order, so that we could correct them for future and/or foreign-language editions. Moreover, we had come to like M. Plantard personally during the course of our previous meetings; we had no wish to antagonise him gratuitously. Finally, we wanted an open channel of communication with him for the sake of further research. Accordingly, we decided to undertake some diplomatic fence-mending.

One night in February 1982, we telephoned M. Plantard from London. We were anticipating a haughtily brusque response, more or less along the lines of his letter. To our surprise, M. Plantard was exceedingly cordial and sounded genuinely pleased to hear from us. He reproved us on the same points as in his letter, but in a friendly, almost avuncular fashion. His letter, he intimated, had been an official document, copies of which had been circulated to other members of the Order. In person, he was prepared to be considerably less frosty. Then, to our amused surprise, he complained that the photograph of himself and his son in the book was not very good. We agreed, explaining that it had been taken by our BBC producer during one of our 1979 meetings. M. Plantard offered to send us a better one for subsequent editions. Even Grand

Masters of the Prieuré de Sion, it seemed, could be subject to vanity.

In the two months that followed, we had several further telephone conversations with M. Plantard, while Louis Vazart continued to meet with our associate in Paris. At last, towards the end of March, as publicity attending the release of our book began to subside and we were no longer required to be available for interviews, we arranged to go to Paris for a personal meeting. In the meantime, an article on the book had appeared in *Newsweek*, with quotations from Jean-Luc Chaumeil.[2] Given M. Chaumeil's disappearance from the scene, this rather puzzled us. What was his interest in the affair? With whose or with what authority was he speaking? Louis Vazart reported that M. Chaumeil's statements were not to be taken seriously. M. Chaumeil, he declared emphatically, no longer spoke for the Prieuré de Sion.

In mid April, we met with M. Plantard in Paris. As usual, he was accompanied by an entourage, consisting this time of Louis Vazart and two journalists, Jean-Pierre Deloux and Jacques Bretigny, who had written *Rennes-le-Château: capitale secrète de l'histoire de France*. Needless to say, Jean-Luc Chaumeil was not present. When we enquired about him, Messrs Plantard and Vazart were vague, off-hand, dismissive, at points abusive. There was one garbled reference to M. Chaumeil apparently possessing, and perhaps trying to sell for an exorbitant sum, documents purportedly issuing from the Prieuré de Sion – though no one clarified what these documents might be or how M. Chaumeil had got access to them. And, M. Plantard added, the night we had telephoned to arrange our meeting with him, he had received another call, from someone claiming to be one of us and managing a passable vocal imitation. The caller said he had just arrived in Paris and asked M. Plantard to meet us that same evening at an hotel. As we had just been speaking with him from London, M. Plantard was not deceived. Prompted by curiosity, however, he had dispatched two associates to the designated rendezvous. No sooner had they arrived than the police did so as well, responding to an anonymous telephone call. Someone had rung, warning of a bomb in the vicinity.

We were mystified by the incident. Was there a genuine connection between the fake call to M. Plantard and the bomb scare? If so, to what purpose? M. Plantard speculated that someone perhaps wanted to photograph him at the site of the hoax. But what would that have achieved? Unless there were some dimension to the episode of which we were wholly unaware, it would seem to have been pointless – an act of petty childish spite, causing no real damage, only inconvenience.

At out meeting in April, 1982, M. Plantard adopted an ambivalent attitude towards our book. On the whole, he endorsed it and offered to correct, for the French edition, certain vague or unclear references. At the same time, he would neither confirm nor deny our thesis that the Merovingian bloodline was descended from Jesus. There was no evidence either way, he said non-committally. It was 'all too far in the past', all 'too long ago'. There were no reliable genealogies. Besides, Jesus had brothers. Nevertheless, he acknowledged the Merovingians to have been of Judaic descent, deriving from the royal line of David.

M. Plantard also challenged our suggestions pertaining to the Prieuré de Sion's involvement in contemporary politics. The Prieuré de Sion, he declared flatly, had no political ambitions. Had it not, we asked, had such ambitions in the past?

'In the past, yes,' M. Plantard acknowledged, 'but not today. Today the Prieuré de Sion's objectives are philosophical.'

'What does that mean?' we asked. 'Is politics determined by philosophy or philosophy by politics?'

'Politics by philosophy, of course,' M. Plantard declared with an ironic smile.

In the course of this meeting, two other fragments of interest emerged. At one point, M. Plantard mentioned, almost casually, in passing, that emissaries of Heinrich Himmler, during the war, had offered him the title of Duke of Brittany if he would pledge allegiance to the Third Reich. M. Plantard had declined the offer. Instead, as we shall see, he edited a curious publication called *Vaincre*, which has been described as a 'Resistance journal'; and he is said, too, to have been imprisoned and tortured by the Gestapo. But why, if his assertion were true, should he have been offered the duchy of Brittany? The very suggestion might at first seem to be absurd. In fact, however, it is not altogether implausible. Certainly the SS did envisage the eventual creation of a state of its own, based upon the medieval principality of Burgundy, resting on a nominally feudal or chivalric foundation and sub-divided into smaller units determined by ancient political frontiers and traditional regionalism. The remainder of France was to be known as 'Gaul', and a duchy of Brittany might well have had a place in SS blueprints. Why it should have been offered to M. Plantard, however, is another question.

The last point of interest raised by our meeting with M. Plantard in April 1982, was even more vague. At several points during the course of our discussion, M. Plantard commented on the 'timing' of our book. Apparently, it had been inopportune. We had published 'too soon', we were told. 'The moment', M. Plantard said at least three times, 'was not yet right.' There was an element of slightly bitter reproof in these statements, as if we had indeed upset some timetable to which the Prieuré de Sion were working. Nevertheless, M. Plantard conceded, as if making the best of the situation, our work would prove valuable when 'the moment *was* right'.

When would it be right? we asked. We received no concrete answer, only nebulous generalities. On several subsequent occasions, however, in meetings and telephone calls with both M. Plantard and others, it was strongly hinted that 1984 would be a critical year in the Prieuré de Sion's plans. During 1984, accordingly, we kept a close watch on events in France. Nothing happened that seemed in any way relevant to the Prieuré de Sion. So far, at least, as public affairs were concerned, 1984 was in this respect resoundingly anti-climactic. But so far as the Prieuré de Sion's own internal affairs were concerned, 1984 was to prove a year of major upheaval.

18

The British Connection

The research which culminated in *The Holy Blood and the Holy Grail* had begun with an apparently local mystery in the south of France, at the village of Rennes-le-Château in the foothills of the Pyrenees. There, in 1891, Bérenger Saunière, the parish priest, had discovered a collection of antique parchments. Apparently as a result of this discovery, he became extraordinarily wealthy, gaining access to, and spending, immense sums of money. One might at first suspect – as did we, along with other writers on the subject – that the parchments in question had led Saunière to some kind of treasure. There was indeed some reason for believing that Saunière might have found the treasure of the Temple of Jerusalem, which had been plundered by the Romans in A.D. 70 and brought to Rome, then plundered from Rome by the Visigoths in A.D. 410 and brought to the vicinity of Rennes-le-Château. As we began to examine the whole matter more closely, however, it became increasingly apparent that, even if a treasure *were* involved, Saunière's primary discovery was a secret – a secret which, as we have said, radiated out from a little backwater village to encompass the whole of Western culture and extend backwards through two thousand years of history.

At the same time, there were still a number of tantalising unanswered questions. Certain of these pertained quite specifically to the parchments allegedly found by Saunière. According to every account of the story we had heard or read, both in Prieuré de Sion documents and in external sources, Saunière had discovered *four* parchments. Three of these were very precisely described. They are cited repeatedly as: (1) a genealogy dated 1244 bearing the seal of Queen Blanche de Castille, mother of King Louis IX, which confirms the survival of the Merovingian bloodline; (2) an updated genealogy, covering the period from 1244 to 1644 and dated 1644 by François-Pierre d'Hautpoul, seigneur at the time of Rennes-le-Château; and (3) the so-called 'Testament' of Henri d'Hautpoul, dated 1695, the contents of which are said to comprise an official 'secret of state' but have never been reported. Why these particular items should be so significant remained unclear. Was there something of consequence perhaps inscribed on the back of the original parchments? Or did they contain other explosive material, in addition to being simply two genealogies and a 'testament'?

Whatever the answer to these questions, three documents were always and consistently cited. At the same time, as early as 1967, the Prieuré de Sion had 'leaked' what purported to be *two* of the parchments supposedly discovered by Saunière. These were the enigmatic biblical texts containing coded messages which have been reproduced in books pertaining to the story, in magazine articles and in our own television films. One text is an extract from the Gospel of John, consisting of chapter 12, verses 1–12. The other is a composite of Luke 6:1–5, Matthew 12:1–8 and Mark 2:23–8. In both, the words of the texts have been run together, though sometimes broken, apparently arbitrarily, at the ends of lines. Mysterious dots appear under certain letters. Other letters have been raised slightly above those surrounding them, or have been inscribed deliberately smaller. Superfluous letters have been interpolated. When deciphered, the text from John's Gospel, yields the message:

A DAGOBERT II ROI ET A SION EST CE TRESOR ET IL EST LA MORT. (TO DAGOBERT II, KING, AND TO SION BELONGS THIS TREASURE AND HE IS THERE DEAD.)

The composite text from Luke, Matthew and Mark is much more intricately coded. Eventually, it yields a longer message:

BERGERE PAS DE TENTATION QUE POUSSIN TENIERS GARDENT LA CLEF PAX DCLXXXI PAR LA CROIX ET CE CHEVAL DE DIEU J'ACHEVE CE DAEMON DE GARDIEN A MIDI POMMES BLEUES. (SHEPHERDESS, NO TEMPTATION. THAT POUSSIN, TENIERS, HOLD THE KEY. PEACE 681. BY THE CROSS AND THIS HORSE OF GOD I COMPLETE – or DESTROY – THIS DAEMON GUARDIAN AT NOON. BLUE APPLES.)[1]

In 1979, when we first met M. Plantard, we were told that both of the ciphered texts were in fact forgeries, concocted in 1956 by the Marquis de Chérisey for a short television programme. We challenged this assertion. The staggering effort required to devise the ciphers seemed inappropriate, indeed ridiculous, for such a purpose. M. Plantard conceded that the forgeries were based very closely on the originals. In other words, they had not been 'concocted' by M. Chérisey at all. They had been *copied*, and M. Chérisey had made only a few additions. When these additions were deleted, what remained were the original texts found by Saunière.

But if these two biblical texts were authentic, and if there were three other parchments – two genealogies and the Hautpoul 'testament' – that made a total of five. Five separate documents. Whereas Saunière was alleged to have discovered only four.

A second, and even more urgent, question was what had become of the parchments. According to one account, they were said to have been 'purchased by fraud' and found their way into the hands of the League of Antiquarian Booksellers – or, at any rate, certain individuals, generally identified as 'Roland Stansmore' and 'Sir Thomas Frazer', posing as representatives of the League of Antiquarian Booksellers. According to another account, they had been plundered from the library of an ecclesiastic in Paris, the Abbé Émile Hoffet, shortly after his death in 1946. They were then said to have found their way into the archives of the Knights of Malta. In our early meetings with him, M. Plantard had confirmed a statement that occurred in a number of specifically Prieuré de Sion sources – that the documents as of then (1979) were in a safe deposit vault of Lloyds International in London. But M. Plantard did not elaborate on how they got there. Finally, in another mysterious addition inserted into Jania Macgillivray's doctored article, the parchments were said to have been removed from their London depository and placed in a safe deposit box in a Parisian bank, located at 4 Place de Mexico. If this was true, the parchments, as of the latter part of 1979, were back in France. But there was no indication of who had transferred them or why, who had access to them, who had been responsible for the shadowy transactions associated with them.

The Notarised Documents

During our meeting with him on 17 May 1983, M. Plantard elaborated on two of the paramount questions pertaining to Saunière's parchments – and, in characteristic fashion, thereby created further mystification. The documents found by Saunière, he said, were indeed only four in number. Three of them were those to which various references had repeatedly alluded – a genealogy dating from 1244 bearing the seal of Blanche de Castille, an Hautpoul genealogy dating from 1644 and the Hautpoul 'testament' dating from 1695. The fourth parchment, he said, was the original on the basis of which the Marquis de Chérisey had devised a modified version. According to M. Plantard, there was one coded message on each side of the page. In some way, apparently, the two texts interacted with each other – if, for example, they were held up to the light and viewed, as it were, in superimposition. Indeed, it was suggested that M. Chérisey's chief 'modification' had simply been to reproduce the two sides of the same page as separate pages, and not to the original scale.

This, of course, immediately resurrected a question with which we had occasionally toyed in the past. Could the other three parchments found by Saunière have been important not because of what they said, but because of something else – something about the actual physical sheets on which they were inscribed? What might be on the reverse, for example? A genealogy of the Hautpoul family, even to people familiar with them and their proprietorship of Rennes-le-Château, would hardly seem to warrant all the fuss it had apparently engendered. But what if there were something else on the reverse of the parchment?

There is certainly documented evidence about the 1644 Hautpoul genealogy which suggests that it was indeed significant. It is known to have been registered on 23 November 1644, by a man named Captier, notary of the town of Esperaza, not far from Rennes-le-Château. After disappearing for a time, it was found again by Jean-Baptiste Siau, notary of Esperaza, in 1780. For reasons unspecified, he deemed it so important that he refused to return it to the Hautpoul family. He declared it to be a document of 'great consequence', which he would not let out of his hands. He offered to travel with it and show it personally to any official authorised to see it, but insisted on returning it afterwards to his strong room.[2] On occasion, the phrase 'state secret' has occurred in relation to this document. Some time after 1780, it again disappeared. Or, more likely, the eruption of the French Revolution dictated that it be concealed. There is evidence that subsequent members of the Hautpoul family were aware of its existence and tried to locate it, but they do not appear to have succeeded.

M. Plantard refused to comment on either of the Hautpoul parchments, or on the 1244 genealogy bearing the seal of Blanche de Castille. He simply asserted that the fourth parchment found by Saunière consisted of the two coded biblical texts, one on each side of the page. But then, with neither preamble nor warning, he suddenly pulled from his briefcase and placed on the table in front of us two impressively be-ribboned and be-sealed documents. The text, as we read it, seemed abruptly to lift the whole question of the parchments out of the realm of hypothesis and speculation, and to anchor it in very concrete, very specifically British, territory.

The documents, M. Plantard showed us, and of which he provided us with photographs, were of two officially notarised statements. The first, dated 5 October 1955, was a request to the French Consulate in London, asking authorisation for the export of three parchments – a genealogy dated 1244 bearing the seal of Blanche de Castille, a genealogy dated 1644 for François-Pierre d'Hautpoul and the 1695 'testament' of Henri d'Hautpoul. The text began:

> I, Patrick Francis Jourdan Freeman, Public Notary ... certify ... that the signature R. S. Nutting which is found at the bottom of the attached request is truly that of Captain Ronald Stansmore Nutting ...

Mr Freeman also declared that he verified the authenticity of Nutting's birth certificate, which was said to be attached – although the birth certificate attached in the photograph was not Captain Nutting's, but that of a Viscount Frederick Leathers.

Leathers's name, at the time, was unknown to us. It seemed clear, however, that Captain Nutting was the person whose name had been garbled to 'Roland' or 'Ronald Stansmore' in a number of references we had encountered previously. In 1981, for example, the Marquis de Chérisey, in a passage quoted above, had spoken of 'Captain Ronald Stansmore of the British Intelligence Service', who, posing as a 'respectable lawyer', had purchased Saunière's parchments allegedly on behalf of the International League of Antiquarian Booksellers. And in the same passage, there had been mention of:

> ... the demand for the recognition of Merovingian rights made in 1955 and 1956 by Sir Alexander Aikman, Sir John Montague Brocklebank, Major Hugh Murchison Clowes and nineteen other men in the office of P. F. J. Freeman, Notary by Royal Appointment.

The first page in the documents shown us by M. Plantard was headed 'Request for Authorisation to the Consulate-General of France'. In the ensuing text, three Englishmen were cited: the Right Honourable Viscount Leathers, CH, born 21 November 1883 in London; Major Hugh Murchison Clowes, DSO, born 27 April

1885 in London; and Captain Ronald Stansmore Nutting, OBE, MC, born 3 March 1888 in London. These three gentlemen requested permission from the Consulate-General of France to export from that country:

> ... three parchments whose value cannot be calculated, confided to us, for purposes of historical research, by Madame James, resident in France at Montazels (Aude). She came into legal possession of these items by virtue of a legacy from her uncle, the Abbé Saunière, curé of Rennes-le-Château (Aude).

There then follows the specific description of the three items in question – the 1244 genealogy, the 1644 genealogy and the 'testament' of 1695. After that, the text goes on to state:

> These genealogies contain proof of the direct descent, through the male line of Sigibert IV, son of Dagobert II, King of Austrasie, through the House of Plantard, Counts of Rhédae, and they are not to be reproduced in any fashion.

The text bears the signatures of Viscount Leathers, Major Clowes and Captain Nutting. At the top of the page is the stamp and seal, dated 25 October 1955, of Olivier de Saint-Germain, the French Consul. In fact, however, all Saint-Germain certifies is that the signature and seal of the notary, P. F. J. Freeman, are correct.

M. Plantard also produced further documents, similar to the first but dated a year later. These introduced a new and, in his way, august personality, whose birth certificate was attached. The birth certificate was that of Roundell Cecil Palmer, Earl of Selborne. On the front, Patrick Freeman, notary attached to John Newman and Sons, 27 Clements Lane, Lombard Street, London, confirmed that the signature at the foot of the attached request was indeed that of Lord Selborne, appended in the notary's own presence. Mr Freeman also confirmed the authenticity and validity of Lord Selborne's birth certificate. The statement was dated 23 July 1956. Below Mr Freeman's signature, there were the seal and stamp of the French Consul-General in London, who, now, a year later, was no longer Olivier de Saint-Germain, but one Jean Guiraud. His signature and seal bore the date 29 August 1956.

The reverse of this statement was headed 'Third Original Example' – implying that there were at least two others. It was sub-headed 'Request to the Consul-General of France in London for the Retention of French Parchments'. In the text that followed, Lord Selborne, 'born 15 April, 1887, in London', declared that, from the office of Patrick Freeman, public notary, he was addressing a request to the Consul-General of France to retain certain French documents. He then proceeded, 'on my honour', to specify the documents in question. In accordance with the wishes of Madame James, who had 'donated' them, Lord Selborne further affirmed that these documents would, after twenty-five years, legally revert to M. Pierre Plantard, Count of Rhédae and Count of Saint-Clair, born 18 March 1920. Should M. Plantard fail to reclaim them, they would pass to the French National Archives.

In the next paragraph, Lord Selborne declared that the documents in question, deposited by Captain Nutting, Major Clowes and Viscount Leathers at the International League of Antiquarian Booksellers, 39 Great Russell Street, London, would be placed 'on this day' in a strongbox of Lloyds Bank Europe Limited. No divulgence of them was to be made. At the bottom of the page there was Lord Selborne's signature.

From these two notarised statements a story of sorts can be pieced together. In 1955, Viscount Leathers, Major Clowes and Captain Nutting appear to have obtained three of the four parchments found by Saunière in 1891. The parchments are said to have been obtained from Saunière's niece, Madame James, then residing in Saunière's own native village of Montazels, not far from Rennes-le-Château. Permission was sought and presumably procured for these parchments to be exported to England. On 5 October 1955, the three Englishmen were in the office of the notary Patrick Freeman and had their request for export notarised – or, if not the request, something pertaining to the request, if only birth certificates and signatures.

In 1956, Lord Selborne sought permission to retain the parchments in England. His request, apparently, was again notarised by Patrick Freeman, on 23 July, and signed by the French Consul-General on 29 August. The parchments, originally deposited with the International League of Antiquarian Booksellers, were then deposited with Lloyds Bank Europe. In twenty-five years – that is, 1980 or 1981 – they were to revert to Pierre Plantard de Saint-Clair, or failing his reclamation of them, to the French government.

Gentlemen of the City of London

From the very beginning of our research into the mystery of Rennes-le-Château, we had encountered references to two Englishmen alleged to have obtained Saunière's parchments. As stated above, their names had previously been cited as Sir Thomas

Frazer and Captain Roland or Ronald Stansmore – who had now proved to be Captain Ronald Stansmore Nutting. The garbling of Nutting's name suggested that the sources responsible for 'leaking' it years ago were themselves uncertain and drawing upon imprecise information.

In 1981, in the doctored text of Jania Macgillivray's article, we had encountered another English name – that of a certain Lord Blackford. And in 1981, too, the Marquis de Chérisey had supplemented the list of English figures connected with the story. Through material provided by M. Chérisey, we had encountered the names of Sir Alexander Aikman, Sir John Montague Brockle-bank and Major Hugh Murchison Clowes, who, together with nineteen others, were said to have 'made a request for recognition of Merovingian rights' – and made it 'in the office of P. F. J. Freeman, Public Notary'.

Now, in 1983, as a result of the notarised documents M. Plantard had shown us, the role of at least some of these men became more concrete, more identifiable. Moreover, the confusion over Nutting's name had been clarified. And two new names had been added – Viscount Frederick Leathers and the Earl of Sel-borne. From diverse sources, then, we had been presented with the names of eight Englishmen who were allegedly connected in some way with the parchments discovered by Saunière – Frazer, Nutting, Aikman, Brocklebank, Clowes, Blackford, Leathers and Selborne. There was also the notary P. F. J. Freeman. And an allusion to 'nineteen others'.

Who were these people? What might have been the nature of their interest in the parchments found at Rennes-le-Château in 1891? Why should those parchments have been so important to this particular group of Englishmen? And what were we to make of the suggestion of some connection with espionage and the intelligence community? Nutting, it must be remembered, had been described as a member of British Intelligence, while Frazer had been called 'the eminence grise of Buckingham'. (Translated, as it is from the French, the implication is probably meant to be Buckingham Palace.) Frazer had received the OBE and been knighted in 1947. His activities, so far as we could ascertain, seemed confined for the most part to the business world. Among his other positions, he was a Director of North British and Mercantile Insurance.

A former captain in the Irish Guards, Nutting had also been prominent in business, especially in shipping and banking. He had served on the boards of directors of no fewer than fourteen companies, including Arthur Guinness and Guardian Assurance.

He had been chairman of the board of the British and Irish Steam Packet Company. And until 1929, he had been a governor of the Bank of Ireland. According to one of his business associates, whom we interviewed personally, he had also been an operative for MI5.[3]

Sir Alexander Aikman had been chairman of the board of EMI from 1946 until 1954, and had played a part in the establishment of the Independent Broadcasting Authority (ITV). Among the company boards on which he had sat as director were those of Dunlop and, again, Guardian Assurance.

Like Nutting, Sir John Brocklebank had been involved in shipping as well as insurance. Indeed, his family had been active in shipping for two centuries, and he himself was chairman of the board of Cunard. He had also been chairman of the Liverpool Steamship Owners' Association and sat on the board of directors of two insurance companies – one of which was a subsidiary of Guardian Assurance.

Major Hugh Murchison Clowes had been active in his family's printing firm, William Clowes and Son, which specialised in the production of Bibles. Among the companies of which Major Clowes was a director was Guardian Assurance.

Prior to the Second World War, Viscount Frederick Leathers had been regarded as an international expert in shipping. During the war, he was a close personal friend of Winston Churchill and served as Minister of War Transport, a role for which his expertise in shipping rendered him particularly qualified. He was active in planning the logistics of the Normandy invasion. Among his directorships were P & O, National Westminster Bank and Guardian Assurance.

During the First World War, Glyn Mason, Baron Blackford, had held a command under General Allenby in Palestine. From 1922 until 1940, he had been a Conservative Member of Parliament. During the Second World War, he had been a sector commander of the Home Guard. Later, he was Deputy Speaker in the House of Lords. Baron Blackford was chairman of the board of Guardian Assurance.

Like Viscount Leathers, the Earl of Selborne was a close personal friend of Churchill's and would certainly have worked with Leathers. From 1942 until 1945, he was Minister of Economic Warfare and, in this capacity, also worked closely with Sir William Stephenson, the 'man called Intrepid'.[4] The primary function of Selborne's ministry was to deny the enemy any and all material that might be of use to the war effort. As Minister of Economic Warfare, moreover, Selborne was overall head of SOE – the Special Operations Executive – which dropped agents into occupied territory, liaised with local resistance groups, pinpointed targets for air raids and undertook sabotage and disruption behind enemy lines. SOE worked closely with the American OSS, precursor of the CIA. And immediately around the corner from SOE's headquarters at 64 Baker Street was the secret London headquarters of all Free French special agents, who also came under Selborne's authority.

Many of SOE's personnel were drawn from the spheres of banking, shipping, journalism – and insurance. In his wartime position, Lord Selborne would necessarily have maintained an intimate contact with insurance companies. According to Sir William Stephenson:

> If you have access to insurance company files, you will see detailed studies of the weak point in any manufacturing process or mining procedure. Insurance companies stand to lose fortunes from an accident, and so they employ experts to figure out every possible way that things can go wrong. Their reports are guide books for saboteurs.[5]

And Sir Colin Gubbins, SOE's last Executive Director, made a point of collecting around him insurance adjustors: 'In peacetime they deal with claims for damage from factories. So they know what puts a machine out of action – fast.'[6]

After the war, Lord Selborne became increasingly interested in religious affairs, in the relations between church and state and in the Church of England's procedures for appointing deans and bishops. In the House of Lords, he was head of the Church Laity Committee. During the late 1950s, he became increasingly conservative – to a degree, at times, that might be considered sinister, cranky or both. In 1956, for example, he proposed a Press Control Bill, designed to make all British newspapers conform to the standards reflected by *The Times* in May of that year. According to his daughter, whom we interviewed, he saw himself 'fighting a rearguard action for empire'. This seems to have extended to an embrace of royalist movements on the continent. His daughter also declared him to have been deeply interested in genealogies, and often to have gone on holiday around the Pyrenees. Among his business activities, he was a director of the North British and Mercantile Insurance Company – the company of which Sir Thomas Frazer was also a director.

Might Lord Selborne have learned something pertinent to Saunière's parchments by virtue of his organisation's work in France during the war? M. Plantard and the Prieuré de Sion were, after all, said to have been active in the Resistance, or in some other way to have aided De Gaulle. If this were true, Selborne would unquestionably have known of them, and SOE would almost certainly have had some degree of contact with them. Such contact might well have occurred through André Malraux, who played a crucial role in Resistance operations, who was in contact with British intelligence and sabotage networks during the war, whose brother was in SOE, and who is repeatedly claimed to have been a high-ranking member of the Prieuré de Sion. But why should Lord Selborne have become embroiled in the Prieuré's affairs more than ten years later?

There seemed, at any rate, some sort of pattern governing the involvement of the Englishmen whose names we had encountered. There were documented connections between most of them, and extremely probable connections between the others. Several of them were engaged not only in high-level wartime planning, but also in clandestine operations of one or another kind. All eight were active in the spheres of shipping and/or insurance. Two – Selborne and Frazer – had been directors of North British and Mercantile Insurance. The remaining six were affiliated with Guardian Assurance (now Guardian Royal Exchange Assurance) – four as directors, one as chairman of the board and one as a director of a subsidiary company.

But this pattern, such as it was, only raised further questions. What, for example, had Guardian Assurance been doing back in 1955 and 1956? Had it served as a screen or a façade for something clandestine? Or had certain members of its governing board been using it as a screen or a façade? What of Frazer and Selborne, who were not affiliated with Guardian Assurance? Why, in any case, should eight men, all of them directors of insurance companies, apparently be interested in obtaining genealogies establishing the legitimacy of a Merovingian claim to the French throne? Might an explanation perhaps lie in French, or in Anglo-French, affairs at the time?

Certainly it was a turbulent period. A year before, in May 1954, the French Army in Indo-China had been defeated at Dien Bien Phu. Internally, France was in a state of upheaval, with spectres of governmental collapse, *coups d'état* and even perhaps civil war looming ominously on the horizon. By the beginning of 1955, 20,000 French troops had already been dispatched to Algeria, and the situation there was careering out of control. Shock waves from the escalating North African crisis were beginning to reverberate back to France. Britain, in the meanwhile, had become increasingly immersed in the situation in Cyprus, which was officially declared an emergency in 1955. In the same year, Churchill resigned and Anthony Eden became Prime Minister. In July of 1956, Nasser appropriated the Suez Canal. In October, Hungary rose in revolt and was crushed by the Soviet invasion. Less than a month later, the Suez Crisis erupted, and British and French troops, together with the Israelis, invaded Egypt.

At the same time, there were other developments, which did not become public until later, gathering momentum behind the scenes during 1955 and 1956. In January, 1957, for example, a plot was discovered by the French army to take over part of Algeria. Blueprints for the EEC were being drawn up, which would lead to the Treaty of Rome in 1957.

Finally, it is worth noting that 1956 seems to have been a crucial year for the internal affairs of the Prieuré de Sion. In 1956, it 'went public' for the first time and registered itself in the French *Journal officiel*.[7] In the same year, material pertaining to the Order began to be deposited in the Bibliothèque Nationale.

Might the transaction which brought Saunière's parchments to England have been connected with certain events of the time – particularly with developments in French affairs and/or in those of the Prieuré de Sion? But if that were the case, in what way? To what end? Were Saunière's parchments brought to England to keep them out of someone's hands? If so, whose? To be used for something? If so, what? Or, alternatively, to ensure that they should *not* be used for something? If so, what again? And on whose behalf were Selborne, Nutting, Leathers and their colleagues working? Might their interest have been wholly personal – the interest of antiquarian scholars, intent on obtaining the parchments for purely academic reasons? Or might there have been some official involvement, pertaining to high-level international politics?

Given their wartime activities, it would hardly be surprising if, ten years later, Selborne, Nutting, Leathers and their colleagues still retained connections with, say, the intelligence community and continued to deal, if only now and then, with government business. There may also have been some formal structure for their work outside the established intelligence community. At the end of the war, Colin Gubbins of SOE formed a Members' Association for former SOE operatives. It was more than a conventional veterans' organisation. Its purpose was to ensure that, in some future emergency, people with special talents and expertise could be contacted and assembled quickly. André Malraux – whose brother, Roland, had been an SOE agent – created a similar unit in

France. By 1947, in fact, he had mobilised what amounted to a private army – the RPF, or Rassemblement du Peuple Français – to secure De Gaulle's position and thwart Communist attempts to seize power in France. The RPF was composed primarily of former Resistance fighters. In 1958, it became the Association for the Support of General de Gaulle, and undertook to deal with any trouble that might arise from De Gaulle's return to power in that year. Malraux's Association would have worked closely with the Committees of Public Safety in mainland France, which also played an important part in returning De Gaulle to power and of which Pierre Plantard claimed to be secretary-general. In 1962, Malraux's organisation of former Resistance fighters was rechristened the Association for the Fifth Republic. If Malraux had indeed been, as claimed, a member of the Prieuré de Sion, he and his Association would in all likelihood have been the conduits for Prieuré interests in England. And, of course, there may well have been links between Malraux and Colin Gubbins's organisation of ex-SOE operatives. From Gubbins, there would have been only a step to Selborne.

In any case, we, in our research, were soon to discover persuasive evidence of mysterious forces at work in the background. These forces were not entirely those of the Prieuré de Sion. It became increasingly difficult for us not to suspect the involvement of one or another secret service – of Britain, of France or even perhaps of the United States.

Preliminary Enquiries

Before we could form any conclusions of our own, we had first, of course, to confirm the authenticity of the notarised documents and learn more about the transaction which had, apparently, brought Saunière's parchments to England in 1955. The information we already had at our disposal offered a number of trails to follow. It was a matter of systematically exploring each of them.

One trail was Lloyds Bank International, where, according to the 1956 notarised document signed by Lord Selborne, the Saunière parchments had been deposited – and from which, according to information received in 1981 from the Marquis de Chérisey, they had recently been moved to a safe deposit box in a bank in Paris. We had talks with two contacts in the banking world. They provided us with two significant pieces of information.

The first was that the firm of the notary, Patrick J. Freeman, was the firm used by Lloyds Bank International themselves. If the transaction in question actually involved a safe deposit box at the bank, and if a firm of notaries was involved, it would most likely be Mr Freeman's.

The second important piece of information obtained from our contacts was that Lloyds had ceased to maintain safe deposit boxes in 1979 – the year in which, according to M. Chérisey, the parchments had been transferred back to France. From 1979 on, there had simply been a strong room in which envelopes could be kept. Apparently, many people had removed their belongings when this change of bank policy was introduced. It was thus perfectly plausible for the parchments, if they had been at Lloyds, to be removed in 1979 and transferred to Paris. We would have liked, of course, to determine whether there had ever actually been a safe deposit box at Lloyds. This proved impossible, because we had no way of knowing in whose name – real or assumed – it might have been registered.[8]

In the 1956 document signed by Lord Selborne, the parchments were said to have been deposited initially with the International League of Antiquarian Booksellers. In our previous research we had already investigated the League, and our renewed enquiries yielded little fresh information. The notarised document of 1956 had specified the League's address as 39 Great Russell Street – directly opposite the British Museum. In 1956, the address was occupied by a bookseller, Henry Stevens, Son & Stiles. And at that time, this shop did indeed serve as headquarters for the British branch of the International League of Antiquarian Booksellers. This trail, however, had long gone cold.

The staff of the French Consulate proved eager to help. We showed photographs of the notarised documents to a vice-consul. She confirmed that, so far as she could judge, the official seal and signature of Jean Guiraud on the 1956 document were authentic. The signature on the 1955 document was unfamiliar to her. A brief check, however, revealed that Olivier de Saint-Germain, the name on the document, had indeed been attached to the staff of the Consulate at the time, and the vice-consul saw no reason to doubt the authenticity of his signature. On the other hand, she found it curious that the Consulate had dealt with the matter at all. Ordinarily, she explained, such a transaction involving old manuscripts would have had to obtain authorisation not from the Consulate, but from the French Ministry of Culture in Paris.

On our request, the vice-consul agreed to check on whether there was any record of a meeting at the French Consulate involving any of the men specified, on the relevant dates in 1955 and/or 1956.

Unfortunately – and this proved to be the case at other points in our research – records dating from that long ago had been destroyed. There was no hope of finding anything pertaining to a transaction which had occurred more than a quarter of a century before.

With the French Consulate, as with Lloyds and the League of Antiquarian Booksellers, everything *seemed* plausible enough, and circumstantial evidence seemed to support the authenticity of the notarised documents. But time itself had contrived to deprive us of both further illumination and definitive proof. Material was becoming available to us in direct proportion to the degree that it was becoming unverifiable. Were tracks being covered, or was it simply an inevitable consequence of the passage of the years?

An English Notary

Patrick J. Freeman, the man who had notarised the documents, was still practising, and we accordingly interviewed him. After examining our colour photographs, Mr Freeman was perplexed. The paper looked like his, he said. The seal was definitely his, as was the signature and, apparently, the typewriter. The documents clearly seemed to have been drawn up in his office. But he had no recollection of any transaction involving parchments brought into England from France.

Shortly after, we met with Mr Freeman for the second time. By now, a check through his files had revealed that on 5 October 1955, there had indeed been a transaction with Nutting, Clowes and Leathers – the men whose signatures appeared on the document of that date. According to the records, Mr Freeman had signed and sealed for each of them individually a statement certifying that their appended signatures were authentic. This, he explained to us, had been normal procedure at the time. In 1955, the French government had decreed that anyone legally representing an insurance company in France must provide a notarised signature. Mr Freeman was thus able to confirm that one part of the document which interested us – namely his notarisation of a signature – was authentic. But Mr Freeman's records made no mention whatever of anything pertaining to Saunière's parchments, to genealogies or the import of such items to England.

Mr Freeman further confirmed that on 23 July 1956, the date of the second notarised document, there had indeed been a transaction with Lord Selborne. Again, however, the records indicated that this had involved nothing more than the notarisation of a signature. Again, there was no mention of anything else.

Mr Freeman continued to express his perplexity concerning everything else about the documents in question – the request in 1955 to import the Saunière parchments to England, the request in 1956 to keep them in England for twenty-five years. It made, he insisted, no sense. He had a good memory, he said, especially for unusual transactions of the sort that this appeared to be. He also indicated that he kept carbon copies of everything drawn up under his auspices. He acknowledged that part, at least, of the documents in question could only have been drawn up by him. Yet neither his memory nor his records could reveal anything further about the matter.

We had reached an impasse. On the one hand, Mr Freeman admitted that the documents would have had to originate in his office, using his paper, his typewriter, his seal. On the other hand, he denied all knowledge of their substance, insisting that he had done nothing but sign an authentication of signature for each of the men involved. We considered the possibility that he had been tricked in some fashion – by being asked to sign something innocuous, for example, while something more important was typed on the reverse of the page afterwards. Such explanations did not seem very likely. The text pertaining to the parchments certainly appeared to have been typed on the same typewriter as the text in which Mr Freeman affirmed the authenticity of the signatures. Nor did it seem possible that the page could afterwards have been inserted into a typewriter without breaking the notary's seal. How, then, could a spurious portion of the text have been added after the fact? What had begun as just an intriguing problem to be resolved had now begun to assume unexpected proportions.

Suspicion of Forgery

We had checked with Lloyds Bank, with the League of Antiquarian Booksellers, with the French Consulate and with Patrick J. Freeman. There remained, of course, Guardian Assurance itself – the company of whose board of directors so many of the men involved were members. In 1968, the old Guardian Assurance Company had merged with Royal Exchange, to produce what today is called Guardian Royal Exchange Assurance. In October of 1983, we met with the company secretary and showed him photographs of the notarised documents, together with the signatures of his company's former directors. Needless to say, he was thoroughly baffled and suggested we speak to a former deputy chairman of the board, Mr Ernest Bigland, who in 1955 and 1956 had been company secretary.

A meeting was arranged for us with Mr Bigland. In the meantime, we were put in touch with the managing director of the company. He, it transpired, had read our previous book, was familiar with the story and relished the opportunity to help us in our research. He personally undertook to check old company records. They yielded one fact of tantalising interest. On the day on which the first document was notarised – 5 October 1955 – there had been a special unscheduled meeting of the board of Guardian Assurance.

A few days later, Guardian Royal Exchange Assurance furnished us with photocopies of the Directors' Attendance Book for the autumn of 1955 – including the day of the special unscheduled meeting on 5 October. The photocopies showed the signatures of the company directors as they had signed the book before entering their meeting. At the top of the page was that of the chairman, Lord Blackford. Further down were the signatures of Viscount Leathers, Major Clowes and Captain Nutting. To our consternation, the signatures did not at all match those on the notarised documents. They were not even rough approximations, not even attempted replicas. They were entirely different!

We were mystified. All of a sudden, our investigation had been diverted, if not derailed, by something for which there was no apparent logical explanation. Were the notarised documents forgeries or were they authentic? If they were forgeries, what was the point of the fraud? And why be so blatant about it? If one wants to forge a man's signature, one attempts to produce some approximation, some reasonable facsimile. One does not use a signature that has no relation whatever to the original. Certainly it would have been easy enough to find the original signatures – in Companies House, in Guardian Assurance's annual reports, in various other possible sources. If, moreover, the signatures on the documents were forgeries, why had not Patrick J. Freeman remarked on the fact? He had done nothing of the sort. On the contrary, he confirmed that on the dates specified in the notarised documents, he had certified the authenticity of the signatures involved.

Then, too, if the notarised documents were forgeries, who might have perpetrated them? And why? What could account for the selection of this particular group of Englishmen? Was it purely coincidental that so many of them were associated with Guardian Assurance, or was this connection between them in some way important to the forger?

The Enigma Compounded

In February, 1984, we met with Mr Ernest Bigland, former company secretary of Guardian Assurance. Mr Bigland was fascinated by the story. What was more, it made a certain sense to him – or, at any rate, did not seem altogether inexplicable.

In the first place, he was less prepared to suspect forgery than we, at this point, were. He was blasé about the discrepancies between the signatures in the Directors' Attendance Book and those on the notarised documents. Such discrepancies, he said, indicated nothing. Men such as those involved often used more than one signature. There might be a casual, slapdash scrawl for routine business or for purely internal purposes. For important or official occasions, there might be something more formal – such as the signatures on the notarised documents. It might even be that a special version of a signature might be employed for some specific transaction – and be notarised accordingly. On the whole, Mr Bigland, who had known all the men involved when they were alive and had dealt with them extensively, was inclined, he said, to accept the signatures on the notarised documents as genuine. And he echoed the point we ourselves had raised. If the signatures were fraudulent, why had the notary, Patrick J. Freeman, not remarked on the fact?

What was more, Mr Bigland said he had a hazy recollection – necessarily hazy, for it was, after all, thirty years ago – of Lord Blackford, chairman of the board, once speaking of certain extremely important documents or parchments arriving from France. He also recalled Lord Blackford speaking of the need to put them in a safe deposit box. These references, if he remembered correctly, had been made informally, in a chat after a board meeting. It had appeared to be a private affair. Needless to say, nothing of this had meant anything to Mr Bigland at the time. He had simply assumed it referred to something of purely antiquarian interest. Such items were often discussed among Guardian Assurance's directors in the 1950s. Mr Bigland cited two other individuals on the board who had a special interest in antiquarian matters. One of them owned a château in the south of France and was an ardent collector of antiques and precious manuscripts. The second was also a collector and owned, among other treasures, an original Magna Carta worth some half a million pounds.

Finally, Mr Bigland spoke of Captain Ronald Stansmore Nutting. Among the other directors of Guardian Assurance, Nutting, according to Mr Bigland, had been closest to Sir Alexander Aikman, Major Hugh Clowes and Lord Blackford. Nutting had also been extremely friendly with Sir John Montague Brocklebank of Cunard. Mr Bigland stated that Captain Nutting had indeed been a former operative of MI5 – as had at least one of Guardian Assurance's departmental chairmen. And, Mr Bigland added in conclusion, the company's representative in France at the time had been an agent of SOE.[9]

Mr Bigland's information, vague though it was, seemed to support the authenticity of the notarised documents. If the former company secretary was prepared to accept the signatures as genuine, we were hardly obliged to do otherwise. The pendulum, so far as we were concerned, had swung from acceptance, to doubt, back to acceptance again. But there was to be one further, albeit partial, swing of the pendulum.

Impasse

Once again, we met with Patrick J. Freeman. Once again, Mr Freeman emphatically denied all knowledge of the transaction to which the notarised documents referred. Once again, he professed his own perplexity about the matter. Once again, he – and we – wondered if the text pertaining to the parchments could somehow have been added afterwards, appended perhaps years later to another text which was legitimate and routine. Until now, we had discounted this possibility because of Mr Freeman's seal. There would, it seemed, have been no way of inserting the page into a typewriter without damaging such a seal. Still less could one type over it. This had seemed to preclude any typed alterations of the documents once they had left Mr Freeman's hands. Now, however, we asked Mr Freeman quite specifically about his seal. No, he said, it was not of wax, but he was still doubtful that one could insert it into a typewriter and type over it. Nevertheless, he produced one. In fact, it consisted of a thin paper disc stuck to the page and then embossed. Using Mr Freeman's own paper and typewriter, we tested. With care, one could indeed insert a page bearing the seal into a typewriter and type over it.

As we considered this new development, Mr Freeman pondered

over the texts which he, and we, had read so many times before. Suddenly, something struck him. It was seemingly trivial, a minor slip which most people, including ourselves, would never have noticed. At the same time, however, it was also a crucial clue which, at least in the case of the 1956 document, gave the game away.

The 1956 document bore Lord Selborne's signature. The text of the document spoke of Saunière's parchments being kept in a safe deposit box at Lloyds Bank Europe. But, as Mr Freeman suddenly realised, and as we confirmed when we checked with Lloyds ourselves, Lloyds Bank Europe had not existed in 1956. In 1956, the European branches of Lloyds were Lloyds Bank Foreign. Lloyds Bank Foreign did not become Lloyds Bank Europe until 29 January 1964. In consequence, this part of the document's text could not possibly date from 1956. It could date only from some time after 1964.

It could thus be definitively established that at least one of the two documents M. Plantard had showed us was not wholly authentic. This, naturally enough, called the earlier, 1955 document into question, but nothing could be proved about it one way or the other.[10] All we could safely say was that part of the 1956 document had been contrived, somehow, after the fact and pre-dated. The seal, Mr Freeman's text, Mr Freeman's signature, Lord Selborne's signature, the stamp of the French Consulate – these were apparently genuine enough. At least eight years later, these valid aspects of the document had been augmented by a spurious text. But for what purpose? And how had the forger obtained the valid part of the document in the first place? If he had, moreover, he would have had a sample of Captain Nutting's customary signature in front of him. Why, then, add a signature so flagrantly different?

A Tentative Resolution

In *The Holy Blood and the Holy Grail*, we published the text of what purported to be the statutes of the Prieuré de Sion. The text was headed 'Sionis Prioratus'. It was dated 5 June 1956, and bore the signature of the Order's alleged Grand Master at that time, Jean Cocteau. The statutes consisted of twenty-two articles. Most of the articles were elaborate, sometimes bureaucratic, sometimes ritualistic, but one of them, Article X, stood out in its mundane simplicity: 'On admission, the member must provide a birth certificate and a specimen of his signature'.

This, of course, is what the documents notarised by Patrick J.

Freeman ultimately involved – an officially verified birth certificate and signature. Part of the 1956 document had been unequivocally established as fraudulent. The corresponding part of the 1955 document was now necessarily suspect, even though nothing could be either proved or disproved about it. But what was indisputable was that Patrick J. Freeman *had* notarised the birth certificates and signatures in question.

Bearing this in mind, one must refer back to the quote ascribed to Lord Blackford in the doctored text of Jania Macgillivray's article and quoted on p. 209, above. According to this text, Lord Blackford says:

> It was the reforms of Jean Cocteau in 1955 which caused the creation [of the new organisation] by denying members of the Order their anonymity. At that time, all members were compelled to furnish a birth certificate and a notarised signature. A necessity perhaps ... but an infringement of freedom.

This statement, it must be remembered, had first appeared when Jania's article was doctored, some time between 1979 and 1981. We had received a copy of it from the Marquis de Chérisey in 1981 – two years before M. Plantard showed us the notarised documents bearing signatures of men connected with Guardian Assurance, over whose board of directors Lord Blackford presided as chairman.

Might the circle of Englishmen involved in the affair have been long-standing members of the Prieuré de Sion? Perhaps they had become associated with the Order through their links with the French Resistance during the Second World War. Perhaps they had been associated with it for longer. And even though Lord Blackford, in the statement attributed to him, apparently rebelled against Article X in Cocteau's statutes, perhaps Blackford's colleagues, however reluctantly, complied. That, certainly, would explain the notarised birth certificates and signatures.

A number of sources, including some issuing from the Prieuré de Sion itself, had spoken repeatedly of a crisis or upheaval within the Order dating from 1955 and 1956. A full-scale schism was reportedly averted only by the diplomatic resourcefulness of Pierre Plantard de Saint-Clair, who is said to have 'reintegrated' the Order. Is it possible that the friction of 1955–6 led certain members of the Order, for reasons that will probably never be known by outsiders, to sequester certain material of value, including Saunière's parchments? If nothing else, this would have constituted something with which to bargain.

We do not think that possibility can be altogether discounted. But there is another possibility as well. If men such as Viscount Leathers, Major Clowes and Captain Nutting had complied with Article X in the statutes, they would have provided – as, indeed, they appear to have done – notarised copies of their birth certificates and signatures. In practice, this would have meant that the hierarchy of the Prieuré de Sion acquired and accumulated a quantity of duly notarised birth certificates and signatures. Presumably, they would have been kept on file. At any time in the future, and especially after the men who provided them were safely dead, they could be recycled. Lord Selborne, for example, died in September 1971. At any time thereafter, his birth certificate and signature could have been exhumed from the files, a text could have been added and dated 1956 – and the deception, if not for the single slip about Lloyds Bank Europe, would have been wholly undetectable.

Certainly there were the shadowy traces of a pattern here. Article X in the statutes, Lord Blackford's alleged statement condemning Article X in the statutes and the apparent adherence to Article X by Nutting, Clowes, Leathers and Selborne could not be entirely coincidental. But the scenario we had woven presupposed that whatever forgery existed in the notarised documents had been perpetrated by the Prieuré de Sion – or, at any rate, by certain of its members. At the same time, however, and plausible though the scenario seemed to us, we could not ignore the evidence of some other hand involved – a hand which appeared to be working not for, but against the Prieuré de Sion.

Although there had been earlier references to the notarised documents, M. Plantard never claimed to have seen them; and he insisted that he had acquired them only in 1983, a short time before he showed them to us. We were inclined to credit this assertion. The garbling of Captain Nutting's name prior to 1983, and the general vagueness of detail, did indeed suggest that members of the Prieuré de Sion in France had not actually seen the documents and had spoken of them wholly on the basis of hearsay. Moreover, when we pointed out the inconsistency of Lloyds Bank Europe, M. Plantard was visibly shocked and upset. He virtually beseeched us to continue our investigation and report back to him on any new developments. He also undertook enquiries of his own, after which he readily, if ruefully, admitted the 1956 document to be spurious. On the basis of all this, it became increasingly apparent that, if there had been an attempt to dupe us, the attempt had not originated with M. Plantard. On the contrary, it appeared that he himself was the intended dupe and we were quite incidental. We, it seemed, had simply been caught up in some shadowy intrigue, some invisible chess game, between the Prieuré de Sion and someone else.

In dealing with the kind of problem posed by the notarised documents, one instinctively tends to polarise possibilities, to reduce the issue to an elementary 'either/or' proposition. Either the documents are legitimate or they are not. If they are not, they cannot be taken seriously and must be dismissed out of hand. And yet it was obvious that things, in this case, were not so conveniently simple. One of the documents, at least in part, was unquestionably spurious. On the other hand, there were too many aspects of the whole affair – Mr Bigland's statements to us, to take but one example – that rested on a solid enough foundation to warrant further enquiry. The more we examined the matter, the more we began to realise that we were not dealing either with straight-forwardly legitimate documents *or* with 'mere' forgeries. On the contrary, we were dealing with something else, something that fell into a category somewhere between truth and falsehood. This category is familiar enough to intelligence agencies. Indeed, it constitutes one of their primary activities. It is called *disinformation*. It involves the deliberate, calculated dissemination of equivocal data, partially true, partially erroneous, in order to conceal something, to divert people from something, to deflect attention in one or another peripheral or tangential direction. But the best lies are always embellishments or variations on the truth, not total fabrications. The most effective disinformation is always structured around a core of validity. It is from this core that the labyrinth of cul-de-sacs and blind alleys invariably radiates.

Both we and M. Plantard had been victims of disinformation. Whoever had devised this disinformation knew quite precisely what M. Plantard had been expecting to find in the notarised documents – knew it well enough to convince him that he had indeed found it. Whoever was responsible not only knew M. Plantard extremely well, but knew also the Prieuré de Sion extremely well, knew the background to the affair extremely well and had access to some impressive resources. The deception could not have been the work of an amateur. It was far too sophisticated, far too professional, for that.

Inevitably, our suspicions gravitated towards the secret services – of Britain, of France or even (though we had as yet no idea why) of the United States. Captain Nutting had been linked with British Intelligence by one associate. We also had grounds for suspecting involvement on the part of the French Internal Security Service. A journalist whom we knew, while on a job in Paris, had been told by an officer of French Security to read *The Holy Blood and the Holy Grail* – because, he intimated cryptically, it was relevant to contemporary political issues. It must be remembered, moreover, that representatives of insurance companies doing business in France in the mid-1950s were obliged by law to provide notarised birth certificates and signatures. The French government would thus have had easy access to the birth certificates and signatures of the men whose names appeared on the notarised documents.[11]

But there was one other intelligence service which came under equally strong suspicion. It had worked with both British Intelligence and the American OSS during the Second World War. It had remained active to the present, maintaining close links with both the CIA and the Vatican. It had, by its very nature, a direct and profound interest in anything pertaining to Christendom in general and Jesus in particular. It included – or so we were later told – certain members of the Prieuré de Sion, even though the two organisations would seem in many respects to be diametrically opposed to one another. And Saunière's parchments were said quite specifically to have found their way into its archives. The intelligence service in question was that of the Knights of Malta.

19

The Anonymous Tracts

When M. Plantard first showed us the originals of the notarised documents in the spring of 1983, he stipulated that we should neither discuss them with anyone, nor reproduce them in print. If word about them leaked out, he said, there could be awkward consequences. Certain interested parties – one of whom, he implied, was the French government – might contrive to seize the parchments found by Saunière, or obtain them by trickery, and they might never be seen again. They would simply disappear into some archive as state secrets. Unlike English and American archives, those in France tend to stay closed.

We assented to M. Plantard's request. We agreed not to discuss the documents publicly until the Prieuré de Sion, or people connected with it, had first done so. We agreed not to reproduce them or their text until they had already entered into the public domain.

In November 1983, Louis Vazart sent us a text he had just completed on Dagobert II and various other historical aspects of the story. It consisted of the typescript for a book, photocopied and bound. To our astonishment, it contained – and not even with much discussion about them – blurred photographs of the notarised documents.

We were perplexed. Why had M. Vazart published the documents if they were inimical to the Prieuré de Sion's interests? And why had M. Plantard sworn us to secrecy if, long before there was any question of our reproducing the documents in a book of ours, M. Vazart was to do so in a book of his? We could not imagine that M. Vazart would undertake such an action without M. Plantard's knowledge and approval. We were about to put these questions to M. Plantard when events suddenly took a dramatic new turn, in an entirely different direction.

In mid-December 1983, we received in the post an anonymous

tract – a 'squib' of the sort not uncommon in French and Italian politics. We learned subsequently that the tract in question had not just been sent to us, but had been widely circulated throughout France. It consisted of a single page, very sloppily typed and then photocopied. The text purported to be an advance publicity notice for a forthcoming book by Jean-Luc Chaumeil, the man who had acted as the Prieuré de Sion's emissary when we first made contact with the Order in 1979. As stated above, M. Chaumeil had subsequently been disowned by the Order.

There is no internal evidence that M. Chaumeil himself actually wrote the tract. This, however, is strongly implied. The reader is clearly intended to be left with that impression. At the upper left-hand corner of the page, there is a logo – a clenched hand brandishing a rose – an established symbol of the French Socialist Party. In capital letters at the top, there is the announcement: 'TO APPEAR NEXT JANUARY IN ALL BOOKSHOPS: THE DOCTRINE OF THE PRIEURÉ DE SION (FIVE VOLUMES) JEAN-LUC CHAUMEIL'. Below, there is the following text:

> 'I was manipulated by the Prieuré de Sion into writing my work, *The Treasure of the Golden Triangle*' – declares J-L. Chaumeil – 'I am now going to reveal the whole truth of this affair.'
>
> The work will reveal that *L'Enigme sacrée* [French translation of *The Holy Blood and the Holy Grail*] is nothing but a vast hoax resting on no serious foundation. Furthermore, since 1981, Pierre Plantard is no longer Grand Master [and] the Prieuré is directed by an Englishwoman named Ann Evans, the true author of this paranoid fiction!
>
> Pierre Plantard is nothing but a ... [here follows a defamatory statement about M. Plantard, M. Vazart and the curator of the museum at Stenay which may well be unwarranted].[1]
>
> Is it necessary to recall that in 1952, Pierre Plantard illicitly effected the transfer from France to Switzerland (to the Union des Banques Suisses) of gold ingots worth more than one hundred million [francs] ...

There then follows a vicious personal libel against M. Plantard, which we cannot legally repeat and which, in any case, has no bearing whatever on our story. After that, the text resumes:

> This affair, like the others, was swept under the carpet because Pierre Plantard was, at the beginning of 1958, a secret agent of De Gaulle, assuming the Secretariat of the Committees of

Public Safety. In 1960, he linked up with ... Gérard de Sède, as well as gaining the support of André Malraux in order to play up the affair of Gisors in which ... another ... individual, Philippe de Chérisey, was involved ...[2]

In 1980, a certain J. P. Deloux and Brétigny set up [the magazines] *Inexpliqué*, *Atlas* and *Nostra* under the aegis of a member of the Prieuré de Sion, Gregory Pons, and launched *Rennes-le-Château: capital secrète*, a booklet in colour published in 220,000 copies. Then, with that job done, it was for *Nostra* to proclaim Plantard future Grand Monarque, and now *Hebdo-Magazine* supports Jacques Chirac, who accommodates himself very well indeed to the resonant appeal of the Prieuré ...

As can be seen, only the opening paragraph of this text constitutes an allegedly direct quote from M. Chaumeil. Everything that follows is intended to sound as though it represents what M. Chaumeil has to say. But there is no indication of whether M. Chaumeil himself is actually saying it, or whether it is being ascribed to him by the tract's anonymous author.

There are obvious points in the text requiring some explanation, which the reader will find in the notes at the end of this book. There are also obvious points which require correction. In one case, at least, we could confirm that the author of the tract does not only jump to conclusions. He positively pole-vaults. In the acknowledgments to *The Holy Blood and the Holy Grail*, we especially singled out Ann Evans, our literary agent – 'without whom', we said, 'this book could not have been written'. Presumably on the basis of this statement, the author of the tract has concluded that an elusive Englishwoman named Ann Evans was in fact the primary source of our information and, indeed, the true author of our book. This kind of solecism immediately called into question the plausibility of what followed. Nevertheless, there are some points worth noting.

In the first place, the tract was patently subject to legal action. Had we wished to do so, we ourselves could have filed a complaint. So could Ann Evans. The insults and allegations directed at Messrs Vazart, Chérisey and Plantard were even more actionable. Whoever wrote the text must surely have known that he was taking a considerable risk, and that exposure could lead to serious consequences. Why, then, was the text written and circulated? To put forward M. Chaumeil's point of view? Or to frame him? And if so, why?

The second point is that the tract's explicit intent is to debunk M. Plantard and the Prieuré de Sion. And yet it contrives, either by crass ineptitude or by cunning design, to do precisely the opposite. Whatever M. Plantard's alleged moral transgressions, he emerges as a powerful figure – a 'secret agent of De Gaulle', a man who can act as Secretary-General for the Committees of Public Safety, can call on the aid of no less a person than André Malraux, can traffic in large sums of money. M. Plantard may appear more sinister as a result of these charges, but he is certainly not diminished. Neither is the Prieuré de Sion. According to the tract, the Prieuré – in a manner unspecified – can 'manipulate' a man into writing a book. It can orchestrate the content of a number of magazines and publicise or withhold material at will. It apparently has access to the media and, one would assume, substantial revenue. It elicits a sympathetic response from Jacques Chirac. Again, one is left with an impression of an organisation more sinister than one perhaps believed, but not any the less influential or powerful. If the purpose of the tract was to debunk and deflate M. Plantard and the Prieuré de Sion, the anonymous author had proceeded in a decidedly singular fashion.

Stolen Archives

At our behest, one of our associates in Paris telephoned M. Chaumeil, arranged a meeting with him and asked him about the tract. At a subsequent meeting, we ourselves did so as well. On both occasions, M. Chaumeil vehemently protested his innocence. He was not responsible for the tract, he insisted. He did not repudiate any of its allegations, but he denied having written them. He was, he maintained, being framed. This was a possibility that could not be discounted. M. Chaumeil has the habit of being rather heavy-handed, not to say vitriolic, in some of his statements, both private and public. In one of his own books (*Du premier au dernier templier*), of which he kindly gave us a copy, he had attacked us in language calculated to make a curate blush. Other victims of his slanging who lacked our sense of humour might have been more than happy to 'set him up'.

In his meeting with our associate, he was reportedly nervous. Apparently, M. Plantard had threatened legal action, and M. Chaumeil, though defiant, naturally found this worrying. If, as he protested, he was innocent, he might now find himself in the position of having to prove it in court.

A few days after we had received the tract from an anonymous source, we received a package of papers from M. Plantard. Not knowing presumably that we had received the tract, M. Plantard enclosed a copy. He also enclosed a riposte to the tract in the form of a well-printed broadsheet entitled *La Camisole Bulletin 'Torchon-Réponse' No. 1*, with a text by Louis Vazart – a text quite as abusive as that of the tract, but in more coherent prose. Enclosed, too, was a copy of a letter from M. Plantard to M. Chaumeil. In this letter, M. Plantard accused M. Chaumeil of having written the tract and demanded a formal public retraction of the allegations. If such retraction were not forthcoming, M. Plantard declared, he would file suit for defamation of character. So, too, would Louis Vazart and the Marquis de Chérisey.

There followed a pause as the Christmas holidays established a transient peace, if not on earth generally, then at least among the feuding parties in Paris. Hostilities resumed with the new year. During the first week of February, we received another package of documents from M. Plantard, intended, like the previous package, to keep us abreast of developments. The most important item in the new sheaf of papers was a two-page text, dated 17 January 1984. At the top of the first page, there was an official Prieuré de Sion letterhead – the first we had ever seen. This was accompanied by a crest with the letters R+C, presumably denoting Rose Croix. There was also what appeared to be the rubber stamp of an official seal – the R+C crest enclosed in two concentric ciricles with the inscribed logo 'Prieuré de Sion – Secretariat Général' and, below, the signature of M. Plantard. In the upper left-hand corner there was some sort of reference number: 3/3/6/84. The document was entitled 'Mise en Garde' (Cautionary Notice') and addressed, with characteristically Masonic abbreviations, 'CONFIDENTIELLE à nos F .·.' – 'Confidential, to our brethren'. Why, we wondered, had it been sent to outsiders such as ourselves? Why were we being drawn into M. Plantard's dispute with M. Chaumeil?

The text of the 'Mise en Garde' clashed rather discordantly with the portentous formalities at the top of the page. It consisted, again, of a torrent of invective and abuse directed at Jean-Luc Chaumeil. It purported to be, for the elucidation of all members of the Prieuré de Sion, a kind of deposition of charges or accusations. Thus, it began:

We are obliged to send this present 'Mise en Garde' against the ... individual known as Jean-Luc Chaumeil, born 20th

October, 1944, in Lille ... against whom an action for libel has been lodged in the High Court at Nanterre 92000 by our G . . . M . . . [Grand Master] on 16th December, 1983.[3]

There followed a selected list of the 'calumnies' Chaumeil was accused of having made – and, to counter his protests of innocence, photocopied extracts reputedly in his own handwriting. On the second page, there were more such excerpts, after which the text of the deposition resumed, speaking of two boxes of Prieuré de Sion archives dating from 1935 to 1955:

> These two boxes were stolen in 1967 from the then home of our Brother Philippe de Chérisey. By whom? ... This modest package contained letters by our late G[rand] M[aster] Jean Cocteau, by our Brethren Alphonse Juin, André Malraux, etc. Was the profane J. L. Chaumeil, then, the receiver of these stolen goods? Be that as it may, he also attempted to palm them off on our friend Henry Lincoln ...

Needless to say, this was flagrantly untrue. At his meeting with us, Chaumeil had denied having any Prieuré documents, or indeed any further interest in the Prieuré. And neither at that meeting, nor at any other time had he tried to sell us, give us or palm off on us documents of any kind. Why, then, were we again being dragged into the affair? In any case, the Prieuré seemed sufficiently concerned about the matter to issue a warning:

> The Prieuré de Sion and its members have no interest in the maunderings of ... J-L. Chaumeil, and those who make themselves accomplices in this traffic of documents and libels risk finding themselves inculpated in this affair at the High Court.

From here, the text moved on to further fulminations against M. Chaumeil. But one striking inconsistency emerged. On the one hand, the prospect of M. Chaumeil writing a book on the Prieuré de Sion was greeted with scorn. M. Chaumeil, it was claimed, could not possibly say anything of validity about the Prieuré. And yet two boxes of the Prieuré's archives, covering the years 1935–55, were said to have been stolen, and it was strongly implied that M. Chaumeil had access to them. How, then, could one be so certain that anything he said would indeed be 'mystification' and 'pure invention'? The Prieuré, it seemed to us, was perhaps protesting a bit too much. It was clear that something had genuinely disturbed them. Quite apart from questions of personal insult and defamation of character, they were obviously worried.

The text of the 'Mise en Garde' provided much food for thought. But there remained one further aspect of the document, more significant and more provocative than anything in the text itself. At the bottom of the second page, the two seals – one for the Prieuré de Sion as a whole, one for its Secretariat-General – appeared again. Below these seals there were four signatures, appended 'on behalf of the Prieuré de Sion'. The signatures, reading from left to right were: John E. Drick, Gaylord Freeman, A. Robert Abboud and Pierre Plantard.

In the doctored version of Jania Macgillivray's article, dating from some time between 1979 and 1981, there had been one reference to Gaylord Freeman. After the death of Jean Cocteau in 1963, the doctored text declared, power in the Prieuré de Sion had been exercised by a triumvirate consisting of Pierre Plantard, Gaylord Freeman and Antonio Merzagora. By virtue of this reference, Gaylord Freeman's name, at least, was familiar to us. The names of John E. Drick and A. Robert Abboud were not. We had never encountered them before.

The Meeting at 'La Tipia'

We had received the package containing the 'Mise en Garde' on 3 February 1984, a Friday. On 6 February, the following Monday, we were scheduled to fly to Paris for a conference we had arranged with M. Plantard. There was no time, before our departure, to track the identities of Messrs Drick, Freeman and Abboud.

At M. Plantard's request, we met him at a brasserie called 'La Tipia' situated on the rue de Rome, immediately adjacent to the Gare Saint-Lazare. M. Plantard remarked that it was a convenient rendezvous point for him. He came into town by train. After meeting with us, he could depart again at once, without having to leave the immediate environs of the railway station. In the months that followed, we were again to meet with M. Plantard at La Tipia on the rue de Rome. Not until later, however, would the place acquire a very provocative significance.

In contrast to every previous occasion. M. Plantard met us alone, without the usual entourage of associates. What was more, M. Plantard seemed genuinely distressed about a number of things and anxious not only to confide in us, but also, in certain respects at least, to enlist our aid. In the course of our conversation, a number of diverse issues were raised. As usual, such answers as we received raised new flurries of questions.

1 Needless to say, we asked M. Plantard who Gaylord Freeman, John E. Drick and A. Robert Abboud were. M. Plantard replied, bluntly but with a slight note of apology in his voice, that he was not prepared to answer that particular question. It pertained, he said, to internal business of the Prieuré de Sion, which he was unable to discuss with outsiders. We attempted to pursue the matter further, asking if the men in question were English or American. M. Plantard only repeated what he had said a moment before – he could not discuss the Prieuré's internal business.

2 Nevertheless, he *did* proceed to discuss the Prieuré's internal business, or at least one aspect of it. The subject seemed to slip out during a moment of casual banter, when M. Plantard had briefly relaxed his guard. Being Grand Master was sometimes a bother, he said half-jocosely, in the tone of a fond parent ironically complaining about parenthood. We expressed vague surprise and M. Plantard briefly elaborated. It was not a major problem, he said in an offhand way, but just now there was a degree of friction within the ranks of the Order, and he had to ensure that this should not turn into internecine strife. The chief difficulty, he said, was being caused by the Prieuré's 'Anglo-American contingent', who apparently wished to move in a different direction from their continental brethren. Beyond this, M. Plantard refused to elaborate. Indeed, he grew reticent on the subject, as if deciding he had already said too much. In consequence, we received no indication of who, precisely, the 'Anglo-American contingent' might be, nor of what might constitute the bone of contention. We were left to speculate in the dark about what – given the Prieuré de Sion as we understood it – might cause dissension in the Order's ranks.

3 Shortly after this fragment of conversation, M. Plantard paused and began to muse. There were at present two vacancies in the Order, he said reflectively. It would be a great advantage to have those vacancies occupied by 'foreigners' who would be sympathetic to the French and continental position. That would serve to counterbalance the influence of the 'Anglo-American contingent'. There was a long and pregnant pause. We said nothing. Then conversation drifted to a different topic. But for a moment, it actually appeared as if M. Plantard had been about to offer us membership in the Order. If our impression was correct and he had indeed considered doing so, why had he not followed through? Presumably he realised that we could not possibly have accepted, could not possibly have pledged ourselves to the

secrecy which such admission would have entailed. Moreover, M. Plantard had said there were two vacancies, and there were three of us. In any case, the moment came and passed. It lingered in our minds long afterwards as a tantalising instant – an instant when, to the extent at least of a crack, a door had opened, then closed again.

4 M. Plantard acknowledged the truth – or, rather, the half-truth – of one of the accusations made in the tract ascribed to Jean-Luc Chaumeil. According to the tract, M. Plantard had illicitly transferred a quantity of gold from France to Switzerland in 1952. M. Plantard admitted that he had indeed transferred substantial funds to Switzerland. But while such a transaction was illicit in 1984, under President Mitterand's government, in the 1950s it had been perfectly legitimate. Moreover, he explained, the transaction had not been on his own behalf. The resources involved in the transfer had had nothing to do with him personally, and he had not in any way profited from them. On the contrary, they had comprised a special fund for use by the Committees of Public Safety; and he, as Secretary-General of the Committees, had undertaken the transaction on their behalf, at the express behest of Charles de Gaulle.

But there was more to the matter than this. The affair, M. Plantard said, had been highly confidential. How had the writer of the tract learned of it, even if only in garbled or distorted fashion? Only, M. Plantard maintained, through some official source in the present French government. What was more, he said, during the last few months additional sums had been transferred to that Swiss account. Why? Presumably to discredit him personally, if not to frame him. Such transactions, by 1984, were indeed illegal, and one could find oneself in serious trouble. Again, the apparently 'inside knowledge' of the affair, the amount of the sums recently transferred and the knowledge of the account number in which they were deposited attested, M. Plantard argued, to the involvement of one or another government office or agency.

5 M. Plantard handed us a book review from a magazine. The review had been written by someone who simply signed himself 'Bayard'. It dealt with a book by (we learned subsequently) a French-Canadian priest, the Reverend Père Martin. Martin's book was entitled *Le Livre des compagnons secrets du Général de Gaulle* ('The Book of the Secret Companions of General de Gaulle'), published by Éditions du Rocher. Its purpose was to explore an alleged group of secret advisers and associates of De

Gaulle, organised into a coherent cabal or order which Martin called 'les Quarante-Cinq' ('the Forty-Five'). In fact, as we discovered when we read Martin's text, 'les Quarante-Cinq' appeared to have no connection whatever with the Prieuré de Sion. In his review, however, 'Bayard' explicitly accused Martin of deliberately trying to sow confusion in the reader's mind by confounding 'les Quarante-Cinq', with the Prieuré. By means of this rather ingenious device, he contrived to publish information about the Prieuré – and to do so as if it were common knowledge. We quote the last column of 'Bayard's' review, which constitutes the most relevant section:

One can also wonder, too, if this book has a hidden purpose, which would seem to be to confuse 'les Quarante-Cinq' with the Prieuré de Sion. There are numerous references to this latter Order, never named by whoever it is who signs himself R. P. Martin (and who is not, however, a member), as though, in speaking of 'les Quarante-Cinq', he wishes to refer us to the forty-five French members of the Prieuré de Sion during the period of Jean Cocteau's Grand Mastership, when Marshal Juin and André Malraux were 'Croisés' [i.e., senior members of the Prieuré].

After Cocteau's death in 1963 and Marshal Juin's in 1967, there remained only forty-three French members. It was at this time that, on the insistence of General de Gaulle (who was not a member of the Prieuré de Sion), Pierre Plantard de Saint-Clair was raised to the rank of 'Croisé'.

On the death of André Malraux in 1976, when the Americans were trying to gain supremacy in the Order, there still remained only forty-three French members.

So – if only by the play made with the number of French members – is one to understand that one of the aims of R. P. Martin is also to indicate, to those aware of contemporary arcana, that he is hinting at the French branch of the Prieuré de Sion and at the same time attributing to it a specific political stance?

The game is a clever one: starting from trustworthy facts (one of Sion's French Commanderies is indeed directed by a woman), or roughly trustworthy facts, the author goes on from them to substantiate the idea of a certain 'Gaullien' vision of the world.

But is this not an attempt to influence the internal equi-librium of the Prieuré de Sion in attributing to the French branch a policy which is not its own – at the very moment when it is attempting to counterbalance the American and English influence and re-establish a natural balance?[4]

We asked M. Plantard if the statements made about the Prieuré de Sion were correct. He replied that they were. We asked him who 'Bayard' was. 'Perhaps R. P. Martin,' M. Plantard replied, with a grin which suggested that 'Bayard' could quite as readily be himself. But whatever 'Bayard's' identity, the statements ascribed to him were extremely interesting. In the first place, he emphasised the same points M. Plantard had made to us verbally – the insistence on friction within the Prieuré de Sion caused by an 'Anglo-American contingent'. He also echoed the ambiguous insistence made elsewhere, that the Prieuré was not political. He stated definitively, for the first time to our knowledge, that Marshal Juin and André Malraux were members of the Prieuré, and he specified their rank in the Order – that of 'Croisé'. According to the statutes, 'Croisé' was the second highest grade in the Order, immediately below that of Grand Master. There were three 'Croisés', then nine 'Commandeurs', the grade which followed.

'Bayard's' comment about De Gaulle was particularly interesting. He stated clearly that De Gaulle was *not* personally a member of the Prieuré de Sion. At the same time, he also made it apparent that De Gaulle was not only privy to the Prieuré's affairs, but also exercised enough influence on the Order to insist on M. Plantard's promotion to the rank of 'Croisé' following the death of Marshal Juin. If this were true, however, it would mean that, prior to 1967, M. Plantard had been a member of some lower grade. Yet according to the Marquis de Chérisey, M. Plantard, as long ago as 1956, had averted a major schism in the Order by his diplomacy. And, according to the doctored text of Jania Macgillivray's article, power in the Prieuré, after Cocteau's death in 1963, had been exercised by a triumvirate consisting of M. Plantard, Gaylord Freeman and Antonio Merzagora. Granted, it is not altogether unusual for a subordinate, especially at a moment of crisis, to assume a role of authority. Yet if this were the case with M. Plantard, it would mean that in all his actions between 1956 and 1967, he had been functioning as a subordinate – and not even a subordinate of the second rank, but of the third or below.

6 We pressed M. Plantard on the notarised documents bearing the signatures of Viscount Leathers, Captain Nutting, Major

Clowes and Lord Selborne. We reminded M. Plantard that he had requested us not to discuss or publicise these documents. And yet Louis Vazart had reproduced photographs of them in his book on Dagobert II. Why, if the documents were thus going to be made public, had M. Plantard asked us to maintain secrecy? M. Plantard looked genuinely distressed. He had not known, he said bitterly, that M. Vazart was going to publish reproductions of the documents. If he had known in advance, he would have prevented it. Had not M. Vazart consulted him then? No, M. Plantard replied, he had known that M. Vazart was working on the book, but had had no idea it was going to include any reference to the documents. But surely, we pursued, M. Plantard had given or at least shown the documents to M. Vazart in the first place. Had he not requested M. Vazart's secrecy, just as he had ours? He had *not* given the documents to M. Vazart in the first place, M. Plantard replied. He had no idea where M. Vazart had obtained them. The first indication that M. Vazart knew anything about them was when they appeared in print, as a *fait accompli*.

We were baffled. M. Plantard had shown us the originals of the documents in April of the previous year. If he had not shown them to M. Vazart as well, then someone else obviously had duplicates. Where had M. Vazart obtained them? M. Plantard shrugged helplessly. He did not know, he said. He found the whole situation disturbing in the extreme. He virtually implored us to investigate the matter further. He would, he said, be grateful for any information our enquiries might yield.

These were the primary points in our conference with M. Plantard in February 1984. Nothing had been resolved, none of the questions lurking in our minds had been satisfactorily answered. At the same time, a veritable welter of new questions had been spawned. Who were John E. Drick, Gaylord Freeman and A. Robert Abboud? What was the role of the 'Anglo-American contingent' in the Prieuré de Sion and why should they be a source of friction within the Order? Had M. Plantard indeed been on the brink of offering us membership in the Prieuré to counter the influence of this 'contingent'? Why should someone in the French government be transferring funds to a secret Swiss bank account in order to discredit M. Plantard? What significance could we ascribe to the information offered by 'Bayard' in his review of the book by R. P. Martin? And from whom, if not from M. Plantard, had M. Vazart obtained the notarised documents bearing the signatures of Viscount Leathers, Captain Nutting, Major Clowes and Lord Selborne?

During our sojourn in Paris, we also had a series of meetings with Louis Vazart. M. Vazart echoed M. Plantard's assertions. No, he said, he had not received the notarised documents from M. Plantard. From where, then, had he obtained them? They had been sent to him, he said. Anonymously. In 'a plain brown envelope'. With British stamps and a London postmark! Once again, we were baffled. Who was playing at what? Was someone perhaps trying to frame *us*, to diminish *our* currency with M. Plantard and the Prieuré de Sion? In any case, if M. Vazart was telling the truth, one thing was clear – someone in London was *au fait* with the whole affair, was keeping closely abreast of developments, was monitoring everything and, at certain key moments, was mysteriously intervening.

20

The Elusive 'American Contingent'

It proved easy enough to establish the identities of Gaylord Freeman, John Drick and A. Robert Abboud. All three men were listed in a number of directories and other standard sources. Given this fact, M. Plantard's evasiveness was all the more puzzling. Why be tight-lipped about men whose lives and activities were so much a matter of public record?

All three men were, or had been, associated with the First National Bank of Chicago. John Drick had been with the bank since 1944, starting as an assistant cashier and within three years becoming an assistant vice-president. In 1969, he became president of the bank and, at the same time, one of its directors. He was also on the board of a number of other American companies – Stepan Chemical, MCA Incorporated, Oak Industries and Central Illinois Public Service.

Gaylord Freeman was originally a lawyer, joining the Illinois Bar in 1934. In 1940, he joined the First National Bank of Chicago as an attorney. In 1960, he became president of the bank. He was vice-chairman of the bank's board from 1962 until 1969, chairman from 1975 until 1980. He was also chairman and director of the First Chicago Corporation, and sat on the board of directors of Atlantic Richfield, Bankers Life and Casualty Company, Baxter Travenol Labs and Northwest Industries. During 1979–80, he had chaired a select 'task force' on inflation for the American Bankers' Association. He was associated with the MacArthur Foundation and was a trustee of the Aspen Institute of Humanistic Studies. The Aspen Institute had been founded in 1949 to acquaint high-level business executives with humanistic disciplines, especially literature. Today, it includes a headquarters in New York, a 2,000-acre estate on the Chesapeake Bay and conference centres in Hawaii, Berlin and Tokyo.

Robert Abboud had followed Gaylord Freeman as chairman of the board of the First National Bank of Chicago, but some years later was dismissed. Subsequently, he became president of Occidental Petroleum Corporation. In 1980 he and others were accused in a shareholders' action of misleading investors about the bank's financial condition during the mid-1970s. According to the *Herald Tribune*, in his defence he insisted that the bank was in dire financial straits when he assumed the chairmanship – in fact, he said its problems of 1974 'had been hidden to prevent a crisis of confidence in the banking system'.[1]

Were these men part of the 'Anglo-American contingent' to which M. Plantard had alluded? If so, that contingent extended into the rarefied spheres of high finance, not only in the United States but, presumably, elsewhere as well. At the same time, if Mr Abboud's *contretemps* with the bank was any indication, the contingent was plagued by its own factional strife.

Shortly after we had discovered the identities of Messrs Drick, Freeman and Abboud, we telephoned M. Plantard. Quite casually, we mentioned that we had learned of their affiliation with the First National Bank of Chicago. '*Vraiment?*' ('Really?') M. Plantard replied laconically, and with a certain irony in his voice, as if commending us for our thoroughness. We stated that, as a matter of course, we would naturally have to contact the three men in question. M. Plantard suddenly became distinctly nervous. Some very important issues were at stake, he declared. Would we please *not* contact the men in question until we had first had another personal meeting with him. Very reluctantly, we agreed, but posed a number of other queries. M. Plantard begged us not to ask for answers on the telephone. The whole affair would have to be discussed in detail, 'face to face'. Could he not, we pursued, elaborate on anything? '*Face à face*,' M. Plantard repeated.

We felt bound to honour our promise to M. Plantard and refrained from trying to contact Messrs Drick, Freeman and Abboud directly. At the same time, however, we promptly contacted friends in the States and requested as much information as could be obtained on the three men, as well as on the various companies, businesses and institutions with which they were associated. A few days later, we received a telephone call from New York. He was not altogether certain, our informant said, and would have to check on the matter; but, if his memory was accurate, he recalled reading that John Drick had died some two years before. How, then, could the man's signature appear on a document' dated 17 January 1984 – unless the Prieuré de Sion possessed some very extraordinary powers indeed?

If John Drick was dead, the signatures on the 'Mise en Garde' must be forgeries. As M. Plantard had also signed the 'Mise en Garde', and had sent a copy of it to us, we could not but suspect his involvement in some way. But from what we had come to know of him, it seemed most unlikely that he could be guilty of so careless and clumsy a blunder. To append the signature of a dead man to an apparently widely disseminated document was not only astonishingly slipshod. It was also downright dangerous, rendering oneself liable to all sorts of serious legal repercussions. Although we had never previously heard of him, John Drick was, after all, a prominent figure in the world of finance. Neither his identity nor his death was a secret, and whoever had contrived the 'Mise en Garde' must have known this.

If the signatures were forgeries, moreover, why these particular signatures? They had not been conjured up on the spur of the moment, nor were they randomly pulled out of a hat. Gaylord Freeman's name had appeared in the doctored text of Jania Macgillivray's article some years before. For some reason, we were being pointed quite specifically in the direction of the First National Bank of Chicago.

We rang the London branch of the First National Bank. Our query undoubtedly sounded peculiar – we asked if John Drick was indeed dead – and we were, accordingly, shunted from office to office. Eventually, we were connected with one of the bank's executive officers, who asked why we wanted to know. We explained that we'd heard John Drick had died some two years ago, but, at the same time, possessed a document apparently signed by him on 17 January 1984. The man at the bank turned cautiously vague. Yes, he said, he too seemed to recall something about Mr Drick having died, but he was not positive. Later in the day, he would be speaking to someone who could clarify the matter definitively. If we cared to leave a number, he would arrange for that person to telephone us.

That afternoon, we received a long-distance call from America. The caller – who, in deference to his request, we shall identify simply as 'Samuel Kemp' – introduced himself as one of the bank's senior officers. He also had a special concern with bank security which maintained a close liaison with Interpol.

We explained the situation – which, needless, to say, whetted 'Mr Kemp's' appetite. There ensued an extremely lengthy conversation, in which we tried to explain as much of the background as was feasible in the circumstances. 'Mr Kemp' was open, candid, thoroughly intrigued and only too willing to undertake whatever enquiries we might entrust to him. But he could confirm, quite definitively, that John Drick had indeed died in 1982, on 16 February. And in the course of this first conversation with 'Mr Kemp', one other item of interest emerged. Until 1983, it transpired, the First National Bank of Chicago had shared its London premises with Guardian Royal Exchange Assurance!

This could hardly be coincidental. But what did it mean? Had someone associated with the bank pilfered documents and signatures from the insurance company? Or had someone at the insurance company pilfered signatures from the bank? Whatever the explanation, there was a discrepancy in chronology. The Guardian Assurance signatures dated from, allegedly, 1955 and 1956. Even if they were appended later, it could not have been after 1971, because Lloyds Bank Europe, in that year, became Lloyds Bank International. Moreover, Major Hugh Murchison Clowes had died in 1956. On the other hand, the joint affiliation of Gaylord Freeman, John Drick and A. Robert Abboud with the First National Bank of Chicago dated from the mid 1970s. Whatever the answers to these questions, one thing seemed evident – someone with an interest in the affair was active in London.

During the weeks that followed, we maintained a constant contact with 'Mr Kemp'. After our initial conversation, he had proceeded to obtain a copy of our first book in order to familiarise himself with the background. We, for our part, sent him a copious dossier of documents pertinent both to material in our previous book and to our present investigation – including, of course, everything relating to the Guardian Assurance connection and the First National Bank of Chicago. This comprised not only the 'Mise en Garde' with the signatures of John Drick, Gaylord Freeman and A. Robert Abboud, but also the doctored text of Jania Macgillivray's article, in which we had seen Gaylord Freeman's name for the first time.

When he had sifted through this welter of material, 'Mr Kemp' was baffled but intrigued. He had had considerable experience in exposing frauds. This served to invest the story with a tantalising appeal, and his curiosity became as great as ours. He agreed to make enquiries of his own and also, at the first favourable opportunity, to speak with Gaylord Freeman personally. In the meantime, he could confirm one thing for us. The signatures appeared to be genuine. Certainly they conformed to every other specimen of the three men's signatures that could be found.

We continued to supply 'Mr Kemp' with additional documents

and with new information as it came to light. He pursued his own investigation, keeping us abreast of his progress, and compiled a detailed report. It appeared to compromise M. Plantard and the Prieuré de Sion irreparably.

From the years when Messrs Drick, Freeman and Abboud had worked together at the bank, 'Mr Kemp' was able to find only one document on which all three of their signatures appeared. This was the 1974 Annual Report of the First National Bank of Chicago and its parent company, the First Chicago Corporation. It had been released on 10 February 1975 and distributed to all the bank's branches, as well as to all shareholders. In this report, the signatures of John Drick, Gaylord Freeman and A. Robert Abboud had appeared together. Not only that. They had appeared in exactly the same sequence as on the 'Mise en Garde'.

'Mr Kemp' had measured the signatures on both documents. Those on the 1974 Annual Report proved to be exactly the same size as those on the 'Mise en Garde'. This was damning evidence indeed. It is virtually impossible for a person to get every letter, every loop and curlicue of his signature precisely the same size on two separate occasions. It was inconceivable that three men could have managed such a feat on the same two documents. There seemed to be little question that the signatures on the 'Mise en Garde' were based on a photocopy. Someone had manifestly photocopied the last page of the 1974 Annual Report, then reproduced the signatures on the 'Mise en Garde'.

Again, however, there remained the question of why. Why these particular men? And why incur the legal risk that using the signatures of these men would entail? As far as we knew, the 'Mise en Garde' had been fairly widely circulated – not only to members of the Prieuré de Sion, but to us, to other researchers on the subect in France and, it was implied, as part of a dossier submitted to the French judiciary. It seemed incredible that M. Plantard would dare expose himself in this way, dare render himself so vulnerable to the consequences of the deception. Other people could surely check as readily as we could. Would it not, then, be only a matter of time before the deception was unmasked? To 'steal' three signatures, one of them belonging to a dead man, was a serious matter. It was no longer merely a practical joke for the purpose of mystification. Nor was it very skilful disinformation.

'Mr Kemp' also reported that he had met with Gaylord Freeman. He had shown to Mr Freeman the 'Mise en Garde' with the three signatures. He had shown to Mr Freeman other documents pertaining to the Prieuré de Sion and to M. Plantard. He had asked, quite directly and explicitly, whether Mr Freeman was a member of the Prieuré de Sion, had ever been a member of the Prieuré de Sion, had ever heard of the Prieuré de Sion or Pierre Plantard de Saint-Clair.

In the dossier we sent 'Mr Kemp', we had included a copy of the Prieuré's statutes. According to Article XXII of these statutes: 'Disavowal of membership in the Prieuré de Sion, made publicly or in writing, without cause or personal danger, shall incur exclusion of the member, which shall be pronounced by the Convent.'[2] If Mr Freeman was indeed associated with the Prieuré, this statute, both we and 'Mr Kemp' reasoned, would oblige him to acknowledge it.

According to 'Mr Kemp', Mr Freeman had denied all knowledge of the matter. He was not a member of the Prieuré de Sion. He had never been a member of the Prieuré de Sion. He had never heard of the Prieuré de Sion, nor of Pierre Plantard de Saint-Clair.

At the same time, Mr Freeman's attitude had apparently been a little puzzling. He had, we were told, appeared slightly quizzical, slightly bemused by the questions put to him, but only distantly so. On the whole, he had been disconcertingly blasé. He had not seemed at all surprised – either by the question, or by his name occurring in so singular a context. He had certainly not expressed anger or indignation at the way in which his name and signature were being used. He had not even asked for further information, and had reacted no more strongly than if the enquiries referred to purely routine business.

Although such insouciance was perhaps striking, 'Mr Kemp' said he did not doubt Mr Freeman's denials. But this, he said, only made the affair more baffling for him. Something of consequence, he suspected, was somehow involved in it all, but he could not imagine what. Through his association with Interpol, he remarked, he had had occasion to investigate literally thousands of frauds. According to all the standards he was accustomed to apply in such circumstances, the present affair made absolutely no sense. Fraud, as he explained, was generally perpetrated for one, or both, of two reasons – for power or for financial gain. So far as the Prieuré de Sion was concerned, however, and especially so far as the specific instance of the 'Mise en Garde' was concerned, neither of these two motivations appeared to come into play. It was difficult to see how the business could possibly involve any jockeying for power. Indeed, the Prieuré had been compromised, rather than reinforced, by the use of apparently spurious signatures whose lack of authenticity could be so readily established. Nor was there any discernible element of financial gain. As we had discovered long ago, the

Prieuré's seeming indifference to money was one of the most convincing things about it. Far from seeking to accumulate revenue, the Prieuré seemed quite prepared to forgo it, even to spend it, in order to get certain material disseminated.

'Mr Kemp' said he had on occasion encountered bizarre and elaborate hoaxes. Now and again, he mentioned, retired members of the intelligence community might, for example, devise some intricate stratagem to amuse themselves and test their younger colleagues. But that, too, seemed irrelevant in the present case. The modern Prieuré had been perpetrating its mystifications for nearly thirty years, since 1956, when M. Plantard was thirty-six years old. Moreover, the implication of such names as Malraux, Juin and De Gaulle argued against a merely frivolous *jeu d'esprit*.

In sum, something was going on which baffled not only us, but also a professional expert in such matters, with years of experience behind him. 'Mr Kemp' concluded this conversation with us on a note of carefully calculated ambiguity, which we would later have reason to recall: 'Trust no one,' he said. 'Not even me.'

In the meantime, we had been pressing M. Plantard for the 'face to face' meeting which he himself had said was necessary. For reasons that became clear to us later, M. Plantard turned elusive. Frequently, we could not reach him on the telephone. When we did manage to do so, he pleaded a fraught schedule, or had to deal with something pertaining to his son's schooling, or was going to be out of Paris, or was suffering from a cold. In the past, he had always been pleased to meet with us. Now he seemed manifestly reluctant to do so. We had other things to occupy us, of course; we were busy researching New Testament history, Celtic Christianity and the material which forms the first part of this book. But we were still frustrated by the way in which time was dragging on and the meeting with M. Plantard continued to be deferred. Both he and the Prieuré de Sion were beginning to appear increasingly suspect.

Not much was happening on other fronts either. Our enquiries about the court case against M. Chaumeil led only to the statement that it was still pending. A book by M. Chaumeil did appear, but it proved to be a reissue of an earlier work, with a new introduction and postscript. It contained no scandalous revelations of the sort promised in the anonymous tract.

At last, we received a letter from M. Plantard. With a frigid formality of tone, he consented to the long overdue rendezvous, but with provisions: 'I will be pleased to meet with you at the end of September on an amicable basis, but I regret that I can give you no information for your publication.'

In the same letter, M. Plantard declared that he had established the 1955 notarised document – the one bearing the signatures of Viscount Leathers, Major Clowes and Captain Nutting – to be authentic. It had, he said, been examined and verified by 'experts'. On the other hand, he acknowledged the 1956 document – the one bearing the signature of Lord Selborne and the reference to Lloyds Bank Europe – to be fraudulent. Then, in capital letters, he reiterated his insistence that the notarised documents 'remain confidential and must not be published' – an insistence all the more perplexing in that the documents, as he himself admitted, had already been published by Louis Vazart and were hardly confidential any longer. Moreover, 'I have had forbidden in France all publications concerning the Prieuré de Sion and myself, this since the month of March, 1984 ...

The phraseology of this statement was interesting. We could not believe, of course, that M. Plantard possessed such sweeping powers of censorship. What he meant, presumably, was that he had instructed all members of the Prieuré de Sion to keep silence. His interdict might not extend to the press at large, but it would certainly encompass the various internal sources who had been leaking material to the public for nearly thirty years.

There was one other statement of interest in M. Plantard's letter. It was appended as a postscript: 'I also formally oppose the publication of correspondence between General de Gaulle and myself, as well as that with Marshal Juin or Henri, Comte de Paris. These documents, stolen from 37 rue St Lazare, Paris, are confidential and remain "state secrets", even though offered for sale ... '[3]

Had M. Plantard, believing we had access to such correspondence, inadvertently betrayed the fact that it existed – and perhaps that it might be in some way compromising? Or did he simply want us to think so? By this time, we were suspicious of everything. Nothing appeared straightforward; nothing could be taken at face value; everything had an alternative explanation. The Prieuré de Sion had begun to seem to us like a holographic image, shifting prismatically according to the light and the angle from which it was viewed. From one perspective, it appeared to be an influential, powerful and wealthy international secret society whose members included eminent figures in the arts, in politics, in high finance. From another perspective, it seemd a dazzlingly ingenious hoax devised by a small group of individuals for obscure purposes of their own. Perhaps, in some fashion, it was both.

A Confrontation with M. Plantard

As our meeting with M. Plantard approached, we assembled the evidence we had accumulated. It included at least three fairly damning items. We could not imagine how M. Plantard would be able to explain even one of them away, much less all three. He, of course, would have had no idea of the directions in which we had pursued our investigation, nor of what we had exhumed. We were confident that we would catch him off guard.

The first item was John Drick's death. How could M. Plantard account for Mr Drick having signed a document on 17 January 1984 when the man had died two years before?

The second point also pertained to the signatures on the 'Mise en Garde'. How could M. Plantard explain the fact that they were absolutely identical with those in the 1974 Annual Report of the First National Bank of Chicago?

The third item involved an entirely different matter. In 1979, M. Plantard – who until then had been known simply as Pierre Plantard – had begun to use a much more resonant title, Pierre Plantard de Saint-Clair, Comte de Sainte-Clair and Comte de Rhédae (the old name for Rennes-le-Château). In *The Holy Blood and the Holy Grail*, we had commented wryly on this apparently sudden acquisition of noble status, and M. Plantard had been affronted by our innuendo. To prove that he was not simply spuriously appropriating or inventing titles, he had shown us his passport and given us a photocopy of a birth certificate. In both documents, he was indeed named Plantard de Saint-Clair, Comte de Saint-Clair and Comte de Rhédae, and in the latter his father was also. But we ourselves, shortly thereafter, had requested a copy of M. Plantard's birth certificate from the Mairie of the 7th arrondissement. The information detailed in the birth certificate we received from this office was in almost every respect identical to that in the one M. Plantard had given us. But on the birth certificate we received from the Mairie, M. Plantard had no titles whatsoever, and his father was cited not as Comte de Saint-Clair or Comte de Rhédae. He was simply cited as a 'valet de chambre'.[4]

Granted, this in itself was not proof of anything. And even if the 'valet de chambre' birth certificate were valid, certain questions remained. How, for example, had M. Plantard been able to produce, so perfectly, an 'official copy' of the original? How had the paper, the official seals and the signatures been duplicated – if, indeed, they had? In any case, the inconsistency between a valet de chambre and a Comte de Saint-Clair and Rhédae warranted some explanation. It would, we felt, especially if presented to M. Plantard suddenly, without advance warning or time in which to prepare a response, at least elicit a revealing reaction. Even a moment of fluster might constitute a giveaway.

There was to be one further enigma before our confrontation with M. Plantard. It would obviously be more telling, we reasoned, if we had with us a copy of the 1974 Annual Report for the First National Bank of Chicago — if we had the original source of the signatures of Messrs Drick, Freeman and Abboud, and could produce it before M. Plantard's eyes. Accordingly, a week prior to our scheduled trip to Paris, we telephoned 'Mr Kemp' and asked him if he could send us a photocopy of the document; and we explained precisely why we wanted it. 'Mr Kemp' replied that there would be no problem and that a photocopy would be put in the post the folowing day.

On the following afternoon, we received a somewhat worried call from 'Mr Kemp's' secretary. He had instructed her, she said, to send us a photocopy of the last page of the 1974 Annual Report — the page bearing the three signatures in question. She had tried repeatedly to comply with these instructions — but the photocopy refused to take! She had tried every machine in the bank, but the signatures would not reproduce.

The next day, we spoke to 'Mr Kemp' again. He had investigated the matter himself, and the explanation appeared to be simple enough. The signatures on the Annual Report — possibly as a security measure to prevent spurious reproduction — had been printed in light blue ink, which had no graphite content. Without some graphite content, a photocopy would not take.

This, of course, was simple enough. But it raised an entirely new question. Along with 'Mr Kemp', we had concluded, pretty much definitively, that the signatures on the Prieuré de Sion's 'Mise en Garde' had simply been photocopied from the 1974 Annual Report. If it was impossible to make such a photocopy, how had M. Plantard contrived to obtain one?

Granted, there were other explanations. The signatures in the Annual Report might, for example, have been photographed, and a photocopy could then have been made from the photograph. But why go to so much bother for the sake of precisely these three signatures? Why not use some others, which *could* simply be photocopied with no difficulty whatever? If a forger were so cavalier, or so sloppy, as to use the signature of a man two years dead, why had he taken so much trouble about it when any other signature might just as well have served his purpose?

For the next few days, this conundrum nagged at us. Nevertheless, we still had three extremely telling pieces of evidence with which to confront M. Plantard. How could John Drick's signature have appeared on a document two years after his death? How could M. Plantard explain the absolute identity of the signatures on the Prieuré de Sion's 'Mise en Garde' with those of the bank's 1974 Annual Report? And how could he explain a birth certificate, obtained from the appropriate official source, which specified his father to have been not a count, but a valet de chambre? Armed with these questions, we embarked for what, amongst ourselves, we wryly called High Noon.

High Noon

On Sunday, 30 September, we made our rendezvous in Paris with M. Plantard at what had become the established venue, the brasserie named La Tipia on the rue de Rome. On previous occasions, we had always got there early and waited for him. This time, however, although we were punctual enough, he was waiting for us. Within a few moments, it became apparent that he had been waiting for us on other levels as well. Before we could even pose the compromising questions, he answered them.

On greeting each other, we exchanged the ritual greetings, then ordered cups of coffee. We produced a small tape-recorder and placed it on the table. M. Plantard glanced at it a little dubiously but made no objections. We then extracted from a briefcase the Prieuré de Sion's 'Mise en Garde' bearing the signatures of John Drick, Gaylord Freeman and A. Robert Abboud. Before we could even say anything about it, M. Plantard pointed to the three signatures.

'Those were made with a stamp, you know,' he said, gesturing with his hand as if rubber-stamping something.

We exchanged furtive glances. The possibility had never occurred to us before, nor had it occurred to 'Mr Kemp'. But yes, certainly, a stamp would serve to explain why the signatures on the 'Mise en Garde and those on the Annual Report were exactly the same size. Large businesses, government bureaucracies, other institutions which have to issue large numbers of documents do indeed use such stamps. A company director does not usually sign hundreds of pay-cheques individually. However, M. Plantard was clearly implying that he had, or had had access to, the stamp in question – the same stamp that had been used on the 1974 Annual Report.

But, we replied, shifting ground rapidly, one of the men whose signatures appeared there ...

Was dead, M. Plantard interrupted quite casually, taking the words out of our mouths. Yes, John Drick had died early in 1982. As a matter of routine, however, the Prieuré continued to use his signature on internal documents until the vacancy created in the Order by his death had been filled.

It was not, for us, the most plausible or the most satisfactory of explanations. To thus continue using a dead man's signature is hardly common practice in an institution of any kind. But we could hardly challenge M. Plantard's assertion. We were in no position to argue with him about the internal policies and procedures of the Prieuré de Sion, however unorthodox these might be.

We had never said anything to M. Plantard about our contact with 'Mr Kemp', nor about 'Mr Kemp's' interview with Gaylord Freeman. Neither did M. Plantard suggest explicitly that he knew anything of these two developments. Instead, as if to pre-empt our raising the point – or perhaps simply to make it apparent to us that he knew after all – he then casually remarked that as of the previous December, Article XXII of the Prieuré's statutes had been officially revoked. For the last nine months, members of the Prieuré were no longer obliged to acknowledge their membership. On the contrary, they were now instructed to repudiate all knowledge of the Order and divulge no information whatever.

We were effectively disarmed. Contrary to all our expectations, M. Plantard had produced an explanation for each of the points on which we were convinced we would trip him up. He had not faltered in producing these explanations, had not had to pause for thought, had not been even slightly flummoxed. What was more, he had quite clearly anticipated each of the points before we could raise them. There seemed only two ways of accounting for this. Either the man was genuinely clairvoyant, which seemed to us unlikely, or he had been 'tipped off'. But the sources of such a 'tip-off' were extremely limited, and we still trusted the discretion of 'Mr Kemp'.

There remained the question of the contradictory birth certificates. Accordingly, we produced them. M. Plantard remained superbly blasé. Again, there was not a moment's pause, not a flicker of uncertainty or embarrassment. He gave us a brief, slightly rueful, slightly ironic smile – as if commending us for assiduousness, even if it had entailed invading his privacy and delving into his personal life. Yes, he said, pointing to the certificate which cited his father as a valet de chambre, that document had been inserted in the Mairie office during the war. It had, he remarked nonchalantly, been common practice. Obviously, the Gestapo had gone through all documents. It was not at all uncommon – especially if one were in any way connected with the Resistance – to substitute falsified information in order to deceive the Germans.

This explanation, at least, we were able to confirm. The next day, we went to the Mairie in person and confronted the officials there with the discrepant birth certificates. Many documents had been falsified, we were told, in order to deceive or mislead the Germans during the war. Many original records had been destroyed or dispersed or removed.[5] The office could vouch for the authenticity of everything subsequent to the war. But on anything pre-dating 1945, there was simply no way of knowing. All they could say was whether something matched those in their archives. If M. Plantard's father had been a count, it would have been perfectly natural to conceal this fact from the Gestapo, who took pains to ferret out aristocrats. M. Plantard might very well have had his birth certificate removed and replaced by a different one. If, after the war, he had not rectified the office's files and records, the only information in the office would of course be false.

The Prieuré's Plans for the Future

In the course of our conversation in La Tipia, a number of other points came up in passing. As on previous occasions, M. Plantard waxed oracular about large-scale public events. Everything was in place now, he said at one stage. All the pieces were aligned on the chessboard in the requisite positions. Nothing could stop 'it' now, he declared, without deigning to clarify or elaborate on what 'it' was. Mitterrand, he added, had been a necessary stepping-stone. Now, however, Mitterrand had served his purpose and was expendable. The time had come to move on, and nothing could now stop 'it' from doing so.

Very explicitly, we asked M. Plantard if he personally knew Gaylord Freeman. Quite emphatically, M. Plantard said yes, fully aware that he was speaking into a tape-recorder. We asked why an important American financier such as Gaylord Freeman should care one way or the other about a Merovingian restoration in France. M. Plantard hesitated. For men like Mr Freeman, he then replied, the primary objective was European unity – a United States of Europe that welded the nations of the continent into a coherent power bloc of its own, comparable to the Soviet Union and the United States. At the same time, M. Plantard also spoke briefly about a kind of expanded Common Market – a financial or economic arrangement, similar to that of the EEC, which, however, included the United States as well. There was another pause, after which M. Plantard, as if reluctantly, added what sounded like an embittered comment. At present, he said, it would be a mistake for us to confuse the Prieuré de Sion's immediate objectives with a Merovingian restoration.

This last point was something new, a development which appeared to have occurred at some point subsequent to the publication of our previous book. Might it, we wondered, perhaps be the source of the difficulty caused by 'the Anglo-American contingent' within the Prieuré de Sion? Might there perhaps have been an internal squabble, with English and American members insisting on a shift of priorities – away from the original monarchical idea so dear to M. Plantard, and towards more mundane, more immediately practicable economic and political principles? When pressed to elaborate on the matter, M. Plantard refused to do so.

What of the Vatican? we asked, casting about for some cue that might prompt M. Plantard to reveal more. Was the present Pope a potential ally or potential adversary in whatever schemes were afoot? There were neither 'good popes' nor 'bad popes', M. Plantard replied. It – whatever 'it' might be – was, rather, a matter of an on-going policy for the Vatican, to which individual popes were bound. In any case, M. Plantard concluded, a rapprochement had been reached with the Vatican. Rome would co-operate. Certain concessions had been necessary in return, but they were essentially nominal.

Our book, by the way, had caused quite a few ripples in the Vatican, M. Plantard added – just to let us know, it seemed, that he was privy to such information.[6]

21

The Vista Widens

M. Plantard's comments had been vague, but we were nevertheless struck by the readiness with which he had discussed the political interests of the Prieuré de Sion. In the past, he had not only refused to discuss such interests. He had denied that they even existed. Why should he now be so loquacious? Did he truly wish to confide in us, or was there some other factor involved?

More perplexing still was the fact that M. Plantard *had*, more or less effectively, defused all the potential evidence with which we had planned to confront him. Not only that. He had been totally unsurprised by this evidence. And everything seemed to indicate that he had been warned in advance. Yet nothing could be proved one way or the other, and 'Mr Kemp', when we reported to him, was equally mystified.

At any rate, we now felt released from the promise we had made M. Plantard earlier in the year. At that time, in our telephone conversation, we had promised not to contact Gaylord Freeman directly until we and M. Plantard had had the 'face-to-face' conversation he requested. That conversation, inconclusive though it proved, had now occurred. We therefore wrote to Gaylord Freeman in Chicago, referring to his meeting with 'Mr Kemp' and asking if he would confirm, in writing, the position he had adopted at that interview. We received a somewhat curt reply. In his letter to us, as in his interview with 'Mr Kemp', Mr Freeman denied membership in the Prieuré de Sion, denied knowledge of M. Plantard, denied involvement in the events that had led us to contact him. He recognised the signatures as 'having been taken' from the 1974 Annual Report of the First National Bank of Chicago. He did not wish to be cited in any book. In his letter, as in his interview with 'Mr Kemp', he appeared uninterested in pursuing the matter further. There was no request for additional information about the way in which his name and signature were being used.

Three weeks after our meeting with M. Plantard in Paris, we received a package from him. It consisted of a brief cover note addressed to us, and copies of two letters addressed to the membership of the Prieuré de Sion. The first letter carried the Prieuré de Sion letterhead that had appeared on the 'Mise en Garde'. It was dated at Cahors, 10 July 1984 – two and a half months, that is, prior to our meeting at La Tipia.

In the text, M. Plantard announced to the Prieuré's membership that he had formally resigned his Grand Mastership and his own membership in the Order. Having been elected Grand Master at Blois on 17 January 1981, he said, he now felt obliged, 'for reasons of health' and 'for reasons of personal and family independence', to renounce his rights, and those of his family, in the Prieuré de Sion. The resignation would take effect in sixty days, 'in accordance with the internal regulations of the Order'. At the bottom of the page, he cited 'the decree of 16 December, 1983', whereby, apparently, Article XXII of the statutes had been revoked. All members of the Prieuré were now 'obliged to maintain their anonymity' and 'to reply in the negative' to any questions about their involvement in the Order. There then followed a cryptic statement to the effect that 'recognition of documents shall only be made by the code' – though it was unclear whether this meant by a cipher or by a code of conduct.

The second letter was dated the following day, 11 July, also at Cahors. This time, the letterhead was that of M. Plantard's personal stationery, bearing his crest in crimson, with a circle enclosing a fleur-de-lis in gold and, beneath, the words 'Et in Arcadia Ego ...'. In the text that followed, addressed to the Prieuré's 'dear brethren', M. Plantard repeated that he had just submitted his resignation as Grand Master, having spent the last forty-one years in the Order – to which, he said he had been inducted on 10 July 1943, on the recommendation of the Abbé François Ducaud-Bourget. During the three and a half years of his Grand Mastership, he explained, he had assumed an enormous burden of work, as well as considerable travelling, which his current state of health no longer permitted him to sustain.

He then added that his resignation had been dictated by other factors as well. He had resigned, he said, because he could not approve 'certain manoeuvres' performed by 'our English and American brethren', and also to ensure the independence of himself and of his family. And there was one other motive which, he stated, had contributed to his decision – namely, the publication, 'in the press, in books and in duplicated pamphlets deposited in the Bibliothèque Nationale', of various 'false or falsified documents' pertaining to him. As instances, he cited birth certificates, reproductions of Prieuré de Sion papers bearing signatures more than ten years old and defamations of his person which had led him to file a complaint at Nanterre on 16 December 1983. He closed by offering his brethren his best wishes 'for your victory in establishing a better society'.

What were we to make of these two letters? On the surface, they seemed straightforward enough. And yet one of the notable things about them was the way in which they effectively, and very precisely, covered each of the points raised verbally in our meeting three weeks before – at which time, it was now apparent, M. Plantard had no longer been speaking as Grand Master or even member of the Prieuré de Sion. It was almost as if the letters of resignation had been composed *after* this meeting. On the other hand, there was no question that something had been in the wind for the last seven and a half months. There had been previous references to difficulty with the 'Anglo-American contingent'. There had been previous references to the revocation of Article XXII in the statutes. And the sheer difficulty we had had even contacting M. Plantard during the spring and summer, still more arranging a meeting with him, might well have been a reflection of some upheaval within the Prieuré.

M. Plantard's cover note to us for the two letters of resignation was, in this respect, particularly interesting. He had written to us, he said, to enclose copies of his confidential documents of resignation, and to confirm that *since March, 1984, he had officially refused all meetings or interviews whose object pertained in any way to the Prieuré de Sion*. The italicised assertion had been underlined emphatically in the text of M. Plantard's letter. It was almost as if this letter constituted an official statement, to be seen and approved (or disapproved) by other members of the Order. M. Plantard was making it clear not to us, but to someone else, that he had discussed nothing of the Prieuré since the previous March. When he met with us at the end of September, it was after the sixty days required for his resignation to take effect had elapsed. When he spoke to us, it was no longer as Grand Master or even member of the Prieuré, but as a private citizen. While we conversed over a table in La Tipia, a new Grand Master had already presumably been chosen, or at least nominated.

M. Plantard's resignation was attended by a general drought of information. Louis Vazart, whom we telephoned upon receiving the news, was palpably upset. He would say nothing, however, except that it was a bitter blow and that significant changes would now probably occur, 'not all of them good'. The Marquis de Chérisey declined to answer any of our numerous letters, and could not be reached by telephone. M. Plantard became equally elusive, except for a ritualised card offering greetings for the New Year.

Contradictory Explanations

There seemed to us at least four possible explanations for M. Plantard's resignation:

1 We had documented an historical Prieuré de Sion from the twelfth century to the sixteenth. After 1619, however, the Order had gone increasingly underground, sometimes operating under the names of other organisations, sometimes vanishing from sight entirely. Perhaps it had ceased to exist, and the modern Prieuré de Sion, registered in 1956, was a mere fabrication – a *jeu d'esprit* of some sort, perpetrated for unknown motives by M. Plantard and a few of his immediate friends, who made use of documents dating from the original Prieuré. Whatever the game might have been, and whatever its objectives, it had been going on for at least the last thirty years, although there had been no obvious attempt to capitalise on the financial possibilities it had generated. But (if this scenario were correct), at some point during the course of 1984, M. Plantard decided he had gone too far – perhaps as a result of our researches, perhaps as a result of something else. The names associated with Guardian Assurance, even more the names associated with the First National Bank of Chicago, may have represented one turn of the screw too many, and raised the spectre of serious legal repercussions or perhaps some embarrassing public exposure. In consequence, M. Plantard had devised a ploy for putting the whole affair to rest. By claiming to have resigned from the Prieuré, he could claim to know nothing further about its activities. In fact, however, with M. Plantard's 'resignation', the Prieuré de Sion would have ceased to exist.

2 The Prieuré de Sion existed as a genuine, bona fide organisation of indeterminate resources and influence, but M. Plantard himself had become compromised. Perhaps he had overstepped the line by sending us the document with the signatures of Messrs

Drick, Freeman and Abboud, and thus divulged something of the Order's workings which he was not authorised to divulge. Perhaps M. Chaumeil or someone else possessed material which, if published, might prove seriously embarrassing, politically or otherwise. Perhaps the French government, or whoever was allegedly depositing funds in the Swiss bank account, was making things uncomfortable. In any case, M. Plantard had become a liability, or a potential liability, to the Order, and could best further its interests by stepping down. He might even have come under pressure to do so – either by external factors, such as the machinations of one or another intelligence service, or by factions within, such as the 'Anglo-American contingent'.

3 The letters of resignation were to be taken at face value, and no ulterior meaning was to be read into them. For the reasons stated in the two letters, M. Plantard had voluntarily chosen to resign. His brethren were as taken aback as Louis Vazart and we ourselves had been, and a new Grand Master would soon be chosen, if one had not been already.

4 The Prieuré de Sion registered in 1956 may have been M. Plantard's invention. It may have been an influential international secret society. It may have been anything in between these two extremes. Whatever it was, M. Plantard deemed it expedient at this point to screen himself from inquisitive outsiders, including ourselves. In consequence, he had gone through what amounted to a charade. Despite his alleged resignation, the Prieuré would continue to function as before; and M. Plantard – while still active as member and even possibly as Grand Master – could plausibly deny all knowledge of its activities. In December 1983, he had revoked Article XXII of the statutes. Indeed, he had positively reversed Article XXII of the statutes, ordering all members of the Prieuré to deny and repudiate their affiliation. By drafting an ostensible letter of resignation, he was simply bringing himself into compliance with his own edict. If this was the case, his apparent resignation was in fact a sham.

There were, so far as we could see, these four possibilities. There were also, of course, variations and combinations of these four possibilities. There certainly seemed to be pressure on M. Plantard from within the Order – presumably from the 'Anglo-American contingent'. There also seemed to be pressure from outside, in the form of some unidentified external intervention. There was, too, the matter of deliberate disinformation. Some of it, unquestionably, had been disseminated by M. Plantard himself, but some of it was issuing from other quarters. We had initially assumed the disinformation to be directed specifically at us, whereas some of it, in fact, had been directed at M. Plantard as well.

As we pondered the situation, another possible explanation for M. Plantard's resignation suddenly crystallised; and, if there proved to be even a shred of substance to it, it would be the most explosive and significant of all. Within a week of receiving M. Plantard's package, we received another anonymous tract – or, rather, pseudonymous. It was signed simply 'Cornelius'. And, as in the case of the earlier tract, it purported to be an advance notice for a forthcoming book, authored by 'Cornelius' and entitled *The Scandals of the Prieuré de Sion*. Unfortunately, we cannot quote the tract in question. In its present state, it is a highly inflammatory document. As none of its allegations has been substantiated, it contains at least half a dozen libels on well-known international figures. We can, however, offer a précis of some of the main points.

1 The former banker Michele Sindona was at that time serving a prison sentence in Italy for fraud and faced further charges of complicity in the murder of an Italian investigator, Giorgio Ambrosoli. (Sindona died in March 1986, from drinking a cup of poisoned coffee.) According to 'Cornelius', Ambrosoli's murder was in fact commissioned by a prominent Italian politician, still active in his country's affairs. The man in question, 'Cornelius' alleges, is also a high-ranking member of the Prieuré de Sion, who played a part in the election of Pierre Plantard as Grand Master in 1981. By innuendo, the murder is linked to the scandal involving the Banco Ambrosiano, the Vatican's former bank, and to the affair which culminated in the mysterious death of the Italian banker Roberto Calvi, found hanging under Blackfriars Bridge in London in 1982.

2 Michele Sindona himself was implicated by 'Cornelius' in certain shady financial transactions involving, directly or indirectly, the Prieuré de Sion. So, too, were other bankers in the United States.

3 In May 1974, Cardinal Jean Danielou, the Vatican's chief spokesman at the time on clerical celibacy, was found dead in circumstances which generated much malicious gossip and rumour. A nightclub stripper was involved. So, too, was a substantial sum of money.[1] As a young man, Cardinal Danielou had been at one time closely associated with Jean Cocteau, and is known in French cultural circles for having made the Latin translation of Cocteau's *Oedipus rex*. Through his association with Cocteau, the Cardinal is likely to have been acquainted with

Pierre Plantard de Saint-Clair. According to 'Cornelius', Cardinal Danielou was involved in secret financial transactions with the Prieuré de Sion. He was also alleged to have played a role in the machinations of Michele Sindona and other bankers. And his death – officially reported as having been caused by a heart attack – is obliquely implied by 'Cornelius' to have been other than accidental.

4 'Cornelius' further alleges the Prieuré de Sion to be closely associated both with the Italian Mafia and with the Italian Masonic Lodge known as P2, which caused a major sensation when its existence, activities and membership were first discovered and made public in 1981. Specific mention is made of the murder of an Italian general – General Dalla Chiesa – by the Mafia, and of two major Italian financial scandals.

5 On 19 January 1981 – two days, that is, after Pierre Plantard de Saint-Clair was elected Grand Master of the Prieuré de Sion – a high-ranking member of the Order is alleged by 'Cornelius' to have had a meeting with Licio Gelli, Grand Master of P2. The meeting is said to have occurred at the brasserie called La Tipia on the rue de Rome in Paris.

It must be stressed that, despite intensive research, none of the allegations made by 'Cornelius' has been in any way substantiated. In the absence of any such substantiation, his tract can only be regarded as libellous in the most malicious of ways, and is, as we said, subject to legal consequences. As far as we know, it was widely disseminated. Its allegations are doubtless currently being investigated by journalists – or have been investigated and dismissed as devoid of substance. But if any of 'Cornelius's' allegations should prove to have even a degree of validity, it will open the lid of a particularly unpleasant can of worms. In any case, and by virtue of his tract alone, 'Cornelius' had contrived to tar the Prieuré de Sion with the same brush as the Mafia and P2. If only in people's minds, he had situated the Prieuré de Sion's activities in the shadowy underworld of European affairs – where the Mafia overlaps with secret societies and intelligence agencies, where big business clasps hands with the Vatican, where immense sums of money are deployed for clandestine purposes, where the demarcation lines between politics, religion, espionage, high finance and organised crime begin to dissolve.

This in itself might well have prompted M. Plantard to resign, or to shroud himself and the Prieuré de Sion in obscurity.

The Prieuré Vanishes

With M. Plantard's resignation, information from the Prieuré de Sion itself dried up completely. M. Plantard himself became more elusive than ever, and it grew increasingly difficult to contact him even by telephone. Louis Vazart became markedly more reticent than before, while other people seemed to have gone to ground. And in July 1985, we, like everyone else who knew him, were saddened to learn of the death of Philippe, Marquis de Chérisey. Whatever the nature of the Prieuré de Sion, and whatever M. Chérisey's role in it, there is no question that he was the most convivial, the most imaginatively resourceful, the most original and perhaps the most brilliant individual we encountered in the course of our research. He was also an extraordinarily gifted novelist, who, on a purely literary level, deserves more recognition than he has received.

Following M. Plantard's resignation, the Prieuré de Sion became, in effect, invisible. Since 1956, it had been more or less accessible to those sufficiently assiduous in researching it. Since 1979, we had had a direct channel to it and to its Grand Master; and for a time, after the publication of our previous book, the Prieuré appeared prepared to assume a fairly high profile. Then, quite suddenly, it receded back into the shadows, drawing a veil over its activities and leaving no trail to follow. Whatever the objectives and priorities of the 'Anglo-American contingent' within the Order, and of such external interests as were involved, they seemed to have succeeded in compromising, if not deposing, M. Plantard – and, in the process, shrouding the entire Prieuré from view.

And yet our own research had already begun to lead us in certain directions, which ran very roughly parallel to those indicated by 'Cornelius'. We could not credit the allegations linking the Prieuré with P2 and the Mafia. There was no evidence whatever to support such claims. Nor could we even say whether such organisations, even if they were involved, stood aligned with the Prieuré or opposed to it. The tract by 'Cornelius' – whose advertised book never in fact appeared – might well have been an attempt to discredit the Prieuré by sheer invention, rather than by exposing any of its secrets.

Nevertheless, it had become increasingly clear that the Prieuré de Sion *did* have interests, and *did* conduct activities, in a somewhat murky sphere – a sphere where Christian Democratic parties of Europe, various movements dedicated to European unity, royalist cliques, neo-chivalric orders, freemasonic sects, the CIA, the

Knights of Malta and the Vatican swirled together, pooled themselves temporarily for one or another specific purpose, then disengaged again. The primary question was where precisely the Prieuré fitted into the web of loosely associated organisations and interests. Was it one of the numerous small associations being manipulated as pawns by more powerful, more shadowy forces? Had it knowingly placed itself at the disposal of those forces, either out of a genuinely shared hierarchy of values or out of a provisional alliance of convenience? Or was it indeed one of the forces that pulled the strings?

22

Resistance, Chivalry and the United States of Europe

In our earlier research, we had endeavoured to trace and thereby confirm the existence of the Prieuré de Sion during past centuries. In other words, we had endeavoured to verify the accuracy, or at least the plausibility, of the claims made by the present-day Order concerning its own pedigree. To a degree that surprised us, and disarmed us of our initial scepticism, we succeeded.

The Prieuré itself claimed that it had been created as the Ordre de Sion in 1090 – or, according to other statements, 1099. We were able to establish, on the basis of first-hand documentary evidence, that an abbey had indeed been established on Mount Sion outside Jerusalem in 1099 and entrusted to the care of an elusive but specific order of 'religieux'.[1] By 19 July 1116, the name of the Ordre de Sion was already appearing on official charters and documents.[2] We found another charter, dated 1152 and bearing the seal of King Louis VII of France, which conferred upon the Order its first major seat in Europe, at Orléans.[3] We found a later charter, dated 1178 and bearing the seal of Pope Alexander III, which confirmed certain land holdings of the Order not only in the Holy Land, but in France, Spain and throughout the Italian peninsula – in Sicily, in Naples, in Calabria, in Lombardy.[4] We learned that, until the Second World War, there were twenty documents pertaining specifically to the Ordre de Sion in the Municipal Archives of Orléans, but that seventeen of these were lost in an air raid.

We were thus able to confirm the statements of the present-day Prieuré concerning its origins and the first century of its existence. Similarly, we were able to confirm other statements pertaining to the Order's subsequent history. In addition to bald dates and lists of land holdings, we were also able to confirm the association with the Prieuré of an interlocked network of noble families, all claiming descent from the Merovingian Dynasty, which had ruled France between the fifth and the eighth centuries. Thus, for instance, the family descended from a fairly obscure knight, one Jean de Gisors, figured prominently in the activities of the Order – and proved to be related to the family of Hugues de Payn, first Grand Master of the Knights Templar. Of comparable importance in the Order's history, and also related by kinship, were the Saint-Clair family, the ancestors of the Prieuré's present-day spokesman and Grand Master between 1981 and 1984, Pierre Plantard de Saint-Clair. Indeed, our research established definitively something only hinted at in the assertions of the present-day Order – that the Prieuré de Sion, throughout its history, had been in large part a family affair, an organisation centred on certain specific royal and aristocratic houses.

The Prieuré was cited by name in references extending from the twelfth to the early seventeenth century. Then, in documents dating from 1619, it was stated to have incurred the displeasure of King Louis XIII of France, who evicted them from their seat at Orléans and turned the premises over to the Jesuits.[5] After that, the Prieuré de Sion seemed to vanish from the historical record, at least under that name, until 1956, when it appeared again, registered in the French *Journal officiel*. And yet the present-day Order had repeatedly cited certain of its activities between 1619 and the twentieth century, certain historical events in which it had played a role, certain historical developments in which it had some sort of vested interest. When we examined the events and developments in question, we found indisputable evidence attesting to the involvement of an organised and coherent cadre working in concert behind the scenes, sometimes using other institutions as a façade. This cadre was not named specifically, but everything indicated that it was indeed the Prieuré de Sion. What was more, it proved to involve precisely the same network of interlinked families claiming Merovingian descent. Whether it was the intrigues and the Wars of Religion in the sixteenth century, the insurrection known as the Fronde in the seventeenth century or the Masonic conspiracies of the eighteenth century, successive generations of precisely the same families were implicated, operating in accordance with a single consistent pattern.

On this basis, we were able to establish that there was indeed some kind of direct lineal connection between the Prieuré de Sion of the present and the Order of the same name which had been evicted from the premises at Orléans in 1619. During the intervening three hundred and thirty or so years, it seemed clear, the Prieuré had survived and continued to function, albeit under various façades or through the medium of various other organisations. We were able to link it, for example, with the Compagnie du Saint-Sacrament in seventeenth-century France, with a conclave of extreme heterodox if not heretical clerics based at Saint-Sulpice in Paris, with the mysterious and elusive 'Rosicrucians' of early seventeenth-century Germany, with certain rites of eighteenth-century Freemasonry, with political conspiracies and esoteric secret societies of the nineteenth century. Through such organisations, and through the recurring association with them of the same families, an unbroken continuum extended from 1619 to our own epoch.

But what of the present? When we first met him in 1979, M. Plantard had stated his position unequivocally. He was quite prepared, he said, to discuss the history of the Order. He would only vouchsafe veiled hints, however, about the future, and was not disposed to say anything at all about the present. Granted, he had modified this position slightly during 1983 and 1984 — to the extent, at any rate, of showing us the notarised documents which allegedly brought Saunière's parchments to England, and the 'Mise en Garde' bearing the signatures of Messrs Drick, Freeman and Abboud. These had led us to the board of directors of the old Guardian Assurance Company and to the First National Bank of Chicago. But nothing had been conclusively established, nothing definitively proved. We had simply blundered into a miasma of disinformation, and our research raised as many questions as it answered, if not indeed more. In pursuing the Prieuré today, we seemed at times to be pursuing a will-o'-the-wisp or a mirage. It receded constantly before us. It turned intangible the moment we seemed to have it in our grasp, only to materialise at some other point a few steps ahead of us. Evidence was forthcoming which, when examined, cancelled itself out, or generated only further mystification, or coiled back upon itself to form a prism of refracting mirrors.

Nor were we alone in these impressions. During the year following M. Plantard's resignation, we engaged the services of a full-time, professional researcher. The woman in question had more than thirty-five years of experience working on projects for a number of prestigious authors. Both she and her husband, a former military man and Resistance fighter, had numerous well-placed connections and access to spheres which we, as outsiders, did not. She certainly had more expertise than we did in dealing with French bureaucracies, whether those of libraries and archives or those of government offices. And being resident in France, she was obviously better placed than we were to spend weeks at a time pursuing one or another individual skein through one or another specific labyrinth. If a particular office was closed at a particular time, or a particular individual unavailable, she could always return the following day, or the following week if necessary.

She provided us with a corpus of extremely valuable information. She exhumed fragments of data from often improbable places, and conducted her enquiries with impressive tenacity. She refused to be daunted, intimidated or deterred by bluster, equivocation or evasiveness. And yet, she confessed to us, at no time in the whole of her experience had she ever encountered so many cul-de-sacs, locked doors, disingenuous denials and mysterious contradictions. On virtually every occasion that she interviewed someone on our behalf, initial courtesy and readiness to help would, as soon as she ventured into certain relevant areas, change to reticence, secrecy and even hostility. We asked both her and her husband what they made of the whole affair, what their investigations had led them to conclude. They were quite emphatic. Unquestionably, they said, there was some kind of cover-up.

The Journal 'Vaincre'

Nevertheless, it did prove possible to exhume at least some information, not only from the Prieuré de Sion itself, but from independent sources. Despite M. Plantard's evasiveness, and despite the screen of disinformation and official reticence, we were able to learn something about the Order and its former Grand Master. The data we obtained enabled us to monitor something of the activities from as far back as the Second World War.

Not long after we first met him, M. Plantard had sent us a deposition dated 11 May 1955 and made in Paris by one Poirier Murat, who described himself as a Chevalier of the Légion d'Honneur, a holder of the Medaille Militaire and a former officer in the French Resistance. According to M. Murat's statement, he had known M. Plantard since 1941. M. Murat further stated that M. Plantard, between 1941 and 1943, had edited a 'Resistance journal' called *Vaincre*. The deposition also declared that M. Plantard had been interned by the Gestapo in the prison of Fresnes from October 1943 until February 1944.

We undertook to check the veracity of M. Murat's assertions. Accordingly, we wrote to the French military, who replied that they did not hold the relevant archives and that we should contact the director general of the Archives of France. They also passed our letter on to the Préfecture of Police in Paris, who advised us to contact the director of the prison at Fresnes. When we wrote to the director general of the Archives of France, we were told to contact the Departmental Archives of Paris. The Departmental Archives of Paris also advised us to write directly to the prison at Fresnes. Fresnes, in reply to our enquiries, demanded to know why we were making them and requested details about our research. We wrote back, enclosing relevant details and photocopies, including the deposition from Poirier Murat. We received no response.

This was the kind of thing we had repeatedly encountered in the course of our research. But it was also the kind of thing with which our researcher proved particularly adept at coping. By dint of persistence, she at last badgered an answer out of Fresnes. It was not, however, very illuminating: ' . . . after research in the registers of those imprisoned in Fresnes, we can find no trace of M. Plantard passing through this establishment between October, 1943 and February, 1944'. Had Poirier Murat − Chevalier of the Légion d'Honneur, holder of the Medaille Militaire and former officer in the French Resistance − been lying in his deposition? If so, why? If not, why was there no record of M. Plantard's incarceration at Fresnes? Had the record been removed? Or had there, for some unspecified reason, never been a record made?

Our attempts to trace *Vaincre*, the 'Resistance journal' with which M. Plantard had been associated, proved markedly more successful. We found six editions of *Vaincre*,[6] which appear to be all that were published. Contrary to our expectations, they were not furtive, cursorily produced broadsheets. There was nothing clandestine about them at all. They were printed on high-quality paper, which was difficult to obtain in France at the time, and included illustrations and photographs. The first issue was openly stated to have been printed by Poirier Murat's company in 1,379 copies. By the sixth issue, a print run of 4,500 copies was claimed. On the whole, *Vaincre* represented a venture that could not possibly have been undertaken without some knowledge on the part of the authorities. It also represented a venture that must have had substantial money behind it.

From the six issues we managed to obtain, it was difficult to regard *Vaincre* as a 'Resistance journal'. The articles in it, by named and in some cases well-known contributors, dealt primarily with a combination of esoterica, myth and pure fantasy. There was much talk of Atlantis, for example. There was particular emphasis on an ancient Celtic 'wisdom tradition' and the mythic themes and images in which it had survived. There was also a liberal seasoning of a kind of neo-Zoroastrian theosophy, with Tibetan initiates and hidden cities in the Himalayas. Above all, however, *Vaincre* purported to be the organ of a specific organisation, or order, called Alpha Galates.

Under the German occupation and the Vichy regime, secret societies, including freemasonry, had been strictly banned, and membership of any such organisation was subject to severe penalties. In consequence, Alpha Galates did not describe itself as a secret society of any kind – although that, clearly, was what it was. Instead, it presented itself, quite explicitly, as a chivalric order, or a neo-chivalric order. The principles of chivalry were stressed repeatedly, and most of the articles in *Vaincre* addressed themselves to chivalric themes – as well as to France as the supreme source of chivalry, and to the role of chivalry in the modern world. According to *Vaincre* and Alpha Galates, chivalry was to be the instrument of national renewal for France: ' ... a chivalry is indispensable because our country cannot be reborn except through its knights'.[7]

When chivalry first evolved during the so-called Dark and Middle Ages, the institution of knighthood had rested on a specifically spiritual basis. Conventional titles of nobility – baron, for example, count or earl, marquis, duke – had denoted social and political status, lands, pedigree. The knight, however, earned his spurs and sword through his own personal virtue – or, more accurately, *vertu* – and moral purity. Subsequently, the concept of knighthood had been progressively debased, eventually coming to be a minor reward for any sort of service – including the refurbishing of a prime minister's public image. *Vaincre* and Alpha Galates, however, insisted on knighthood in its original and traditional sense: 'The Chevalier cannot live without the spiritual ideal, which is the reservoir for moral, intellectual and spiritual force through coming generations.'[8]

According to *Vaincre*, Alpha Galates had been registered in the French *Journal officiel* on 27 December 1937. A check of the *Journal officiel* for June 1937 to April 1938, however, revealed no such entry. The French Ministry of Defence, when we wrote to them, said they had never heard of either *Vaincre* or Alpha Galates, and had no record of the names. The French Préfecture of Police likewise denied all knowledge – although we learned subsequently that the French equivalent of Special Branch did indeed have a dossier on Alpha Galates and its leaders. In any case, and despite official denials, *Vaincre* indisputably existed, as did its contributors, who appear to have included a number of members of Alpha Galates.

One of the contributors to *Vaincre* was Robert Amadou, now a well-known writer on esoteric and Masonic subjects, a Martinist and an official of a lodge belonging to the Swiss Grand Lodge Alpina.[9] Another prominent contributor was Professor Louis Le Fur, a well- known right-wing publicist prior to the war. Subsequently, of course, he was discredited for his support of the Vichy regime. During the German occupation, however, he did enjoy a certain repute as a thinker and cultural commentator, and was named to an important educational post by Pétain.[10] At the time, Louis Le Fur was a name to be reckoned with. He would not have been publicly associated with a journal such as *Vaincre* unless he regarded it as a serious and laudable enterprise. In one of his articles, Le Fur declares himself to have been a member of Alpha Galates for eight years. Among the Order's other members, he names Jean Mermoz, a famous aviator who died before the war, and Gabriel Trarieux d'Egmont, a writer on esoteric subjects and a minor mystical poet whose work still commands a certain qualified respect.

According to *Vaincre*, the membership of Alpha Galates consists of two general groupings, the 'Légion' and the 'Phalange'. The role of the 'Légion' is not specified. The role of the 'Phalange' is said to be that of philosophical research and the instruction of future Chevaliers. What is interesting is that, according to the 1956 statutes deposited with the French Préfecture of Police at Annemasse, the Prieuré de Sion was also divided into the two groupings of 'Légion' and 'Phalange'.

Partly on this basis, we at first assumed Alpha Galates to be yet another façade for the Prieuré de Sion. Apparently, however, that was not the case. M. Plantard stated to us personally that he did not enter the Prieuré until 10 July 1943. In the letter accompanying his resignation, he repeats this assertion and adds that he was inducted into the Prieuré under the auspices of the Abbé François Ducaud-Bourget. His association with *Vaincre* and with Alpha Galates dates, on the other hand, from at least a year earlier. From this chronology, it would seem that Alpha Galates and the Prieuré de Sion were two separate organisations – unless, of course, the former was a kind of adjunct, or perhaps a recruiting service, for the latter. In any case, the Prieuré, in order to induct M. Plantard, must have liked what Alpha Galates was doing. And the orientation of the two Orders would seem, in many respects, to be very similar, if not indeed identical. This is particularly apparent in the emphasis on chivalry. Moreover, certain of the contributors to *Vaincre* figure later in publications associated with the Prieuré.

The very first issue of *Vaincre* names its editor and director as 'Pierre de France' and publishes his photograph. The photograph is unquestionably one of a young M. Plantard, who would have been twenty-two at the time. On 21 September, Pierre de France is reported by *Vaincre* to have been made Grand Master of Alpha Galates. In the fourth issue of *Vaincre*, 21 December 1942, Pierre de France's name is amended to Pierre de France-Plantard. His address – 10 rue Lebouteux, Paris 17 – is given as the headquarters or central office of Alpha Galates.

Despite its mythic and chivalric character, *Vaincre* is not without political orientation. As the involvement of Louis Le Fur would seem to indicate, the journal is explicitly pro-Vichy in its sympathies, and at times effusively fervent in its support of Pétain. The first issue contains a hymn dedicated to Pétain, and Alpha Galates is described as 'a Grand Order of Chivalry', 'in the service of the homeland' and 'with the Marshal'. There are also, in the pages of *Vaincre*, occasional ugly anti-Semitic statements which echo the more rabid ravings of Nazi propaganda. 'To restore our homeland to its rank ... it is necessary to eradicate ... false dogmas ... and the corrupt principles of the formerly democratic Jewish-Masonry.'[11]

On the other hand, one must remember the time and circumstances in which *Vaincre* was published. Most of France was occupied by German troops, the Gestapo were everywhere and very little could find its way into print that escaped the German authorities and their French minions. M. Plantard could hardly have published a well-produced journal such as *Vaincre* and endorsed De Gaulle. Everything that appears in the pages of *Vaincre* must be regarded with caution, because it was printed with the expectation of being read by German eyes. In order to survive, the magazine had perforce to make certain propitiatory statements and not deviate too markedly from the official establishment line. When we confronted him with certain potentially compromising statements from *Vaincre*, M. Plantard, not unduly embarrassed, stressed this point. He hinted that, beneath its pro-Vichy and Pétainist patina, *Vaincre* contained coded messages and instructions which would have been decipherable only to the Resistance.

Whether this was indeed the case or not, it is still difficult to describe *Vaincre* as a 'Resistance journal'. But it is equally difficult to take it at face value and dismiss it as nothing more than a cranky esoteric publication with straightforward Vichy and Pétainist sympathies. Although politically and religiously conservative, the Abbé

François Ducaud-Bourget played an active role in the French Resistance and in fact received the Resistance Medal. If he did indeed sponsor M. Plantard's induction into the Prieuré de Sion, it is hardly likely that M. Plantard, Alpha Galates or *Vaincre* were as inclined to collaborate with the Germans as might at first appear. Moreover, *Vaincre* had been printed by Poirier Murat, Chevalier of the Légion d'Honneur, holder of the Medaille Militaire and officer in the French Resistance. Murat is not likely to have underwritten a journal of the sort that *Vaincre* appears to be, unless it *was* indeed functioning on another level as well and performing some service to the Resistance. Finally, there is, as will be seen shortly, M. Plantard's later association with Charles de Gaulle. De Gaulle's unswerving hostility to former collaborators is well enough known. Had M. Plantard actually been a collaborator, he could not have attained the rapport he subsequently enjoyed with De Gaulle.

There is one other piece of evidence which weighs heavily in favour of M. Plantard, Alpha Galates and *Vaincre*. Among the most scurrilous publications in occupied France during the war was a vicious satirical magazine named *Au pilori*. *Au pilori* was fervently pro-Nazi, rabidly anti-Semitic and anti-Masonic. It was devoted to ferreting out Jews and Freemasons or alleged Jews and Freemasons, publishing names and addresses and generally seeking to help, as well as to curry favour with, the Gestapo. Anyone attacked by *Au pilori* cannot have been 'all bad'. And on 19 November 1942, *Au pilori* published a sneeringly satirical commentary on M. Plantard, on Alpha Galates and on *Vaincre*. It made no explicit accusations. But it sought, most maliciously, to ridicule all three. And it published M. Plantard's address – which, in the circumstances, was tantamount to encouraging harassment and vandalism by party thugs, if not by the Gestapo.

The whole of the third issue of *Vaincre* consisted of a defence against the attack by *Au pilori*. One member of Alpha Galates was declared to have been expelled, and it was implied that he had leaked information to *Au pilori*. In attemping to rebut *Au pilori*, *Vaincre* re-stated the objectives of Alpha Galates. These were described as:

1 the unity of France within her geographic frontiers and the abolition of the line of demarcation between German-occupied zones and those under Vichy control;
2 the mobilisation of all French energy and resources for the defence of the nation and, particularly, an appeal to the young for obligatory service;

3 the creation of a 'new western order', a 'young European chivalry' whose keynote was to be 'Solidarity'. Within each European nation, this organisation, known as 'Solidarity', was to represent 'the first stage of the United States of the West'.[12]

To judge from the circumstances, *Vaincre*'s defence against *Au pilori* was neither convincing nor successful. Within another three issues, *Vaincre* closed down, and the evidence suggests that it did so under pressure. With the disappearance of *Vaincre*, M. Plantard's activities and career seem to pass into a period of temporary obscurity. But certain of the themes enunciated by *Vaincre* would later surface again, not only under the auspices of the Prieuré de Sion, but under those of other organisations as well.

For our purposes, the most important of these themes is that of a United States of Europe. As we have noted, *Vaincre*, in defending itself against *Au pilori*, declared a United States of Europe – or a 'United States of the West' – to be one of Alpha Galates's primary objectives. In fact, the idea of a United States of Europe recurs repeatedly in the pages of *Vaincre*. Along with the idea of a new European chivalry, it is one of the journal's most dominant themes. In the first issue, for example there is an illustration of a knight on horseback riding down a road towards a rising sun on the horizon. The ribbon of the road is labelled 'United States of the West'. The beginning of the road is demarcated by the year 1937. The rising sun at the end of the road is inscribed with the year 1946. One side of the road is labelled Brittany, the other Bavaria.[13]

Long before the war, Professor Louis Le Fur had co-founded a small group called 'Énergie'. Among this group, and among Le Fur's closest associates, was a man named Robert Schuman, who subsequently became a prominent French politician.[14] Schuman dreamed of uniting the coal and steel industries of Western Europe. This, however, he saw as only a preliminary step to a much broader political entity – a European federation, or a United States of Europe. In the years that followed, Schuman, echoing ideas expressed by Le Fur and others in *Vaincre*, became one of the principal architects and guiding spirits of the EEC.

The Kreisau Circle

The fifth issue of *Vaincre*, dated 21 January 1943, contains an article by Louis Le Fur which praises Alpha Galates's new Grand Master, Pierre de France-Plantard. In the course of his text, Le Fur quotes 'a great German, one of the Masters in our Order'. The 'great German' in question, then in his fifty-eighth year, makes an extraordinary statement apropos the 23-year-old Pierre de France:

> I have the pleasure to say, before my departure for Spain, that our Order has at last found a chief worthy of it in the person of Pierre de France.
>
> It is therefore with total confidence that I depart to perform my mission; for while not deluding myself about the perils I run in discharging my duty, I know that until my last breath my watchword will consist in recognition of Alpha and fidelity to its chief.[15]

This statement is ascribed to Hans Adolf von Moltke, a career diplomat from one of the most prestigious and influential aristocratic families in Germany. In 1934, he had been German ambassador to Poland. In 1938, he was tipped to be the next German ambassador to Britain. At the time of the statement attributed to him, he had just been appointed ambassador to Spain, where he died in March, 1943.

Although ostensibly friendly with both Hitler and Himmler, Moltke was, in fact, a 'good German'. He was a first cousin and a close associate of Count Helmut James von Moltke. He was also a cousin of Claus von Stauffenberg. And he was married to the sister of another cousin, Peter Yorck von Wartenburg. Helmut James von Moltke, together with Peter Yorck von Wartenburg, was the leader of the so-called Kreisau Circle, the civilian wing of the German Resistance to Hitler. Count Claus von Stauffenberg was the architect and guiding spirit of the military conspiracy against the Reich, which culminated with the Bomb Plot of 20 July 1944 – the attempt to assassinate Hitler in his headquarters at Rastenburg.

In short, the man who in *Vaincre* endorses M. Plantard, and declares himself a member of Alpha Galates, was in the forefront of the effort, originating within Germany, to overthrow the Nazi regime. At the time of his appointment to Spain, his cousin, Helmut James von Moltke, was making secret peace feelers to the Allies through Sweden, seeking to enlist their aid in deposing Hitler and endeavouring to secure favourable peace terms for the new, democratic German government which would follow. From his ambassadorial post in Spain, Hans Adolf von Moltke was soon to embark on similar clandestine negotiations. Although it was not publicly known until after the war, this was the 'mission' he was departing to discharge; and he was quite correct in not deluding himself about the perils he was running.[16]

Today, Claus von Stauffenberg, Helmut James von Moltke, Peter Yorck von Wartenburg and their fellow conspirators against the Third Reich are regarded as heroes, both in Germany and abroad. The anniversary of the Bomb Plot, 20 July, is a national holiday, officially known as Stauffenberg Day. Until now, however, there has never been any evidence to suggest that the German Resistance had links of any kind with any other resistance movement on the continent. It is believed by historians to have been totally independent of the network of clandestine operations elsewhere in Europe. It may indeed have been so. But Hans Adolf von Moltke's statement in *Vaincre* indicates that he was a member of Alpha Galates – a species of secret society functioning under the public guise of an esoteric neo-chivalric Order. It also indicates that his primary allegiance was to Alpha Galates and its Grand Master. Can Alpha Galates in fact have provided a link between the German Resistance to Hitler and resistance movements in France, if not elsewhere?

In a letter, Helmut James von Moltke admits that there was no contact between his circle of conspirators and any French organisation prior to late 1942. After considerable difficulties, he reports, links have been established with groups ' ... in the various occupied territories with the exception of France, where, as far as we can tell, there is no effective opposition based on fundamental principles'.[17] Shortly thereafter, however, he begins to allude to 'our man in Paris', though history has not yet discovered the identity of the man in question. Perhaps coincidentally, but perhaps significantly, the first issue of *Vaincre* did not appear until late 1942 – until October of that year.

Certainly the objectives of Alpha Galates, as reported in *Vaincre*, had much in common with those of Moltke's Kreisau Circle. Both were intent on youth movements and on mobilising the resources of European youth. Both insisted on a moral and spiritual hierarchy of values as a foundation for European renewal – an opposition, in Moltke's words, 'based on fundamental principles'. Both were essentially chivalric in their orientation. And both were dedicated to the eventual creation of a United States of Europe. Even before the war, such a federation had been extolled and promoted by members of the Kreisau Circle. Subsequently, this idea became for Moltke and his colleagues a fundamental cornerstone of any post-war policy. According to one commentator, the Kreisau Circle's 'long-term aim was a European federation of states, the United States of Europe'.[18]

In pursuit of this aim, the Kreisau Circle, by the beginning of

1943, was in touch with representatives of the British Foreign Office based in Switzerland. It was also in close touch with an important American official based in Switzerland – Allen Dulles, Head of Station, Switzerland, for the OSS, precursor of the CIA.

23

The Return of De Gaulle

With the disappearance of *Vaincre* early in 1943, all trace of M. Plantard seemed to vanish as well. We, at any rate, were unable to find any trace of him during the next dozen years. Then, in 1956, the Prieuré de Sion formally registered itself in the French *Journal officiel*. At the same time, it deposited what purported to be a copy of its statutes with the Sub-Préfecture of Saint-Julien-en-Genevois near Annemasse on the Swiss border, copies of which we obtained. Subsequently, we were told that these statutes were spurious and were given a copy of what were supposed to be the real ones. But spurious or not, the statutes deposited with the Sub-Préfecture once again placed M. Plantard in the public eye. He is named specifically as Secretary-General of the Prieuré de Sion. The Prieuré itself is said to be divided, like Alpha Galates, into 'the Légion' and 'the Phalange'. The former is described as being 'charged with the apostolate'. The latter is described as 'guardian of the tradition'. According to the statutes, the Order consists of nine grades, all of them bearing chivalric titles. The organisation, in the portentously enigmatic jargon of the statutes, was as follows:

> The general assembly is composed of all members of the association. It consists of 729 provinces, 27 commanderies and an Arch designated 'Kyria'.
> Each of the commanderies, as well as the Arch, must consist of forty members, each province of thirteen members.
> The members are divided into two effective groups:
> a The Légion, charged with the apostolate.
> b The Phalange, guardian of the tradition.
> The members compose a hierarchy of nine grades.
>
> The hierarchy of nine grades consists of:
> a in the 729 provinces

1	Novices:	6,561 members
2	Croisés:	2,187 members
b	in the 27 commanderies	
3	Preux:	729 members
4	Écuyers:	243 members
5	Chevaliers:	81 members
6	Commandeurs:	27 members
c	in the Arch 'Kyria'	
7	Connétables:	9 members
8	Sénéchaux:	3 members
9	Nautonier:	1 member

Neither in *Vaincre* nor in any other document or publication has there been anything to suggest that M. Plantard or the Prieuré de Sion was specifically Catholic. In *Vaincre*, the orientation of M. Plantard had appeared to be esoteric, pagan and theosophical. In later sources, both he and the Prieuré draw upon a broad spectrum of diverse traditions, including gnosticism and various forms of heterodox or heretical Christianity. According to these 1956 statutes, however, the Prieuré de Sion is a specifically Catholic chivalry. The Order is said to function under the subtitle of 'Chevalerie d'Institutions et Règles Catholiques, d'Union Indépendante et Tradionaliste' ('Chivalry of Catholic Rules and Institutions of the Independent and Traditionalist Union'). This abbreviates to CIRCUIT, the name of a magazine which, according to the statutes, is published internally by the Order and circulated within its ranks.

Whether the 1956 statutes are genuine or not remains uncertain. For our purposes here, they are significant first because of their emphasis on chivalry, and second because of their resemblance to the statutes of Alpha Galates as published in *Vaincre*. Moreover, they brought M. Plantard's name before the public eye for the first time in twelve years. From then on, he and the Prieuré de Sion were to be increasingly associated with the burgeoning interest in the enigma of Bérenger Saunière and Rennes-le-Château. Before long, however, M. Plantard was to figure in a much more familiar and resonant context.

Committees of Public Safety

On 7 May 1954, the French Army in Indo-China suffered a disastrous and decisive defeat at the Battle of Dien Bien Phu, which led to the loss of France's empire in south-east Asia. Within six months of this débâcle, a bitter and brutal terrorist campaign erupted in Algeria under the auspices of Algerian nationalists. Determined not to incur another humiliating defeat, France, within a month, had dispatched 20,000 troops to her North African colony. Eventually, this number would swell to 350,000. Nevertheless, the Algerian situation continued to deteriorate, leading to a vicious struggle which would prolong itself for eight years.

Unlike Indo-China, Algeria was close to France — just across the Mediterranean. The French population of Algeria was not an isolated enclave of foreigners, but a long-established community of settlers. Algeria's cities were, in many respects, more French than they were North African. Algeria was regarded not as an overseas possession, but as an integral part of mainland France. In consequence, the events in Algeria produced major repercussions in the mother country.

As the turmoil in Algeria escalated, so, too, did the turmoil within France. By the end of 1957, France was not only in disarray, but in a state of chronic crisis. Governments were falling with terrifying rapidity. Twice, France was without any government at all for a period of more than four weeks while parties wrangled and failed to negotiate coalitions. A general sense of panic began to prevail; and in the background loomed the ominous spectre of fully fledged civil war.

Amidst the proliferating chaos, conspiracies flourished. The army, in particular, was involved in much clandestine intrigue. In Algeria, a network of semi-secret societies began to appear, the Comités de Salut Public (Committees of Public Safety). Modelled on the Committees of Public Safety during the French Revolution, the Algerian network undertook to weld French interests, the French Army and the French population of North Africa into a cohesive and unified force which would constitute a bulwark against Algerian independence and keep the colony permanently attached to France. At the same time, the Committees began to agitate for a strong guiding hand in France which would be sympathetic to their cause. Only one person was deemed capable of providing such a hand — Charles de Gaulle. Thus, the Committees in Algeria began to press insistently for De Gaulle to assume power in France, if necessary by means of a military coup. They received support from a number of high-ranking military men, including Marshal Alphonse Juin, who is alleged to have been an important member of the Prieuré de Sion. They also received support from a coalescing pro-Gaullist movement in France, the Social Republican Party, whose leaders included Michel Debré — who became De

Gaulle's Minister of Justice and, shortly after, between 1959 and 1962, Prime Minister of France. Another important pro-Gaullist figure was Georges Bidault, a former Resistance hero. Between 1945 and 1954, Bidault had worked closely with Robert Schuman – Professor Louis Le Fur's old friend – in drawing up the blueprints for the EEC.

Perhaps naively, the Algerian Committees assumed, as a matter of course, that De Gaulle could be counted on to keep Algeria French. De Gaulle did nothing to discourage this assumption. As subsequent events were to prove, however, he had no such intention.

In April, 1958, the newly elected French government signalled a desire to resolve the Algerian crisis by granting independence to the colony. The Committees of Public Safety in Algeria responded on 13 May by staging a *coup d'état* in Algiers and forming their own government. At the same time, they issued an appeal to De Gaulle to assume power in France, reunify the country and preserve Algeria's colonial status. In a statement of 15 May, De Gaulle would say only that he held himself in readiness should he be called upon. France remained in a state of chaos.

By 23 May, reports had begun to surface of Committees of Public Safety already being established in mainland France. On 24 May, a Committee assumed power in Corsica, while Algerian broadcasters urged France and her people to 'choose between the star of Moscow and the Cross of Lorraine'. In opposing Algerian independence and supporting De Gaulle, former Resistance fighters of the Free French forces found themselves allied with former Vichy officials and even more extreme right-wing elements.

At some point during that week, it appears to have become an open secret that a military coup was planned for the 28th and that the army would seize power in France. Rumours abounded of an imminent drop of paratroops on Paris.[1] Accordingly, on 28 May, the government resigned, leaving the field clear for De Gaulle. On 29 May, every Committee of Public Safety in Paris was mobilised and thousands of supporters poured on to the streets. Later that afternoon, De Gaulle appeared in the capital, accepted the Presidency of the Fifth French Republic and proceeded to form a government, with Michel Debré and André Malraux in his cabinet. The Committees of Public Safety had obviously played a key role in the process whereby the new President was swept into office – and, apparently, effectively forestalled any serious opposition. On 29 May – the day De Gaulle assumed power – a spokesman reported 120 Committees to be active in metropolitan France.[2]

In so far as such generalisation is possible, there appear to have been differing priorities between the Committees of Public Safety in Algeria and those in France. For the Algerian Committees, the primary objective was to ensure that the colony's status remained unchanged, and De Gaulle was seen as a means to this end. For at least some of the French Committees, on the other hand, the primary objective seems to have been installing De Gaulle in the Presidency, and Algeria may have been wholly incidental, if not irrelevant. It is difficult to be certain about this, however, simply because the Committees themselves, especially in France, were so shadowy. They were obviously widespread, obviously very well organised – a true 'secret army', with many links with the regular army. But firm information about them is virtually impossible to obtain, and reliable documentation is virtually non-existent. That they existed no one questions, nor is there any doubt about the general nature of their role. But little else about them is known. It is deemed probable that De Gaulle was in personal contact with their command structure, for he kept his options always open. But it is equally probable that he destroyed whatever records there were, if any, attesting to such contact. Indeed, we were told by a biographer of De Gaulle that he would have contacts of this sort via intermediaries, and that commonly nothing would be put in writing.

In any case, De Gaulle, once he had assumed power, found his position in relation to the Committees extremely delicate. He was in large part indebted to them for having helped install him as head of state. He had encouraged them to believe that Algeria, under his auspices, would remain French. Now he was about to renege on his part of the implicit 'bargain' and negotiate with Algerian nationalist leaders for the colony's independence. This, of course, would render him subject to accusations of betrayal.

He must certainly have anticipated a backlash from the Algerian Committees. This backlash was not long in coming. It took the form of the OAS, the Organisation de l'Armée Secrète, or Secret Army Organisation, which pledged itself to avenge what it saw as De Gaulle's treason. Composed of hard-line officers, veterans of the Algerian conflict and former French settlers and officials in Algeria, the OAS, in the years that followed, made a number of assassination attempts on the French President. Even today, there are ex-members of the OAS to whom De Gaulle's very name is anathema.

Ultimately, however, the Algerian Committees did not pose a truly major threat to the stability of De Gaulle's new regime in France. The French Committees were an altogether different matter. They, if they embarked on a full-scale campaign of opposition, might constitute a much more serious problem. In consequence, the membership of the French Committees had to be won round, persuaded to disband or direct their energy elsewhere and eventually to accept the new President's *volte face* on Algeria. This would have entailed a substantial effort in public relations. So far as records exist, that effort appears to have been orchestrated by Pierre Plantard.

When we first met M. Plantard in 1979, he told us that Charles de Gaulle had personally requested him to direct the French Committees of Public Safety and, when their task of installing the General in power had been completed, to preside over their dissolution. In a mimeographed pamphlet deposited with the Bibliothèque Nationale in 1964, Anne Lea Hisler – M. Plantard's first wife – states:

> Under the authority of Marshal Alphonse Juin, the seat of the Secretariat-General of the Committees of Public Safety in metropolitan France was at Aulnay-sous-Bois [Paris suburb]. This Committee was directed by Michel Debré, Pierre Plantard known as Way, and André Malraux.[3]

Madame Hisler also quotes a letter reportedly sent by De Gaulle to M. Plantard on 3 August 1958, some two months after the new government had been formed:

> My dear Plantard,
> In my letter of 29 July, 1958, I said to you how much I appreciated the participation of the Committees of Public Safety in the work of renewal I have undertaken. Now that the new institutions have been established which will enable our country to rediscover her rightful status, I believe the members of the Committees of Public Safety can regard themselves as released from the obligations they have until now assumed, and can demobilise.[4]

Anne Lea Hisler's pamphlet was not widely circulated. Indeed, the text in the Bibliothèque Nationale may well be the sole existing copy. Both of the above quotations, however – Madame Hisler's account of M. Plantard's role in the Committees of Public Safety and the text of the letter ascribed to De Gaulle – were subsequently reproduced in a book by Louis Vazart, which has been in print for some seven years. To our knowledge, no one has ever impugned, challenged or even questioned the authenticity or veracity of either quotation.[5]

We ourselves were not wholly satisfied, however. Accordingly, we sought to obtain some further confirmation and, if possible, information. We checked all published compendia of De Gaulle's letters, notes and notebooks. Not surprisingly, perhaps, there was no reference to M. Plantard, to the pseudonym 'Way' or to a letter of either 29 July or 3 August. Neither did the Institut Charles de Gaulle – depository of all archives pertaining to De Gaulle – know of any contact between the General and a man named Plantard or Way. When we consulted historians associated with the Institut, they were sceptical. They found it incredible that a subject sufficiently important to elicit two letters from De Gaulle in four days had left no trace in the official records. The director of Archives at the Institut declared that, to his knowledge, he held the whole of De Gaulle's correspondence and that the names of neither Plantard nor Way appeared in it.

We had begun to doubt Madame Hisler's reliability when we received a letter from the Institut. The director still had no record of the letter quoted, but he had indeed, and at last, found references to the names 'Plantard' and 'Way'. To his embarrassment, these references appeared not in his own archive, but in old copies of Le Monde, generally regarded as the most reliable of French newspapers.

In its edition of 18–19 May 1958, Le Monde ran a short article entitled 'A Clandestine Committee of Public Safety in Paris?' The text was as follows:

> The American agency United Press has disseminated the text of an appeal emanating from a 'Committee of Public Safety in the Paris region' in support of General de Gaulle. Communiqués of this Committee are reserved for foreign agencies 'to the extent that the arrangement (presumably of secrecy) about their source is respected'. The appeal bore neither address nor signature.[6]

On 6 June, there appeared a longer article, 'How Many Committees of Public Safety Are There in France?' It reports that one of the Algerian coup leaders had disclosed to two journalists that the Committees in metropolitan France numbered no less than 320. The article then proceeds to quote a communiqué from the Paris Central Committee of Public Safety:

> The Committees of Public Safety must express the wishes of the people, and it is in the name of liberty, of unity and of solidarity that all French citizens must participate in the task of reconstructing our country. All volunteers who have answered

> our appeals during the last fifteen days must be present today
> to aid General de Gaulle ... Patriots, to your posts, and have
> confidence in the man who has already saved France ...[7]

This communiqué, the article in *Le Monde* reports, was signed by a certain 'Captain Way', which is assumed to be a pseudonym.

On 8–9 June, *Le Monde* published a third article, 'Committees of Public Safety have been well established in Paris, in the Paris Region and in Fourteen Departments'. The article cites a communiqué which makes it clear that a Paris Committee of Public Safety had already existed at the time of the *coup d'état* in Algeria on 13 May. Between 16 and 18 May, this Committee established others in six Paris arrondissements, twenty-two communes of the Seine and fourteen metropolitan departments. The communiqué stresses that the primary objective of the Committees is 'national rehabilitation' under the auspices of General de Gaulle. The Committees are declared to be working in concert with 'various associations of war veterans'. Having cited this communiqué, the article in *Le Monde* then refers back to the communiqué quoted on 18–19 May and bearing the signature of 'Captain Way':

> Following its publication, its author was made known to us by a letter in which he stated:
> 'The central committee was created on 17 May, and its objective was propaganda and establishing a liaison between all Committees of Public Safety in Paris.
> 'Considering that France is a land of liberty, where everyone has the most absolute right to his convictions, our action is to be placed beyond all politics, wholly on the patriotic level, to gather the maximum of our resources for the renovation of France.
> 'As we have declared by letter of 29 May to General de Gaulle, "we adhere strictly to the directives we receive from public authorities".'[8]

This letter, the article then states, was signed by M. Plantard. He can be contacted, apparently, at his personal telephone number by dialling the words 'WAY' and 'PAIX' ('Peace').

On 29 July – the day on which De Gaulle allegedly sent his letter of thanks to M. Plantard – *Le Monde* published another article, in which the dissolution of the Central Committee for the Paris Region was announced:

> We have received the following communiqué:
> 'The effective dissolution of the central Committee of Public

Safety for the Paris region, which entails that of the Committee of Public Safety in Paris and other localities, thus discharges the militants who responded to the appeal of 17 May.

'Those responsible for the central Committee have resolved to institute federations for ... a national movement whose programme assures the defence of the country and of liberty.

For the bureau of the Committee,
Captain Way'

'Captain Way', signatory of this communiqué, has already published, during the month of May, several appeals and declarations in the name of the 'Central Committee of Public Safety for the Paris Region'. As we have already indicated, he is M. Pierre Plantard ... who, together with certain friends, took the initiative of establishing this Committee.

The 'Movement' which will comprise the successor to the Committee is directed by M. Bonerie-Clarus, a journalist. Its treasurer is M. Robin; M. Pierre Plantard is secretary and in charge of propaganda ...[9]

From all of this, a pattern begins gradually to emerge. De Gaulle no doubt welcomed the support of the Committees of Public Safety, both in Algeria and in metropolitan France. At the same time, he must, as we said before, have been worried by the prospect of a backlash when his position on Algeria became clear. Moreover, the French Revolution, and the fates of Danton, Desmoulins and Robespierre, had demonstrated that Committees of Public Safety were potentially extremely dangerous, liable to turn impetuously on those they had previously supported. In consequence, it was necessary to create some form of centralised directorate which (1) would unify and co-ordinate the mainland French Committees; (2) would bring the mainland French Committees into accord with the new government's programme; and (3) would dissolve the mainland French Committees when required, thus leaving the Algerian Committees isolated. It would appear to be for these reasons that M. Plantard established the Central Paris Committee, which imposed itself as a kind of *ad hoc* authority over the other Committees already in existence and proceeded, in effect, to hijack them. De Gaulle, in the meantime, was able to maintain a serene Olympian aloofness from the apparently 'grass-roots' movement which swept him to power – as well as from the potentially awkward process of having personally to dismantle the organisational apparatus of that movement before it could be turned against him.

Assuming this analysis of the situation to be more or less correct, the ploy was quite ingenious – an example of Machiavellian statecraft at its most sophisticated. It could not possibly have been implemented without very close, and very covert, collusion between De Gaulle and M. Plantard.

CIRCUIT

As we have noted, the Prieuré de Sion, according to the 1956 statutes deposited with the French police, identified itself by the acronym CIRCUIT, which was also said to be the name of the Order's internally circulated magazine. There are, in fact, two series of the magazine *Circuit*, the first dating from 1956, the second from 1959.[10] The 1956 series is baffling in its apparent irrelevance. There is one article on astrology, extolling the use of a thirteen-sign, rather than the conventional twelve-sign, zodiac. Apart from this, the journal would appear to be nothing more consequential than the publication of a housing association. It contains much lengthy discussion of low-cost housing, crossword puzzles, contests for children on a housing estate, advertisements for pencils. There is only one statement of any ostensible note, to the effect that the housing association to which the magazine is addressed reportedly maintains close contact with a network of other housing associations. It is certainly reasonable to suspect that housing associations in *Circuit* functioned as a façade for something else, and that the journal itself employed complex codes such as those purportedly employed by *Vaincre*. These 'housing associations' may even have been the organisational apparatus which, two years later, emerged to regulate the French Committees of Public Safety. But while such suspicions cannot be disproved, neither can they be verified. They remain confined to the realm of pure speculation.

The 1959 series of *Circuit* is an altogether different matter. The first issue is dated 1 July 1959, and its director is listed as Pierre Plantard. But the magazine itself does not pretend to be connected with the Prieuré de Sion. On the contrary, it declares itself to be the official organ of something called the Federation of French Forces. There was even a seal, and the following data:

Publication périodique culturelle de la Fédération
des Forces Françaises
116 rue Pierre Jouhet, 116
Aulnay-sous-Bois – (Seine-et-Oise)
Tél: 929-72-49

In the early 1970s, a Swiss researcher checked the above address. As far as he could ascertain, no magazine had ever been published there. The telephone number, too, proved to be false.[11] All attempts to track the Federation of French Forces, by the researcher in question, by ourselves and by others, have proved futile. To this day, no information on any such organisation has been forthcoming. But it would hardly seem coincidental that the address in Aulnay-sous-Bois is the same as that ascribed by Anne Lea Hisler to the Secretariat-General of the Committees of Public Safety in metropolitan France. Moreover, the second issue of the magazine reports M. Plantard as having received another letter of thanks from De Gaulle, this one dated 27 June 1959 – eleven months after the letters discussed above. It would seem evident that the Federation of French Forces was some sort of continuation of the administrative apparatus of the Committees, perhaps a means of keeping members in touch with each other. If this is so, it indicates that the Prieuré de Sion was using its magazine for something other than its own internal business.

The 1959 series of *Circuit* refers the reader repeatedly to *Vaincre*, indicating that *Vaincre* at the time must still have been available and obtainable. And indeed, *Circuit* echoes many of the themes and issues raised in *Vaincre*. As in *Vaincre*, much space is devoted to esoterica, mythology and matters of chivalry. There are articles by Anne Lea Hisler and others, including Pierre Plantard, sometimes writing under his own name, sometimes under the pseudonym of 'Chyren'. The Text includes statements such as the following: 'Everything is found in symbolic form. Whoever knows how to interpret the hidden meaning will understand. Humanity is always in a hurry, preferring solutions always to be given out ... '[12]; 'The place which seems the most solid is perhaps the most unstable. We have a tendency to forget that we live on a volcano, at the centre of forces of great strength ... [13]; ' ... all is accomplished in accordance with well-determined cycles. A "Nautonier" guides the ark ['arche'] in the flood'[14]. And finally:

> We are not strategists and we stand above all religious denominations, political perspectives and financial matters. We give to those who come to us moral aid and the indispensable manna of the spirit. We are but messengers, addressing believers and unbelievers alike with the sole object of transmitting fragments of truth. We do not subscribe to the conventional and erroneous astrology. The stars in themselves exert no influence. They are but reference points in space.[15]

There then follows another endorsement of the thirteen-sign zodiac, which M. Plantard uses to predict something of France's future. Interestingly enough, he forecasts that 1968 will be a cataclysmic year.

This, however, is not the only kind of material to be found in *Circuit*. There are articles on vines and viticulture – the grafting of vines – and a lengthy exegesis on the wine trade. There are also patriotic statements, echoing the tone of both *Vaincre* and the communiqués issued by the Committees of Public Safety. In one of these statements, for example, signed Adrian Sevrette, the author asserts that no solution for existing problems can be found:

> ... except through new methods and new men, for politics are dead. The curious fact remains that men do not wish to recognise this. There exists only one question: economic organisation. But do there still exist men who are capable of thinking *France*, as during the Occupation, when patriots and resistance fighters did not bother themselves about the political tendencies of their comrades in the fight?[16]

And, in another article:

> We desire that the 1500 copies of *Circuit* be a contact which kindles a light; we desire that the voice of patriots be able to transcend obstacles as in 1940, when they left invaded France to come and knock on the office door of the *Leader* of Free France. Today, it is the same. Before all, we are French. We are that force which fights in one way or another to construct a France cleansed and new. This must be done in the same patriotic spirit, with the same will and solidarity of action. Thus we cite here what we declare to be an old philosophy.[17]

There then follows a detailed plan of government to restore to France a lost lustre. It insists, for example, on the dismantling of departments and the restoration of provinces:

> The department is but an arbitrary system, created at the time of the Revolution, dictated and determined by the era in accordance with the demands of locomotion (the horse). Today, it no longer represents anything. In contrast, the province is a living portion of France; it is a whole vestige of our past, the same basis as that which formed the existence of our nation; it has its own folklore, its customs, its monuments, often its local dialects, which we wish to reclaim and promulgate. The province must have its own specific apparatus for

defence and administration, adapted to its specific needs, within the national unit.[18]

The blueprint that follows is organised under nine sub-headings: Council of the Provinces; Council of State; Parliamentary Council; Taxes; Work and Production; Medical; National Education; Age of Majority; and Housing and Schools.

Yet despite such specifically, even obsessively French preoccupations, M. Plantard, writing in another *Circuit* article, stresses another theme enunciated in *Vaincre*,

> ... the creation of a Confederation of Lands becomes a Confederation of States: the United States of Euro-Africa, which represents economically (1) an African and European community of exchange based on a common market, and (2) the circulation of wealth in order to serve the well-being of all, this being the sole stable foundation on which peace can be constructed.[19]

24

Secret Powers behind Covert Groups

It is a truism that politics make for strange bedfellows. A nation or an institution under pressure, fighting for its objectives and even for its survival, will make alliances when and where they can be made – and often, if expedient, with nations or institutions theoretically inimical. History, on one level, is a compendium of strange, ill-assorted coalitions, grotesquely mismatched marriages. For most of the last seventy-odd years, the Soviet Union has been perceived by the West as a threat and an adversary, potential or actual; and yet there was a period between 1941 and 1945 when the West united with the Soviet Union against a foe whom both perceived as more dangerous. On a smaller scale, there are numerous other examples. In 1982, the rabidly anti-Soviet military junta in Argentina announced its preparedness to receive Soviet arms and equipment in order to wage war against Britain over the Falklands. In the Gulf War today, Iran fulminates against Israel yet reportedly receives arms through Israel because Israel regards Iraq as potentially a greater threat. After his meeting with Mikhail Gorbachov in 1985, Ronald Reagan, characteristically reducing international relations to the level of Disneyland, claimed to have pointed out the way in which all the peoples of the world, including those of the United States and the Soviet Union, would unite in the face of an invasion from another planet. Even Ronald Reagan can have flashes of lucidity. Confronted by purple people-eaters from Sirius wielding death rays that carbonised their adversaries, even Ian Paisley and Gerry Adams might be prevailed upon to pool their resources (although we ourselves, at the prospect of such an alliance, might well be inclined to side with the people-eaters).

According to all the evidence we have been able to cull, as well as to statements 'leaked' to us by M. Plantard, the Prieuré de Sion seeks a United States of Europe partly as a bulwark against the

Soviet imperium, but primarily as a separate power bloc, a self-contained and neutral power bloc capable of holding the balance of power between the Soviet Union and the United States. In this respect, the Prieuré's position would appear to be almost identical to that of Pan Europa, the organisation for European unity currently directed by Dr Otto von Habsburg which, like the Kreisau Circle and others, uses as a symbol a Celtic cross in a circle. At the same time, there are other organisations and institutions which seek a united Europe primarily as a bulwark against the Soviet imperium, seeking to tie it closely to the United States. To what extent will each camp subordinate its differences with the other to the aims that both have in common? To what extent will each make concessions simply in order to obtain a united Europe, and be prepared to sort out priorities and allegiances afterwards?

In so far as it pursued the idea of a united Europe of any kind, or in any form, the Prieuré de Sion would necessarily have had to establish contacts, and quite probably accords, with a diverse spectrum of other organisations. In attempting to trace the history of the united European idea, one finds a tangled welter of allegiances and marriages of convenience. Just as the Algerian crisis prompted ex-Resistance fighters and veterans of the Free French Forces to align themselves with former Vichy officials and collaborators, so the dream of a united Europe has sometimes impelled moderate conservatives or Christian Democrats to align themselves temporarily with much more sinister, much more extreme and even 'neo-Nazi' right-wing groups. It is not therefore surprising that our quest for the Prieuré de Sion should have led us into the murky territory of the tract signed by 'Cornelius' – the territory in which 'the good guys', acting with what they conceive to be the best of intentions, prove to be working hand-in-glove with organisations such as P2.

The European Movement

As we have seen, the idea of a United States of Europe had been endorsed during the war by *Vaincre* in France and by Helmut James von Moltke's Kreisau Circle in Germany. These, of course, were not the only, nor even the most influential, sources of support for the idea. It was widely embraced in the French Resistance, for example, especially in border areas such as the Ardennes, where the individual's national loyalties were often split between France, Belgium, Luxemburg and Germany. The idea was enthusiastically espoused by André Malraux, who as early as 1941 was advocating a 'European New Deal, a federal Europe excluding the USSR'. It was espoused by Marshal Alphonse Juin, who, unlike Malraux, was to fall out bitterly with De Gaulle over Algeria. It was espoused by Georges Bidault, who as head of the OAS, in the wake of De Gaulle's *volte face* on Algeria, was to conspire for the General's assassination. It was also espoused by Winston Churchill, who, in a speech on 19 September 1946 at the University of Zurich, declared that 'we must build a kind of United States of Europe'. As early as October 1942, in fact, Churchill had written to the British War Cabinet: 'Hard as it is to say now, I trust that the European family may act unitedly as one under a Council of Europe. I look forward to a United States of Europe.'[1]

In the aftermath of the Second World War, Europe was exhausted, devastated and disillusioned. At the same time, Europeans, whatever their allegiances, felt they had been drawn together by a shared and collective tragedy – a tragedy which seemed increasingly to resemble civil war on a massive scale. For post-war Europe, the chief priority was at all costs to avoid another such conflict, another such fratricidal strife. Perhaps the most obvious means of doing so was European unity; and thus a call for European unity arose from a multitude of diverse quarters.

Late in 1947, the various individuals and institutions intent on European unity formed, from amongst themselves, a committee to co-ordinate their action. By May 1948, this committee had organised a Congress of Europe, similar to the council Churchill had advocated five and a half years before. It convened at The Hague and included representatives from sixteen countries. The President of Honour was Winston Churchill. At the final session, a communiqué stated: 'We desire a united Europe throughout whose area the free movement of persons, ideas and goods is restored.'[2]

Shortly after this, the European Movement was created – an unofficial but permanent body to pursue and promote the concept of a united Europe. Winston Churchill was again one of the Presidents of Honour.

In July, 1948, Georges Bidault, then Foreign Minister of France, became the first member of a government officially to propose the creation of a European parliament. Bidault, together with Jean Monnet, now regarded as a godfather of the EEC, and Robert Schuman, Louis Le Fur's old associate, proceeded to work in concert for what they described as a 'federation of the West'.

Another immensely important figure in the movement towards European unity was a Pole, Dr Joseph Retinger. Since the 1920s,

Retinger had been active in support of European unity and seems to have had contact with both Helmut James von Moltke, leader of the Kreisau Circle, and Hans Adolf von Moltke, self-proclaimed member of Alpha Galates. During the Second World War, he was based in England and served initially as political adviser to the Polish General Sikorski – who also seems to have been associated with Hans Adolf von Moltke when the latter was German ambassador to Poland.[3] In 1943, Retinger joined the British Special Operations Executive and, at the age of fifty-six, parachuted into Poland as an SOE operative. After the war, he again assumed an active role in promoting European unity. He helped to organise the Hague Congress of Europe in May, 1948. In July of that year, he travelled to the United States with Winson Churchill, Duncan Sandys and the former Belgian Prime Minister, Paul-Henri Spaak, in order to elicit financial support for the recently formed European Movement. This trip led to the creation, on 29 March 1949, of the American Committee on a United Europe, or ACUE. With ACUE, a process was inaugurated whereby successive organisations working for European unity were effectively hijacked by American agencies working for American interests.

The seeds were thus sown for the growth of a shadowy subterranean sub-culture in which secret and semi-secret societies – religious, political and financial – would soon begin to flourish. By the late 1950s, this sub-culture had assumed a momentum of its own, comprising a milieu which, although invisible to the outsider, began to exercise a more and more pervasive influence on public affairs.

Moves by the CIA

The man perhaps most responsible for initiating American interest in united Europe movements was Count Richard Coudenhove-Kalergi, who had founded Pan-Europa in 1922 as the Pan European Union. Although it accomplished little on a practical level, Pan-Europa, in the period between the wars, was a prestigious organisation. Its membership included a number of esteemed political figures, such as Léon Blum and Aristide Briand in France and Eduard Beneš in Czechoslovakia, as well as Winston Churchill. The membership also included Albert Einstein, and such cultural luminaries as Paul Valéry, Miguel de Unamuno, George Bernard Shaw and Thomas Mann.

Driven out of Austria by the German *Anschluss* of 1938,

Coudenhove-Kalergi, in 1940, fled to the United States. Here, he lobbied tirelessly for his Pan-European ideal, insisting that European unity must be a priority for American policy after the war. His efforts served to convince a number of important American political figures, such as William Bullitt and Senators Fulbright and Wheeler. When America entered the war, some of Coudenhove-Kalergi's thinking offered a blueprint for action. It was to be adopted as such by the OSS, precursor of the CIA.

The OSS, or Office of Strategic Services, was created in emulation, and with the aid, of Britain's MI6 and SOE. Its first director was General William ('Wild Bill') Donovan. Donovan's agents were to provide the nucleus for the post-war CIA. One of them, Allen Dulles, became director of the CIA from 1953 until the Bay of Pigs débâcle forced him to resign in 1961. During the war, Dulles had been based in Switzerland, and he maintained the contacts he had made there with Helmut James von Moltke and the Kreisau Circle.

As director of the OSS, William Donovan was quick to realise the potential significance of the Vatican to intelligence operations. Thousands of Catholic priests were scattered across Europe, in every country, every city, virtually every town and village. Thousands of Catholic priests were also serving as chaplains in the armed forces of every combatant nation. This network was already engaged in intelligence activity, passing vast quantities of information back to the Vatican's own internal intelligence department. One of the four section leaders of Vatican Intelligence was Monsignor Giovanni Montini – later Pope Paul VI.[4] Donovan therefore undertook to establish close links with the Vatican.

Shortly after America's entry into the war, Donovan forged an alliance with one Father Felix Morlion, founder of a European Catholic intelligence service called Pro Deo ('For God'), based in Lisbon. Under Donovan's auspices, Pro Deo moved its headquarters to New York and the OSS undertook to finance its operation. When Rome was liberated in 1944, Donovan and Father Morlion proceeded to install Pro Deo in the Vatican itself.[5] Here, it was particularly well situated to draw on information from Catholic priests who had been, or were still, in Germany or with the German armed forces. The Jesuits, with their sophisticated training, rigorous discipline and tight-knit organisation, proved an especially valuable source of intelligence material.

In the period following the war, the United States hastened to capitalise on the apparatus Donovan had established, particularly in Italy. In 1948, with Italian elections scheduled, the newly formed

27 The grave of Jean Cocteau, Milly la Forêt, chapel of Saint-Blaise des Simples. Cocteau himself decorated the interior and designed the stained-glass windows.

N° 1 - 1ère Année   21 Septembre 1942

VAÍNCRE

POUR UNE JEUNE CHEVALERIE

DIRECTION-RÉDACTION, 10, Rue Lebouteux, PARIS (XVIIe)

ΑΛΦΑ GALATES — HONNEUR-PATRIE

VAINCRE...

par
Pierre de FRANCE

« Vaincre », mot prestigieux qui eut toujours le pouvoir de rassembler les peuples, est aujourd'hui le titre de cet organe qui doit redonner à la patrie la puissance de vivre, avec un idéal chevaleresque et l'abnégation du soi.

Le plus beau parti, voyez-vous, c'est l'ensemble de tous les hommes penchés sur leur travail, à l'atelier, dans les Facultés, dans les bureaux, coordonnant leurs volontés dans un même idéal d'entr'aide et qui parfois lèvent la tête en sentant qu'ils doivent vaincre pour assurer leur avenir.

L'avenir pour eux, ce n'est ni l'intrigue politique, ni un baquenard de vendu, ce n'est ni la haine, ni l'anarchie, ce n'est ni la guerre, ni la révolution avec leurs cortèges sanglants; il est beaucoup plus simple.

L'avenir, c'est vaincre pour être dans la sécurité, avec la certitude que le salaire ne sera plus synonyme de mauvaise surprise, que le travail aura des lendemains réconfortants.

Vaincre, c'est en rentrant chez soi, le soir, après le travail, trouver une présence sous la lampe, et, dans un coin, le berceau sur lequel deux fronts vont se pencher.

Vaincre, c'est constituer, sous le petit pécule qui assure la quiétude aux heures de maladie, et permettra peut-être l'achat de la petite reine de la route même de la petite maison dont on rêve, ou d'un supplément à la ration journalière.

C'est aussi constituer une dot pour les filles ou les fils qui, le moment venu, devront s'établir à leur tour.

Vaincre, c'est organiser sa vie comme on trace un sillon en profondeur et en rectitude.

Vaincre, c'est l'entr'aide nationale et l'entente des Peuples, unis dans un véritable socialisme, bannissant à jamais les querelles créées par des intérêts capitalistes.

Je connais beaucoup de ces braves travailleurs qui doutent du lendemain, qui vont, chancelant, de déception en déception, durement éconduits par les riches de ce monde aux égoïsmes confortables, ou bien douloureusement déçus par des meneurs cyniques travestis en apôtres.

Ceux-là, que pensent-ils donc?

Ils songent avec anxiété au pain quotidien, à l'avenir proche, à leur sort et à celui des leurs.

C'est toute cette grande famille que je veux grouper sans distinction d'origine ou de parti.

L'âge lui-même n'est pas une limite, parce qu'il y a de faux vieillards et de faux jeunes gens. Il y a des hommes d'âge pour qui le nombre des années n'est jamais un âge accumulée, et des jeunes qui ont toujours eu le sens de la direction.

Il faut d'abord être unis, être groupés; il faut être nombreux,

Pierre de FRANCE

c'est-à-dire former un Grand Ordre de Chevalerie, parce que, si nous sommes *nombreux et disciplinés*, nous serons forts, parce que, si nous sommes forts, nous serons craints et pourrons *vaincre*, c'est-à-dire imposer aux foules une doctrine et un idéal.

En outre, je veux ouvrir le cahier des revendications des travailleurs, centraliser leurs doléances, leurs récriminations, en dégager leurs aspirations communes, les traduire, en être devant les foules le porte-parole tenace et passionné. *Je veux vaincre avec eux, pour eux.*

C'est pourquoi je veux d'abord créer un état d'esprit, puis appeler les hommes à l'action.

Il s'agit de cristalliser les volontés.

Il s'agit de grouper tous les hommes que n'a pas atteint le microbe politique, *dans une coalition qui dominera le présent et sauvera l'avenir.*

Qu'on le sache bien, pour poursuivre cette tâche, je n'ai pas besoin de l'aide des partis organisés, JUIN 1943, complaisantes ou des fanatiques politiciens.

— ORGANE GRATUIT —

SYNTHÈSES DE FORCES

« ...Quand un ruisseau est pollué, il est nécessaire pour trouver l'eau pure de remonter à la source; il en est de même pour la *tradition*, elle n'est restée pure qu'à son origine. »
Paul LECOURT,
Directeur de l'*Atlantis*.

« ...La nouvelle *construction d'Occident* puisera ses forces dans le vieil ordre Celtique, et la Bretagne qui conserve le dépôt inaltéré de la science sacrée, sera très certainement le berceau de l'Ordre Chevaleresque. »
G. THARIEUX d'EGMONT,
Écrivain et Poète.

« ...C'est très beau les discours, mais quelle est leur utilité? Voyez-vous ce qu'il faut à notre Patrie, c'est l'action, une *action chevaleresque*, dégagée des intrigues politiques où nos éminences s'embourbent... »
Henry COSTON
Directeur de la *Libre Parole*.

« ...Un Ordre de Chevalerie, mais c'est la pierre de base d'une nation, la France est justement morte pour avoir remplacé ses Chevaliers par des Cavaliers... »
FRANCHET d'ESPÉREY
Maréchal de France.

« ...Certes, une Chevalerie est indispensable, car notre pays ne peut *renaître que par ses Chevaliers...* »
Geneviève ZAPPELLI
Directrice
de l'*Arche Nationale*.

Notre ordre n'est pas en quête d'hommes avides de titres ou de rubans.

Ces lignes s'adressent uniquement aux forces saines de mon pays, à ceux qui sont capables de faire don de leur personne pour une cause désintéressée, à ceux qui ont juré, comme nous, de vaincre pour sauver la France.

28–9 Illustrations from the first issue of *Vaincre*, 21 September 1942. *Left*, front page, including a photograph of the journal's publisher and editor, 'Pierre de France', the pseudonym of Pierre Plantard de Saint-Clair. *Above*, the road towards the 'United States of the West – 1937 to 1946', between Brittany and Bavaria.

30 *Right*, Pierre Plantard de Saint-Clair, Grand Master of the Prieuré de Sion from 17 January 1981 until 10 July 1984, shown here in Paris, 1982.

31 Charter recording the donations in 1152 by King Louis VII of the Abbey of Saint Samson, Orléans, to the Order of Sion.

32 Charter recording Pope Alexander III's confirmation of the Order of
Sion's possessions in Palestine, Sicily, Naples, Calabria, Lombardy,
Spain and France; this is an official copy, made in 1337, of the original,
dated 1178.

33–4 *Left*: *above*, Rennes-le-Château, seen from Le Bézu; *below*, the Sals valley, looking from Roque Nègre towards Rennes-les-Bains.

35 *Right*, a section of paved Roman road between Rennes-le-Château and Rennes-les-Bains. The complex and extensive road system in the area attests to a much greater population in earlier times.

36–7 *Below*, the first and second documents found by Abbé Saunière in the Rennes-le-Château church in 1891. In the first, the Latin text is a combination of Luke 6:1–5, Matthew 12:1–8 and Mark 2:23–8; the second is from John 12:1–11. Both conceal ciphered messages.

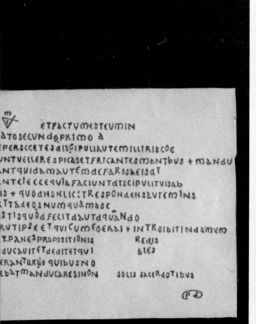

38 The Arch of Titus, Rome, showing part of the treasure of the Temple at Jerusalem being carried to Rome.

CIA embarked on a complex clandestine operation to preclude any prospect of a Communist victory. Under the auspices of James Angleton, former OSS station chief in Rome, and later CIA head of counter-intelligence, millions of dollars were covertly filtered to the Christian Democrats, while additional funds were pumped into newspapers and other vehicles of propaganda.[6] This procedure was also used to good effect in France.[7]

As stated above, Dr Joseph Retinger's trip to the United States on behalf of the European Movement led, on 29 March 1949, to the creation of the American Committee on a United Europe, or ACUE. Its chairman was William Donovan. Its vice-chairman was the former OSS Head of Station in Switzerland, Allen Dulles. Its secretary was George S. Franklin, who was also director of the private Council on Foreign Relations and subsequently became a co-ordinator of the Trilateral Commission. The executive director of ACUE was a serving CIA operative, Thomas Braden, then chief of the agency's International Organisations Department. Under the auspices of these men, ACUE decided to underwrite the European Movement of Joseph Retinger.[8] Funds from American State Department sources were discreetly filtered to the European Movement's Brussels headquarters. As the Soviet Union extended its influence across Eastern Europe, the epoch of the 'Cold War' began. Conceived originally to foster European unity, the European Movement was gradually being conscripted to help build a 'bulwark against Communism' – and this bulwark conduced to the atmosphere in which clandestine organisations flourished.

Now partially financed by the CIA, Joseph Retinger and other members of the European Movement forged ties with Prince Bernhard of the Netherlands, with the Italian Prime Minister and with Sir Colin Gubbins, former director of Britain's SOE. Together with the then director of the CIA, General Walter Bedell Smith, this group proceeded to create a 'think tank' which met for the first time in May 1954 at the Hotel de Bilderberg, in the Dutch town of Oosterbeek. Thus arose the Bilderberg Conferences.

In the meantime, the CIA had been proceeding on its own initiative as well, embarking on a large-scale programme of covert action to support any institutions that might help consolidate the 'bulwark against Communism'. Political leaders, political parties and pressure groups, unions, newspapers and publishers were all heavily subsidised, providing their orientation was sufficiently pro-Western and anti-Communist. During the 1950s, an average of between twenty and thirty million dollars[9] a year was reportedly spent in Italy to support cultural activities, youth schemes, publishing ventures and Catholic groups of one kind or another. Enterprises sponsored by the Church, including missions and orphanages, were often co-funded by the CIA. CIA money was dispensed to many bishops and monsignors, one of whom was the future Pope Paul VI. And, needless to say, the Christian Democratic Party in Italy remained a particular focus of attention. In fact, the future Pope's father, Giorgio Montini was co-founder in 1919 of the party which became called the Christian Democratic Party, and his elder brother was a Christian Democrat senator.

Dr Joseph Retinger's CIA-sponsored European Movement was also active in Italy, further consolidating the bonds between the American intelligence agency and the Vatican. Retinger enlisted the support of Dr Luigi Gedda, an old personal friend, who was medical advisor to Pope Pius XII and also the head of Azione Cattolica, or Catholic Action, the power behind the Christian Democratic Party. Through Gedda, Retinger was also able to conscript the services of the future Pope Paul VI, and Catholic Action became another primary recipient of CIA funds.[10]

The rapport between the CIA and the Vatican became closer in 1963, when Pope John XXIII died and was succeeded by Paul VI, formerly Giovanni Montini, Archbishop of Milan. As we have already noted, Montini was already associated with the agency and had already received funds from it. Even during the war, he had worked with the American intelligence services, passing information to and fro between the Vatican and the OSS. After the war, as Archbishop of Milan, he turned over to the CIA comprehensive dossiers on politically active priests. These were to be used to influence the Italian elections of 1960.

The relationship between the Vatican and the CIA has continued to the present. According to Gordon Thomas and Max Gordon-Witts, there occurred, in November 1978, a private meeting between Pope John Paul II and the CIA's station chief for Rome. As a result of this meeting, an accord was reached whereby the Pope was to receive regular weekly intelligence briefings from the CIA.[11] What the CIA received in return was not specified, but one can make an educated guess.

Another of the CIA's most influential allies within the Church was Cardinal Francis Spellman of New York. In 1954, he acted directly for the CIA in Guatemala, helping to stage a coup there which was orchestrated by the agency. But Spellman was also deeply involved in affairs in Italy. He played a crucial role in obtaining large sums of US Government 'black money' for the use of the Roman Catholic Church. He was intimately associated with

Bernardino Nogara, the mastermind behind the Vatican Bank, and with Count Enrico Galeazzi, who with Michele Sindona watched over Vatican investments and banking in the early 1960s.[12] And it was Cardinal Spellman, who, in 1963, first brought to the Pope's attention Father Paul Marcinkus of Chicago. By 1971, Marcinkus, now Archbishop, was head of the Vatican Bank, a close friend of P2 members such as Michele Sindona and Roberto Calvi, and an alleged member of P2 himself.

The origins of the Masonic Lodge P2 are obscure, but it is believed to have been formed in the early 1960s.[13] Whatever its orginal priorities and objectives may have been, its ultra-right-wing Grand Master, Licio Gelli, had soon brought it into the phalanx of groups and organisations which constituted the 'bulwark against Communism'. Certain of its members received generous CIA subsidies. And through individuals such as Calvi and Sindona, P2 provided a means of furnishing anti-Communist institutions in Europe and Latin America with both Vatican and CIA funds. Calvi also claimed that he personally had arranged the transfer of $20,000,000 of Vatican money to Solidarity in Poland, although the overall total sent to Solidarity is believed to have exceeded $100,000,000. Prior to his indictment for murder, Michele Sindona was not only P2's financier, but the Vatican's investment counsellor as well, helping the Church to sell its Italian assets and re-invest in the United States. His services for the CIA included passing funds to 'friends' in Yugoslavia, as well as to the Greek colonels prior to their seizure of power in 1967. He also channelled millions of dollars into the funds of the Christian Democrats in Italy.

When the existence of P2 first made international headlines in 1981, the scandal surrounding its stranglehold on the upper echelons of government, police and finance was focused primarily on Italy. According to David Yallop, however,

> ... there are still branches functioning in Argentina, Venezuela, Paraguay, Bolivia, France, Portugal and Nicaragua. Members are also active in Switzerland and the U.S.A. P2 interlocks with the Mafia in Italy, Cuba and the U.S.A. It interlocks with a number of the military regimes of Latin America, and with a variety of groups of neo-Fascists. It also interlocks very closely with the C.I.A. It reaches right into the heart of the Vatican. The central common interest of all these elements is apparently a hatred and fear of Communism.[14]

It is now generally acknowledged that P2, however influential and powerful it may have been, was (and probably still is) controlled by some even higher, more shadowy authority, which transmitted its instructions through Licio Gelli, the Lodge's Grand Master. According to an Italian parliamentary commission, the organisation behind P2 lay 'beyond the frontiers of Italy'.[15] There has been much speculation, both plausible and otherwise, about this organisation. Some have identified it as the American Mafia. Some have suggested the KGB, or some other intelligence agency from Eastern Europe. Some have even suggested the Prieuré de Sion. In 1979, however, a defector from P2 – a journalist named Mino Pecorelli – accused the CIA. Two months after this accusation, Pecorelli was murdered.

In March 1981, Italian police raided Licio Gelli's villa. They discovered comprehensive lists of the Lodge's membership. They also discovered an index to Licio Gelli's files – although the files themselves had vanished, apparently being of greater importance than the membership lists. Some of the headings in the index were published in Italian newspapers. They included Opus Dei. They included Giulio Andreotti, currently Italian Foreign Minister and alleged, in a document we received, to be a member of the Prieuré de Sion. And they included the organisation known officially as the Sovereign and Military Order of the Temple of Jerusalem – the organisation, that is, which today claims a direct lineal descent from the Knights Templar.

The Order of Knights

The Sovereign and Military Order of the Temple of Jerusalem dates, in its present form, from 1804, when it announced itself publicly and was officially acknowledged by various other institutions. It claims a much older pedigree, however. According to its own assertions, Jacques de Molay, last Grand Master of the Templars, left, on his execution in 1314, a charter designating his successor[16] Although officially dissolved by the Papacy, the Templars, acting on this charter, are said to have perpetuated themselves through the centuries. The authenticity of the charter remains a source of contention among historians, though there is a certain body of evidence in its favour. The issue has never been one of pressing importance because the Sovereign and Military Order has never made any explicit bid for power of any kind, never actively endeavoured to wrest back the prerogatives, privileges and holdings of the Knights it claims as its predecessors. Today, it is devoted largely to antiquarian research and charitable works. Its internal procedures are reminiscent, at times, of certain rites of Freemasonry, at times of other heraldic orders such as those of the Golden Fleece, the Holy Sepulchre and Saint Maurice. Its current Grand Master is the Portuguese Count Antonio de Fontes.

In 1982, we had the first of several meetings with an official of the Sovereign and Military Order of the Temple. During the course of our conversations, he described to us the factional strife and schism which, during the last decade, had obtained within the institution he represented. One faction of the membership had broken away to form its own separate neo-Templar body in Switzerland. This faction had, in turn, spawned yet another 'renegade' faction, which, under the leadership of one Anton Zapelli, had adopted a new, higher profile and a more aggressively ambitious programme. Zapelli's headquarters were also in Switzerland – at Sion. The membership of Zapelli's organisation was said to include a number of people associated with the Swiss Grand Lodge Alpina, whose name had previously appeared on a number of Prieuré de Sion documents.

None of this would have been of any particular significance to us had it not been for the fact that we had already encountered Zapelli's name in another context. In 1979, when we were first attempting to establish contact with the Prieuré de Sion and with M. Plantard, an informant in Paris had cited Zapelli. He was said, on that occasion, to be the real power behind the Prieuré de Sion – although this assertion may well have resulted from simple confusion, Zapelli's Templar organisation being based in Sion and bearing the name of Grand Prieuré de Suisse.

Struck by the reappearance of Zapelli's name in connection with the Sovereign and Military Order of the Temple, we asked whether he was indeed associated with the Prieuré. The representative of the Sovereign and Military Order did not know. He was aware, he said, of the Prieuré de Sion. Within his own organisation, the Prieuré was known to have been active in the French Resistance during the war. But he had no idea whether Zapelli was in any way affiliated with it. In fact, he declared, he would be very grateful if we could find out and let him know. He seemed to fear that the Prieuré, working through Zapelli, might perhaps be attempting to hijack his own Order.

When we asked M. Plantard whether he knew Zapelli, he only smirked cryptically and said, 'I know everybody.' Subsequently, however, we were given a document produced for circulation within Zapelli's organisation. Two themes emerged as of paramount concern. One was banking and international finance. By

1982, Zapelli's organisation had apparently established its own bank or 'mutual society'. The other principal theme was a united Europe and 'the role of modern Templars in the unification of Europe'. The original Templars, Zapelli's document argued, had sought to create a united Europe. Their latter-day successors were now urged to emerge from the shadows, embrace something more important than purely antiquarian interests, involve themselves in politics, work for European unity and promote 'the European idea'. The structure Zapelli advocated was roughly similar to that of the Swiss Confederation. Europe was defined as stretching from the Atlantic and the Mediterranean to the Urals.

We found no reliable evidence linking Zapelli to the Prieuré de Sion. Neither have we found any evidence linking Zapelli to Licio Gelli or other members of P2. Like them, however, he appears to be functioning in a kind of twilight region, where secret societies link with high finance and Pan-European politics, where national frontiers do not constitute an obstacle and where no established legal guidelines obtain. And the fact remains that the index to Licio Gelli's files betrays an interest, on the part of P2, in the Sovereign and Military Order of the Temple.

The precise role, and the effective power, of the modern Templars remains uncertain. On the other hand, there is another organisation, closely associated with the Templars historically, whose role and power are much more thoroughly documented and tangible. This organisation is the original Templars' traditional rival, the Knights Hospitaller of Saint John – or, as their primary offshoot is known today, the Sovereign Military Order of Malta.

The Order of Saint John originated with a hospital dedicated to Saint John in Jerusalem and established around 1070, some thirty years before the First Crusade, by Italian merchants to minister to pilgrims. It seems to have constituted itself officially as an order around 1100, just after the First Crusade, when it took its first Grand Master. The Hospitallers thus pre-dated the Templars, but they were not initially involved in military activity, only in hospital work. By 1126, however, some eight years after the Templars appeared publicly on the scene, the Knights of Saint John had begun to assume an increasingly military character, which was soon to eclipse, though not altogether supplant, their hospitaller services. In the years that followed, they came to comprise, along with the Templars and subsequently the Teutonic Knights, the major military and financial power in the Holy Land, and one of the major such powers in all Christendom. Like the Templars, they became immensely wealthy. Their Order developed into a vast military, ecclesiastic and administrative edifice with hundreds of knights, a standing army, numerous ancillary services, a network of castles and fortresses and enormous holdings of land not only in Palestine, but across the Christian world. At the same time, the Order remained loyal to its hospitaller origins, maintaining well run and clean hospitals staffed by its own surgeons.

In 1307, the Templars were charged with a catalogue of offences against Catholic orthodoxy, and by 1314 they had been officially suppressed. Between 1309 and their secularisation in 1525, the Teutonic Knights were periodically subjected to similar charges – though their primary theatre of operations, in Prussia and along the Baltic coast, placed them safely beyond the reach of any authority disposed to act against them. In contrast, the Knights Hospitaller of Saint John never incurred any such stigma. They continued to enjoy the favour of the Papacy. In England and, to a lesser degree, elsewhere, former Templar holdings were turned over to them.

After the fall of the Holy Land in 1291, the Knights of Saint John retired for a time to Cyprus. Then, in 1309, they proceeded to establish their seat and headquarters on the island of Rhodes, which they governed as their private principality. Here they remained for more than two centuries, withstanding two major sieges by the Turks. At last, in 1522, a third siege forced them to abandon the island, and in 1530 they re-established themselves on Malta. In 1565, Malta in turn was besieged by the Turks in one of the most ambitious such operations in military history. In an epic defence, 541 Knights Hospitaller and sergeants, aided by a garrison of some 9,000 men-at-arms, repelled the repeated assaults of between 30,000 and 40,000 attackers. Six years later, in 1571, the Order's fleet, together with warships from Austria, Italy and Spain, won a decisive victory at the naval Battle of Lepanto, definitively shattering Turkish maritime power in the Mediterranean.

The sieges of Rhodes and Malta, and the Battle of Lepanto, were the high points of the Hospitallers' history, exceeding even their exploits in the Holy Land during the Crusades. In the mid sixteenth century, they were still one of the supreme military and naval powers of the Christian world, with strength and financial resources comparable to most kingdoms. Already, however, the seeds of decline had been planted. In Germany, Switzerland, Holland, Scotland and England, the Protestant Reformation had begun to fracture the unity of Catholic Europe; and the fissures erupting throughout Western Christendom were mirrored, in microcosm, within the Order of Saint John. English and German brethren of the Order proceeded to defect and create their own rival institutions. By the seventeenth century, the Knights still resident on Malta had been left behind by the tide of history, a staunch Catholic enclave still adhering to obsolete chivalric tenets while the rest of Europe moved on into a new age of mercantilism, industrialisation and middle-class hegemony.

In 1798, however, the Knights were still on Malta, albeit reduced to the status of a quaint anachronism, impotent, led by an inept Grand Master and with their Catholic allegiances eroded by Freemasonry. Then Napoleon swept through the Mediterranean, en route to his disastrous campaign in Egypt. The Knights who had withstood the Turks two and a quarter centuries before were unable to offer resistance. They were summarily expelled by Napoleon, who claimed Malta for France, only to lose it again to the British fleet under Horatio Nelson. For the Order of Saint John, a period of confusion ensued. At last, in 1834, the Knights were able to establish a new base for themselves in Rome. Despite the loss of their island home, they adopted the title of Order of Malta to differentiate themselves from the Protestant Orders of Saint John then being formed in Britain and Germany. They devoted themselves once again to hospital work which, during the century and a half that followed, earned them increasing prestige. In the immediate aftermath of the Second World War, before the creation of the state of Israel, there was actually some talk of entrusting the Knights of Malta with sovereignty over Jerusalem.

In 1979, the Order numbered 9,562 full Knights, a thousand of whom were American and more than three thousand Italian.[17] Today, from their headquarters at Palazzo Malta on the Via Condotti in Rome, the Knights of Malta maintain a world-wide hospitaller organisation. There is an emergency aid section to provide help in cases of natural disasters. There are hospitals and leper camps run by the Order in many countries. And, like their kindred Protestant Orders of Saint John in Britain, Germany, Holland and Sweden, the Knights of Malta have their own ambulance service. In Northern Ireland, ambulances of the English Order of Saint John and of the Knights of Malta are on the streets simultaneously, ministering to the needs of their respective denominations and communities.

In international law, the current status of the Knights of Malta is that of an independent sovereign principality.[18] The Grand Master is recognised as a head of state, with a secular rank equivalent to a prince and an ecclesiastical rank equivalent to a cardinal. The Order maintains formal diplomatic relations with a number of countries, especially in Africa and in Latin America, and in those countries its ministers enjoy standard diplomatic privileges. The upper grades of the Order are still fastidiously aristocratic. The highest Knights must be able to display a coat of arms dating back at least three hundred years, in unbroken succession from father to son.

The twentieth-century Order of Malta is, needless to say, ideally placed for intelligence work. Its network of membership is international and at the same time well organised. Its hospital and medical services often place it strategically at points of crisis – as in Northern Ireland. Its membership extends from medical staff and ambulance drivers to important figures in politics, business and finance who have access to spheres that ordinary priests would not. In consequence, the Knights of Malta became closely associated with the Vatican's own intelligence department. The Order seems not to have been hostile to such an association. On the contrary, it seems to have welcomed the opportunity to resume, on a clandestine level, the role it had first begun to perform during the twelfth century – that of spearheading a crusade.

Today, the Order of Malta is believed to be one of the primary channels of communication between the Vatican and the CIA. There is ample evidence for such an assertion. In 1946, James Angleton – former OSS and then CIA station chief in Rome, who filtered millions of dollars from his agency to the Italian Christian Democrats – received a decoration from the Order of Malta for counter-intelligence work.[19] So, too did Dr Luigi Gedda, the head of the group called Catholic Action, who served as liaison between the CIA, Joseph Retinger's European Movement and the future Pope Paul VI.[20] In 1948, the Knights awarded their highest decoration, the Grand Cross of Merit, to General Reinhard Gehlen, head of the West German secret service, which at that time was little more than a department of the CIA.[21] Previously, Gehlen had been in charge of Hitler's intelligence services for Russia. As early as the late 1940s, then, the Order of Malta was becoming involved in the secret war against Communism beginning to escalate across Europe.

The Order's work in intelligence would naturally have been facilitated by the number of highly placed American officials in its ranks. As the 'Cold War' gained momentum, the American contingent of the Order increased substantially. The most influential figure in this contingent was, again, Cardinal Francis Spellman of New York – who had worked for the CIA in Guatemala and whose network of personal associates led directly to P2. Spellman became 'Protector and Spiritual Adviser' of the American Knights. He also became their effective *de facto* head. In this capacity, he raised immense sums of money, each of the many Knights created annually having to pay tens of thousands of dollars as an enrolment fee. It has been alleged that only a portion of this revenue ever found its way back to the Order in Rome, the bulk of it being deployed for other purposes. Spellman was also in league with a cardinal who, during the 1950s, made an attempt to hijack the Order and use it for his own political ends.

It is not uncommon for CIA directors to be Knights of Malta. John McCone, for example, was a Knight. The agency's current Director, William Casey, is also a Knight. Former Director William Colby was reportedly offered membership in the Order but is said to have declined with the words 'I'm a little lower key.'[22] The Order's membership at present includes William Wilson (United States ambassador to the Vatican), Clare Boothe Luce (former United States Ambassador to Italy), George Rocca (former deputy chief of CIA counter-intelligence) and Alexander Haig.

But it is not only from such prestigious American spheres that the Order recruits its ranks. Licio Gelli, Grand Master of P2, is associated with the Order, probably as a Knight, but confirmation is now impossible. However, Gelli's closest associate in P2, Umberto Ortolani, is a Knight of Malta and served as the Order's ambassador to Uruguay where he owned a bank. Other Knights include Alexandre de Marenches (former chief of French Intelligence), Generals de Lorenzo and Allavena (former chiefs of the Italian Secret Service), General Giuseppe Santovito (former chief of Italian Military Intelligence) and Admiral Giovanni Torrisi (Chief of the Italian General Staff). The last three were also members of P2.[23]

It would, of course, be erroneous and unfair to regard the Order of Malta as nothing more than 'a CIA front'. The Order remains an autonomous institution pursuing charitable and diplomatic work of its own, much of which is laudable. Nevertheless, there is a persuasive body of evidence attesting to its involvement in intelligence activity. Some of this activity need not necessarily even be the Order's official policy. Thus, for example, a cardinal, say, and a high-ranking intelligence officer, both of whom happen to be Knights, may come together at one or another of the Order's social functions. Each may introduce the other to an influential banker, or a prominent politician. In this way, a project may be implemented and co-ordinated at the highest level without official directives, written instructions or formal procedures that might ultimately demand accountability. There would be no tell-tale paperwork to be discovered afterwards – paperwork which can often be compromising and is notoriously difficult to dispose of without trace. Like the Lodge in Freemasonry, the Order of Malta, by its very nature, conduces to such procedures. It functions, in effect, as an ideal conduit. And its freedom of manoeuvre is facilitated by its diplomatic prestige, its relatively low profile, its international network and the respect accorded its humanitarian endeavours.

The current situation in Central America is regarded by a number of commentators as indicative of the way in which the Order of Malta can be utilised – indicative, indeed, of the way any such organisation can be suborned to the aims of one or another political ideology. The present head of the Order in the United States is a prominent businessman, J. Peter Grace. Prior to 1971, Grace was associated with Radio Liberty and Radio Free Europe, both of which had been established by Reinhard Gehlen and funded by the CIA. Today, Grace, whose aides include another Knight of Malta, former United States Treasury Secretary William Simon, runs an organisation called Americares, of which he is chairman. A primary objective of Americares is to raise money for aid to Central America. The agency in charge of distributing this aid is the Order of Malta, working through its field organisation in El Salvador, Guatemala and Honduras.

At the same time, Americares seems to share certain interests with the World Anti-Communist League (WACL), now directed by ex-Major General John Singlaub, who in 1978 was required to resign for defying the President. When the White House failed to win Congressional support for funding the Contras in Nicaragua, Ronald Reagan enlisted the support of the World Anti-Communist League and others. Singlaub's organisation openly undertook to supply the Contras with money and material. American journalists have legitimately wondered how much of this money and material is in fact being provided by Peter Grace's Americares organisation and distributed through the Knights of Malta. If any of it is, there remains the question of whether Grace and Americares are simply exploiting the Knights of Malta, or whether the entire Order, as a matter of its own policy, is involved.

The Unknown Factor

In our October 1984 meeting with M. Plantard – when, unknown to us at the time, he was no longer speaking as Grand Master of the Prieuré de Sion – the Order of Malta was mentioned. The Prieuré de Sion, M. Plantard said – almost, it seemed, a little resentfully –

included a number of Knights of Malta. We did not find this unduly surprising. The Knights of Malta, as we had already discovered by then, seemed to be everywhere. Why not in the Prieuré de Sion as well? In fact, the Abbé François Ducaud-Bourget – who, by M. Plantard's own admission, had sponsored his induction into the Prieuré and was publicly stated to have been the Order's Grand Master – was from 20 September 1947 to 18 November 1961 Magistral Chaplain of the Knights of Malta. Given the Knights' liaison with the OSS during the war, such a role seemed perfectly in keeping with the Abbé's activities on behalf of the French Resistance, when he was based in Paris yet managed to supply arms to Resistance groups – a feat which was rewarded by a Resistance medal after the war.

The French press, in a brief article on M. Plantard's election as Grand Master in 1981, had stated that 'the 121 high dignitaries of the Prieuré de Sion are all *eminences grises* of high finance and of international political or philosophical organisations'. Something very similar could clearly be said about the Knights of Malta. By virtue of their intrinsic natures, both Orders could be expected to function in much the same sphere, the twilit underworld where politics, finance, religion and the work of various intelligence agencies converge. Undoubtedly, too, the Knights of Malta and the Prieuré de Sion had certain interests and certain objectives in common. Both Orders, though perhaps for different reasons and with differing priorities, were apparently intent on the creation of some sort of United States of Europe. And the history of both Orders, assuming the Prieuré's pedigree to be authentic, would have been closely intertwined. Both claimed a heritage dating back to the Crusades, and such a heritage would have dictated that their respective paths intersect at numerous points during the ensuing centuries. Each was an explicitly neo-chivalric institution, and each could be expected to figure prominently in the other's archives. Each could be expected to have had a long familiarity with the other, and probably some considerable knowledge of the other's secrets. The very fact of such a shared past would inevitably have created some bond.

At the same time, there would have been certain crucial points of contention between the two Orders. The Knights of Malta had always been unswervingly loyal to the papacy and the Roman Catholic Church, and this loyalty still obtains today. The Prieuré, on the other hand, presented itself as traditionally hostile to the Vatican and seemed, indeed, to constitute its own clandestine, alternative papacy. And as the protector of a bloodline descended through Jesus or his family from the House of David, the Prieuré would naturally be perceived as inimical by the Church. Thus their respective positions vis-à-vis Rome would necessarily have cast the Prieuré and the Knights of Malta as adversaries.

There might also have been a dispute between the two Orders about present priorities and theatres of operation. So far as M. Plantard was concerned, the Prieuré's proper sphere of interest seemed to lie primarily in Europe. Although the Knights of Malta obviously retained a vital interest in Europe, much of their energy of late – like that of Opus Dei, P2 and the CIA – had been diverted to Latin America. In some sense at least, the Knights of Malta have been partially conscripted by the CIA. If the Prieuré de Sion included a number of Knights of Malta in its ranks, might it not have feared being hijacked in turn? Might not M. Plantard have been perturbed, perhaps to the point of resignation, by elements within the Order who advocated a shift of attention from Europe to Latin America? And might these elements, who included perhaps a number of Knights of Malta, have comprised the 'Anglo-American contingent' which M. Plantard had blamed for creating dissension in the Prieuré's ranks?

Whether this was the case or not, there remained one other major point of contention between the Prieuré de Sion and the Knights of Malta. This was the sheaf of parchments found by Bérenger Saunière at Rennes-le-Château in 1891. To the extent that these parchments might have compromised the papacy, or even aided the Prieuré in its clandestine struggle with the papacy, they would have been of interest to the Knights of Malta. According to the Prieuré's own statements, the parchments in question had been obtained and brought to England 'by fraud' and found their way into the Knights of Malta's archives.[24]

In attempting to track Saunière's parchments, we had encountered a bewildering labyrinth of fraud, red herrings, falsified documents, apparently forged signatures and carefully disseminated disinformation. We had reached the inescapable conclusion that some other agency was involved – that we had blundered inadvertently into the middle of an invisible feud between the Prieuré de Sion and someone else. At first, we had been inclined to suspect the involvement of one or another intelligence service. But might it have been the Knights of Malta? Or perhaps some intelligence service working through the Knights of Malta? We cannot, of course, definitively confirm our suspicions. But there remains an unknown factor in the equation. It is impossible not to wonder whether this factor might be the Order of Malta, acting on someone else's behalf or on its own.

Epilogue

We had endeavoured to learn more about the Prieuré de Sion today. We had sought to ascertain something definitive about its membership, its power and resources, its specific objectives. We had hoped at some point to reach the centre of the labyrinth, not necessarily to slay whatever minotaur lurked there, but at least to confront it. At the same time, however, we could not escape the rueful recognition that we were often being outmanoeuvred by individuals who contrived, with great subtlety and skill, to remain consistently one step ahead of us.

Certainly, the Prieuré does exist. Its activities, and those of its former Grand Master, are matters of historical record. *Vaincre* was published during the war, and probably seemed as elusive to the German authorities then as it does to us today. Alpha Galates enjoyed some form of existence, and does seem to have included such individuals as Hans Adolf von Moltke. Elusive and enigmatic though he be, M. Plantard did wield a very real influence and was associated with individuals such as Cocteau, Malraux, Juin and De Gaulle. And documentary evidence makes it impossible to doubt either his role in the Committees of Public Safety or the role of the Committees in returning De Gaulle to power in 1958. Indeed, De Gaulle's return to power bears testimony to the activity of an extremely sophisticated, resourceful, well-organised and disciplined apparatus, adept at political manoeuvring.

So far as we are concerned, the chief uncertainty pertains not to the Prieuré's existence or status, but to its present activities and to the company it currently appears to keep. Is not at least some of that company decidedly insalubrious? And has not the Prieuré, despite its avowedly lofty objectives, thereby become sullied and tainted? How can an organisation which traffics with the likes of

P2 retain its integrity? And how can such an organisation be reconciled with the exalted image it seeks to purvey of itself?

But perhaps we were naïve in expecting anything else. Such alliances, after all, were hardly unique in the Prieuré's history. So far as we could trace them, neither the Prieuré nor its Grand Masters had ever shrunk from the taint of political power. On the contrary, both the Order and its governing hierarchy, all through the centuries, appeared to have been constantly embroiled in machination and intrigue. During the Wars of Religion in the sixteenth century, for example, and during the insurrection known as the Fronde in the seventeenth, the Prieuré had apparently availed itself of all the resources, all the conventions, of the age. It had, in short, been 'realistic'. In order to survive, it had had recourse to the same measures and techniques as other organisations and institutions operating in the 'real world' – including the Roman Catholic Church.

If the modern Prieuré functions in an insalubrious underworld, making compromising alliances, sacrificing idealism to expediency, this does not mean it has been newly corrupted. It means, rather, simply that the Order is running true to form, and is probably neither more nor less corrupt than in the past. Survival, for an organisation such as the Prieuré de Sion, necessarily entails dirtying one's hands with political power. To the extent that dabbling with political power is tantamount to some degree of corruption, the Prieuré has always been corrupt. So, too, have most such institutions which have not in their purity refined themselves out of existence. As we have seen, the Knights of Malta are subject to the same charges as might be levelled against the Prieuré, as, for that matter, is the Vatican, both in the past and today. Pope John Paul II, despite his dogmatic intransigence, may be above reproach personally. But a cloud hangs over the Vatican itself. Indeed, the exposure of P2, the scandal involving the Banco Ambrosiano and the mysterious death of Roberto Calvi – 'God's Banker' – have all demonstrated the Vatican's hierarchy and adminstration to be operating in precisely the same murky, clandestine, subterranean spheres as the Order of Malta and, it would appear, the Prieuré de Sion. If the Prieuré is tainted, the Vatican is no less so.

Had they been perpetrated by the regime of a Western-style democracy, the activities of the Vatican during the last quarter of a century would unquestionably have led to a major enquiry, and probably to the fall of a government. In the case of Rome, however, such activities have caused but surface disturbances, and the Church itself has remained fundamentally unshaken. Not only that. It still continues to perform its traditional pastoral function. It can still furnish solace and comfort. In certain areas of the world – in Latin America, for example, in Poland and Czechoslovakia, in the Philippines – it can serve as a beacon of freedom and hope. And though its congregation, especially in the West, may be dwindling, it can still provide for that congregation a repository of trust and of meaning.

The point is that, behind the sordid dealings of the Church's temporal hierarchy at any given epoch, there stands what might be called 'the archetypal Church', the structure conceived as a 'vessel', as 'an ark breasting the sea of time'. Behind all transient vicissitudes there stands an ideal, a structure of exalted principles, a 'communion of souls', which by its very nature is proof against corruption. This psychic conception of the Church will remain unsullied, whatever the activities of the Vatican or the papacy. A pope such as Alexander VI, for example, may be guilty of everything from simony to incest and murder. He may quip cynically that 'it has served us well, this myth of Christ'. But he is still 'Christ's vicar on earth'.

A similar principle obtains for the Prieuré de Sion. Like the papacy, the Prieuré has centuries of dirt on its hands, and seems, of late, to have acquired fresh deposits of grime. And yet just as the archeytpal Church stands behind the papacy, there stands behind the Prieuré de Sion an equally lofty conception – that of the archetypal chivalric cabal. Whatever its activities at a given moment, the idealised Prieuré, like the idealised Church, remains supernally aloof and immune. On this supernal level, the Prieuré is not a mere secret society plotting and conspiring behind the scenes with other secret societies. Rather, it is the self-appointed custodian of an exalted tradition to which a great many people are eager to subscribe. It is also, in its emphasis on chivalry, the embodiment of a code of conduct held to link humanity with the divine.

The doctrine of chivalry as promulgated by the Prieuré de Sion is indeed archetypal. It is not confined to the knighthood of Christian Europe during the Middle Ages. It can be found in institutions as diverse as the patrician caste of ancient Sparta, the Red Branch of pre-Christian Ulster, the warrior fraternities of such tribes as the Sioux and Cheyenne in the American West, the Samurai in Japan – and the Sicarii or Zealots of Jesus's time. All these institutions were regulated and governed by a code which was not just ethical or moral, but cosmological – a code intended to place human activity in harmony with the order of the cosmos. They involved not just a social and a military discipline, but a spiritual discipline as well. By virtue of this discipline, the adherent was held to function in accordance with divine law.

As we stated in Part Two of this book, politics today is very much a matter of effective packaging. If it is packaged effectively – packaged, that is, in such a way as to assuage anxieties and elicit trust – chivalry can make a potent appeal to the modern mind. It can offer ritual, colour, pageantry and spectacle to a world increasingly denuded of those things and increasingly haunted by their absence. It can offer a sense of continuity to a world which feels cut off from the past and rootless. It can offer dignity and grandeur to people ever more oppressed by the conviction of their own smallness and insignificance. To individuals chafing against their helplessness, loneliness and isolation, it can offer the prospect of belonging, of community, of participation in a lofty fraternal enterprise. It can cater to most people's secret desire to partake of an 'élite', unfashionable though that word itself may currently be. It can offer a hierarchy of values and a code of conduct which are not arbitrary or haphazard, but which rest on a hallowed traditional foundation – a foundation held to reflect some intimation of a divine pattern or plan. It can offer a ritualised, and so sanctioned, channel for emotional expression. Thus chivalry can be made to constitute a principle of coherence and a repository for trust and meaning. In the appropriate circumstances, trust can be reposed in it, and meaning obtained in return. The potency of a resurrected chivalry was illustrated during the Second World War by Japan, where the Samurai code of Bushido imparted a governing principle to an entire culture, culminating in what, to Western eyes, seemed the terrifying 'fanaticism' of the kamikazes.

Although markedly less belligerent and militaristic, the Prieuré de Sion is particularly well equipped to put itself forward as a vehicle for chivalric ideals. It is also particularly well equipped to put itself forward as something more. Unlike many other social, political and religious institutions, the Prieuré, as we noted in Part Two of this book, has considerable psychological sophistication. It understands the depth and magnitude of humanity's internal needs. It understands how to manipulate archetypes – archetypal images and themes – in such a way as to invest them with maximum appeal.

One of the most resonant of archetypal symbols, for example, is that of the 'roi perdu', or 'lost king' – the supernaturally aided monarch who, having completed his task on earth, does not quite die, but retires into some other dimension where he bides his time until the need of his people dictates his return. English-speaking readers are familiar with this archetype through King Arthur. In Wales, Owen Glendower conforms to the same pattern, as does Friedrich Barbarossa in Germany. The '*roi perdu*' who figures most prominently in the Prieuré de Sion's mythos is Dagobert II, the last effective Merovingian monarch. Dagobert is presented by the Prieuré in such a fashion that his image becomes fused in people's minds with that of the supreme lost king, Jesus himself. On a psychologically symbolic level, quite independent of any question of a blood descent, Dagobert becomes an extension of Jesus. With this psychological association established, even if unconsciously, the idea of a literal and historical blood descent becomes that much easier to propagate. It is by just such techniques that the mystery attached to Rennes-le-Château has been invested with such magnetic attraction, not only to us as authors, but to our readers as well.

The Prieuré also understands the intimate relationship between trust and power. It understands the potency of the religious impulse and knows that this impulse, if activated and channelled, is potentially as puissant a force as, say, money – so puissant, indeed, as to represent perhaps an alternative principle of power. Finally, the Prieuré knows how to sell itself, knows how to purvey an image of itself that accords with its own objectives. As we said before, it is able to orchestrate and to regulate outsiders' perceptions of itself as an archetypal cabal, if not the supreme archetypal cabal. Whatever the ultimate authenticity of its pedigree, it can convey the impression of being what it wishes people to think it is, because it understands the dynamics whereby such impressions are conveyed.

But psychological sophistication and an ability to 'market' itself are not the only points the Prieuré de Sion has in its favour. In 1979, M. Plantard had said to us, quite categorically, that the Prieuré was in possession of the treasure of the Temple of Jerusalem, plundered by the Romans during the revolt of A.D. 66 and subsequently carried to the south of France, in the vicinity of Rennes-le-Château. The treasure, M. Plantard stated, would be returned to Israel 'when the time is right'. If the Prieuré does indeed possess the treasure of the Temple, and could produce it today, the implications are staggering. Not only would it be an archaeological sensation eclipsing such discoveries as the ruins of Troy or the tomb of Tutankhamun. It would also be fraught with contemporary religious and political repercussions. What, for example, would be the implications for modern Israel, as well as for both Judaism and Christianity, if – on the basis of records or other evidence issuing from the Temple of Jerusalem – Jesus stood revealed as the

Messiah? Not the Messiah of later Christian tradition, but the Messiah expected by the people of Palestine two thousand years ago – the man, that is, who was their nation's rightful king, who married, sired children and perhaps did not die on the Cross at all. Would it not rock the foundations of two of the world's major religions, and possibly the foundations of Islam as well? Would it not, at a single stroke, eradicate the theological differences between Judaism and Christianity, and at least some of the antipathy of Islam?

In any case, and quite apart from the treasure of the Temple, the Prieuré de Sion can promulgate a claim which would enjoy considerable currency even in today's world. On behalf of the families it represents, it can establish a dynastic succession extending back to the Old Testament House of David. It can establish, quite definitively and to the satisfaction of the most fastidious genealogical enquiry, that the Merovingian Dynasty was of the Davidic line – and was formally recognised as being so by the Carolingians who supplanted them, by other monarchs and by the Roman Church of the period. Aided by the techniques of modern public relations, modern advertising and modern political packaging, the Prieuré could thus present to the modern world a figure who, by the strictest scriptural definition of the term, could claim to be a biblical Messiah. It may seem preposterous. But it is no more preposterous, surely, than the conviction of tens of thousands of Americans who are prepared to be 'raptured' upwards from their cars at various points on the freeway between Pasadena and Los Angeles.

This does not mean, of course, that we can expect an imminent press conference and the media circus which would follow. For the moment, it probably does not mean a public announcement of any kind. A lineal descent from the House of David – or, if provable, from Jesus and his family – could never in itself be used as a stepping-stone to secular power. The Prieuré de Sion and/or the Merovingian bloodline could never simply unmask themselves, divulge their identity and rely on popular fervour to do the rest. There would be too many sceptics. There would be too many people who were simply not interested. Even among those prepared to acknowledge the legitimacy of Merovingian descent, there would be too many objectors – too many people who, whatever their religious affiliations, would have no greater desire to be ruled by a Messiah than by anyone else. And there would be too many people already in power, or jockeying for it, who would hardly be disposed to welcome a new challenge on the scene. In 679, the

Roman Church had betrayed the pact made a century and three-quarters earlier with Clovis, and knowingly colluded in the assassination of Dagobert II. Could one seriously believe that those holding or seeking power in the world today would show any more compunction, would have any more inhibiting scruples? Once again, Dostoevsky's parable of the Grand Inquisitor comes irresistibly to mind.

Moreover, it is unlikely that the Prieuré itself has any desire to create upheaval. If we have assessed it correctly, it seeks to bring about a monarchical or imperial United States of Europe, not a situation of chaos in which existing institutions are compromised, undermined or overturned. As far as we can discern, the Prieuré has nothing to gain from revolution, whether political or of any other kind. It would seem to be much more interested in 'inheriting' or perhaps hijacking an already established order and gradually transforming that order from within – in such a fashion as to entail minimal fuss, minimal disorientation, minimal turmoil. This, of necessity, would dictate a policy of discreet infiltration, rather than one of overt challenge – a policy of the sort that characterises organisations such as P2 and Opus Dei.

For all these reasons, then, a pedigree cannot be used as a stepping-stone to power. Rather, it is a trump card which can be played only to consolidate power once power has already been obtained. A man cannot say 'Look who I am', and expect on that basis to be elected or promoted pope, president, king or emperor. But if he were already pope, president, king or emperor, and more or less securely installed as such, he could then say 'Look who I am', and thereby not only consolidate his position, but also invest it with a new aura, a new credibility, a new and more resonant significance.

In consequence, the Prieuré, so far as the immediate future is concerned, is unlikely to do anything sudden, startling or dramatic. It is much more likely to employ the techniques which seem to have served it and the families associated with it – the House of Lorraine, for example – more or less effectively in the past. These techniques would include a programme of gradual, methodical but discreet infiltration of existing institutions. They would include a network of high-level dynastic intermarriages, so as to bring certain influential families – not only royal and aristocratic families, but families involved in politics, finance and the media as well – 'into the fold'. And they would include the manipulation of archetypes in such a way as to foster a climate congenial to the implementation of certain long-term objectives. Thus, to take an extreme example, a sudden *coup d'état* which restored the monarchy in, say, Greece or

Portugal would be counter-productive. Even if it could be accomplished, many people would object and many people would remain indifferent, regarding it as simply another change of regime to be accepted with more or less sympathy or cynicism. If, on the other hand, a charismatic monarchical figure were swept dramatically to power by a tide of popular acclamation, his mandate would be altogether different.

Since the First World War and the fall of most of Europe's ruling dynasties, republican democracy has become the established norm in Western society. As we have seen, however, monarchy has not lost either its archetypal appeal or its purely functional utility. During the Second World War, Churchill, together with many others, regarded the collapse of the monarchical system as one of the primary factors conducing to the rise of totalitarianism and, especially, to the phenomenon of Nazism. In secret discussions, he and Roosevelt are reported to have concurred that monarchical restoration was the best means not only of holding the shattered shell of post-war Europe together, but also of ensuring there would be no resurgence of the tendencies which had culminated in the Third Reich. They talked of restoring the Habsburgs to the throne of Austria and possibly Hungary, with Otto von Habsburg presiding over a form of imperial confederation of the Danube. According to Otto von Habsburg himself, they also discussed the possibility of installing Lord Louis Mountbatten as emperor of a new German confederation.

Nor has the dream of monarchical restoration subsided even today. In Spain, King Juan Carlos is entering upon the second decade of his reign, presiding over the first democracy his country has known for some thirty-five years, and this arrangement has thus far proved successful. In France, royalist movements continue as vigorous as ever, while the president himself assumes an ever more regal air. Whenever she visits Vienna, Otto von Habsburg's mother, the former Empress Zita, a woman now in her nineties, draws adulating crowds of the kind usually associated with the Pope. During 1984 and 1985, certain newspapers again began to speculate about a possible Habsburg restoration in Austria.

If monarchy itself continues to exercise such appeal, how might that appeal be augmented if a specific monarch or monarchical candidate could also claim, in strict conformity with the original meaning of the term, to be a Messiah?

We, as authors, do not wish to be seen as proselytes or propagandists for the Prieuré de Sion. Indeed, we are wary of the Prieuré de

Sion. If we are sympathetic towards certain of its theoretical objectives, we are decidedly sceptical, even dubious, about others. And quite apart from all theoretical considerations, the fact remains that any concentration of power in the hands of a small group of individuals – especially a group of individuals who function primarily in secret – is potentially dangerous. It is a truism that most of history's greatest transgressions and atrocities have been perpetrated by people acting with what they believed to be the best of intentions. We would prefer to see individuals creating a sense of meaning from within themselves, rather than accepting one proffered from without, however ostensibly lofty or laudable.

And yet our age appears determined to embrace one or another form of Messianic myth in order to obtain a sense of meaning. If it must perforce do so, we would prefer to see a mortal Messiah presiding over a united Europe than a supernatural Messiah presiding over Armageddon. The Prieuré de Sion cannot provide a Messiah of the sort which that word has come erroneously to connote for, say, American fundamentalists. We question whether anyone other than the special effects department of a Hollywood studio can provide that. But if we are correct in our assessments, it would seem that the Prieuré de Sion can provide a Messiah of the kind that Jesus himself, as an historical personage, actually was.

Bibliography

ABERG, N., *The Occident and the Orient in the Art of the Seventh Century*, Part I, *The British Isles* (Stockholm, 1943–7)

AGEE, P., and WOLF, L., *Dirty Work: The CIA in Western Europe* (London, 1978)

ALLEGRO, J. M., *The Dead Sea Scrolls*, 2nd edn (Harmondsworth, 1975)

ANDERSON, A. O., *Early Sources of Scottish History*, 2 vols (London, 1922)

ARMSTRONG, H. W., *The United States and Britain in Prophecy* (Pasadena, 1980)

ATIYAH, A. S., *History of Eastern Christianity* (London, 1968)

ATTWATER, D., *The Christian Churches of the East*, 2 vols (London, 1961)

BAIGENT, M., LEIGH, R. and LINCOLN, H., *The Holy Blood and the Holy Grail* (London, 1982)

BAUER, W., *Orthodoxy and Heresy in Earliest Christianity* (London, 1972)

BENTINE, M., *The Door Marked Summer* (London, 1981)

BERNIER, G., *Les Chrétientés bretonnes continentales depuis les origines jusqu'au IXème siècle* (Université de Rennes, 1982)

BILLIG, M., *Psychology, Racism and Fascism* (Birmingham, 1979)

BOWEN, E. G., *Saints, Seaways and Settlements in the Celtic Lands* (Cardiff, 1977)

BRANDON, S. G. F., *Jesus and the Zealots* (Manchester, 1967)

——*The Fall of Jerusalem and the Christian Church*, 2nd edn (London, 1974)

Britain's Triumphant Destiny (pub. by the British Israel World Federation, London, 1942)

BUGLIOSI, V., and GENTRY, C., *Helter Skelter* (New York, 1982)

BULL, G., *Inside the Vatican* (London, 1982)

BULTMANN, R., *Jesus and the Word*, 2nd edn, trans. Louise Pettibone Smith and Erminie Huntress (New York, 1934)

BUTLER, A. J., *The Ancient Coptic Churches of Egypt*, 2 vols (Oxford, 1884)

CHADWICK, N., *The Age of the Saints in the Early Celtic Church* (London, 1961)

CHADWICK, H., *The Early Church* (Harmondsworth, 1978)

——*The Circle and the Ellipse* (Oxford, 1959)

——*Priscillian of Ávila* (Oxford, 1976)

CHADWICK, H., and OULTON, J. E. L., *Alexandrian Christianity* (London, 1954)

CHAMBERLAIN, H. S., *The Foundations of the Nineteenth Century*, trans. John Lees, 2 vols (London, 1911)

CHAUMEIL, J.-L., *Du premier au dernier templier* (Paris, 1985)

CHÉRISEY, P. de, *L'Or de Rennes pour un Napoléon* (Liège, 1975)

——*L'Énigme de Rennes* (Paris, 1978)

CHITTY, D. J., *The Desert a City* (London, 1977)

Circuit, Bulletin d'information et defense des droits ... H.L.M. (Annemasse, 1956)

Circuit, Publication périodique culturelle de la Fédération des Forces Françaises (Aulnay-sous-Bois, 1959)

CONWAY M., 'Burgundian Buckles and Coptic Influences', *Proceedings of the Society of Antiquaries of London*, 2nd series, vol. xxx (London, 1917–18), pp.63ff.

COONEY, J., *The American Pope* (New York, 1984)

COTTINEAU, L. H., *Répertoire topo-bibliographique des abbayes et prieurés*, 3 vols (Macon, 1935–70)

COUDENHOVE-KALERGI, R. N., *Europe Must Unite* (Plymouth, 1940)

——*From War to Peace* (London, 1959)

——*An Idea Conquers the World* (London, 1953)

CRAWLEY, A., *De Gaulle* (London, 1969)

CROSS, F. M., *The Ancient Library of Qumran* (New York, 1961)

CUPITT, D., *The Sea of Faith* (London, 1984)

DANK, M., *The French against the French* (London, 1974)

DEANESLY, M., *The Pre-Conquest Church in England* (London, 1961)

DE CLERCQ, V. C., *Ossius of Cordova* (Washington, 1954)

——'Ossius of Cordova and the Origins of Priscillianism', *Studia patristica*, vol. i, part 1 (Berlin, 1957)

DELARUE, J., *L'OAS contre De Gaulle* (Paris, 1981)

DESCADEILLAS, R., *Rennes et ses derniers seigneurs* (Toulouse, 1964)

DESCHNER, G., *Heydrich: The Pursuit of Total Power*, trans., Bance, Woods and Ball (London, 1981)

DI FONZO, L., *St Peter's Banker* (Edinburgh, 1983)

BIBLIOGRAPHY

DROWER, E. S., *The Mandaeans of Iraq and Iran* (Leiden, 1962)

DULLES, A. W., *The Craft of Intelligence* (London, 1963)

——*Germany's Underground* (New York, 1947)

DUMVILLE, D. N., 'Biblical Apocrypha and the Early Irish: A Preliminary Investigation', *Proceedings of the Royal Irish Academy*, vol. lxxiii, section C, no. 8 (Dublin, 1973), pp.299ff

EISENMAN, R. H., *Maccabees, Zadokites, Christians and Qumran* (Leiden, 1983)

——*James the Just in the Habakkuk Pesher* (Leiden, 1986)

EISLER, R., *The Messiah Jesus and John the Baptist*, trans. Alexander Haggerty Krappe (London, 1931)

Encyclopaedia judaica, ed. Cecil Roth, 16 vols (Jerusalem, 1974)

EPIPHANIUS, *D. epiphanii episcopi Constantiae Cypri, contra octoaginta haereses opus*, ed. Iano Cornario, (Basileae, 1578)

ERINGER, R., *The Global Manipulators* (Bristol, 1980)

EUSEBIUS, *The History of the Church from Christ to Constantine*, trans. G. A. Williamson (Harmondsworth, 1981)

FLAMINI, R., *Pope, Premier, President* (New York, 1980)

FOLZ, R., *The Concept of Empire in Western Europe*, trans. Sheila Ann Ogilvie (London, 1969)

FOOT, M. R. D., *SOE in France* (London, 1966)

——*Resistance* (St Albans, 1978)

FOOTE, A., *Handbook for Spies*, 2nd edn (London, 1964)

FORD, C., *Donovan of O.S.S.* (London, 1971)

FREEMANTLE, B., *CIA: The Honourable Company* (London, 1983)

FREND, W. H. C., 'Early Christianity and Society: A Jewish Legacy in the pre-Constantinian Era', *Harvard Theological Review*, vol. lxxvi, 1 (Jan. 1983)

FREY, A., *Cross and Swastika*, trans. J. Strathearn McNabb (London, 1938)

GALVIN, J., *The History of the Order of Malta* (Dublin, 1977)

GAMBLE, W., *Irish Antiquities and Archeology* (Redhills, 1946)

GASTER, T. H., *The Dead Sea Scriptures* (New York, 1956)

GETTINGS, F., *The Hidden Art* (London, 1978)

GLADWYN, Lord, *The European Idea*, (London, 1967)

GLOVER, F. R. A., *England, the Remnant of Judah and the Israel of Ephraim* (London, 1861)

GOODENOUGH, E. R., *Jewish Symbols in the Greco-Roman Period*, 12 vols (New York, 1953)

GOODRICK-CLARKE, N., *The Occult Roots of Nazism* (Wellingborough, 1985)

GURWIN, L., *The Calvi Affair* (London, 1984)

GUTMAN, R. W., *Richard Wagner* (Harmondsworth, 1971)

GWYNN, A., and HADCOCK, R. N., *Medieval Religious Houses: Ireland* (London, 1970)

HAMMER, R., *The Vatican Connection* (Harmondsworth, 1983)

HARDINGE, L., *The Celtic Church in Britain* (London, 1972)

HEDIN, S., *German Diary*, trans. Joan Bulman (Dublin, 1951)

HENNECKE, E., *New Testament Apocrypha*, ed. W. Schneemelcher, trans. ed. R. McL. Wilson, 2 vols (London 1963–5)

HERRIOT, É., *The United States of Europe*, trans. Reginald J. Dingle (London, 1930)

HERVET, F. (pseud.), 'Knights of Darkness', *Covert Action Bulletin*, no. 25 (Winter, 1986), pp.27ff

HILLGARTH, J. N., 'Visigothic Spain and Early Christian Ireland', *Proceedings of the Royal Irish Academy*, vol. lxii, section C, no. 6 (1962), pp.167ff

HINE, E., *The English Nation Identified with the Lost House of Israel by Twenty-seven Identifications* (Manchester, 1870)

——*Forty-seven Identifications of the British Nation with the Lost Ten Tribes of Israel* (London, 1874)

HISLER, A-L., *Rois et gouvernants de la France* (Paris, 1964)

HITLER, A., *The Speeches of Adolf Hitler (1922–1939)*, ed. and trans. Norman H. Baynes, 2 vols (London, 1942)

——*Mein Kampf* (London, 1939)

——*Hitler's Table Talk*, trans. Norman Cameron and R. H. Stevens (London, 1953)

HÖHNE, H., *The Order of the Death's Head*, trans. Richard Barry (London, 1981)

HOPKINS, J., *The Armstrong Empire* (Grand Rapids, 1974)

HOWARTH, P., *Undercover* (London, 1980)

HUGHES, K. *The Church in Early Irish Society* (London, 1966)

HUGHES, P., *The Church in Crisis* (London, 1961)

HUNTINGTON, D., 'Visions of the Kingdom. The Latin American Church in Conflict: Cross Currents', *NACLA Report on the Americas* vol. xix, no. 5 (Sept/Oct. 1985), pp.14ff

HÜSER, K., *Wewelsburg 1933 bis 1945* (Paderborn, 1982)

HYDE, H. Montgomery, *The Quiet Canadian* (London, 1962)

IRENAEUS, *Adversus omnes haereses* (selected passages in *Documents Illustrative of the History of the Church*, vol. i, ed. B. J. Kidd, London, 1928)

JOYCE, P. W. *A Social History of Ancient Ireland* (London, 1920)

JUSTIN MARTYR, *Dialogue with Trypho the Jew* (in *The Works now Extant of S. Justin the Martyr*, trans. E. B. Pusey, Oxford, 1861)

KAZANTZAKIS, N., *The Last Temptation*, trans. P. A. Bien (London, 1975)

KEE, A., *Constantine versus Christ* (London, 1982)

KERSTEN, F., *The Kersten Memoirs*, trans. Fitzgibbon and Oliver (London, 1956)

KIDD, B. J., *A History of the Church*, 3 vols (Oxford, 1922)

KIEWE, H. E., *The Sacred History of Knitting*, 2nd edn (Oxford, 1971)

KING, A. A., *Liturgies of the Past* (London, 1959)

KING, E. and LUKE, H., *The Knights of St John in the British Realm* (London, 1967)

KOESTER, H., 'Apocryphal and Canonical Gospels', *Harvard Theological Review*, vol. lxxiii, 1–2 (Jan–April, 1980), pp.105ff.

KRAUSE, C. A., *Guyana Massacre* (London, 1979)

KRAUT, O., *Jesus was Married*, 2nd rev. edn, (*s.l.*, 1970)

LACOUTURE, J., *André Malraux* (London, 1975)

LANGER, W., *The Mind of Adolf Hitler* (London, 1973)

LANIGAN, J., *An Ecclesiastical History of Ireland*, 2nd edn, 4 vols (Dublin, 1829)

LEE, M. A., 'Their Will Be Done', *Mother Jones* (July, 1983), pp.21ff.

LE MAIRE, F., *Histoire et antiquitez de la ville et duché d'Orléans*, 2nd edn, (Orléans, 1648)

LINDSAY, H., *The 1980s: Countdown to Armageddon* (Basingstoke, 1983)

MACCOBY, H., *Revolution in Judaea* (New York, 1980)

McNAMARA, M., *The Apocrypha in the Irish Church* (Dublin, 1975)

McNEILL, J. T., *The Celtic Churches* (London, 1974)

Manual of the Council of Europe (London, 1970)

MARCHETTI, V., and MARKS, J. D., *The CIA and the Cult of Intelligence* (London, 1974)

MARSHALL, A., *The Interlinear Greek–English New Testament* (London, 1967)

MARTIN, M., *The Decline and Fall of the Roman Church* (London, 1982)

MASON, A. J., *The Persecution of Diocletian* (Cambridge, 1876)

MASSÉ, D., *L'Énigme de Jésus-Christ* (Paris, 1926)

MEHTA, G., *Karma Cola* (London, 1981)

MENDEL, A. P., *Michael Bakunin: Roots of Apocalypse* (New York, 1981)

MOMIGLIANO, A., ed., *The Conflict between Paganism and Christianity in the Fourth Century* (London, 1970)

MOORE, G., *The Lost Tribes* (London, 1861)

MONNET, J., *L'Europe unie* (Lausanne, 1972)

MOULY, R. W., 'Israel: Darling of the Religious Right', *The Humanist* (May–June, 1982), pp.5ff.

McCORMICK, W. J. McK., *Do Herbert W. Armstrong and Garner Ted Armstrong speak the Plain Truth?* 2nd edn (Belfast, 1968)

331

NEGRI, M., 'The Well-Planned Conspiracy', *The Humanist* (May–June, 1982), pp.40ff.

NEMOY, L., 'Al-Qirqisani's Account of the Jewish Sects', *Hebrew Union College Annual* vol. vii (1930), pp. 317ff.

NEUSNER, J., *Judaism in the Beginning of Christianity* (London, 1984)

ORIGEN, *Origen against Celsus*, trans. James Bellamy (London, 1660)

PAOLI, M., *Les Dessous d'une ambition politique* (Nyon, 1973)

PATRICK, J., *The Apology of Origen in Reply to Celsus* (London, 1978)

PAYNE, R., *The Life and Death of Lenin* (London, 1967)

PEYREFITTE, R., *The Knights of Malta* (London, 1960)

PHELPS, R. H., 'Before Hitler Came: Thule Society and Germanen Orden', *Journal of Modern History*, vol. xxxv, no. 3 (Sept. 1963), pp. 245ff.

PHILO JUDAEUS, *A Treatise on the Virtues and on the Office of Ambassadors addressed to Caius*, trans. C. D. Yonge (London, 1855)

PHIPPS, W. E., 'Did Jesus or Paul Marry?', *Journal of Ecumenical Studies*, vol. v, no. 1 (Fall, 1968), pp.741ff.

PIEPKORN, A. C., *Profiles in Belief*, 4 vols (San Francisco, 1979)

PINES, S., 'The Jewish Christians of the Early Centuries of Christianity According to a New Source', *Proceedings of the Israeli Academy of Sciences and Humanities*, vol. ii (1968), pp. 237ff.

PLANTARD, P., *Gisors et son secret* (Paris, 1961)

POMIAN, J., *Joseph Retinger* (Brighton, 1972)

POWERS, T., *The Man Who Kept the Secrets* (London, 1979)

PRITTIE, T., *Germans Against Hitler* (London, 1964)

RADER, S. R., *Against the Gates of Hell* (New York, 1980)

RAMSAY, R. L., 'Theodore of Mopsuestia and St Columban on the Psalms', *Zeitschrift für celtische Philologie*, vol. viii (1912), pp. 421ff.

RAMSAY, R. L., 'Theodore of Mopsuestia in England and Ireland', *Zeitschrift für Celtische Philologie*, vol. viii (1912), pp. 452ff.

RAUSCHNING, H., *Hitler Speaks* (London, 1939)

REITLINGER, G., *The SS: Alibi of a Nation 1922–45* (London, 1981)

REVILLOUT, E., 'Évangile de Saint-Barthélemy', *Patrologia orientalis*, tom. 2 (Paris, 1907), pp. 185ff.

REY, E-G., 'Chartes de l'abbaye du Mont-Sion', *Mémoires de la Société Nationale des Antiquaires de France*, 5ème série, vol. viii (1887), pp. 31ff.

RÖHRICHT, R., *Regesta regni Hierosolymitani* (Oeniponti, 1893)

ROON, G. van, *German Resistance to Hitler: Count von Moltke and the Kreisau Circle*, trans. Peter Ludlow (London, 1971)

Salthair na Rann, ed. Whitley Stokes, in *Anecdota oxoniensa*, Medieval and Modern series, I:III (Oxford, 1883); see also *The Poem-Book of the Gael*, ed. Eleanor Hull (London, 1912)

SANDERS, E., *The Family* (St Albans, 1977)

SANDERS, E. P., *Jesus and Judaism* (London, 1985)

SCHONFIELD, H. J., *Secrets of the Dead Sea Scrolls* (London, 1956)

——*The Authentic New Testament* (New York, 1958)

——*Those Incredible Christians* (London, 1968)

——*The Pentecost Revolution* (London, 1974)

——*The Passover Plot* (London, 1977)

——*The Essene Odyssey* (Longmead, 1984)

SERBANESCO, G., *Histoire de l'ordre des Templiers et les croisades*, 2 vols (Paris, 1970)

SEWARD, D., *The Monks of War* (St Albans, 1974)

SMALLWOOD, E. M., *The Jews under Roman Rule* (Leiden, 1976)

SOYER, J., 'Annales prioratvs sancti sansonis avrelianensis ad monasterivm beatae Mariae de Monte Sion in Hiervsalem pertinentis', *Bulletin de la Société Archéologique et Historique de l'Orléanais*, tom. xvii, no. 206 (1914), pp. 222ff.

STEINSCHNEIDER, M., *Die arabische Literatur der Juden* (Frankfurt, 1902)

STEPHENSON, W., *A Man Called Intrepid* (London, 1982)

STOKES, G. T., *Ireland and the Celtic Church*, 7th edn, rev. Hugh Jackson Lawlor (London, 1928)

TACITUS, *The Annals of Imperial Rome*, rev. edn, trans. Michael Grant (Harmondsworth, 1979)

TEICHER, J. L., 'The Dead Sea Scrolls – Documents of the Jewish Christian Sect of Ebionites?', *The Journal of Jewish Studies*, vol. ii, no. 2 (1951), pp. 67ff.

THOMAS, G., and MORGAN-WITTS, M., *The Year of Armageddon* (London, 1984)

Trial of the Major War Criminals before the International Military Tribunal, 42 vols (Nuremberg, 1947–9)

TOURNIER, M., *The Erl King*, trans. Barbara Bray (London, 1972)

TURNER, Sharon, *The History of the Anglo-Saxons*, 4 vols (London, 1799–1805)

——*The History of the Anglo-Saxons*, 2 vols, 2nd edn (London, 1807)

TURNER, Stansfield, *Secrecy and Democracy* (London, 1986)

Vaincre, 'Pour une jeune chevalerie' (Paris, 1942–3)

VERMASEREN, M. J., *Mithras, the Secret God* (London, 1963)

VERMES, G., *Jesus the Jew* (London, 1977)

——*Jesus and the World of Judaism* (London, 1983)

——*The Dead Sea Scrolls in English*, 2nd edn (Harmondsworth, 1977)

——*The Dead Sea Scrolls* (London, 1977)

WAECHTER, M., *How to Abolish War: The United States of Europe*, rev. edn (London, 1924)

WARREN, F. E., *The Liturgy and Ritual of the Celtic Church* (Oxford, 1881)

WEBB, J., *The Harmonious Circle* (London, 1980)

WEBER, E., *Action Française* (Stanford, 1962)

WIESENTHAL, S., *The Murderers Among Us*, ed. Joseph Wechsberg, (London, 1967)

WILSON, E., *The Dead Sea Scrolls 1947–1969* (London, 1977)

WILSON, I., *Jesus: The Evidence* (London, 1984)

WILSON, J., *Our Israelitish Origin*, 3rd edn (London, 1844)

——*The Millennium or World to Come* (Cheltenham, 1842)

——*The Book of Inheritance* (London, 1846)

WINTERBOTHAM, F. W., *The Nazi Connection* (London, 1978)

WYKES, A., *Himmler* (London, 1972)

ZURCHER, A. J., *The Struggle to United Europe 1940–1958* (New York, 1958)

YADIN, Y., *The Temple Scroll* (London, 1985)

YALLOP, D., *In God's Name* (London, 1984)

Notes and References

Note
The full bibliographical details, when not cited here, are to be found in the Bibliography.

1 Scholarship and Public Understanding

1 Roger Martin du Gard, *Jean Barois* (Paris, 1912), p. 51.
2 Ibid., p. 52.
3 Bultmann, *Jesus and the Word*, p. 8.
4 All biblical quotations, except where specified, are taken from *The Jerusalem Bible* edited by Father Roland de Vaux. English edition edited by Alexander Jones (London, 1966).
5 Wilson, *Jesus: The Evidence*.

2 Jesus as King of Israel

1 Maccoby, *Revolution in Judaea*, p. 75.
2 Judas of Galilee and his son, Manahem. Josephus, *Wars*, II:xvii.
3 Dr H. L. Ginsberg writing in the *Encyclopaedia judaica*, vol. xi, p. 1407.
4 See Micah 5:1–2:

But you, (Bethlehem) Ephrathah,
the least of the clans of Judah,
out of you will be born for me
the one who is to rule over Israel ...

5 It is on the basis of Mark 6:3 that the story of Jesus as a carpenter developed. However, Dr Geza Vermes of Oxford University, in *Jesus the Jew*, points out the common metaphorical use of the terms

335

'carpenter' and 'carpenter's son' in ancient Jewish literature (pp. 21–2).

6 Baigent, Leigh, Lincoln, *The Holy Blood* . . ., pp. 292–3.

7 Matthew 26:7, Mark 14:3–5. The significance is that this expensive oil, which was one of the components of the Temple incense, was poured upon Jesus's head. As the *Encyclopaedia Judaica* states: 'In the anointing of kings the whole head was covered with oil . . . ', vol. iii, p. 31.

8 John 12:3–5. He is attempting to remove the significance of this anointing by specifying that only the feet of Jesus were touched by the oil. This is despite the assertions of Matthew and Mark's gospels.

3 Constantine as Messiah

1 Baigent, Leigh, Lincoln, *The Holy Blood* . . ., pp. 325–8. Much of the following few pages comes directly from this text.

2 Chadwick, *The Early Church*, p. 125.

3 Goodenough, *Jewish Symbols*, vol. vii, pp. 178 ff.

4 Kee, *Constantine versus Christ*, pp. 117–18.

5 Ibid., p. 120.

6 Ibid., p. 136 (quoting Eusebius).

7 Ibid.

8 Ibid., p. 41 (quoting Eusebius).

9 Ibid.

10 Ibid., p. 42.

11 Ibid., p. 47.

4 Jesus as Freedom-fighter

1 Josephus, *Antiquities*, XVIII:i.

2 Brandon, *Jesus and the Zealots*, p. 204, note 1. He notes too that some old Latin MSS render the name as Judas Zelotes.

3 Crucifixion in general, and that of the Gospels in particular, receives a detailed discussion in *The Holy Blood* . . ., pp. 312–17. However, the details need some slight modification in the light of the work of Joseph Zias of the Israeli Department of Antiquities and Eliezer Sekeles of the Hebrew University Medical School. See Zias and Sekeles, 'The Crucified Man from Giv'at ha-Mivtar: A Reappraisal' in *Israel Exploration Journal*, vol. xxxv (1985), pp. 22–7.

4   Tacitus, *Annals: Nero*, p. 365.

5   Neusner, in *Judaism in the Beginning of Christianity*, p. 30, states that after A.D. 6, when Judaea became part of the Roman provincial territory of Syria, the Sanhedrin lost the authority to impose capital punishment. However, it must be said that other experts such as Haim Cohn and Paul Winter disagree with Neusner here. Mary Smallwood, in *The Jews under Roman Rule*, p. 150, concludes that the Sanhedrin could pass a death sentence in religious cases, but of course that sentence would be carried out by stoning.

6   When Jesus enters the Temple he accuses the populace of having turned it into a 'robbers' den' (Mark 11:18). This refers back to Jeremiah 7:11, 'Do you take this Temple that bears my name for a robbers' den?' The precedent for this action of Jesus is in Nehemiah 13:8. The latter, upon his return from the Persian court, found someone living inside the Temple court and proceeded to throw out all the furniture.

7   See *The Jerusalem Bible*, Mark 15:16 and John 18:12. The latter makes it clear that there were troops *in addition* to the cohort: 'The cohort and its captain and the Jewish guards seized Jesus ... '.

8   See Smallwood, *The Jews under Roman Rule*, p. 146.

5   **The Zadokite Movement of Qumran**

1   Neusner writes of the period that '... no such thing as "normative Judaism" existed, from which one or another "heretical" group might diverge. Not only in ... Jerusalem, do we find numerous competing groups, but throughout the country and abroad we may discern a religious tradition in the midst of great flux.' *Judaism in the Beginning of Christianity*, p. 29.

2   Josephus, *Wars*, II:viii.

3   Cross, *The Ancient Library of Qumran*, p. 198.

4   Josephus, ibid.

5   Baigent, Leigh, Lincoln, *The Holy Blood ...*, pp. 336–7. The text of Eleazar's speech is found in Josephus, *Wars*, VII:viii.

6   Cross, op.cit., p. 69.

7   Vermes, *The Dead Sea Scrolls in English*, p. 119.

8   Eisenman, *Maccabees ...*, pp. 4–6.

9   Schonfield, *The Pentecost Revolution*, p. 190.

10 Eisenman, *Maccabees ...*, pp. 19ff; see also p. 45, note 36.

11 Acts 21:20; see Marshall, *The Interlinear Greek-English New Testament*.

· 12 Eisenman, op. cit., p. 96, note 180.

> The whole question of the physical relationships of these 'Messianic' families is something which remains to be investigated. The parallel developments of Judas' (also from Galilee) and Jesus' families ... and the almost contemporary crucifixions of 'Jacob and Simon' (equivalent also to the names of two of Jesus' brothers – the second of whom, Eusebius insists, 'won the prize of an end like that of the Lord') and the *stoning* of Menachem, an event both parallel to and contemporary with the stoning of Jesus' brother James ... must give historians some pause.

13 Eisenman, *James the Just*, p. 3. James, according to Epiphanius and Jerome, was able to enter the Holy of Holies in the Temple, a privilege accorded only to the High Priest. That, and information deriving from both the Acts and Qumran literature, makes it clear that James was the opposition High Priest, head of the Jerusalem community at least and likely head of the entire Zadokite movement. And whatever James was, then his brother Jesus was before him.

6 The Formation of Christianity

1 None of the biblical experts agrees on the dating of the Gospels and Acts: the field is open. We propose the following arguments and dating:
   – We make the assumption that all the books were written after the fall of Jerusalem, when the destruction of the 'Christian' Church and its authority made a compilation of traditions from oral sources necessary.
   – Matthew and Mark conceal the fact that Simon was a Zealot. Hence we argue that these books were written when the subject of Zealots was still an emotive issue for Gentile readers. Thus a date of A.D. 70+ for Mark and c.75 for the later Matthew.
   – Luke and the later work, Acts, feel able to state that Simon was a Zealot, indicating that the issue had faded somewhat. They cannot be later than A.D. 90 since at this date Josephus was writing and lecturing, raising again the issue of the Zealots whom he blamed for the destruction of Jerusalem. Thus we propose a date of c.80 for Luke and c.85 for the Acts.
   – In A.D. 95 the persecution of Domitian began and so gives us a final point. It seems likely that John was written about this time, along with the Revelation.

2 Acts ends with Paul's meeting with Agrippa II in Caesarea, in A.D. 60, and the briefly described trip to Rome, when the chronicle abruptly ceases. Acts bears all the hallmarks of emerging from a

'Herodian' milieu in Rome some time after the revolt. Its basis is very likely a diary from Agrippa II's library brought to Rome in A.D. 68 during Agrippa II's exile there.

3   The dating of the Crucifixion is still very uncertain: good cases can be made for three dates, A.D. 30, 33 and 36. The New Testament says only that the event occurred after the execution of John the Baptist, at a passover when Pontius Pilate was governor of Judaea and Caiaphas was High Priest. As both Pilate and Caiaphas lost their positions in A.D. 36 this provides a last date. The execution of John the Baptist cannot be dated with any accuracy but there is a strong suggestion that it was as a result of his criticising the marriage of Herod and Herodias (see Matthew and Mark). This marriage took place, it is agreed, in A.D. 35, the year when John was very likely executed. Hence, it follows that Jesus must have been crucified at passover A.D. 36. See Schonfield, *The Pentecost Revolution*, pp. 45–55. (Schonfield's timing involving Sabbatical and Census years is not universally accepted among scholars; see Vermes, *The Times Literary Supplement*, 17 Jan. 1975, p. 65. See also Schonfield's reply in the same journal, 14 Feb. 1975, pp. 168–9, where he adds the support of Yigael Yadin to his arguments on timing.)

4   Eisenman, *Maccabees* ..., p. 5, referring to Eusebius, *History* 2:23. Note that in Arabic James is *Saddiq Ja'aqob* (Eisler, *Messiah Jesus*, p. 449).

In Hebrew the title of 'Zaddik' is given to Jesus in Acts 3:14, 7:52 and 22:15. Of importance here is the speech by Stephen in Acts 7:51–3 where he says, 'they killed those who foretold the coming of the Just One [= Zaddik]'.

5   Eusebius, *History*, 3:11.

6   Eisenman, *Maccabees* ..., p. 89, note 163, suggests that this flight may have been not to Pella but to Sela – an unidentified Dead Sea valley location. He points out that this could have been either Qumran or Masada. In other words, he is suggesting that the defenders of Qumran and Masada may have included members of the Jerusalem Church of Jesus and James.

7   Josephus, *Wars*, II:xx.

8   It is a possibility that Paul went not to Damascus but to the monastery of Qumran, for the community there referred to their site as 'the land of Damascus' (Eisenman, *Maccabees* ..., p. 27; also p. 69, note 122).

In a lecture, 'Paul as Herodian', given to the Society of Biblical Literature in 1982, Professor Eisenman develops the theme of Paul being an agent of the 'Herodian' Sadducee party and opposed to all that James and the Zadokites stood for. His sojourn, then, in the Nazarean community, perhaps the one at Qumran, would be akin to that of a spy or *agent provocateur*.

9   Jesus did not consider himself to be divine – or, at least, no more divine than anybody else. When Jesus was accused of claiming to be God he pointed out that the Jewish law says that all to whom the word of God is proclaimed are themselves gods. See John 10:33–5.

10   The destruction of Jerusalem and the central governing body of the Nazarean community is very important, for part of the later success of Paul's approach to Christianity rests on the absence of any strong and centralised opposition to his wild claims regarding the person of Jesus.

11   Vermaseren, *Mithras*, p. 104.

12   Wynn-Tyson, *Mithras*, p. 73.

13   It is just possible that Simon Peter is in fact the brother of Jesus: that brother listed as Simon (Matthew 13:55; Mark 6:3). Eisenman, *Maccabees ...*, p. 67, note 118, says he is Simeon bar Cleophas. Then, by the intermediate step of Simeon Keophas, this tradition from the Jerusalem Church is sufficiently garbled to produce Simon Peter (personal communication from Professor Eisenman).

14   Zechariah 11:12; see also Zechariah 12:10, 13:7 and 14:21.

15   Matthew 27:9.

16   Kazantzakis, trans. Bien, *The Last Temptation*, pp. 430–1.

17   John 17:12.

18   Matthew 13:55 and Mark 6:3.

7   **The Brothers of Jesus**

1   Vermes, *The Dead Sea Scrolls in English*, pp. 47–51.

2   Eusebius, *History*, 3:1.

3   The 'Acts of Thomas' in Hennecke, *New Testament Apocrypha*, vol. ii, pp. 442–531. See also on this subject Rendel Harris, *The Twelve Apostles*, especially pp. 23–57.

4   Hennecke, *New Testament Apocrypha*, vol. ii, p. 448.

5   Koester, 'Apocryphal and Canonical Gospels', p. 130.

6   Hennecke, *New Testament Apocrypha*, vol. ii, p. 464.

7   Ibid., p. 470.

8   See Revillout, *Évangile de Saint-Bathélemy*, 2e Fragment, p. 197. The Coptic text is broken off in the middle of the relevant word, which Revillout translates into Greek as *krestos*: 'faithful'. However,

his translation is arbitrary since it could as legitimately be translated as *kristos*: 'christ'. An expert on the Coptic language we consulted thought the latter the most likely original reading.

Incidentally, it is clear that, despite Revillout's assertion, this fragment does not belong in the 'Gospel of Bartholomew'. See Hennecke, *New Testament Apocrypha*, vol. ii, p. 507. It would fit better as part of some Coptic 'Acts of Thomas'.

9   In the painting of the Last Supper, the second figure from the left of the painting, in profile, is the twin of Christ. He is dressed similarly, the only difference being that Christ's robe is draped over his left shoulder and arm.

For a discussion of the medieval heresy of the Twins see Gettings, *The Hidden Art*, pp. 33ff. He says (p. 55) ' ... the source of the tradition in Renaissance thought is so far unknown. Perhaps Leonardo da Vinci was himself an initiate, a secret adept ... '.

10   Eusebius, *History*, 1:7.

11   1 Corinthians 7:8. The point is obscured by the translation of the Greek for 'widowers' as 'unmarried men'. See Phipps, 'Did Jesus or Paul Marry?', p. 743.

12   See Clement of Alexandria, *Strom*, vol. iii, 6:52.

13   Eusebius, *History*, 3:19.

14   Martin, *Decline and Fall of the Roman Church*, p. 42.

8   The Survival of Nazarean Teaching

1   Justin Martyr, *Dialogue with Trypho*, 49 (pp. 127–9).

2   Irenaeus, *Adversus haereses*, I:26 (see also V:1).

3   Eusebius, *History*, 3:27.

4   Epiphanius, *Contra octoaginta haereses*, XXX (p. 45).

5   Schonfield, *Those Incredible Christians*, p. 158 (quoting the Clementine *Recognitions*, IV:34–5).

6   Pines, 'The Jewish Christians ... according to a new source', p. 276.

7   Kidd, *History of the Church*, vol. iii, p. 201.

8   Of importance to the history of Nestorianism and the survival of the Nazareans and their teaching was the great Theological School of Antioch and the 'heresy' of Adoptionism. This latter considered Jesus as a man who became god, not as a god who became man. He was the 'son of God' not by nature but by grace. Furthermore, as a consequence, Mary was not held to be either a virgin or the mother of God. Rather, she was human and the birth of Jesus was as all births.

An early Bishop of Antioch, Paul of Samosata (A.D. c.260) was an Adoptionist and a major influence upon Arius and Nestorius.

The School of Antioch continued the tradition of Paul of Samosata and, under such great teachers as Diodore and Theodore of Mopsuestia, influenced the Christianity of Syria and Mesopotamia – at the least. Theodore was in fact the teacher of Nestorius – who was later to have an entire branch of Christianity named after him.

Obviously the surviving Nazareans found it easy to reach an accommodation with Nestorian thought and it seems clear that many made the small compromise and became Nestorians. Others, though, evidence suggests, only nominally joined the Nestorian Church, remaining, in all practical matters, Nazareans (or, as scholars insist, 'Jewish–Christians'). Pines says of the source of the Jewish Christian texts he studied that they may well have been 'preserved by the Nestorians. Indeed, some of the latter may have been crypto–Jewish Christians.' (Pines, 'The Jewish Christians ... ', p. 273.) He sums up by quoting another text which 'seems to corroborate the hypothesis that the Nestorian Church included Jewish Christians or crypto-Jewish Christians.' (Ibid., p. 279.)

9   Schonfield, *Secrets of the Dead Sea Scrolls*, pp. 1–7.

10 Schonfield, *The Essene Odyssey*, pp. 162–5.

11 Josephus (*Wars*, VII:x) records that many zealots fled to Egypt; indeed, some 600 were immediately apprehended though many more fled up the Nile.

Professor Brandon, in *The Fall of Jerusalem*, pp. 169–78, argues that the original Nazarean Church went not to Pella but through to Egypt. He makes the point (p. 222) that the silence in the later Christian tradition about Christianity in Alexandria is curious. He concludes that after the fall of Jerusalem in A.D. 70 the Church of Alexandria would be the sole remaining strong centre of primitive Christianity (p. 225).

12 It needs to be noted that there was, in Egypt, a division between the urban Church, based upon the theological centre of Alexandria, and the remote monastic centres populated by Christians who had fled the doctrines and intolerance of the urban Church. The monasteries used texts drawn from both Christian and pagan philosophers, as can be seen in the list of works found at Nag Hammadi. Needless to say, these works would have been condemned by the urban Church.

13 It is useful to remember that certain of the works of Plato and Asclepius were found at Nag Hammadi, along with the Gnostic texts for which the site is famous.

14 Chadwick, *Priscillian of Avila*, pp. 166–7.

15 Eisler, *The Messiah Jesus ...*, p. 449.

16 Chadwick, *Priscillian of Avila*, p. 233.

17 We owe this information to the Spanish writer and researcher Juan G. Atienza, whose speciality is the heretical and mystical past of Spain. He is a fine source of information on the Templars in the Iberian peninsula and the Balearic Islands.

18 Hugues, *The Church in Early Irish Society*, p. 34.

19 Hardinge, *The Celtic Church in Britain*, p. 55.

20 See: Dumville, 'Biblical Apocrypha and the Early Irish', p. 322; Hillgarth, 'Visigothic Spain and Early Christian Ireland', pp. 167 ff.

21 Originally at this site stood the Celtic monastery of Maximi, later known as Santa Maria de Bretoña. It is first mentioned in 569 at the Council of Lugo. Three years later, a Celtic bishop, Mailoc, was a signatory at the second Council of Braga. And in 633 the fourth Council of Toledo makes it clear that the Celtic tonsure was in use. The original settlement was destroyed in 830 by the Moors, but the bishopric continued to maintain an independent existence until the late tenth century. See Bernier, *Les Chrétientés Bretonnes ...*, pp. 115–21, and Bowen, *Saints, Seaways and Settlements*, p. 76.

22 Aberg, *The Occident and the Orient ...*, p. 35.

23 For lists of correspondences, see King, *Liturgies of the Past*, pp. 228 ff.; Kiewe, *Sacred History of Knitting*, pp. 70–80.

24 *Salthair na Rann* is a long work of poetry: the opening poems describe the creation of the universe and the workings of the cosmos. This information derives from pseudepigraphical works such as 2 Enoch, 3 Baruch, which would have been used by the Nazareans (2 Enoch is published by Charles, *Pseudepigrapha*, p. 425, as 'The Book of the Secrets of Enoch'). Poems XI and XII describe the penance of Adam and Eve and the death of Adam. This derives from the 'Book of Adam and Eve' which is only known elsewhere in Egypt.

25 See above, note 23.

26 Ramsay, 'Theodore of Mopsuestia ... ', p. 430.

27 Ibid., p. 450.

28 McNeill, *The Celtic Churches*, p. 109.

29 Ibid.

30 Hardinge, *The Celtic Church ...* , p. 37, quoting Boniface.

31 Anderson, *Early Sources of Scottish History*, vol. i, p. 341.

32 From the 'Passion of Peter and Paul' which is itself derived from the 'Acts of Peter', which was in the Nag Hammadi corpus.

33 'New manuscripts are constantly coming to light and fresh studies are being made,' writes McNamara in *The Apocrypha in the Irish Church*, p. 6. This remains the standard list of all the known

apocryphal works which, to date, have been found in manuscripts of the Celtic Church. Of a total of ninety-seven works cited, thirty-four derive from Old Testament apocrypha and pseudepigrapha, fifteen are infancy narratives, and there are twenty-four apocryphal apostolic works. On this subject, see Dumville, 'Biblical Apocrypha ... '.

11 The Loss of Faith

1 Hitler, *Table Talk*, p. 251 (evening of 25 Jan. 1942).

12 Substitute Faiths: Soviet Russia and Nazi Germany

1 Mendel, *Michael Bakunin*, p. 372.
2 Ibid., p. 430.
3 Webb, *The Harmonious Circle*, p. 45. This was some time between 1894 and 1899. Stalin's daughter fled to the USA and joined a Gurdjieff group there (Webb, p. 425).
4 Payne, *The Life and Death of Lenin*, pp. 609–10.
5 Langer, *The Mind of Adolf Hitler*, pp. 55–6.
6 Ibid., p. 56.
7 Ibid.
8 Rauschning, *Hitler Speaks*, p. 209.
9 Ibid., pp. 209–10.
10 Hitler, *Mein Kampf*, p. 395.
11 Rauschning, *Hitler Speaks*, p. 236.
12 Ibid., p. 237.
13 For the definitive exploration of these occult influences upon Hitler, see Goodrick-Clarke, *The Occult Roots of Nazism*. Hitler's ideas on race, politics, extermination of non-Aryans and the founding of a Germanic millennium derived in the main from the magazine *Ostara* of Lanz von Liebenfels, founder in 1907 of the Order of New Templars, the flag of which carried a swastika; see pp. 194–5. See also Phelps, 'Before Hitler Came ... '
14 Frey, *Cross and Swastika*, p. 5.
15 Ibid., p. 79.
16 Ibid., p. 78.
17 Stated by Baldur von Schirach at his trial, Nuremberg, 1946. See *Trial of the Major War Criminals ...* , vol. xiv (May 1946), p. 481.
18 Rauschning, *Hitler Speaks*, p. 58.
19 Frey, *Cross and Swastika*, pp. 85–6.
20 Tournier, trans. Bray, *The Erl-King*, pp. 261–2.

21 Frey, *Cross and Swastika*, pp. 92–3.

22 Wykes, *Himmler*, pp. 121–2.

23 The definitive work on Wewelsburg is Hüser, *Wewelsburg 1933 bis 1945*.

24 Communicated to Michael Bentine and repeated to us. See Bentine, *The Door Marked Summer*, p. 291.

16 Towards an Embrace of Armageddon

1 See Krause, *Guyana Massacre*.

2 See Sanders, *The Family*, and Bugliosi, *Helter Skelter*.

3 Mehta, *Karma Cola*, p. 7.

4 Ibid., p. 5.

5 Wilson, *Our Israelitish Origin*, p. 97.

6 Ibid., p. 100.

7 Glover, *England, the Remnant of Judah and the Israel of Ephraim*, p. 167.

8 Hine, *Forty-seven Identifications* ... , p. 12. By 1910, there were a claimed 405,000 copies sold. Hine, in his earlier work ... *Twenty-seven Identifications* ... , derived some interesting political conclusions from his research: 'If we are Israel,' he says, 'then we can safely reduce our war expenditure' (vol. ii, p. 68), and further, 'It is an utter impossibility for England ever to be defeated ... ' (vol. ii, p. 71).

9 Hine, ... *Twenty-seven Identifications* ... , p. v.

10 Apart from the Fundamentalist churches, the major successors to the work of Wilson, Glover, Hine, et al. is the 'British Israel World Federation', based in London but with branches all over the Commonwealth. Once boasting a wide and socially respectable membership, it has now become a small organisation on the fringe of Fundamentalist religion and right-wing politics. In October 1969 the 50th Congress was held at the Royal Pavilion, Brighton, where the secretary gave an address from which this quote is taken; see *A Jubilee of Witness*, BIWF (London, n.d.), p. 10.

11 Ibid., p. 11.

12 Armstrong, *The United States and Britain in Prophecy*, p. 174; Lindsay, *Countdown to Armageddon*, pp. 104, 108–10, 131.

13 Armstrong, *The United States* ... , p. 174. Armstrong's organisation publishes the glossy magazine *The Plain Truth* which is sent free to all who request it. In this there is a much more muted approach to the apocalyptic predictions. For the full extent of his thought it is

345

necessary to request a second level of information, a set of explanatory booklets, again sent free on request. Speaking of the move to European unity, for example, *The Plain Truth* says 'This will not be good news for the United States – decoupled from Europe – or Britain either.' (*The Plain Truth*, July-Aug. 1981, p. 24.) The booklet *The United States and Britain in Prophecy* pulls no such punches, stating: 'That YOKE of SLAVERY without mercy is to be laid on the United States and Britain by the coming united nations of Europe!' One well-known politician who had been interviewed for the magazine *The Plain Truth* informed us that he considered the organisation to be pro-European, apparently being unaware of the anti-European stand this organisation takes. His position is not uncommon. We sent him a dossier detailing the anti-European stand of the organisation for his perusal; within a week the organisation was attempting to contact us to discover more about our own position.

14 Armstrong, *The United States . . .*, p. 183.

15 For example, see Lindsay, *Countdown to Armageddon*, pp. 170–1.

16 *Guardian*, 21 April 1984, p. 19.

17 Ibid.

18 Ibid.

19 Ibid.

20 Ibid.

21 Ibid.

22 *Observer*, 25 Aug. 1985, p. 6.

23 *The Humanist*, July-Aug. 1981, p. 15.

24 *Guardian*, op. cit.

25 Ibid.

26 *The Globe and Mail*, 8 Oct. 1984, p. 7.

27 *Sunday Times*, 5 Dec. 1982, p. 15.

28 Ibid.

29 *Evening Standard*, 4 Sept. 1985, p. 7.

17 Fragments in the Post

1 Chérisey, *L'Énigme de Rennes*, p. 8.

2 *Newsweek*, 22 Feb. 1982, p. 55.

18 The British Connection

1 For the story of these codes, see *The Holy Blood . . .*, pp. 5ff.

2 Descadeillas, *Rennes et ses derniers seigneurs*, pp. 7–8.

3 Communicated to us by Mr Ernest Bigland, former deputy chairman of the board of Guardian Royal Exchange Assurance, on 21 Feb. 1984.

4 Sir William Stephenson was the wartime chief of BSC (British Security Coordination), the secret wartime organisation based in New York which represented the British Secret Service groups MI6 and SOE in the United States. Stephenson was a long-time friend and business associate of Viscount Leathers. Another friend of Leathers, Sir Connop Guthrie, also a shipping executive, headed the security department of BSC in New York. See Hyde, *The Quiet Canadian*, pp. 29–30, 66.

5 Stephenson, *A Man Called Intrepid*, p. 64.

6 Ibid., p. 131 (quoting Sir Colin Gubbins).

7 *Journal officiel*, 20 July 1956 (no. 167), p. 6731. It was registered with the sous-préfecture of Saint-Julien-en-Genevois, who kindly supplied us with photocopies of the Prieuré's 'statutes' and the letter requesting registration. Both are dated Annemasse, 7 May 1956 and signed by Pierre Plantard as secretary general and André Bonhomme as president.

8 Naturally we had the records checked for all the names which immediately came to mind. No safe deposit boxes had been listed under these.

9 The former deputy chairman of Guardian Assurance, Stanley Adams, who was also chairman of Cooks, was, according to Mr Ernest Bigland, immediately taken into British Intelligence on the outbreak of the Second World War. The head of Guardian Assurance in France, Mr Robert Sprinks – who was on the last boat out – was taken into SOE on his arrival in the UK. In addition, Captain Nutting was also on this last ship; he had been in Paris in 1940 as military assistant to General Dill, the commander of the BEF. Upon his return to London Dill became CIGS, retaining Nutting as assistant. Nutting was a close friend of Stanley Adams and General Alexander.

10 One error was found in the text of this document, but it does not constitute proof of forgery, as it could be a simple error. The reverse lists Captain Nutting's birth-place as London, when in fact it was Dublin.

11 These notarised birth certificates were all sent, so the French Consulate informed us, to the French Economic Ministry, Paris. We visited the archives section and spoke on several occasions with the director, yet could get nowhere. Our essential query was: if we have held in

our hands documents which were sent to you in 1955 and 1956 it follows that they must have been removed from your archives. Do you have any record of having destroyed these documents, or all documents for that year, or do you expect still to have them in your files? Could you please check your files, if they have not been destroyed, and tell us the result? After much stonewalling and demands to know why we were concerned with this at all, we did find out through a slip of the tongue by one official that there was some problem with 1956 documents relating to the insurance company we specified, and that the dossiers were with the Ministry of Justice. We could find no more about this, or even if it related to our enquiries. We pursued our enquiries, making a thorough nuisance of ourselves, and after several visits finally received the definitive stonewall, the definitive statement. The officials at the archival centre did 'not understand how we received the documents'. At this point, further effort seemed to promise little reward, so we gave up.

19 The Anonymous Tracts

1 Louis Vazart has founded the 'Cercle Saint Dagobert' which is concerned to perpetuate the memory of this Merovingian king and to promote the archaeology of Merovingian sites. One of its first moves was to organise the return of some small relics of Saint Dagobert to Stenay; a ceremony to mark this return was held at the site of Saint Dagobert's assassination, in September 1984. M. Vazart is associated with the small archaeological group centred on the Museum of Stenay which is directed by M. Philippe Voluer.

2 In 1961 Pierre Plantard wrote his *Gisors et son secret*, a mimeographed document of thirty-two pages with appended maps. In 1962 the writer Gérard de Sède wrote his *Les Templiers sont parmi nous*, which dealt at length with Gisors and carried a long interview with M. Plantard on the subject at the end of the book. The interview contained certain references to the Prieuré de Sion. In the same year André Malraux expressed interest in the affair, and later that year the French government decided to undertake excavations at the château of Gisors.

Page 1 of Plantard's document states that on 23 March 1961 copies had been sent to the Librarian at Caen, the Mayor of Gisors and Gérard de Sède.

3 We checked with the High Court early in 1985 to see how the action was progressing. We received the reply that the action had been lodged for some time but that the affair was now marked 'no further action'.

4 *Nostra*, 28 Oct.–4 Nov. 1982 (no. 542), p. 6.

20 The Elusive 'American Contingent'

1 *International Herald Tribune*, 20 June 1984, p. 9.

2 This text appears in the statutes carrying the signature of Jean Cocteau; they are undated but claim to incorporate the 'modifications of the convent of the 5th June, 1956'. The statutes sent to us by the sous-préfecture of Saint-Julien-en-Genevois dated 7 May 1956 are quite different and do not have 22 articles. These were signed by Pierre Plantard and André Bonhomme. The Marquis Philippe de Chérisey sent us the Cocteau statutes.

3 37 rue St Lazare, Paris, was the apartment of Philippe de Chérisey.

4 The question of the birth certificates is curious. The original is hand-written in a large bound volume. There are hand-written additions mentioning M. Plantard's first marriage, to Anne Lea Hisler, on 6 December 1945, and his second marriage, to France Germaine Cavaille, on 18 March 1972. This is to be found at the Mairie of the 7th arrondissement, Paris. In this the name is given as Plantard, and his father's profession as 'valet de chambre'.

There exists a certified 'Extrait des Minutes des Actes de Naissance' from this same Mairie dated 22 August 1972 and with the serial number C 658785. This is typewritten and follows the wording of the hand-written original faithfully except for the additions of 'Comte de Saint Clair et Comte de Rhédae, architecte' after the mention of M. Plantard's father (also called Pierre). This also reproduces the additions listing M. Plantard's two marriages. It is stamped and signed. A copy of this is deposited in the Bibliothèque Nationale, Paris.

We have a copy of a third document issued by the Mairie of Garenne-Colombes which is dated 14 May 1977 and which lists the births of M. Plantard's two children. This too gives M. Plantard's name as 'Plantard de Saint Clair'. This name appears on his cheques and in his passport. All appeared legitimate.

5 Of possible relevance is that the particular page containing M. Plantard's birth notice in the bound volume was completely loose, having broken away from its binding.

6 We had already received reports of this sort from other researchers working on stories concerning the Vatican.

21 The Vista Widens

1 See *New York Times*, 25 June 1974, p. 2. Cardinal Danielou died at 4 p.m. on 20 May 1974 in the fifth-floor apartment of Mme Mimi Santini, a 24-year-old stripper. A large sum of money was reported as having been found on him. He had died of a heart attack. The Church remained silent for three weeks (presumably while they conducted their own investigation), then issued a strong statement against what it called 'grave insinuations'.

In an interview, Mimi Santini confirmed that the Cardinal had indeed died in her flat, but said it was because of a heart attack caused by the effort of climbing all the stairs to the fifth floor. She added that she did not know Danielou was a Cardinal, since he rarely wore clerical vestments when he called (*Sunday Times*, 9 June 1974, p. 3). Cardinal Danielou was a member of the Académie Française, author of fourteen books and head of the Paris University theological faculty. His area of special study was in the primitive Christian Church and the doctrines of the Jewish Christians (the 'Nazareans'), and he wrote an important book on the subject. He also led the Roman Church's counter-attack on those (especially Dutch) bishops who argued that the Church should accommodate both married and celibate priests. Danielou conceded that celibacy derived from discipline and tradition rather than from theological doctrine.

22 Resistance, Chivalry and the United States of Europe

1 This is recorded in the charter of 1178, sealed by Pope Alexander III.

2 Röhricht, *Regesta regni Hierosolymitani*, no. 83 (p. 19). The Prior, Arnaud, was still mentioned as late as 1136.

3 Archives du Loiret, D.357, pièce 2.

4 Ibid., pièce 5. A discussion of this document, together with the text in modern Latin, appears in Rey, 'Chartes de l'abbaye du Mont-Sion'.

5 Le Maire, *Histoire et antiquitez de la ville ... d'Orléans*, Part 2, pp. 96–9; Cottineau, *Répertoire topo-bibliographique ...*, p. 2138; Soyer, 'Annales prioratvs sancti sansonis ... ', pp. 222ff.

6 In the Bibliothèque Nationale, Paris: no. L^2c 7335 (Quarto).

7 *Vaincre*, 21 Sept. 1942 (no. 1), p. 1.

8 Ibid., 21 Oct. 1942 (no. 2), p. 3.

9 We contacted Robert Amadou in order to gain some idea of the milieu in which this magazine appeared. He told us that in 1942, as an 18-year-old philosophy student with a fervent interest in esotericism, he did not miss any opportunity to get in contact with

movements operating in this field. This was the year he met M. Plantard and was received into Alpha Galates, but without any ceremony and without, apparently, any follow-up. He wrote one article for *Vaincre* and met M. Plantard three or four times, but after that had no more contact.

M. Amadou is a Freemason, friend of Dr Pierre Simon, the Grand Master of French Freemasonry. Amadou is also a Martinist, editor of the French Martinist journal and a member of the Paris lodge 'Memphis and Misraim'. Despite his obviously good knowledge of esoteric groups in France, he refused to be drawn on the subject of the Prieuré de Sion. He did say, however, that 'For my part, I have never been involved in political activity, neither before nor since ... My only desire was and remains philosophical order and religious order.'

10 As one of the governors of the Institute d'Études Corporatives. Le Fur also contributed to the collaborationist journal *Je suis partou* from spring 1941. Another member of the Right was Henry Coston, quoted on the front page of issue no. 1 of *Vaincre*. He was an extreme right-wing journalist, a collaborator, anti-semite and head of the 'Centre d'Action Masonique', which held all the looted Masonic archives. Ironically, he was one of the regular writers for *Au pilori*.

11 *Vaincre*, 21 Sept. 1942 (no. 1), p. 2.

12 Ibid., 21 Nov. 1942 (no. 3), p. 1.

13 Ibid., 21 Sept. 1942 (no. 1), p. 3.

14 Weber, *Action française*, p. 153, note *d*, and p. 444.

15 *Vaincre*, 21 Jan. 1943 (no. 5), p. 2.

16 Van Roon, *German Resistance to Hitler*, p. 183. When in Madrid, Hans Adolf von Moltke was making overtures to the Allies, it seems most likely through either the British Ambassador or via some channel to General Sikorski. On 3 January 1943, General Sikorski visited Lord Halifax and told him to expect Hans Adolf von Moltke to get in touch with the British Ambassador in Madrid, since he or his colleagues had already been trying to make contact with peace feelers. See Halifax's report to the Foreign Office, FO 371 34559, paper *c*205, at the Public Record Office, Kew.

17 Van Roon, *German Resistance ...*, p. 210.

18 Ibid., p. 201. Also (p. 256): 'The documents make it clear that the foreign policy proposals of the Kreisau Circle were based upon a fundamental belief in a Europe integrated into a federal state.'

23 The Return of de Gaulle

1 See Crawley, *De Gaulle*, p. 349. One paratroop commander had his

precise order: he was to drop with his men at Colombey and take de
Gaulle to Paris.

2 The spokesman was M. Delbecque, one of the Algiers leaders. See
The Times, 2 June 1958, p. 8.

3 Hisler, *Les Gouvernants et rois de France*, p. 103.

4 Ibid., p. 103, note 2.

5 We contacted M. Debré and told him of these allegations. He was
surprised and said that he did not recall ever having had dealings
with any M. Plantard, and that anyway he was not involved with the
Committees of Public Safety.

6 *Le Monde*, 18–19 May 1958, p. 3.

7 Ibid., 6 June 1958, p. 1.

8 Ibid., 8–9 June 1958, p. 2.

9 Ibid., 29 July 1958, p. 7.

10 Kept at the Versailles annexe to the Bibliothèque Nationale, Paris:
Circuit (1956) carries the no. Jo 12078 (Quarto); *Circuit* (1959)
carries the no. Jo 14140 (Quarto). Not all of these are available.
When we checked, only nos 2, 3, 5, and 6 were there. However, we
have seen nos 8 and 9, and obviously nos 1 and 4 existed at one time.
It would appear that some have been stolen.

11 The Swiss researcher Mathieu Paoli presented his findings in *Les
Dessous d'une ambition politique*.

12 *Circuit*, Nov. 1959 (no. 5), p. 1.

13 Ibid.

14 Ibid.

15 Ibid.

16 Paoli, *Les Dessous d'une ambition politique*, p. 94.

17 Ibid.

18 Ibid., pp. 94ff.

19 *Circuit*, Sept. 1959 (no. 3), p. 8.

24 Secret Powers behind Covert Groups

1 *Manual of the Council of Europe*, p. 3.

2 Ibid., p. 4.

3 See Chapter 22, note 16, above.

4 Flamini, *Pope, Premier, President*, p. 22.

5 Ibid., p. 56; Lee, 'Their Will Be Done', p. 21.

6 Marchetti and Marks, *The CIA and the Cult of Intelligence*, p. 25;
Freemantle, *CIA: The Honourable Company*, pp. 29–30; Gurwin,
The Calvi Affair, p. 185; Agee and Wolf, eds, *Dirty Work: The CIA
in Western Europe*, pp. 168–73.

7   Turner, *Secrecy and Democracy*, p. 76.

8   Agee and Wolf, *Dirty Work* ... , pp. 202–3.

9   The CIA did not usually provide funds directly to these groups, but used various other groups as intermediaries. A common procedure was for a CIA-funded 'private' foundation to fund in turn the chosen group. Lists of the contributors to Radio Free Europe, for example, reveal the names of the various conduits for such financing.

10 Pomian, *Joseph Retinger*, p. 236; Lee, 'Their Will Be Done', p. 23. Dr Luigi Gedda, head of Catholic Action, was decorated by the Knights of Malta.

11 Thomas and Morgan-Witts, *The Year of Armageddon*, pp. 17–18, 71.

12 Huntington, 'Visions of the Kingdom', p. 21.
    Spellman had been an old friend of 'Wild Bill' Donovan, former head of OSS, and Donovan had enlisted his help in the Italian election campaign of 1947–8. Details of his actions in South and Central America and especially in Guatemala are found in Cooney, *The American Pope* ... , pp. 231–6. For his role in obtaining US Government finance see Cooney, ibid., pp. 42, 275 and 278.

13 Some writers will have it that the Lodge was long established before it was taken over by Gelli. Be that as it may, the standard story has it that Gelli became a Freemason in 1963, joined P2 in 1966, became an officer in the Lodge in 1971, then in May 1975 became Grand Master. P2 Lodge was suspended by the Grand Orient of Italy shortly *before* (according to an Italian Freemasonic source) Gelli's assumption of Mastership. According to Italian law, all Masonic Lodges are required to furnish annual lists of members to the police. P2 Lodge refused to do this, and so was suspended pending investigation.
    Some researchers working in the field have claimed that City of London Lodge no. 901 is implicated in the P2 scandal, as Roberto Calvi at least was a member. The story has been published in the national press in Britain. United Grand Lodge of England state that a check of the Lodge register for the years 1940–86 confirms that neither Calvi nor Gelli were ever members of this Lodge. Why this Lodge should come into such notoriety is unclear – the present membership includes professions as varied as florist, engineer, publican, chauffeur and builder. It is certainly not packed with high-level bankers.

14 Yallop, *In God's Name*, pp. 117–18.

15 The commission reported that there was a foreign organisation running the P2 Lodge. The image they used to describe the situation was that of two pyramids. One pyramid sitting on its base represents

the Lodge P2 with Gelli at the top, the apex. Upside down and above the first is the second pyramid, the two being joined at the apex. The higher pyramid represents the controlling organisation which acted via Gelli, who sat at the connecting link between the two. See the *Guardian*, 11 May 1984, p. 6 and 7 June 1984, p. 8.

16 The Charter of Larmenius.

17 *Le Monde*, 25 Sept. 1979, p. 12.

18 The UK does not recognise the Order of Malta, and passports issued by the Order are not considered valid. In fact, the wearing of any decoration or insignia of the Order in the UK is forbidden by the Queen. See *Foreign and Commonwealth Regulations*, A:7; B:1, 5.

19 Lee, 'Their Will Be Done', p. 23.

20 Ibid.; see also Hervet, 'Knights of Darkness', p. 31.

21 Lee, 'Their Will Be Done', p. 23; Hervet, 'Knights of Darkness', p. 33.

22 Lee, 'Their Will Be Done', p. 24.

23 Hervet, 'Knights of Darkness', p. 34–5.

24 Article by Edmond Albe contained in the *Dossiers secrets d'Henri Lobineau*, 1967 (Bibliothèque Nationale, Paris, ref. no. Lm^1 249 (Quarto)). There is no indication that the archives in question are those of the English branch of the Order of Malta. A query addressed to the historian and archivist of the English branch elicited the reply that no such documents were or are in the Order's archives in England.

Index

355